Debts to Pay
The Future of Federalism in Quebec
Third Edition

John F. Conway

D1328179

James Lorimer & Company, Publishers
Toronto

James Lorimer & Company Ltd. acknowledges the support of the Ontario Arts Council. We acknowledge the support of the Government of Canada through the Book Publishing Industry Development Program (BPIDP) for our publishing activities. We acknowledge the support of the Canada Council for the Arts for our publishing program. We acknowledge the support of the Government of Ontario through the Ontario Media Development Corporation's Ontario Book Initiative.

The Canada Council | Le Conseil des Arts
for the Arts | du Canada

ONTARIO ARTS COUNCIL
CONSEIL DES ARTS DE L'ONTARIO

Canadian Cataloguing in Publication Data
Conway, John Frederick
   Debts to pay : the future of federalism in Quebec / John Frederick Conway. – 3rd. ed.

Includes bibliographical references and index.
ISBN 1-55028-814-8

1. Canada – English-French relations. 2. Québec (Province) – History – Autonomy and independence movements. I. Title.

FC144.C65 2004   971.4   C2004-900472-7

James Lorimer & Company Ltd., Publishers
35 Britain Street
Toronto, Ontario
M5A 1R7

www.lorimer.ca

Printed and bound in Canada

CONTENTS

	Acknowledgements	4
	Preface	7
	Note	9
1	Dangerous Impasse	11
2	Quebec as a Defeated Nation: The Conquest	21
3	The Re-conquest and Isolation of Quebec	31
4	The Quiet Revolution	57
5	Lévesque, the Referendum and Patriation	91
6	The Meech Lake Accord	123
7	The Charlottetown Referendum	139
8	The 1993 Federal Election	166
9	The 1994 Quebec Election	186
10	The 1995 Sovereignty Referendum	199
11	Ottawa's Plan B	212
12	The 1998 Watershed	227
13	The Fall of Lucien Bouchard and the Rise of Paul Martin	246
14	Charest Defeats the PQ: Plan B Vindicated?	260
15	Separation or Special Status?	276
	Bibliographic Note	292
	Selected Bibliography	294
	Appendix I: The Charlottetown Agreement	305
	Appendix II: The Supreme Court Case	
	The Reference Questions and the Court's Answers	319
	Bill C-20: *The Clarity Act*	324
	Quebec's *Fundamental Rights Act*	329
	Index	334

For Patricia Vivian Conway Robitaille,

born, 17 November 1940 at Moose Jaw, Saskatchewan,

died, 6 March 1988 at Montreal, Quebec,

who attempted a reconciliation of the two nations

in her personal life

ACKNOWLEDGEMENTS

The manuscript was read by historian Dr. Lorne Brown, University of Regina, and by production editor Chad Fraser at James Lorimer and Company. The idea was also discussed at length with Jim Lorimer. Their suggestions helped to produce a better book. The copy-editing expertise of Robin Hunter greatly improved the final text. Cheryl Heinnemann and Leanne Overend typed the manuscript, showing constant patience with my interminable changes and revisions. To all six, to my family, and to my many students and colleagues, both in Quebec and English Canada, with whom I have debated the "Quebec question" over the years, my heartfelt thanks.

In days of yore, from Britain's shore,
Wolfe the dauntless hero came,
And planted firm Britannia's flag
On Canada's fair domain.

Here may it wave, our boast, our pride,
And joined in love together
The Thistle, Shamrock, Rose entwine
The Maple Leaf for ever!

from "The Maple Leaf For Ever"
Alexander Muir, 1890

Je me souviens.

Quebec's national motto since 1883

I am convinced that much of our
problem is simply that people do
not know enough about their history…

Joe Clark
Minister Responsible for Constitutional Affairs
The Globe and Mail, 31 December 1991

Those who cannot remember the past
are condemned to repeat it.

George Santayana

PREFACE

When I was growing up in Moose Jaw, Saskatchewan, we regularly sang "The Maple Leaf For Ever" during morning assembly at Empire School. It was not until much later that I noticed that the fleur-de-lis did not entwine with the rose, shamrock, and thistle. That it did not is not, of course, surprising. During those days the song was English Canada's unofficial anthem, usually sung with more gusto than "God Save the King."

Quebec and the entire "French fact" were more or less absent from my direct experience, except when we studied history (and those classes never left any doubt that the best thing that ever happened to New France was the Conquest). I can't recall meeting a French Canadian from Quebec during my childhood, but I heard a lot about them. And we had our local, semi-assimilated variety. I learned the usual epithets — pea-souper, frog. A lot of the prejudice we absorbed in my home mixed Orange hostility to Rome with ethnic contempt. What I learned about French Canadians was either uniformly negative — disloyal to Britain and Canada, untrustworthy, unwilling to fight in the war while our boys died, lazy, backward, priest-ridden — or patronizing — overly emotional, good-natured, simple. Both these stereotypes were also portrayed in the movies I went to see at the Royal Theatre — French Canadians were either evil villains or happy-go-lucky, good-hearted buffoons.

There was one jarring exception to this general attitude. Like most working men in Moose Jaw in that era, my father joined in the harvest. He used to bring home stories of the French Canadians he met who had come out on the harvest trains to help take off the wheat. At the time it didn't strike me as odd that these men he worked with were quite different from all other French Canadians. They worked hard, did their fair share, were easy to get along with and enjoyed a good time.

Like most English Canadians, I was shaken out of my ignorance about Quebec by the Quiet Revolution. At university I was exposed to books and courses on Quebec. I heard touring speakers like Pierre Bourgault and René Lévesque. I followed political events in Quebec avidly. I travelled to Quebec. On my first extended trip there in 1965 I learned something of both the anger and the reasonableness of the people when I discovered that my inability to speak or to understand French provoked hostility only until the Quebeckers in question learned I was not from either Montreal or Ontario, but from the West. Then they would warm up. It was okay to be an English-only speaker from Western Canada.

On an extended trip to Quebec in the autumn of 1987 for language training at Laval University I learned something of the determination of the Québécois in securing their nation. This was a period when many in English Canada, and not a few in Quebec, were gleefully crowing that Québécois nationalism was dead for at least a generation. The Québécois were too busy earning money, and they had even voted Tory in 1984, an unthinkable act! Yet I failed to find any evidence of this death of nationalism. Quite the contrary. I was in Quebec City when René Lévesque died, and I was amazed by the massive outpouring of deep love and grief for the man and strong support for his ideals.

I've put my children in French immersion. I have learned enough French to function haltingly at professional meetings. I do not want Quebec to separate. Yet I know that my linguistic gestures are not enough, are not even what Quebec wants. I believe today, just as I believed at the height of the Quiet Revolution, that Quebec will eventually separate unless English Canada offers a serious accommodation to Québécois nationalism. This is an appeal to my fellow English Canadians to open their hearts and minds to Quebec in an effort to help save the Canada we know and love.

NOTE

The use of the term "English Canada" may bother some readers, but it is still the most convenient and historically accurate term. The facts are clear. Canada is composed of two nations: the Québécois nation, with the province of Quebec as its political and constitutional home; and the English-Canadian nation, with a considerably stronger political and constitutional home — nine provinces and three territories. The latter also has hegemony in the House of Commons, the Senate and all other federal institutions and a well-protected minority status in Quebec. Canadians have now agreed to add a third nation to the equation of Canada's constitutional design, the aboriginal or First Nations.

About 70 per cent of Canada's current population is of British or French extraction, or some combination thereof. Those of British extraction make up the largest single population bloc, often an overwhelming majority, in every province except Quebec. In Quebec, about 80 per cent of the population is of French origin. Granted, the English-Canadian nation is characterized by a high degree of tolerance of ethnic and cultural diversity, and this diversity has continued to transform and enrich it. Perhaps we will soon reach the point when we can drop the adjective "English" and just speak of the Canadian nation.

The Québécois nation is similarly undergoing transformation as diverse ethnic and cultural groups adopt French as their language of work and education. Sixty-eight per cent of Canadians speak English, 23 per cent speak French, while only 8 per cent speak a different language at home.

The English-Canadian nation's distinctive roots remain in its British origins, now significantly modified, and the English language;

the Québécois nation's distinctive roots remain in its French origin, also significantly modified, and the French language. All the other ethnic groups that have come to Canada have integrated, to varying degrees, to one or the other of these nations.

Dangerous Impasse

Canadians live in a fool's paradise as Canada undergoes an extended constitutional crisis. Those aware of the seriousness of the situation are ignored, accused of exaggeration and hysteria. Those with the power to reverse the trend — incumbent politicians in Ottawa and the nine English-Canadian premiers — perversely express pride at refusing to discuss a constitutional resolution. The recent setbacks experienced by the sovereignty movement in Quebec — fewer Bloc seats in the House of Commons after 2000, the departure of Bouchard in 2001, the defeat of the PQ government in 2003, further Bloc losses expected in the 2004 federal election — are seen by many in English Canada as the end of the crisis. But we have heard about many endings in the Quebec/Canada impasse during the last forty years and more.

Supporters of the Charlottetown Agreement told Canadians that approval would bring an end to constitutional bickering so national reconciliation could begin. The defeat of the Agreement on 26 October 1992 in both Quebec and English Canada, and the deep divisions provoked by the referendum campaign, were damning testimony to a monumental miscalculation on the part of our political elite. The Charlottetown referendum became the first upheaval in what became a sustained and rolling political earthquake that shook Canada to its foundations. Echoes of the referendum result reverberated in the results of the 25 October 1993 federal election. The two parties that campaigned strongly against Charlottetown were rewarded by their regional electorates. In Quebec, where sovereigntist sentiment surged, the Bloc Québécois took 54 of 75 seats with 49.3 per cent of the popular vote and became, ironically, Her Majesty's Loyal Opposition in the House of Commons. In the West, the Reform party won 51 of 86 seats with 38 per cent of the vote, annihilating the Tories and almost doing the same to the NDP in the region. Forty-six Reform seats were in Alberta and British Columbia, the seedbed of the greatest hostility to Quebec in English Canada. Thus the extremes of the two solitudes in opposition to Charlottetown fared well — the Reform party in the West, which argued that Charlottetown gave Quebec too much and Quebec should learn to love Canada or leave it; the Bloc, which argued that Charlotte-town gave Quebec nothing of significance and sovereignty was now the only dignified option for the Québécois nation. Clearly, between these two there was no middle ground and if they had had their way, each for their own reasons, we would have wit-nessed the end of Canada.

The rolling political earthquake impacted again during the 12 September 1994 provincial election in Quebec. Though the Parti Québécois won only a narrow popular-vote victory — less than one per cent — Jacques Parizeau won a comfortable majority of seats (77 of 125), easily enough to move, as promised, to a quick referen-dum on sovereignty. Despite this narrow victory, in which many in English Canada sought delusional solace, the pro-sovereignty popu-lar vote in Quebec had, in fact, edged up to 51.21 per cent when one added in the vote won by Mario Dumont, the former leader of the Young Liberals in Quebec and leader of the pro-sovereignty Action démocratique du Québec (ADQ). This was a significant gain over Lévesque's 1976 victory with 42 per cent.

The final seismic shock resulting from the Charlottetown fiasco occurred on 30 October 1995 when 49.4 per cent of Quebec voters supported a much harder sovereignty question than that presented by Lévesque in 1980. This was an incredible indictment of the failure of federalist leadership, both in Ottawa and in the nine English-Canadian provincial capitals, particularly given the campaign of political, economic and territorial threats against a sovereign Quebec leading up to the referendum vote. The inescapable fact was that Quebec sovereignty had come ominously close to winning the magic number required in any democratic system, 50 per cent plus one vote.

After that near-death experience, Ottawa and the English-Canadian provinces mounted a campaign of bullying and threatening rhetoric to frighten the Québécois from following the sovereigntist road. This proved temporarily successful: it drove Bouchard from office, it chipped away at the Bloc's representation in the House of Commons and it defeated the PQ government. Some now declare the separatist threat dead. Others, wiser to the ebb and flow of Canadian history, warn that this is but a temporary lull in what has become an increasingly bitter impasse without apparent end. When the sovereignty movement again bursts onto the scene, English Canada will again be unprepared and shocked. Why? Because the impasse continues. Quebec still has not accepted the 1982 constitution, while Quebec's minimum demands for recognition and security of the Québécois nation in the Canadian federal system remain unacceptable to Ottawa and English Canada.

How did we reach this impasse? Though the conflict between English Canada and Quebec has been with us since the Conquest in 1759, its current sharp expression exploded with the death of the Meech Lake Accord in 1990. Many Québécois interpreted the failure of Meech as a rejection of their minimum demands. When Meech died, public opinion in Quebec hardened on the option of either sovereignty or a satisfactory renewal of federalism. In English Canada positions also toughened as a result of the death of Meech. In the period following its failure, sympathy for Quebec fell to a low ebb, where it has remained. The meteoric rise of the Reform party (which later became the Canadian Alliance) reflected the way many English Canadians had hardened their hearts against the concerns of the Québécois. The party leapt almost overnight from relative obscurity in the 1988 election to prominence in English Canada. The Canadian Alliance's support remained wholly concentrated in English Canada, especially in the West, and Alliance leaders have shown little interest in offering themselves to the people of Quebec, while toying with the idea of appealing to extreme elements among Quebec's non-francophone minority. (In an effort to break out of their western ghetto and make a breakthrough in Central and Atlantic Canada, in 2003 the Canadian Alliance merged with the Progressive Conservatives to form the Conservative Party of Canada.)

Though Manning and the Reform party got their kick-start in the late 1980s by voicing western alienation and demanding a Triple-E Senate, much of Reform's and the Alliance's national rhetoric was, and continues to be, carefully designed to capture the minority strain of anti-French, anti-Quebec bigotry that has always ebbed and flowed in English-Canadian politics. Manning's position on Quebec was probably given its most disturbing expression in a speech he made in April 1991 in New York, counselling Americans to look to the U.S. Civil War in order to understand what was happening in Canada. He spoke of the Civil War as the "model for secession." In that speech, Manning came perilously close to suggesting civil war as a possible outcome in Canada's constitutional crisis. During Manning's one foray into Quebec during the 1992 Charlottetown referendum campaign, he spoke at the Loyola campus of Concordia University in the heart of anglo-Montreal. In the sole episode during that campaign at which a speaker required police protection, he reiterated his determination to confront the separatists head-on, forcing the Québécois "to choose once and for all" between Canada and independence. The Canadian Alliance maintained that hard-line position: Quebec must accept Canada largely as it is or leave it.

At the opposite end of the spectrum were Canada's main-stream anglophone intellectuals. During the Quiet Revolution and the Lévesque era, these intellectuals, particularly those in the cen-tre and on the left, were largely sympathetic to Quebec. Though unable to persuade Ottawa and most provincial governments that Quebec needed some special constitutional accommodation, Eng-lish-Canadian intellectuals played a significant role in tilting public opinion toward a softer line on Quebec. This positive atti-tude largely ended with the free trade election of 1988 when many of these intellectuals were angered and deeply disappointed by Quebec's strong support for Mulroney and free trade, particu-larly by the aggressive support of Québécois nationalists. The events at Oka in 1990, which provoked sympathy for the Mohawks across English Canada but hostility in Quebec, further undermined the progressive reputation of Québécois nationalism among the English-Canadian intelligentsia.

In a sense, Québécois nationalism lost an influential ally in English Canada. At the same time, the minority intellectual current in English Canada that had always been hostile to Québécois nationalism was pushed to prominence. Books that formerly would have had only a narrow appeal, such as Mordecai Richler's *Oh Canada! Oh Quebec!*, became best-sellers. Views that would have formerly been largely beyond the pale were taken seriously: Canada would be better off without Quebec; military force ought to be contemplated to keep Quebec in Confederation; a separating Quebec would be carved up and partitioned; an independent Que-bec would not be welcome in any post-separation economic or other association; and so on. Before free trade and the collapse of Meech, intellectuals who took such positions were seen as cranks. In the Meech aftermath, they were not, a fact that indicates how far the polarization had gone. These poisonous voices resonated on the fringes of the No campaign in English Canada during the Charlottetown referendum, and a year later they played a central role in the success of the Reform party in Alberta and British Columbia during the 1993 federal election campaign.

The referendums of October 1992 and 1995 are behind us. Instead of reconciliation, the "two solitudes" have hunkered down even further into their respective enclaves than before the Quiet Revolution or the bitter World War I Conscription Crisis, or perhaps even since the hanging of Riel. The Bloc Québécois and the Canadian Alliance represent the logical extreme of each solitude, looking inward and brooding over their own grievances. Perhaps one could take a fatalistic view, arguing that this was an inevitable outcome that has been coming ever since the Conquest. But many of us do not share that view. Rather, we believe that history, both long past and recent, informs us that English Canada must largely shoulder the blame for our present circumstances.

The Bloc Québécois and the Parti Québécois reflect a conviction, present in Québécois nationalism from the beginning, that in order to save the Québécois nation a separate and sovereign state must be constructed. This conviction has been a clear provincial choice for the Québécois ever since René Lévesque was spurned by the Quebec Liberal Party and proceeded to build the Parti Québécois.

But in the past, it was a choice exercised only in the secure context of simultaneously choosing among the Conservatives, Liberals or NDP in federal elections. When the Bloc Québécois began winning significant numbers of Quebec seats in the House of Commons, the situation became more dangerous. It was one thing to joke during the Lévesque-Trudeau era that the Québécois wanted an independent Quebec within a strong federal system. The election of sovereigntists at both the provincial and federal levels representing the people of Quebec was no joking matter. Quite simply, the federal government had much less political legitimacy in Quebec or in world councils when dealing with the Quebec question. Today, after the losses experienced by the Bloc in the 2000 federal election, the defeat of the PQ government in 2003 and the further Bloc losses expected in 2004, the immediate critical crisis has passed. This relative calm has not, however, led to negotiation and reconciliation, but rather it has led to gloating and a continuing contemptuous dismissal of the legitimacy of the aspirations of the Québécois nation.

After Meech and Charlottetown, Canada endured a period of serious political instability and rancour, a period that almost witnessed the departure of Quebec. It did not have to come to pass, just as what has happened since the Quiet Revolution need not have come to pass, and perhaps it is not too late to learn from our history in order to avoid repeating past mistakes. During the Quiet Revolution, when English Canada opened up to Quebec as never before, there was an opportunity to renegotiate Confederation. English Canada refused to do so. After Lévesque lost the referendum in 1980, there was another opportunity to renegotiate Confederation. English Canada again refused. After the failure of Meech, there was another chance. Initially, the wide-open process which culminated in the Charlottetown Agreement raised many hopes, but then the English-Canadian premiers intercepted the process and badly fumbled the ball. British Columbia's Minister Responsible for Constitutional Affairs, Moe Sihota, put it most graphically when he said Quebec's Premier Bourassa "ran into a brick wall formed by nine other governments...[which] said: 'Look, there is no way you are going to get special status...'" After the Yes side was narrowly defeated in the 1995 referendum there was another opportunity. But again English Canada refused, and through its governments in Ottawa and the provinces, embarked on a sustained campaign of rhetorical terrorism and bullying.

Again and again, English Canada failed to rise to the challenge of the Quebec question, harshly refusing to make the accommodations for which Quebec has been asking, episodically from the Conquest onward and most insistently for the last forty years. What Quebec wants is straightforward: that English Canada affirm an acceptance of the right of the Québécois to national self-determination and that negotiations begin to reconstruct Canada's constitutional order in ways that give Quebec the special powers it needs to protect and enhance the Québécois nation. That was what the Royal Commission on Bilingualism and Biculturalism more or less told us in 1967. That was what the Task Force on Canadian Unity told us in 1979. That was what Lévesque first asked of the Quebec Liberal Party and then asked of Canada through the PQ. And that's what Bourassa, who may well go down in history as the last credible federalist in Quebec provincial politics, asked in 1992 when he warned us against "domineering and authoritarian federalism."

After the English-Canadian premiers and Ottawa arrogantly and unsuccessfully presented Charlottetown to Quebec on a "take it or leave it" basis, warning there would be no new offers or concessions, a campaign of intimidation against the Québécois began in a desperate effort to deflect them from the sovereigntist course. Warnings about partition, territorial claims, the establishment of ethnic enclaves, the possible enforcement of a general principle of the infinite divisibility of a separating Quebec (a piece here for the Cree, there for the Innu; here for the allophones, there for the anglophones; perhaps a chunk including communities in western Quebec; etc.), no negotiations, no association, no legal or constitutional path to sovereignty despite any democratic decision by the Québécois, economic reprisals, these and more were all tossed into Quebec politics like so many bombshells. The campaign of intimidation largely failed, as affirmed in the federal and provincial election results in Quebec in 1993 and 1994. And only a last-minute gesture of conciliation by Ottawa and English Canadians narrowly forestalled a victory for the Yes side in the 1995 sovereignty referendum. Rather than seizing the opportunity, English Canada responded with an even more aggressive campaign of intimidation. As a result, the federation totters on the abyss, and Quebec and English Canada continue in a face-to-face polarized standoff in which the options continue to be clarified and simplified for the Québécois as never before since 1837–38: surrender or sovereignty. In a sense, Charest's victory in April 2003 can best be seen as a temporary cease-fire, giving a serious renewal of federalism another chance.

A large part of the problem is that English Canada and Quebec premise their actions on two very different versions of the same history. English Canada recalls the Conquest of 1759 as a simple battle on the Plains of Abraham. Quebec recalls it for what it was, the final confrontation in a long, bloody military campaign that stretched from Acadia up the St. Lawrence. English Canada recalls the uprising of 1837–38 as a comic sideshow in the irresistible march to responsible government. Quebec recalls 1837–38 as another bloody suppression of the Québécois nation. English Canada celebrates Confederation in 1867 as the birth of a nation. Quebec views it as the imposition of a two-layered constitutional stranglehold on national aspirations. English Canada sees the hanging of Louis Riel as unfortunate, an event best forgotten, and ambivalently contemplates making Riel a hero. Quebec views the hanging of Riel as yet another English-Canadian declaration that the French fact ought to stay locked up in Quebec. And so it goes, each solitude with its own version of the same history, even up to the present.

English Canada now views the imposition of the *War Measures Act* in 1970 as a regrettable, if understandable, over-reaction. Quebec considers it another military occupation designed to subjugate, warn and humiliate. English Canada sees the victory of the federalist option in the 1980 Quebec referendum as affirming Quebec's commitment to Canada. Quebec, contemplating all the broken promises made during that referendum campaign, views it as yet another example of English Canada's political duplicity. English Canada sees the isolation of Lévesque in 1981 as another small gambit in the constitutional chess game where Quebec's leader was outmatched by the English-Canadian team. Quebec regards it as an affront to the Québécois nation and a deliberate slap in the face. English Canada was divided on Meech and Charlottetown. Some regarded both accords as craven surrenders to blackmail by Québécois nationalists while others regarded them as reasonable and generous offers to Quebec. Quebec regarded Meech as a bare minimum on which English Canada choked, and Charlottetown as yet another effort by English Canada to impose unilateral constitutional solutions. Late in the 1995 referendum campaign, faced with looming defeat, Prime Minister Chrétien offered distinct society status and a veto to Quebec voters if they would support him in defeating the Yes side, only to renege on the promise very soon after. English Canada views this action as just another example of the effectiveness of a shrewd federalist politician. Quebec sees it for what it was — an act of bad faith.

English Canada has not yet been able to go through the process of recognizing the oppression of the Québécois — and other francophones — and undertaking a resolute effort to make amends. It has gone through such a process regarding the oppression of aboriginal people. Now we appear prepared to pay our debts. Even the Acadians were offered an official apology in 2003 for their violent deportation. Similarly, Canadians have acknowledged the debts owed to Japanese-Canadian victims of the World War II internment infamy. And we have gone partway, from time to time, with the Québécois. Indeed, many English Canadians believe that we admitted our oppression during the Quiet Revolution with the Commission on Bilingualism and Biculturalism. They believe we paid our debts amply, perhaps too amply, to the Québécois through French power in Ottawa, official bilingualism, allowing French to become the language of work and education in Quebec and various economic development concessions. But the Québécois do not agree and never have. English Canada's most recent effort, finalized at Charlottetown and forcibly presented to both the Québécois and English Canadians on a "take it or leave it" basis, only served to deepen the divisions both within and between the two solitudes, as did the outcome and aftermath of the 1995 referendum.

The idea that Quebec is oppressed is a hard sell in English Canada. Canadians have many diverse grievances and oppressions that are uniquely rooted both in the design of Confederation and in our free market political economy. Confederation was, after all, a scheme hatched and carried out by the British Colonial Office to salvage the fortunes and futures of the traditional colonial elites in Britain's North American possessions. It involved the construction of a sea-to-sea federation that would remain loyal to Britain while containing the troublesome French fact. Confederation was a last resort for our elites, who had stumbled from option to option and crisis to crisis after the defeat of the rebels in 1837–38 and whose separate futures would doubtless have culminated in their falling into the tender embrace of Uncle Sam. Confederation had only minority popular support throughout the British colonies, except in Canada West (Ontario). Atlantic Canada, British Columbia and the Prairies all continue to have grievances rooted in the political and economic design of Confederation. It is, therefore, understandably hard to win sympathy for the Québécois nation from the poor and unemployed of Cape Breton or Newfoundland, from Saskatchewan farmers driven off the land because of low prices and debt, from B.C. lumber and mining communities that live through booms and busts always mindful that a total shutdown is possible.

But that sympathy must be won if we want Canada to survive. Whatever the grievances and the regional oppressions faced by English Canadians, we must never forget what sets the oppression of the Québécois apart. No other province or region has faced the routine use of military force, or the threat of such force, throughout its history. No other province or region can claim to be the political and constitutional homeland of a unique nation with its own language, culture and history. And the Québécois and the aboriginal nations are the only "peoples" or "nations" who can claim that their defeat and oppression laid the basis for the emergence of Canada as we know it. The Québécois nation exists, justifiably festering with historical grievances and resentments arising from unjust treatment by English Canada. These are the facts that English Canada refuses to face and avoiding them has been the object of an elaborate constitutional dance begun long before 1867. The dance must end; the facts must be faced.

And if we in English Canada want Canada to survive we must set about paying our debts to the Québécois nation, a nation we continue to deny at Canada's peril.

Quebec as a Defeated Nation: The Conquest

The first historical fact to remember is the military conquest of Quebec, for it must colour our interpretation of all subsequent events. It was much more than the defeat of the French by British forces in a contest for North America, a contest whose geopolitical outcome was only a matter of time. The Conquest was also the defeat of a nation — the *Canadiens* — a people who no longer saw themselves as French citizens on a temporary sojourn in the New World. They had, in fact, built a new *habitant* culture from which, for most, there was no going back.

English Canada no longer celebrates the Conquest. One rarely hears "The Maple Leaf For Ever" any more. School children do not recite 18 September 1759, the date of Quebec City's final surrender to the British, as a singular founding event in Canada's history. But the fact of conquest is not ignored. It is duly recorded as the inevitable outcome in a continental struggle between the 60,000 to 70,000 French, largely in Acadia and New France, and the more than 1.5 million British, largely in the Thirteen Colonies. It is also duly recorded that this was more than a local continental skirmish; it was a confrontation between the French and British world empires, a confrontation only finally resolved at Waterloo.

Historians in English Canada frequently refer to Versailles' neglect of New France and indifference to the growing gap between the French from France and the Québécois. In this context, the quip by Montcalm's aide Bougainville is often quoted: "It seems that we are of a different nation, even an enemy one." These historians also like to recount stories about the generosity of the British conquerors and the good, even kindly, relations between the

British troops and the people of Quebec City, especially during that first terrible winter of 1759–60.

General James Murray, Wolfe's replacement as troop commander and the first governor of Canada, was generous and humane in victory, once referring to the Québécois as "the bravest and the best race upon the Globe." Scarce food and fuel were shared, and troops who misbehaved were punished severely. During the worst of the winter, the British troops, ill-prepared and poorly equipped for the harsh climate, suffered terribly from the cold and hunger. Over a thousand soldiers died. The kindnesses of the conqueror were repaid by the conquered. The Ursuline nuns, who had tended the mortally wounded Montcalm and buried him in their convent's walls, knitted knee warmers for the bare-legged Highlanders. Such events should be remembered and celebrated, as should other, less admirable actions. They are not well remembered in English Canada, but they are among the Québécois.

This final war to conquer France in North America continued from 1754 to 1760 and, until the final year, the British did not fare well. Indeed, until the spring of 1760 neither the French nor the British knew for certain who would win the final day, since that depended on which country's supplies and reinforcements arrived in the St. Lawrence first. Montreal had not been taken, and the French army of seven thousand (including three thousand *Canadien* militiamen) had regrouped there and intended to retake Quebec City. General Murray had only three thousand troops fit to fight. The British fleet arrived first, and Montreal surrendered in September 1760.

However, because their campaign had gone badly until 1759, the British took some desperate measures. About 15,000 French lived on the Nova Scotia peninsula, which was ceded to Britain by the 1713 Treaty of Utrecht. Angry that many Acadians remained actively loyal to the French cause and fearful that a majority might share similar sentiments, the English decided, in 1755, to exile the Acadians forcibly and disperse them throughout the Thirteen Colonies. The orders were brutal — the Acadians were rounded up by military units and the homes and crops of those evading deportation were torched. In this way, an estimated 6,000 Acadians were dispersed, their land seized without compensation and later redistributed to loyal British settlers, largely from New England.

Before the battle on the Plains of Abraham, a frustrated Wolfe ordered a scorched-earth policy, burning homes, villages and farms along the St. Lawrence and shooting any *Canadien* who carried a gun. Further frustrated by Montcalm's effective defences at Quebec City, Wolfe had the city bombarded from across the river, a tactic without military merit that served only to inflict terror and suffering on the city's civilian population. The later generosity of Governor Murray could not completely erase such events from the collective memory of the Québécois. And the fact that Murray was forced out in 1766 by the minuscule but powerful bloc of British merchants, who chafed and bridled under the restrictions on their right to exploit Britain's newest possession freely, could not have been reassuring to the Québécois, who, above all, feared sharing the fate of the Acadians.

After the Conquest, the British occupation had two faces, military and economic. Of the two, the military occupation was the milder, and the economic occupation would have been even harsher, but for Murray and his successors. The newly arrived British merchants wanted to make profits, and anticipated easy plunder. The profitable fur trade of New France was rerouted from French to British hands and from French to British ports. But the merchants wanted more. Because the Québécois could not hold office, the British merchants sought an elected assembly and other rights for British subjects. Had they been successful, the Québécois would have been delivered, shackled, to a pitiless commercial fate. But Governor Murray, and later Governor Guy Carleton, who once described the British merchants as "the scum of the earth, masquerading as its salt," refused to accede.

Upon reflection, this contrast — economic occupation held in check by military occupation — makes sense. The British merchants had little interest in agriculture, except insofar as it fed land speculation. Their primary interest was the fur trade and the resulting commercial traffic across the Atlantic. Furthermore, for them, the Québécois were merely a source of cheap labour to staff this fur trade, a small but significant captive market, and the annoying occupiers of potentially profitable land. If the merchants could have exiled all the Québécois they considered either surplus to their pecuniary needs or impediments to profit, they would have done so without a second thought. After all, the Québécois were not only conquered and therefore subject, but they were also French and Catholic. On three counts, therefore, they were of little consequence.

The British military, and later the governors appointed from London, were concerned with both day-to-day and long-term order in the context of the long-range global interests of the British Empire. They were acutely aware that a handful of British occupiers could never hold the colony against a united, determined and aroused population. As military commanders and politicians, they knew the population had to be placated and reassured that their worst fears were groundless and that local leaders had to be won over to, at least, passivity and indifference. Wisely, therefore, they turned a blind eye to the practice of Catholicism and they spoke French when dealing with the population. The law was administered as fairly and as reasonably as possible under the circumstances. Charity was given. Kindnesses were shown.

Thus, even though the Royal Proclamation of 1763 outlined what appeared to be a draconian program of forced assimilation, its implementation was another story altogether. The Proclamation clearly intended to remake the new colony in the mould of British colonies. It imposed English civil and criminal law and customs and the use of English. Catholics were effectively barred from public office because of the oath requiring allegiance to the British monarch as head of church — the very oath that had provided the pretext for the exile of the Acadians. In this way, the Québécois were excluded from all influence in the society and effectively enjoyed no status as citizens. The size of the colony was severely reduced: the northern boundary now ran northeast from Lake Nipissing to Lake St. John and thence up the north shore of the St. Lawrence; the southern boundary ran due east from Lake Nipissing across the St. Lawrence and thence up the south shore of the river. The Proclamation also promised to introduce an elected assembly — which would effectively have been English and Protestant — in an effort to promote an influx of British settlers. The Proclamation was legally, but imperfectly, implemented and life for the ordinary Québécois went on much as before. Introducing an assembly was left to the governor's discretion, a discretion Murray and Carleton chose not to exercise.

While it may be true that the Conquest and its aftermath were benign by the standards of the day and that the governors did hold in check some of the more rapacious tendencies of the British merchants, these facts should not deflect us from the long-term sociological consequences of the Conquest. Québécois society lost its leadership. The British victory led to the dismantling of the French political and administrative apparatus, the displacement of the French and Québécois merchant elite and the emigration of many landowners. How many people actually returned to France and how many remained, or returned later to be absorbed in a transformed and defeated society, is the subject of scholarly controversy. Sociologically it makes little difference. These elements largely ceased to exist as leaders with real power in the larger community, and those who remained, did so on the conqueror's terms. British domination led to a massive rural retreat during which, like other conquered people, the Québécois turned inward and hunkered down in their parishes. Since their society was deprived of effective secular leadership, the Church and the local priest became a key focus of community life, a central source of leadership and a rampart for linguistic and cultural resistance. With no significant outside contact, Québécois society became increasingly homogeneous and rural, rooted in a subsistence economy and overseen by British masters. The extent of the "ruralization" of Québécois society was dramatic and quite contrary to world trends: at the Conquest it is estimated that 25 per cent of Québécois were urban dwellers. By 1825 only 12 per cent were urban, and in Quebec City and Montreal the British were in the majority. This rural character of Québécois society remained predominant until World War II.

Cut off from the usual sources of population renewal and growth available to colonial societies through immigration, the Québécois commenced what became known as "the revenge of the cradle," which saw the Québécois population, from the Conquest to the Quiet Revolution two hundred years later, increase eighty fold, rising from sixty or seventy thousand to five million, not counting the loss of another million or so to immigration to the United States. Today, Quebec has among the lowest fertility rates in Canada, a fact serving to increase the anxiety of the Québécois.

These, then, were the survival responses of a conquered nation determined to thwart the conqueror's plans. Certainly, the hope that the Québécois would ultimately be swamped by a huge British immigration was misplaced, at least initially. The slowness of British immigration, combined with the relentless rate of natural increase of the Québécois, made it clear that the French fact was in Canada to stay. The imposition of the English language and English laws, customs and administration had been met with passive resistance, and long-run prospects of a significant rate of assimilation appeared more and more elusive as the Québécois nation remained vital. Thus conqueror and conquered reached a potentially unstable standoff. British power and British numbers could never withstand the Québécois, should their resistance become active. This concern was always foremost in the minds of the wiser among the British, and it became even more central as the Thirteen Colonies moved from defiance to rebellion.

Under the circumstances, the loyalty of the Québécois could not be counted on, and even elements among the British merchants contemplated throwing in their lot with the American rebels. As relations deteriorated between the Thirteen Colonies and the British, Governor Carleton moved to forestall revolt in Quebec. The informal pact the British had made with the Québécois clergy and the remnants of the French merchant and landowning elite was carefully cultivated in order to ensure that the Québécois masses were not swept up in the coming American contagion. Now, however, the Québécois leadership, forever conservative but also nationalist, demanded a quid pro quo — the worst of the chains binding the Québécois nation would have to go. Furthermore, the bases of the Québécois leadership would have to be consolidated since the Québécois as a whole did not blindly love their elite.

The *Quebec Act* of 1774 was adopted just in time, only months before open military hostilities broke out between British troops and American rebels. The Act was a complete reversal of the policies embodied in the Royal Proclamation of 1763. The Québécois nation got its language, its old civil law and the freedom to practise its religion. With official, legal status, however, Québécois leaders were a step removed from their community, especially since they led by British selection rather than by Québécois election and therefore became more securely a part of the British apparatus of domination than before.

Furthermore, the *Quebec Act* explicitly forbade an elected assembly — "it is at present inexpedient to call an Assembly" — and established an appointed council to advise the governor. In this way, the overall governance of the Québécois remained essentially despotic. The British had, deliberately or otherwise, misinterpreted the Québécois' earlier resistance to an elected assembly from which they would be excluded as a resistance to elected assemblies in general. No one asked them if they wanted an assembly elected fairly by both Québécois and British residents, nor did their conservative leaders propose such a radical measure. The Québécois were not yet considered fit to enjoy the rights of Englishmen. In a final act, both to please the Québécois and to put the American rebels on notice, the *Quebec Act* also restored the boundaries of the colony to their pre-Conquest dimensions. The fact that much of this territory was part of future expansion plans of the Thirteen Colonies was far from accidental. The new province of Quebec was, therefore, made up of equal measures of desperation and expediency on London's part.

The *Quebec Act* was sufficient to ensure the passive neutrality of the Québécois during the American War of Independence. Contrary to some British expectations, the Québécois did not jubilantly hail this measure as a great victory, because for them it was not. But it was enough. While many sympathized with the American cause and more than a few joined the Americans to fight the British, the Québécois, as a nation, did not rise up and join the Americans to throw off the British yoke. But neither did they join the British. When the Americans invaded, the Québécois not only refused to join the American cause but also actively resisted efforts to conscript them to fight on the British side. They did not view the Americans as enemies and invaders, treating them more often as a first wave of bothersome tourists creating noise and disturbances in their tranquil communities. The Québécois did not want to fight on either side. Many, of course, did agitate on behalf of the Americans, and some suffered excommunication as a result. Others did act as guides for the Americans and even fought with them. Consequently, the neutrality of the Québécois remained uncertain until the very end. The *Quebec Act* of 1774 and the alliance that the measure cemented among the British, the Church and landlords was enough. But had Montgomery and Arnold's winter 1775 siege of Quebec City been successful, and had Quebec City surrendered to the Americans as Montreal had, Canada's and Quebec's stories would have been entirely different.

The *Quebec Act* granted the Québécois a portion of their national rights. It also briefly consolidated the conservative leadership bloc among the Québécois while setting in motion a process that ultimately undermined it. Professions that served the people and their culture were now legitimate: teaching, law, medicine and the notariat joined the priesthood, which resulted in the growth of an alternative secular and middle-class leadership potentially more independent and progressive than the old bloc. These professional occupations, and to a lesser extent the Québécois merchant class, provided a fertile field for ideas and ideals spawned by the American and French revolutions. Though the British continued to select Québécois office-holders "from a group...of 'followers' of the English," as the early Patriote Pierre Bédard put it in 1814, alternative leaders with substantial popular support began to emerge from among the new Québécois middle class. Only the lack of an elected assembly prevented these leaders from proving their legitimacy and then, when an assembly was granted, the absence of responsible government kept them from holding offices with real power.

The victory of the Americans had a final echo in Quebec with the arrival of the United Empire Loyalists to settle in the Eastern townships, the Gaspé and what was to become Ontario. These were the most loyal of British subjects, having faced and passed the ultimate test of civil war and having lost everything as a result of their commitment to Britain and the Empire. Of the estimated forty thousand Loyalists who came to British North America, most went to Nova Scotia, but a large group of about seven thousand arrived in Quebec and provided that colony with its first British population of any great significance.

The Loyalists both sustained and subverted the traditional British colonial merchant elite. They sustained the elite just by being there in numbers as ballast to the large Québécois population. They also sustained it by their deep pro-British patriotism, their anti-Americanism and their anti-republican conservatism. Their demands for loyalty to the British flag and Empire were implacable, and their standards were high. In payment for their losses, the Loyalists received an immediate tangible stake in the colony. Each Loyalist was granted one hundred acres of land, as well as another fifty acres for each additional person in their family. But the Loyalists who came to Quebec were largely farmers and therefore committed to further immigration and agricultural settlement. They found little support among the British merchant elite, whose vision was still limited by the blinders of mercantilism. The Loyalists also brought with them the expectation that they would enjoy the rights of Englishmen, including the election of assemblies and the right, as owners of property, to participate actively in the political life of the commonwealth. Inevitably, there was a clash of interests between the merchant elite and the Loyalist farmers, who were joined by other British immigrants who anticipated a well-settled agricultural society firmly based on a loyal landowning yeomanry. The contradiction between the commercial designs of the British merchant elite and the agricultural designs of the Loyalists could not be long contained merely by appeals to patriotism and loyalty.

The growing British population was unhappy both with the *Quebec Act*'s considerable concessions to the Québécois in law, language and land tenure and with its explicit prohibition of an elected assembly. Furthermore, they did not see the prospect of an assembly elected generally by both British and Québécois electors as a solution. They wanted British institutions, rights, laws and customs. And they wanted English to be the language of daily life, business and politics. These things the British population could never have without turmoil and controversy as long as they were confined in a political home with the Québécois. The Québécois, for their part, newly confident and assertive as a result of the assurances in the *Quebec Act*, and more and more led by a progressive middle-class leadership, were attracted to the idea of an elected assembly to provide a representative political voice for their nation. The demand for an elected assembly thus united the British and the Québécois against London and the local administrative elite. But they were very much divided on the other issues.

A reconciliation of sorts was achieved with the *Constitutional Act* of 1791. The Act imperfectly divided the British and Québécois populations into Upper and Lower Canada, respectively. The line of division, just west of Montreal, included in Lower Canada a small but powerful British minority. The Act allowed for elected assemblies, but appointed governors and councils. The rights of the British minority in Lower Canada were well protected: the appointed governor and a majority of the appointed council remained British, and the boundaries for election to the assembly were craftily drawn to give considerable over-representation to the British minority. For example, the Québécois, making up well over 90 per cent of the population of Lower Canada, were apportioned about 70 per cent of the assembly seats, while the British minority were granted the other 30 per cent. This practice of providing considerable over-representation to the British minority in the assembly only ended during the October Crisis in 1970. Nevertheless, in Lower Canada the stage was set for confrontation as the assembly rapidly became the democratic voice of the Québécois nation, or at least of those with property, and the appointed governor and council increasingly took on the character and appearance of external impositions, which, of course, they were.

Since the *Quebec Act* was not repealed, the effect of the *Constitutional Act*, which was, in fact, passed as an amendment to the *Quebec Act*, allowed each colony to decide which provisions of the *Quebec Act* would continue to be in effect. Needless to say, Upper Canada quickly opted out and established a truly British colony. Lower Canada, however, retained the comforts granted to the Québécois by the *Quebec Act*, while making careful arrangements to secure and protect the privileges of the British minority. At least in that sense, long before Confederation, Quebec was recognized as an atypical and "distinct" British colony. The forerunner of modern Quebec was therefore born in 1791, having been conceived in 1774.

The Québécois moved into the nineteenth century with some remarkable gains. They had been granted concessions that made it clear that London had finally abandoned the notion of making the French fact disappear through a combination of assimilation and British immigration, and they had secured their civil law, language and religion. Though their homeland had been considerably reduced with the creation of Upper Canada, the very act of creating Lower Canada provided the Québécois with a geographical and constitutional homeland. Granting elected assemblies — something that London could not very well give to British Canadians and not the Québécois — provided the nascent structures necessary for the democratic evolution of the Québécois. The only things that separated the Québécois nation from full mastery in their homeland were the appointed British governor and council, a powerful, privileged and dominant British minority, and British military might. To some of the more progressive middle-class leaders among the Québécois, who enjoyed growing popular support, responsible government and real national independence were only a small, if momentous, step away.

The Re-conquest and Isolation
of Quebec

The four decades following the *Constitutional Act* of 1791 occupy an uncertain place of honour in Canada's official history as the era dominated by the struggle for democratic and responsible government in Upper and Lower Canada. The Québécois of Lower Canada and the English Canadians of Upper Canada were largely united in this struggle, which pitted elected assemblies against the Family Compact and the Château Clique.

There was much that united the middle-class democratic movements in the two colonies: anger at, and hatred for, a corrupt economic and political oligarchy, which ruled as if the colonies were the personal fiefdoms of its members; fury at distant colonial masters in London who failed to respond to petitions with speed and justice; and the affliction of an unworkable political system based on elected assemblies with the limited power of supply and appointed governors and executives jealously holding all political and administrative authority. The result was an obvious impasse; the desire for colonial economic policies designed to encourage immigration, local industry and agricultural settlement, as opposed to the oligarchy's increasingly irrational determination to cling to the old mercantilist strategy. These grievances, in retrospect, made the Rebellions of 1837–38 inevitable.

There was, however, a central issue that divided the democratic movements in Lower and Upper Canada from each other. In Lower Canada the movement was both nationalist and democratic, shaped by the Québécois majority's resentment of the national oppression of British colonial rule and its local expression through a privileged, powerful and arrogant English minority. In Upper Canada the basic democratic issues were unclouded by the issue of national oppression and, as a result, both the Rebellion and its aftermath were much less bloody and bitter.

In Upper Canada the conflict between the assembly and the Family Compact was a more clear-cut constitutional question. The Family Compact dominated the London-appointed governor and his executive council. Furthermore, the gulf between the elite, the assembly members and the electors was not complete. The elite enjoyed some popular support and maintained a strong loyal presence in the assembly, and elections were not always foregone conclusions. The Reform movement won majorities in the assembly in 1828 and again in 1834, but only a minority in 1830, and in 1836 was defeated, amid charges of fixed votes, unfair counting, bribes and intimidation. Apparently, the governor's appeal in 1836 to British loyalty and patriotism was effective. The electorate's loyalty was uncertain and wavering, to be sure, and it was severely tried by London's refusal to accept the call for responsible government. But it was sufficient to hold most Upper Canadians, indeed most Reform sympathizers, back from leaping into the abyss of armed insurrection.

A new society was emerging in Upper Canada, one based on agriculture and small industry. It was composed largely of land-holding farmers locked in a structure of government and economy over which they had little or no control. Even when their representatives came to dominate the assembly, the appointed council remained in the hands of the dominant merchant class. This elite group had appropriated for themselves much of the land as its value increased. It was the land monopoly issue more than anything else that sparked the Rebellion. Indeed, the increasingly irreconcilable political conflict between the legislative and executive branches of government merely reflected this conflict between the new agricultural and industrial majority and the old mercantile minority, which blatantly used its control of the colonial state to defend its privileges. Lord Durham later agreed and reported the "deep-seated impediments in the way of industrial progress," including "the possession of almost the whole soil...by absentee proprietors, who would neither promote nor permit its cultivation, combined with the defective government which first caused and has since perpetuated the evil." It is not therefore surprising that William Lyon Mackenzie's 1837 Navy Island Proclamation most prominently promised freedom of trade and the redistribution of land when independence was won.

Independence, however, was not won. The Rebellion failed

miserably. The military confrontation involved only a few skirmishes in 1837 and its outcome was never in doubt: the Reform
forces were outnumbered, outgunned and very badly led. Canadians thereby learned the lessons learned by European revolutionaries
that same decade. You do not storm barricades and topple governments with ideals, passion and a just cause alone.

The repression was severe but not brutal, involving few casualties and no widespread punitive lootings or burnings against
populations sympathetic to the Reform cause. Two military leaders, Peter Matthews and Samuel Lount, were tried and hanged,
after being hugged and kissed by a tearful executioner. During the
1838 raids four captured Reformers were summarily executed
after they surrendered. Nine others were tried and executed, and
about sixteen were transported to Australian penal colonies. In
total, some 855 fighters were officially named as arrested or
escaping arrest. Most had their sentences of death or imprisonment commuted.

The 1837–38 Rebellion in Upper Canada is not accorded a
great deal of honour in English-Canadian history. When seeking
heroes from the event, English Canada has tended to honour
those who sided with the authorities against the Reformers. A
notable exception, of course, was the leader, William Lyon
Mackenzie, though he has hardly been lionized in Canadian history. The Rebellion is very often viewed as the unnecessary
actions of impatient hotheads whose extremism probably slowed
down rather than speeded up London's benevolent devolution of
responsible government to British North America. The Rebellion
in Upper Canada is often painted as faintly ridiculous, involving
a great deal of bombast, a lot of running and hiding, and very little shooting. No significant historical monument memorializing
the Rebellion in Upper Canada exists, with the exception of that
to the executed leaders Lount and Matthews located in the
Toronto Necropolis.

The Rebellion in Lower Canada was a different matter. The
national question dominated every other issue contested. While
Mackenzie envisioned an independent confederation of colonies if
the Rebellion succeeded, Louis-Joseph Papineau, the Patriote
leader, played coy with Mackenzie and toyed with the vision of an
independent Québécois nation-state emerging from success. Papineau and his followers favoured a democratic republican form of
government. They did not embrace proposals for universal male
suffrage, which were called for by the radical elements, nor did

they embrace some of the more thoroughgoing anti-seigneurial and anti-clerical tendencies. Thus the democracy envisioned was imperfect and designed primarily to transfer political, economic and social power from the English minority, and their British colonial masters, to the Québécois middle classes.

On the land question, Patriote concerns were different from those of the Reformers, since land and nation were inevitably emotionally intertwined in Lower Canada. The Patriotes were concerned about a land shortage resulting from both overpopulation and the fact that British immigrants with capital were taking up more and more land. Emotions concerning the land issue were intensified by the fact that the rural retreat after the Conquest had tied the survival of the nation to the land and the *habitant* way of life. Furthermore, British immigration into Lower Canada was viewed as ominous, particularly in the context of the recurring British dream of obliterating the French by drowning them in an irresistible tide of immigrants. The fact that the major urban areas were now the centres where economic, political and administrative power was held largely by the British did little to alleviate this fear. While the Reformers' economic program might be characterized as wide-open frontier capitalism, the Patriotes' was very much one of restrained capitalism managed in ways to sustain and nurture the nation. Though there was a radical wing in the Patriote party that wanted to go beyond the moderate policies to a more popular, anti-clerical and anti-seigneurial program, they only began to reach ascendancy in the dying days of the Rebellion and then only because of their military courage and dedication to the cause.

There were other fundamental differences between the Upper Canadian Reformers and the Lower Canadian Patriotes. Both movements opposed the colonial system as a corrupt and undemocratic barrier to economic progress. But the Patriote complaints could never be separated from the fact that they suffered under a British colonial regime and that the Québécois nation — the overwhelming majority of the population — suffered endless national oppressions and humiliations. Those few Québécois co-opted into positions of power and privilege were denounced as *les gens en place*, and such promotions were counted against those who took them. The British minority dominated the economy, particularly in trade, industry and finance, the sectors of growth, dynamism and progress. The relentless pressure of this British domination and encroachment denied land to many Québécois, drove others into emigration to the United States, and left the Québécois excluded from the economy in the growing cities. All this fit into the sense of national grievance and could only intensify Québécois fears that the long-run project of the British was the ultimate extinguishment of the Québécois nation, or at least its reduction to the status of a rootless minority in what was formerly its national home. The Rebellion, therefore, was seen as more than a fight for democratic and responsible government. It was also seen as the necessary means, first to save, and then to reassert, the Québécois nation's right of primacy of place on the soil of Lower Canada. Perhaps such emotions alone are sufficient to explain the Patriotes' greater courage, determination and more general willingness to die for the cause in comparison to their counterparts in Upper Canada.

After almost a generation of struggle for national recognition and democratic political reform, there was no doubt about the population's support for the Patriote party. In the 1827 election, the Patriotes won an overwhelming victory, reducing the English party opposition to four. Many Patriote assembly members were of British origin, but they were committed to both the democratic program and the struggle for national independence of the Patriotes. In the general election of 1834, held to the tune of Papineau's denunciation of "the aristocracy of the banks, the government and trade," and fought on almost entirely nationalist grounds, the Patriotes swept in with 77 per cent of the vote, winning seventy-eight seats (forty-one of these by acclamation) to the English party's nine seats. Just prior to the election, the assembly adopted Papineau's "Ninety-two Resolutions," a passionate distillation of Patriote grievances and remedies. The government of Lower Canada reached a stalemate between the appointed British-dominated executive and legislative councils and the elected assembly, which controlled public funds.

After the 1834 election, the Patriotes held a series of huge rallies demonstrating their popular support. Clearly, Papineau and the Patriotes were determined to use the decisive 1834 election results and their palpable support to force concessions from London. Popular anger against the British minority and Québécois "traitors" increased, scuffles broke out and tensions mounted. The situation was worsened by an economic crisis. A drastically small harvest resulted in a sharp rise in the price of bread and in the cost of living. The economic downturn adversely affected all sectors of the economy and increased popular anger as farmers plunged into debt, workers could find no work, merchants saw profits fall and professionals adjusted to shrinking incomes.

Meanwhile, grain that could not be found for local consumption was somehow found for the export market. The situation became a classical pre-revolutionary one, with political and economic grievances coming together into a hardening of positions and a widespread anticipation of a looming final confrontation. At this point, the impasse could have been broken, and the Rebellion avoided, had London agreed to serious reforms toward responsible government. Instead, on advice from the local British elite, London acted provocatively when the British House of Commons adopted Lord John Russell's infamous "Ten Resolutions" in the spring of 1837. The resolutions, in effect, rejected any concessions to the Patriote reform program, while stripping the elected assembly of its powers. The message was clear. Not only was London rejecting any reform in response to the years of tireless democratic agitation culminating in an unmistakable expression of popular will, but it had also decided to strip the Québécois of what little political power they enjoyed, the very instrument that had allowed them to mobilize and shape this expression of the nation's will. It was a provocation that could have had only one outcome, presenting the Patriotes with a stark choice: abject surrender or insurrection.

That the Patriotes had not seriously planned insurrection from the beginning is well known. No military preparations of any significance had been made. A Patriote militia had not been organized, though some Patriote activists secured positions in the established militia. Military plans had not been made. Talk of military action usually occurred as mere rhetorical flourishes in flights of political oratory. Typically, such talk was not followed up with any practical actions. These were not serious revolutionaries, though they were in love with the idea of revolution and naively convinced that revolution was justified in the circumstances.

The Church, long suspicious of the anti-clerical tendencies among the Patriotes, and the government took counteraction quickly and ruthlessly, catching the Patriote leadership off guard. The Church announced that there would be neither absolution nor religious burial for those rebelling against constituted authority. The Patriotes were denounced from the pulpits as "heathens, hypocrites, and manipulators." This effort to shatter the Patriotes' popular support largely failed, since many local priests did not comply with the bishop's directives. But the message could not help having some inhibiting effect. There was now a yawning gulf, according to the Church, between the rebels and devoted God-fearing Québécois.

The government banned public meetings, called in troops and commenced military preparations. Arrest warrants for Patriote leaders were prepared, but most went quickly into hiding. The ranks of the magistrates and militia were purged of known and suspected Patriote sympathizers. London and the local government had opted for a final, military solution of both the present crisis and the previous decades of impasse.

The actual two-year civil war in Lower Canada was quite extensive, involving a number of pitched battles between poorly armed Patriotes and British regulars and volunteers. In most major battles the Patriotes were inadequately led. The only significant Patriote victory occurred at St. Denis in the early phase of the war. Very soon, however, the war became a punitive expedition as British troops, particularly the volunteers with years of scores to settle, embarked on a campaign of killing, looting and burning. At St. Charles, surrendering Patriotes were killed and the village was burned. St. Denis was also burned to the ground in reprisal for being the site of the early victory. Patriote leader Dr. Jean-Olivier Chénier died during the defeat at St. Eustache. His body was put on display at the inn, it was rumoured that his heart was cut out, and the village was torched. Outnumbered Patriotes at St. Benoit offered to surrender, but their offer was refused and the village was attacked and burned to the ground. Burning villages and farms became so general that the British military commander and later governor of Lower Canada, Sir John Colbourne, was nicknamed *Vieux Brûlot* (Old Arsonist), and when he was later made Lord Seaton, many Québécois deliberately mispronounced his name as "Satan."

There are no precise figures for the total number of dead and wounded, but most accounts speak of hundreds. Of the estimated 515 locked up in jail at the end of the war, not counting those prematurely freed by Lord Durham, ninety-nine were condemned to death, and twelve were finally hanged. Fifty-eight were deported to penal servitude in Australia, and two were banished. Many hundreds fled into exile and later trickled back as pardons were granted. Chevalier DeLorimier, a Montreal notary who was among those executed, left a political testament in which he said, "I die without remorse; all that I desired was the good of my country, in insurrection and in independence...My efforts have been for the independence of my compatriots; thus far we have been unfortunate...I die with the cry on my lips: *Vive la Liberté, Vive l'Indépendance!*"

The full story of the uprising in Lower Canada is rarely recounted among English Canadians. We conveniently overlook it or diminish its significance. Among the Québécois it is different. The story is told and retold in all its detail. It is a deep part of the national heritage. The Patriotes are presented as heroes of the nation, and their names and the details of their lives are taught in school. Statues and monuments to the Patriotes dot the province. The most striking is that raised at St. Denis, the site of the only Patriote victory; topped by a Patriote partisan in fighting stance, it bears the simple inscription in French and English, "*Honneur aux Patriotes 1837*." The events of 1837–38, and the agitations leading up to them, mark the birth of the modern Québécois nation. Though the nation was reconquered and suppressed by military force and the noose, and though its leadership was broken and dispersed, slowing down its development, the Québécois nation did not disappear.

Lord Durham's report on the events, issued in January 1839, was a scurrilous, anti-Québécois document that once again reflected the English determination to extinguish the French fact. The document blamed the rebellions on the Québécois and proposed, most importantly, that measures be taken to prevent the Québécois from ever controlling an elected assembly again. Since Durham himself, as a radical lord, was committed to responsible government and since it was inconceivable for him to deny democracy to Englishmen, he took local advice and recommended that the stillborn 1822 idea of uniting Upper and Lower Canada into one colony, Canada, be resurrected. The estimated 400,000 British in Upper Canada would combine with the 150,000 in Lower Canada, providing a working majority against the 450,000 Québécois. Durham also recommended adopting a policy of assimilation. The English language would prevail as the language of government and business. Excluded from the vital mainstream, the language and customs of the Québécois would be pushed to the margins of society where they belonged. Durham's view was that, while the backward among the Québécois might continue their resistance by clinging to the old ways, the best and the brightest would be attracted to, and finally absorbed by, the opportunities and the progressive dynamism of a bustling, British-dominated colony. Furthermore, an aggressive encouragement of British immigration would doom the Québécois to the status of a declining minority.

London implemented many of Durham's recommendations with the *Act of Union* in 1840, which set the stage for the pattern that has continued ever since. The Québécois were locked up in a political and constitutional home they could never hope to control, a measure intended to ensure their long-term fate as a declining, marginalized minority. Upper and Lower Canada were united into a single colony with an elected assembly in which each former colony received forty-two seats. Thus, the seats for the old Upper Canada, combined with the over-representation provided the British minority in the old Lower Canada, would ensure a British-dominated assembly. French was denied official status as a language either of public record or of debate in the assembly. A very high property qualification was established for eligibility to run for election (in the old Lower Canada there had been no restrictions on who could run for the assembly, and a fairly low property qualification determined eligibility to vote). Furthermore, money bills could be presented to the assembly only by the government. Durham's major recommendation — responsible government — was flatly denied. The governor and council were appointed, and there was no requirement for equal representation from the two former colonies in the appointed councils nor was there a requirement for the representation of both language groups.

London did not, however, go the whole route in national oppression. French civil law remained in place for Canada East (Lower Canada), and the religious rights of the Catholic church were respected, as was the principle of the local control of education. Thus, Canada was an administrative nightmare with two systems of law, two legal bureaucracies, two attorneys-general, and two school systems with two different languages of instruction. The *Act of Union*, then, pleased no one completely, but neither did it offend anyone completely. The Reformers were angry that responsible government was not granted, but they were pleased that Governor Lord Sydenham promised nearly responsible government by a careful selection of his council to ensure that its members had the support of the assembly. The British Tory bloc was happy to get union, an assured British majority in the assembly and a postponement of full responsible government. The Québécois were angry, but they were also marginally relieved that the national oppression was not as thoroughgoing as they feared. The Québécois still had the right to elect representatives to the assembly, the comfort of their civil law and the assurance that their key cultural and linguistic institutions — schools and the Church — would be permitted to carry on. But it was to prove a largely unworkable system, ensuring that deadlock would again inevitably result.

London, Governor Lord Sydenham and the local British elite's biggest fear was that the Reformers of Upper Canada and the Patriotes of Lower Canada might coalesce around another reform program and achieve control of the new assembly. For the first election the governor left nothing to chance or to the unfettered exercise of democracy. The high property qualification served to keep out some of the radical riff-raff. In addition, the governor personally gerrymandered the electoral boundaries to reduce Québécois representation, and he actively campaigned in Canada West to encourage the election of moderate and/or conservative members. He also made clear he did not want too active a campaign, advising the public to "avoid useless discussion upon theoretical points of government." The tame press helped considerably in this effort to de-politicize the situation by warning the people "to shun as they would a pestilence the contaminating presence of an itinerant preacher of grievances…[and] to cast politics to the winds and devote themselves…to their farms and their warehouses as if…the turmoil of an election had never been heard by their peaceful firesides."

The effort was successful, and the first assembly saw only a handful of committed Reformers elected from Canada West. Though a significant group of Patriotes was elected in Canada East, the heir to Papineau's mantle, Lafontaine, was defeated. In the end, the governor had an assembly he felt he could work with — a moderate majority of around fifty to sixty members, with a strong but not unmanageable Patriote/Reform opposition on the left and a rump group of hard Tories carping on the right.

With a relatively tame assembly, the Québécois nation again contained and a sort of half-way house to responsible government in place, the resurrection of the old mercantile dream seemed plausible, even irresistible. Prosperity returned, and the future seemed to hold prospects unlimited for the elite, which, though somewhat transformed and a bit subdued, had survived the worst fear of elites everywhere — a popular insurrection. The St. Lawrence trade route would dominate the heart of the continent — British and American — carrying raw or partly finished staples to Europe and bringing British manufactured goods back. Both trips would fill merchant and forwarding pockets. Settlers would rush in. An imperial loan on good terms and a doubling of the revenue tariff assured the new colony's fiscal recovery, making it possible to complete the St. Lawrence canal system. Alas, for the elite, the golden future was not to be; the house of cards began to collapse.

To the dismay of Canadian merchants and Tories, Britain began to dismantle its worldwide mercantile system and move to free trade. This process began in 1842 with measures that reduced the preference for Canadian wheat and timber; next, the Corn Laws and Timber and Sugar Duties were repealed and finally, in 1849, the protection given by *The Navigation Acts* ended. These moves swept away the foundation of Canada's commercial system, which relied on imperial preference and protection for its exports and *The Navigation Acts* for its shipping industry. Furthermore, to emphasize London's conviction that British colonies had to find their own niche in the world economy and become responsible for themselves, in 1842 Canada was granted de facto responsible government, followed by formal and final measures in 1847. In an irony of history, what the Reformers and Patriotes had failed to win in 1837–38 was granted by the imperial Parliament: economic self-determination and responsible government. The ideological descendants of 1837–38, now more moderate, came to ascendancy; the old Tory bloc was more or less excluded from power; the French language returned to official status in 1848; and a complex and comprehensive reform program was carried out.

Britain's moves to free trade precipitated an economic disaster in Canada. Exports of wheat and flour collapsed, property values declined and bankruptcies accelerated. Even with the changes following on responsible government, Canada's new political and economic elite had no alternative economic strategy for recovery, and consequently the government lurched from crisis to crisis. Eventually Canada's choices became clear, even to the old Tories. The alternatives were not attractive; they were all through perilous uncharted waters, and none included the old secure special mercantilist bond with Britain.

The cruelly orphaned colony could move to a policy of economic protection, keeping the home market for local manufacturers and encouraging industrialization. It could adopt free trade, carving out an economic niche in a world already dominated by European industrial powers. It could embrace annexation and throw its lot into a continental American empire. It could seek reciprocity with the United States in an effort to exchange benefit for benefit in the hopes of ultimate prosperity. Or, the colony could adopt a mixture of such policies. This last prudent course was adopted as Canada's elite opted for a judicious application of protection and reciprocity, but with considerable energy also devoted to maintaining a special relationship with Great Britain. The shadow blueprint for Confederation began to be drawn.

The first step to Confederation was the Intercolonial Reciprocity Agreement of 1850 between Canada, New Brunswick, Nova Scotia and Prince Edward Island, which provided for preferential duties for each colony's products in the others. This worked so well for Canada West that pecuniary enthusiasm for Confederation increased rapidly. In 1854 the Reciprocity Treaty with the United States was signed. Again, Canada West did very well, particularly as the growth in markets began to stimulate Canada's small manufacturing base. There was a brief period of prosperity until the 1857 depression. It resulted in another fiscal crisis, spurring a further strategic innovation, as Minister of Finance Alexander Galt proposed his famous "fiscal tariff with incidental protection." With one bold stroke more revenue was generated at the same time as the government responded to demands from Canada's emerging industrialists for targeted protection of the home market. Growing discontent with the Reciprocity Treaty in Canada, especially among farmers, fishermen and lumbermen, who were becoming unhappy with the free flow of natural products, was now joined by American annoyance at these moves to protection. The protectionist North's victory in the American Civil War in 1865 and the subsequent abrogation of the treaty by the U.S. government simply confirmed the wisdom of the already well-prepared underpinnings of Confederation: westward expansion, an east-west transcontinental railway and industrialization through protection.

This colonial project, though largely conceived in London, received its strongest support in Canada West, soon to be Ontario. London's interests were clear: to preserve a British North America from sea to sea. To realize it, London had to beg, cajole and threaten the elites of Britain's North American possessions, except in Ontario. There Confederation, particularly the economic prospects of a vast westward expansion, captured the imagination. Canada, as a transcontinental national economy, was to be Ontario's. More importantly, the West was to be Ontario's frontier.

What of Canada East, soon again to be Quebec? In the period leading to Confederation, Québécois nationalism had divided between the conservative Bleus and the more radical Rouges. The Bleus entered into a pact and shared power with the English moderates of Canada West. Radical nationalism ebbed and became more and more isolated. Anti-clericalism and freethinking became increasingly unacceptable and the Church enjoyed a renewed status in the society, joining the governing coalition. The pact, quite simply, was to accept the defeat of the Québécois nation in 1837–38 and to attempt to salvage the essence of the nation — its language, religion and culture — through accommodation and compromise with the dominant English. And, though the *Act of Union* imposed strict limits on the Québécois nation, significant concessions had been secured.

As the Confederation scheme unfolded, supported by the Bleus in Canada East, a promise was held out to the Québécois nation. Canada would be divided into two provinces: Ontario and Quebec. Thus, the Québécois would again be granted a political and constitutional home in which they would enjoy a certain hegemony within the considerable constitutional limits of Confederation. The French language and civil law would prevail in Quebec, and significant powers would be granted to both provinces with respect to education, health, local government, property, resources, civil rights and a large say in agriculture. These powers would be, in turn, sufficient to defend the cultural and linguistic foundation of the Québécois nation. The powerful English minority in Quebec would be reassured by Article 80 of the *British North America Act* (*BNA Act*), which established seventeen protected English provincial constituencies in the Eastern Townships, the Ottawa Valley and northwestern Quebec. These constituencies were to remain protected until a majority of the seventeen sitting members agreed otherwise. And, for the first time since 1837, the Québécois nation would be able to express its democratic political will, however circumscribed by the *British North America Act*, through a National Assembly.

For the British-dominated Canada West, the dangers inherent in defying Durham's advice never again to allow the Québécois domination in an elected assembly were offset by being rid of the burden of having constantly to reconcile the divergent interests of the united Canada. Establishing Ontario as the biggest, richest and most dynamic and powerful province, freed of all the messy history of the old colony, would allow the province's elite to get on with nation-building and westward expansion — British nation-building and westward expansion. With the Québécois nation safely secured in a separate province under a strong central government dominated by Ontario, the elite of Ontario could turn its mind to other more important matters.

Yet the Québécois in their new province could pose a threat. With its large population, economic base and strategic location on the St. Lawrence, Quebec was the only province that could present itself if not as an alternative leader of Confederation, then at least as a serious counterweight to Ontario. This might prove a serious problem if the Québécois nation decided to play a significant role in westward expansion through settlement. This was unlikely to happen since Québécois nationalism was obsessively rooted in Quebec soil. Nevertheless, it could occur if opportunities arose for those with a broader vision of the role that the Québécois nation could play in Confederation, a vision that might include the co-development of the West to include a significant French population. After all, the Québécois had not been reluctant to move in droves to the United States to seek their fortunes. Why would they not move in large numbers to a West that was welcoming and congenial to them? It was one thing to lock up the Québécois nation in the province of Quebec, but it also had to be isolated and confined there, and the rest of Canada, especially Ontario's frontier in the West, quarantined from the French fact. The vision of Canada as a British nation from sea to sea — except for Quebec — could not be realized if the West were to become a series of New Brunswicks. And it was, indeed, in the West that any emerging aspirations of the Québécois nation to play a significant role in building Canada outside Quebec were firmly thwarted.

In March 1992, the House of Commons honoured Louis Riel by adopting a resolution recognizing his "unique and historic role" in founding the province of Manitoba and in defending the rights of the Métis. Riel has long been viewed by western Canadians as a hero in the West's battle against Central Canadian domination. And it goes without saying that he has been held in deeper reverence by both Indian and Métis.

Louis Riel led two rebellions resisting the terms of incorporation of the Prairie West into Confederation — one in 1869–70 in Red River, the other in 1885 in the Saskatchewan region. In 1670 the Prairie region and most of the vast northern territory had been granted by the British Crown to the Hudson Bay Company, which for two hundred years exercised relatively complete economic and political control over the region and its inhabitants. In 1867–68 Canada negotiated the purchase of the entire region from the Company for 300,000 pounds sterling, retention of one-twentieth of the "fertile belt" in the region (about seven million acres) and further land grants around the Company's many trading posts. In 1869, Canada dispatched a governor to take control of the entire region as a colonial possession of Ottawa. At no time were the Red River inhabitants consulted. Sixteen hundred white settlers, 5,700 French-speaking and 4,000 English-speaking Métis lived in the region.

The local people responded with something less than enthusiasm to their annexation by Canada. The French-speaking and Catholic Métis feared for their language, education and religious rights. White settlers and the Métis as a whole shared a concern that their rights, particularly land rights, would be overridden without prior guarantees. Both groups wanted some form of responsible government and full provincial status, and rejected the prospect of exchanging the dictatorship by the Company for one by Ottawa. When the Canadian governor, William McDougall, declared his authority over the region, the overwhelming majority of white settlers and Métis united under the leadership of Riel, proclaimed a provisional government, issued a list of rights and demanded negotiations with Ottawa. Ottawa agreed to negotiate, and as a result the province of Manitoba was established in 1870. The French and English languages were both granted official status, local control of education was assured, the recognition of the rights to tenure on existing farms was promised and 1.4 million acres of land were designated for the settlement of outstanding Métis land claims. This was a significant victory, though it was somewhat offset by Ottawa's decision to constrict Manitoba's size to just 10,000 square miles around what is now Winnipeg and to deny the new province control of its lands and resources.

The grievances in Saskatchewan in 1885 were similar, again uniting white and Métis. This time there was also significant support from the native nations, who faced starvation and were angered at the failure of Ottawa to live up to treaties. The 1885 "Bill of Rights" demanded more just treatment for Indians, a redress of Métis land grievances and guarantees of security of tenure on existing farms for whites and Métis alike. Additionally, the demands included responsible government, representation in the House of Commons and the cabinet, control of lands and natural resources, improvements in the homestead laws, vote by ballot, improvements in rail transportation and tariff reductions. The central political demand was again full provincial status and involved a threat of separatism: "We may settle up with the East and form a separate federation of our own in direct connection with the Crown," Riel warned in his Bill of Rights.

When the Red River Rebellion occurred, Québécois opinion insisted that the Canadian government negotiate Riel's Bill of

Rights, which included education and language equality for French and English. Ontario opinion wanted to send an army to crush this affront to Canadian law and sovereignty. In Quebec, Riel was celebrated as a Québécois hero battling against British arrogance. In Ontario, he was viewed as a rebel and, after the execution of Thomas Scott, a villainous murderer. British refugees from Red River wanted nothing less than a war of conquest, followed by the imposition of a stern regime until British immigration could increase the loyal population sufficiently to outvote the French in the colony. Ontarians largely shared this view.

Prime Minister John A. Macdonald initially tried to appease both sides. He agreed to negotiate Riel's Bill of Rights, but he also agreed to send a military expedition. In an effort to reassure Quebec, Macdonald promised that the military expedition would not be punitive and let it appear that he agreed an amnesty would be granted to the rebels. This amnesty was widely understood in Quebec, and among the rebels, to be a general one, including Riel. When some twelve hundred troops were raised for the expedition, an effort was made to include Québécois. But the Québécois proved reluctant, and the Quebec battalion that finally went west included mostly British volunteers. In Ontario, there was no problem recruiting for this *cause célèbre*, since many did see the main object of the expedition as avenging the executed Scott. Given the mood, an amnesty was simply unthinkable in Ontario.

Increasingly, the debate about Riel and Red River became a more fundamental one about the character of Confederation in the West. The Québécois hoped to assert that the West was not the private possession of Ontario and the Orange Order. Ontario was determined to claim just that: the West did belong to Ontario, and Quebec ought not to meddle.

In the end, the Québécois felt betrayed. Riel did not get amnesty and fled into exile, where he lingered despite his continuing popularity in both Quebec and Red River. In 1873 and 1874, he was elected to the House of Commons *in absentia*. The military expedition turned out to be sufficiently punitive to drive many Métis westward. The land settlement the Métis gained was more or less annulled through deliberate administrative delays and harassment and the issue of scrip negotiable for cash. But the defeat was not complete by any means. The province of Manitoba was established, both French and English were established as official languages and two school systems were guaranteed. The French fact had an official and legally equal foothold in the West.

The script was more or less replayed in the North-West Rebellion in 1885. Riel was called back by his people, Métis and white, French and English, to lead the region's campaign for settlement of its grievances. Riel had, after all, despite his personal banishment, been successful in winning the establishment of Manitoba. But English Ontario immediately vilified him as a rebel, a murderer and a traitor. Again, the Québécois praised Riel as a patriot, almost equal to the 1837 leader Papineau, fighting the good national cause against English domination and injustice. Opinions were somewhat harder and more polarized this time. Many in Ontario saw the Rebellion as a determined effort to impose the French language and culture on what should be English Canada's western preserve. Facing overwhelming odds, including eight thousand men, artillery and machine guns, Riel's forces were easily defeated at Batoche. This time there was no pretence that the military expedition was not punitive. Métis communities and farms were looted and burned and the population was dispersed westward and northward. Riel surrendered, was taken to Regina, tried before an English and Protestant jury, found guilty of high treason and condemned to death despite the jury's recommendation for mercy.

With the death sentence pronounced, the national debate between Orange and English Ontario and French and Catholic Quebec became intense and bitter. Many Québécois now saw Riel as a potential martyr on an equal footing perhaps with Joan of Arc, and certainly with the Patriotes of 1837–38 who went to the scaffold. The Québécois demanded that Riel be pardoned. English Ontario saw him as a twice-over traitor who must not be allowed to escape the noose again.

Macdonald played his usual double game, but in the end he had to make a decision amid a great deal of political pressure and turmoil, some of which had spilled from the editorial pages and the meeting halls onto the streets in minor riots. If Macdonald agreed to allow Riel to hang, he risked his loyal Conservative base in Quebec. On the other hand, given the intensity of passions aroused in Ontario, if Macdonald agreed to pardon Riel he risked his base in Ontario and perhaps in the rest of English Canada. Reasoning that he had survived the 1869 Red River controversy and that nationalist passions in Quebec usually died down with time, Macdonald decided to yield to Ontario. Macdonald's personal preference was revealed in a remark that has echoed through the pages of Canadian history ever since: "He shall hang though every dog in Quebec bark in his favour." And so, on 16 November 1885 Riel was hanged. Macdonald seriously miscalculated this time, for the bark of Québécois nationalism turned out to have a serious bite indeed. The hanging of Riel, and the bitter division between Québécois and English Canadians created by that sorry event, resulted in the rise of a Québécois nationalism strong enough both to defeat the Conservative provincial government in Quebec and ultimately to ruin the federal Conservative party in Quebec for almost a hundred years.

The message to Quebec was obvious. The Québécois nation could play no significant role in westward expansion. The West belonged to English Canada. The Québécois had earlier made some symbolic, even practical, gains, thanks to the apparent victory at Red River. French and English were made official languages in Manitoba in 1870, and in the North-West Territory in 1875. In the aftermath of the 1885 Rebellion and Riel's execution, these gains were quickly and unconstitutionally erased. In 1890 the Manitoba legislature declared that French was no longer an official language, and in 1892 the North-West Territory legislature followed suit. In 1912, French was eliminated from public education in Ontario. In 1916, after a series of crises and unsatisfactory compromises, Manitoba abolished French, or any language other than English, in its schools.

* * *

From the defeat of Riel in 1885 until the Quiet Revolution of the 1960s, enormous impediments were thus put in the way of those francophones in English Canada who wished to retain their language and to educate their children in French. It was in this period that the incredible and moving stories of the Québécois diaspora outside Quebec emerged, stories of assimilation, ridicule, prejudice, and discrimination — even of training children to hide their French texts when the education inspectors came to town. In Quebec, by contrast, the English minority enjoyed enormous privileges. The message that the Québécois were unwelcome in Confederation if they ventured outside of Quebec was taken to heart by the Québécois. At the turn of the century, just over 7,000 francophones resided in Saskatchewan and Alberta, which had a total population of 165,000. Another 16,000 could be found among Manitoba's population of 255,000 and 5,000 among British Columbia's population of 179,000. In other words, from the western border of Ontario to the Pacific, at the height of the western settlement boom, there were fewer than 30,000 francophones in a total population of approximately 600,000. Among those deciding to seek their futures outside of Quebec, few came to the western frontier where they were obviously not wanted, while more than 500,000 immigrated to the United States. Had this tidal wave of Québécois come west there is no doubt Canada would have become an entirely different country. But that, of course, is the point. English-Canadian opinion in Ontario was determined that Canada could never be allowed to become such a place.

It should be understood clearly that the Québécois nation backed down from the immediate confrontation over the 1885 Rebellion and Riel's fate. Many historians express admiration for this statesmanlike behaviour, as well as for Québécois reasonableness over the subsequent suppression of French-language rights outside Quebec. Had Québécois political leaders pushed the issue further, the very foundations of Confederation might have broken asunder just before success began with the 1896 Wheat Boom. It was clear to the Québécois that English Ontario had no intention of backing down. But was their behaviour an act of statesmanship, or was it a frank recognition of yet another defeat? Conquered in 1759, reconquered in 1837–38, having had the apparent Red River victory turned into defeat and then having been defeated by proxy in 1885, the Québécois nation again retreated into a degree of passivity.

Ontario had carried the day. The Confederation project, including the development of the cherished western frontier, would proceed on Ontario's terms without any significant compromise. Though the national pride and sensibilities of the Québécois had again been wounded and a more aggressive nationalism had briefly stirred, the Québécois nation remained locked up in Quebec, deliberately isolated from Confederation's western realization. Across English Canada the mocking stereotypes of the Québécois held sway, and within Quebec the population played the passive role of being a captive market and the source of cheap labour, overseen by English-Canadian economic masters, as wave upon wave of British and then Eastern European immigrants passed through the Québécois national enclave on the St. Lawrence. Yet, it was also self-evident that the Québécois nation had to be handled with care. If the events of 1837–38, 1869–70 and 1885 proved anything, they proved that there were limits to the endurance of the Québécois, limits that English Canada transgressed at the peril of keeping Confederation intact. During the conscription crises of World Wars I and II, the limits of that endurance were again tested significantly by English Canada. By far the most serious crisis of the two was World War I.

When Great Britain declared war on Germany in August 1914, Canada, as a loyal dominion in the British Empire, was automatically at war as well. It may seem incredible that a nation could go to war without a decision of its people or their representative institutions, but the war was completely, even enthusiastically, accepted by English Canada. Among the Québécois, there was no such enthusiasm. Nationalists in Quebec had long attacked British imperialism and warned that Canada would be dragged into distant wars it had no tangible reason to fight. Ever since the Boer War, Québécois nationalists had taken the position that the Québécois should eagerly share the burden in dollars and blood of defending Canada but absolutely oppose fighting British wars of imperialism. Rather than with enthusiasm, then, the Québécois accepted Canada's role in World War I with resignation, insisting that fighting in the war remain voluntary and that Canada not jeopardize the national treasury. Resigned to their isolation and exclusion, yet still annoyed over the loss of French education in Ontario, and even more annoyed by Manitoba's English-only education decision in 1916, the Québécois made it clear that military service by conscription could not be imposed on the Québécois and that if it were attempted, it would not be tolerated.

The glorious "war to end all wars," which many expected to be over by spring of 1915, dragged on and on into a bloody stalemate, and the new industrial techniques of mass war combined with the military tradition of fighting from fixed positions to produce staggering casualties. The demand for fresh troops could not be met by voluntary recruitment, despite the government's information campaign, which combined censorship to hide the truth of what was happening with a duplicitous propaganda effort. From the beginning, the Québécois had not been eager to enlist, and that resistance grew as the war continued. Even in English Canada, where early efforts at voluntary recruitment had been quite successful, eagerness subsided, especially as the truth trickled home from the trenches to families of men undergoing the horror. Criticism of the war was not then limited to Quebec. Québécois voices of dissent were joined by those from farm and labour movements in English Canada, especially in the West. Though English Canada was divided, the loudest clamour still came from those supporting the war, and they increasingly began to point an accusing finger at Quebec for not carrying its fair share.

In this context, Prime Minister Robert Borden approached what he viewed as the need for conscription gingerly, aware that the Tory government could go down to defeat on the issue. He first tried to make the recruitment effort more effective, but he declared he would move to conscription if necessary in order to raise sufficient troops to fulfil Canada's commitments. In 1917, after voluntary recruitment had failed to reach acceptable levels, Borden decided to institute conscription. Acutely aware of the anger his action would provoke in Quebec, Borden approached Wilfrid Laurier to join a coalition government in order to prosecute the war effort. Laurier refused and Borden then approached members of the English-Canadian wing of the Liberal Party, most of whom joined him in the Union government. Though Parliament passed the conscription measure, serious implementation awaited an election on the issue. Deeply uncertain of victory, given both Québécois and growing English-Canadian opposition, the Union government passed *The Military Voters Act* and *The War-time Elections Act* just before calling the 1917 election.

The first law gave the vote to all those in the armed forces, including women (who as a group did not yet have the vote), without any residency or citizenship requirements. Leaving nothing to chance, the military ballots were cast simply for or against the Union government and not for candidates. Furthermore, if the military voter did not designate his or her home constituency, the vote was assigned by the elections officer. The second law gave the vote to all female relatives of people in the armed services, including wives, mothers, daughters and sisters. Even Borden did not dare include grandmothers, female cousins, sisters- and mothers-in-law. Furthermore, the law took the vote away from conscientious war objectors and all immigrants from enemy countries who had come to Canada since 1902. As the election campaign came to a close, Borden was still worried about continuing farmer opposition. Just two weeks before the vote, the cabinet issued an order-in-council exempting farmers' sons from conscription. Taken together, these efforts were probably the most comprehensive (and perfectly legal) attempt to fix or steal an election in Canadian history.

It worked. The Union government won an overwhelming victory, 153 seats to 82 with a popular vote of 57 per cent. English Canada delivered massively: 12 of 16 seats in Nova Scotia; 7 of

11 in New Brunswick; 74 of 82 in Ontario; 14 of 15 in Manitoba; all sixteen in Saskatchewan; and all thirteen in British Columbia. In Quebec the results were quite different. The Québécois gave 62 of 65 seats to Laurier with 73 per cent of the vote, and the three seats that went to Borden were English-speaking. But the actual vote was closer than it appears. Just under 320,000 votes separated the Union government and Laurier's anti-conscription Liberals. Of this victory margin, 200,000 came from the military vote and only 100,000 from the civilian vote. Had *The Military Voters Act*, *The War-time Elections Act* and the last-minute exemption of farmers' sons (which was withdrawn the following spring) not been put in place, the Union government might well have either gone down to defeat or achieved such a narrow majority that Borden could not have proceeded the way he did without risking losing the confidence of the House of Commons.

The Union government's efforts to impose conscription on the Québécois were a monumental disaster. The mood of the Québécois had been made clear when the bill was first introduced and passed: virtually the entire Québécois press opposed the measure; opponents carried out a massive lobby effort; protest rallies were held; the home of the pro-conscription owner of the Montreal *Star* was bombed; and serious rioting occurred in Montreal. And in January 1918, on the heels of the Union victory, a Québécois member of Quebec's National Assembly introduced a motion offering to separate from Canada if English Canada found Quebec's presence distasteful. The motion was short and blunt: "That this House is of the opinion that the province of Quebec would be disposed to accept the breaking of the Confederation Pact of 1867, if in the other provinces it is believed that she is an obstacle to the unity, progress and development of Canada." The motion provoked a lively debate and received a lot of headlines, but it was withdrawn before a vote was taken. Clearly, the purpose of the motion was to warn English Canada just how serious the situation had become.

The Union government failed to heed the warning and proceeded to implement the law. In defiant response, the Québécois engaged in a mass resistance to it. Local boards granted wholesale exemptions. Draft dodging and aiding draft dodgers became nearly universal. Deserters fled to the United States. Even the Quebec legal system could not be counted on for systematic enforcement. The situation became an ugly confrontation between an English-Canadian government with no Québécois representation, a government that, furthermore, appeared to have rigged an election and thus had little democratic or moral legitimacy, and the Québécois nation. Never since 1837 had the divisions been so deep. The Union government, under relentless pressure from English Canada, was determined to impose the law of the land upon the Québécois. The Québécois were just as determined to defy it.

Matters came to a head in Quebec City on Easter weekend, 1918. On the evening of 29 March, Dominion police officers detained a Québécois on the street, and when he could not produce his draft exemption papers, briefly arrested him and took him to his home, where he produced the proper papers. However, his public arrest was the spark for bloody rioting, which lasted until 2 April. The crowds burned a police station, vandalized a newspaper and stormed and burned the office of the registrar of *The Military Service Act*. The police asked for military help. Martial law was declared. In an act of complete stupidity, or of deliberate provocation, a battalion of English-Canadian soldiers from Toronto was sent to relieve the civil authorities. Their clumsy and brutal efforts to contain the crowds with bayonets and clubs were completely unsuccessful and served only further to enrage the local population. On the evening of 1 April, the military authorities claimed that snipers had fired on troops, and they responded by firing back. Others claim the troops fired on an unarmed crowd. In all, five civilians were killed, a great many were wounded and scores were placed under military arrest without bail. The authorities produced four wounded soldiers, which suggests that the snipers, if there had indeed been any, were remarkably bad shots. At an inquiry, a local jury laid the entire blame for the incident at the feet of the authorities.

The situation was reduced to a stalemate after the Easter riot. The Union government refrained from enforcing the law too vigorously, and the Québécois continued their passive resistance. When all special exemptions from the draft were withdrawn later that month, rioting and draft resistance became significant in English Canada. Then refraining from a zealous enforcement of the law seemed an even wiser course for the government to pursue. Furthermore, as the war began to turn in the Allies' favour and the end came in sight, the only effect of enforcing conscription would have been to create an even deeper chasm between Quebec and English Canada. By the end of the war, English Canada could claim only partial victory over Québécois war resistance. About the same number of Québécois submitted to conscription as resisted it. The

Québécois nation had a chance to pass judgement on conscription in the 1919 provincial election when the Quebec Tories won only five seats with less than 24 per cent of the vote, the lowest Bleu vote since Confederation. And in the 1921 federal election, the Québécois gave all sixty-five seats and more than 70 per cent of the vote to the Liberals, entirely shutting out the Tories.

The World War II conscription crisis was much less serious, but it again revealed the deep chasm between English Canada and Quebec. When Canada's Parliament declared war, Prime Minster Mackenzie King, remembering Quebec and World War I, made an early promise that no Canadian would be conscripted for the war effort and that Canada would focus on supplying war material and equipment rather than cannon fodder. This promise mollified Quebec, and the provincial Liberals actually defeated the Union Nationale when Duplessis called an election to criticize Canada's involvement in the war. But King's position pleased neither English Canada nor its allies. As the war continued to go badly, with victory after victory by Germany, and particularly after Japan entered the war with stunning success at Pearl Harbor, pressure for conscription mounted. In fact, English Canada clamoured for conscription. But the Québécois made equally clear their determination to resist it. The King government tried to extricate itself by holding a plebiscite asking the Canadian electorate to release the government from its no-conscription promise. English Canada said "yes" with a resounding 80 per cent. Quebec said "no" with an equally resounding 73 per cent. The stage was again set for an ugly confrontation. King, however, adroitly implemented his "conscription if necessary, but not necessarily conscription" compromise. There would be conscription, he said, but no one who did not volunteer would be sent overseas to combat. Those who were conscripted for home defence and refused to volunteer for overseas service became known as "zombies," a term that did not sit well with the Québécois. Even though the King government later reneged and repealed the measure limiting overseas service to volunteers, the practice of sending only volunteers overseas largely continued. Nevertheless, holding the plebiscite and breaking the no-conscription vow led directly to the re-election of Duplessis and the Union Nationale in the 1944 Quebec election. Only military victory in 1945 and the fact that the federal Tories were now totally unpalatable to the Québécois saved King from a similar fate in the federal election of 1945.

* * *

By the end of the era of the world wars, Québécois nationalism had changed considerably, but it remained largely divided between two great ideological streams. One stream, which adhered more or less to the Liberal Party, argued that Quebec should seek to affect the Canadian identity in ways that pulled it away from the British Tory tradition in order to achieve a more significant place for the Québécois in Canadian national life through the positive use of the Québécois presence in federal institutions. At the same time, this group held, the Québécois should sustain and develop their unique cultural and linguistic identity as a small nation within the larger one. The larger nation of Canada, which included both Québécois and British traditions, should develop a unique Canadian nationalism, simultaneously incorporating both traditions and accommodating the inevitable divergences when they occurred. This stream, though federalist, could still be fiercely and assertively nationalist when confronted by threats to the Québécois nation and its cultural and linguistic life.

The other stream of Québécois nationalism remained largely turned inward on itself and its political enclave in Quebec. It was more intensely nationalistic and viewed the Québécois role in Canadian federal institutions merely as one of protecting Quebec from encroachments by English Canada. In a sense, federal institutions were seen as agencies that could be used when necessary, but not as ones to be embraced positively. There was no commitment to an effort to build a unique Canadian nationalism blending British and Québécois traditions. Such a project was seen either as an illusory fool's paradise or as a dangerous trap that would lead to assimilation. The proper nationalist project was to defend and sustain the Québécois nation and to take every opportunity to empower it further. This stream was further divided into a variety of smaller tendencies, ranging all the way from a right-wing, ultra-religious nationalist tradition to varieties of progressive and anti-clerical nationalism. The conservative stream tended toward a defensive strategy, rooted largely in fond remembrances of the past, reacting aggressively only to attacks and outrages on national sensibilities. The more progressive stream tended toward a more assertive and aggressive nationalism, advocating programs of modernization and sometimes of radical social change.

Despite obvious and often bitter divisions, there were basic core beliefs that united the entire Québécois nation, whether federalist/nationalist or nationalist. The Québécois people were a nation whose political and constitutional home was Quebec. That nation had experienced oppression at the hands of the English-Canadian nation, and such oppression had to be resisted. Above all, the Québécois nation had to survive and its institutions, if they were changed, had to be changed according to the Québécois' own desires. Changes could never be imposed by English Canada. And, however federal institutions were used, they should never be used to violate the integrity of the Québécois nation. Typically, the Québécois supported the strongly nationalist stream in provincial elections and the federalist/nationalist option in federal elections, a shrewdly effective hedging of bets.

English Canada was also changing. The British Tory traditions were slowly dying as the old generations died off, and many of the traditional British myths died with them. Furthermore, many English Canadians reacted defensively to longstanding Québécois nationalist claims that the Québécois nation was the only true Canadian nation firmly and uniquely rooted in Canada and that English-Canadian nationalism, such as it was, was overly devoted to the British connection and sustained itself too often by anti-Quebec posturing. Finally, as non-Anglo-Saxon immigrants streamed into Canada, especially into the West, the British flavour of English Canada was increasingly diluted as subtle, sometimes even dramatic, modifications of the "Canadian identity" began to occur.

Whether it was the demand for a separate seat at Versailles after World War I, winning a separate seat at the League of Nations, establishing an independent foreign policy after 1922, achieving true legislative independence with the *Statute of Westminster*, the independent declaration of war in 1939 or the attraction to the Red Ensign over the Union Jack, English Canada was evolving, albeit slowly and reluctantly from the Québécois point of view, toward a sense of identity incrementally separate from its British roots. In the past, English-Canadian nationalism had shown only brief episodes of an intense sense of unity of purpose, usually as a negative reaction, sometimes against a real or perceived external American threat, but more often against a perceived and exaggerated Québécois threat. That negative feature of English-Canadian nationalism was slowly disappearing and being replaced more and more by an open, frank, even naive search for a new sense of national purpose. When the Québécois nation once again asserted itself, English Canada's reaction was thus more ambivalent than before, swinging from openness and sympathy on some occasions, to the old hostility and anger on others, but always in the context of a willingness to accommodate Québécois nationalism to an extent unthinkable in the past.

The Quiet Revolution

From 1936 to 1939 and 1944 to 1959, conservative Union Nationale premier Maurice Duplessis governed Quebec through a close alliance with the English business establishment and the Catholic Church. It was a period in Quebec's history marked by patronage, corruption and the manipulation of anti-communist hysteria to justify the repression of trade unions, movements for reform and progressive ideas. Consequently, in Quebec, the period became known as *La Grande Noirceur* — the Great Darkness. The end of the darkness and the beginning of *La Révolution Tranquille* — the Quiet Revolution — is marked by the death of Duplessis in 1959 and the election of Liberal premier Jean Lesage in 1960. These events, however, were merely external confirmations of long-developing social and economic changes that would have inevitably burst through. While conservative Québécois nationalism had continued to dominate the province's politics under Duplessis, it was a doomed domination based on resisting disquieting changes the ideology could neither understand nor ultimately control. In fact, the 1960 victory of Jean Lesage, and of his leading minister René Lévesque, merely accelerated the long overdue transformation of Quebec.

Between Confederation and World War I investors were primarily attracted to Quebec by its copious supply of cheap labour and its large market. Consequently, much of Quebec's industrial development was labour intensive and heavily dependent on low wage costs. This relatively narrow industrial sector co-existed with a large and backward rural economy rooted in a small-holding, inefficient agriculture. After World War I Quebec was suddenly thrust into the modern era by rapid industrialization based on the discovery of important new resources — copper, pulp, iron, asbestos, chemicals — and the development of an apparently endless supply of cheap hydro-electric power. These developments were less dependent on cheap labour, more on cheaply available natural resources. Indeed, the modern industrial sector tended to be capital intensive, using advanced technologies that required skilled rather than unskilled labour. The speed of change was breathtaking with, for example, industrial employment during the single decade of World War II growing by the same amount as it had during the previous century.

After World War II the dual trends of industrialization and urbanization totally transformed Quebec, laying the material basis for the Quiet Revolution. The rural farm population, comprising 41 per cent of all Québécois in 1941, plummeted to 13 per cent in 1961, while urban dwellers went from 55 to 71 per cent. This dramatic change, coupled with very large natural population increases during the 1940s and 1950s, resulted in the rapid emergence of an entirely new way of life for the Québécois nation. Conservative Québécois nationalism still faced firmly backward, nostalgically regretting a disappearing past, and remained rooted in a rural way of life remote from the concrete experience of a whole new generation.

One of the consequences of rapid urbanization was the reconquest of Montreal by the Québécois. After the Conquest in 1759, Montreal became the centre of the English minority, and for a time in the nineteenth century the English even outnumbered the Québécois in the city. Even in the 1950s, almost one in four Montrealers was English, and the centre of the great city, dominated by English cultural and business institutions, remained essentially English-Canadian. By the 1960s, with the rapid urbanization of the Québécois, the English share of Montreal's population had declined to less than one in five, and it was continuing to fall. Nevertheless, the tendency to Québécois cultural dominance, including accepting French as the language of city life, was still successfully resisted by the English minority. It is not, therefore, surprising that Montreal became the focus of the contest between the new assertive nationalism of the Québécois and English-Canadian resistance. The English-Canadian minority of Montreal was, if you like, English Canada's cultural and economic garrison in the heart of a conquered Quebec. And that garrison became increasingly beleaguered, first materially, then intellectually and culturally and, finally, politically.

Initially, however, it was among the Québécois themselves in

Montreal that the soil was tilled for the Quiet Revolution. Since Montreal was the emerging centre of the new Quebec, the intellectual ferment there was greater than elsewhere, if only because of the ever-present weight of the English fact. But the ferment reached out and touched the Québécois everywhere, even those in the diaspora. In one sense, it was a replay of an old scenario, whose issues remained the common themes of Québécois nationalism since Papineau and before. How shall the nation be preserved as an island in a continental sea of English speakers? How shall the nation affirm itself, grow and change to meet the new challenges of modernization? How shall the nation best deal with English Canada and Ottawa: confrontation? accommodation?

Increasingly, this intellectual ferment achieved a certain uneasy but clear consensus. The Duplessis mixture of manipulative, right-wing and paranoid nationalism, relying on patronage, corruption and the cultivated ignorance of the masses, had to be swept away. The new trade unions, locked in a fierce battle with English and/or American bosses backed by the Duplessis regime, had to be supported in their bitter struggle. The Catholic Church, which held a central position in the conservative power bloc and which intruded heavily on daily life, had to be trimmed, tamed, set aside and directed to focus on spiritual concerns, leaving worldly power and administration to democratic and secular forces. Quebec had to catch up quickly if the Québécois nation was to determine its future effectively. Beyond that, there was much disagreement.

At first, the debate was between the new nationalism, reflected in *Le Devoir*, and the new liberalism, reflected in *Cité Libre*. Though they shared a common political foe in Duplessis and conservative nationalism and a common project in bringing Quebec society into the modern era, they disagreed deeply on ideology, methods and ultimate objectives. The new nationalism argued that Quebec had to be secularized, modernized and democratized but that the objective of the reform program also had to be to win and consolidate Québécois power in Quebec, to make French the working language of life in all public spheres in Quebec and to shape the provincial state into a modern political and constitutional tool for the Québécois nation. The new liberalism opposed nationalism, whether in its backward Duplessis guise or in its modern, enlightened guise. In the process of modernization, secularization and democratization, liberalism argued, Quebec must abandon and reject the nationalist project and substitute concepts of individual and social rights for those of national collective rights.

Both nationalists and liberals wanted to construct and use an interventionist and technocratic provincial state. But the nationalists insisted that the state must always serve the nation in the task of progress and nation-building. The two streams also divided deeply on the correct approach to federalism and Quebec's place in Confederation. The new nationalism argued that the Quebec provincial government apparatus had to be used, as nationalists had always maintained, as an instrument to protect and to enhance the place of the Québécois in the federal system. Thus, they insisted that, given its unique role as the political and constitutional home and political instrument of the Québécois nation, Quebec had to strive to win increased powers from Ottawa, particularly fiscal, social and cultural powers. The new liberalism did not see the need for new or enhanced powers and appeared content to argue that existing arrangements, coupled with a flexible and reasonable government in Ottawa, were sufficient for Quebec's assured future.

These, of course, were the polar streams, and many tried to bridge the gap, wanting to serve both masters. Indeed, Jean Lesage and the Quebec Liberal Party made an effort to do so. In fact, in its first phase, the Quiet Revolution was very much a successful effort to create a hybrid of liberalism and nationalism, a hybrid that took much more from the new nationalism than from the new liberalism. As events unfolded these two dominant streams divided into three, each represented by one of the leading politicians of the era. René Lévesque became the most prominent advocate of the new nationalism. In the face of an unyielding federalism, he believed that some form of sovereignty was essential for the Québécois nation. Robert Bourassa became the leading advocate of Quebec liberalism. He sought special status and significantly increased powers for Quebec within the federal system. Pierre Trudeau became the symbol of an uncompromising federalism determined to block the inevitable secessionary tendencies of the newly aroused and progressive Québécois nationalism. The three men began their careers as friends and colleagues who met together in intense face-to-face debates in countless kitchens and living rooms during the early phase of the Quiet Revolution. At the end of the process, they had become bitter political foes.

In 1960 Lesage and the Liberal Party campaigned on the slogan *"C'est le temps que ça change!"* There were few across Canada who did not applaud his victory in 1960 — the Duplessis regime had come to epitomize corruption and extreme reaction; it was an embarrassing relic from the past. Indeed, many English Canadians were smug about the Duplessis era. That the Québécois would tolerate and continue to elect such a government could be cited not only as evidence of the backwardness of the entire population but also as further confirmation of the dangers of Québécois nationalism. What Lesage appeared to propose seemed self-evidently good and necessary; that is, reform, modernization, catch-up and the integration of Quebec into the mainstream of modern Canada. What followed, however, was less reassuring.

During its first brief term from 1960 to 1962, the Lesage government took the obvious reform steps, many of which had begun during Paul Sauvé's Union Nationale government. Most of the program amounted simply to beginning to provide in Quebec what were considered normal government services across English Canada in areas like health, education, labour law and social welfare. Then, in 1962, under the influence of nationalists like René Lévesque, who was the minister of natural resources, and Paul Gérin-Lajoie, who was the attorney-general, Lesage successfully sought a new and stronger mandate, using the more dramatic slogan, "*Maîtres chez nous!*" This slogan, and the palpable quickening of the Quiet Revolution, were more disturbing to English Canada. For the Québécois to want obviously needed changes to catch up to the rest of the country was one thing, but for them to want to be masters in their own home, whatever that meant, was quite another.

Gérin-Lajoie pushed a more aggressive line for Quebec in constitutional matters, seeking what was, in effect, "special status" in a variety of areas as well as the right to enjoy international recognition and representation, particularly in areas of exclusive provincial jurisdiction. Lévesque ardently pushed the need for the Quebec state to become more interventionist on behalf of the Québécois nation, advocating the nationalization of the Quebec power industry and the establishment of Hydro-Québec as a Crown corporation. This proposal, in fact, became the central issue in the 1962 election. Furious and enraged at the paternalistic attitude of the many English Canadians who believed the Québécois lacked the necessary skills and qualifications to do the top jobs, Lévesque was determined to use Hydro-Québec as a model of what the Québécois could accomplish if they had the necessary powers. Lévesque also pressed the idea of special status for Quebec, going so far as to propose that Quebec be granted the status of "associate state" in Confederation. There was no doubt that the decisive 1962 victory of the Lesage Liberals confirmed an overwhelming desire among the Québécois both to get on with, and to speed up, the Quiet Revolution.

"Maîtres chez nous!" enjoyed a variety of meanings in Quebec. At a minimum, the slogan called for a cultural and linguistic revolution to bring the Québécois a real sense of cultural and linguistic domination in the daily life of the province. This was reflected in an enormous proliferation of the arts and letters, cinema and drama, and a push to make French the language of work and common usage. This cultural and linguistic revolution had a couple of false starts during the Duplessis regime. Back in 1937, Duplessis' Union Nationale government passed a law officially making French the pre-eminent language in the province's legislation and administration. In 1938, under pressure from the English lobby, he backed off. Though they were fearful that the move might be misinterpreted as secessionary in English Canada, the Union Nationale also adopted the fleur-de-lis as the official flag of Quebec, a nice gesture. But Duplessis had not been a true friend of Québécois culture, certainly not in its progressive and secular manifestation. In contrast, during the Quiet Revolution, the Lesage administration supported Québécois culture as no regime ever had, and the provincial government's efforts to make French the language of business and government, as well as of cultural life, resulted in a surprisingly aggressive assertion of the French reality in Quebec.

But the meaning and implications of the slogan quickly began to expand. Lévesque and other nationalists in the Lesage government interpreted the slogan as meaning that Québécois mastery in Quebec had to extend beyond culture and language into both the economy and Quebec's place in the federal system. The state had to become an instrument to build Québécois economic power and influence from the bottom to the top. It had to be used as an instrument to achieve social and economic justice for the Québécois, which necessarily meant that the state had to be used to attack and dismantle the two-hundred-year-old structure of English privilege in Quebec. Furthermore, the state had to be used to defend Quebec from unwarranted intrusions of federal power into the national life of the Québécois. This expanded meaning of *"Maîtres chez nous,"* more and more shared among the Québécois, was enormously disquieting to the English establishment, both within and outside Quebec.

It is not surprising that the speed of change and the growing dominance of Québécois nationalism led to an explosion of expectations among the Québécois. By 1964, in terms of modernizing programs and infrastructures in health, education and social policy, Quebec had more or less caught up with English Canada. But the Québécois had not caught up economically. The new labour law, the most progressive and pro-labour in Canada, extended the right to strike to the public sector and provided an important means for catching up. During the period from 1964 to 1966, Quebec was hit by an astonishing wave of labour militancy. Strikes by taxi drivers, police, postal workers, engineers at Hydro-Québec, teachers, hospital workers and civil servants rocked the province. For example, in 1966 almost two million person days, five times the 1964 figure, were lost as a result of strikes. Everywhere the demand was the same — income parity with English-speaking equivalents in Canada (usually in Ontario). In the case of the taxi strike, the demand was that the airport monopoly be taken away from the English firm, Murray Hill. For more and more among the Québécois, "*Maîtres chez nous*" meant nothing less than economic equality with English Canadians and an end to the system of English privilege in Quebec.

Nationalists frequently evoked the image of Quebec as a colony of English Canada. And reality suggested the image was apt. The Québécois nation was confined in a federal system that prevented self-determination and imposed constraints according to the will of English Canada. The system treated the Québécois as second-class citizens economically and gave them fewer opportunities and lower incomes than English Canadians. The Québécois language and culture were confined, suppressed and marginalized. Most telling, of course, was that in Quebec itself a small, powerful English minority enjoyed enormous economic, political and cultural privileges while the Québécois majority languished at the bottom of the heap. It was not surprising that Québécois nationalists often compared Quebec to Rhodesia, where a tiny English white minority ruled an overwhelming majority of blacks. Nor was it surprising that leading Front de Libération du Québec (FLQ) intellectual Pierre Vallières wrote a best-seller entitled *Nègres blancs d'Amérique*.

The emergence of the Front de Libération du Québec further provoked growing English-Canadian anxiety. In 1963, the FLQ commenced a terrorist campaign of bank robberies (called "voluntary taxes"), armoury raids and bombings. The campaign began in 1963 with the bombing of the Wolfe monument in Quebec City and stretched over six or seven years. The targets were carefully selected symbols of English privilege, English political and/or economic power and the federal presence in Quebec. Westmount, a wealthy English residential neighbourhood, and McGill and Loyola, English universities, were targeted because they represented privilege. Eaton's and the Montreal Stock Exchange were selected as bastions of English economic power. Federal targets included various military and paramilitary headquarters and other symbols of Ottawa's power, such as the National Revenue building and CNR headquarters. In addition to the Wolfe monument, a monument to Queen Victoria and the office of the Queen's Printer were also hit. Though the objective of the bombings was clearly symbolic, six people died during the campaign. These events increased the tensions caused by the wave of strikes and the almost routine occurrence of demonstrations. Taken together, they profoundly disturbed English Canada. To many it appeared that changes they had warmly supported in 1960 were getting out of control, heading in unforeseen and undesirable directions.

Nevertheless, the reaction in English Canada remained ambivalent, and feelings often cleaved along generational lines. Among the younger generation, particularly those touched by the growing radicalism of the 1960s, there was a great deal of openness and support for what was happening in Quebec. Increasingly critical of the establishment, its old ways and outdated attitudes and symbols, many young English Canadians enthusiastically endorsed Quebec's right to special status and ultimately to self-determination. Within the older generation, especially among those supportive of tradition and the establishment, there was confusion. For many, their old hatred of the Québécois was rekindled. Yet many of the strongest voices defending Quebec were English. English Canada, therefore, from the outset of the Quiet Revolution was seriously split.

Prime Minister John Diefenbaker seemed to have won the forgiveness of the Québécois for past Tory sins when he swept the country in 1958. In some ways, the Quiet Revolution was initially seen merely as the Quebec reflection of the mood for change igniting the entire country. In Quebec, the Diefenbaker landslide included fifty of the seventy-five seats with 50 per cent of the popular vote. This was a remarkable achievement compared to the dismal Tory showings in the five previous elections, which ranged from one seat and 20 per cent of the vote in 1940, up to a meagre nine seats and 31 per cent of the vote in 1957. But Diefenbaker neither understood nor responded effectively to the Quiet

Revolution. Some of his well-intentioned gestures only exacerbated the situation and made the Québécois angrier. In 1958, for example, his government introduced simultaneous translation in the House of Commons, a sensible and long overdue measure. But this was hardly *un beau geste*, since it called attention to the fact that for almost a hundred years the two solitudes of Canada had made speeches to each other that neither understood. Most members of Parliament on both sides of the language barrier were unilingual, and it seemed bizarre that no federal government had ever set up translation services. Quebec saw it as a reaffirmation of a basic truth — Quebec's voice, on most national issues, was irrelevant when English Canada's Parliament made decisions. The 1962 decision to issue all federal cheques in both languages was again perceived as more of an insult than anything else in Quebec — as if bilingual cheques addressed the issues raised by the Quiet Revolution!

While Diefenbaker was preoccupied with his "Northern Vision," events in Quebec were showing that Canada would be made or unmade there and not in the north, a point the prime minister never understood. So it was that the Québécois, who had embraced Diefenbaker so warmly in 1958, sent him firmly into Opposition in 1963. He never forgave Quebec, constantly attacking the aspirations of the Québécois in a vendetta that shredded his own party when he fought the "two nations" concept without compromise. In 1958 Quebec, and the rest of Canada, had given Diefenbaker a great opportunity to move the nation forward in new ways by bestowing on him the greatest measure of trust ever given to a prime minister. Sadly, Diefenbaker squandered this opportunity. Even more sadly, he never realized that such an opportunity had been placed into his hands. He went to his grave without remorse, without regret, without any doubt, firm in his conviction that he had stayed the course for the cause, deluded that the masses loved him deeply and unaware that in Quebec he had become a laughing stock.

Liberal prime minister Lester Pearson, in contrast to Diefenbaker, was well aware of the depth of the crisis Canada had entered as a result of developments in Quebec. Having won his first minority government in 1963 thanks largely to Quebec, Pearson knew that both his future as prime minister and Canada's future as an intact federation depended on more effectively winning the hearts and minds of the Québécois. His regime took steps to deal with Quebec that were denounced on both sides at the time; in Quebec as much too little and much too late and in English Canada as much too soft.

As a result, these measures took considerable political courage. But the overwhelming *raisons d'état* always weighed heavily on Pearson — if Ottawa did not do something and only replaced Diefenbaker's policy of hostile indecision with one of friendly indecision, then events in Quebec could spiral out of control. Above all, if Canada were to survive, the federal state had to act decisively, or at least appear to act decisively. And any such actions had to be sufficient to produce two almost contradictory results: to begin to win over English Canada to the need for accommodation and a willingness to yield; and to convince the Québécois that real change and accommodation were possible within Confederation.

In 1963 the Pearson government established the Royal Commission on Bilingualism and Biculturalism (the B and B Commission), whose interim report in 1965 asserted that Canada was in the midst of "the greatest crisis in its history." The basic premise of the inquiry was politically courageous and will endure as a major feature of Pearson's legacy. The commission was directed to base its recommendations on the controversial doctrine of Confederation as "an equal partnership between the two founding races." For the Pearson government this move not only provided breathing space but also ensured that the eventual recommendations would focus on seeking a significant accommodation with the Québécois. Convinced that pro-federalist elements in the new Quebec had to be co-opted into national leadership to replace the traditional old Liberal guard in Quebec, Pearson persuaded three leading Quebec personalities to join his government: the intellectuals Pierre Trudeau and Gérard Pelletier and the prominent labour leader Jean Marchand. Then, as a significant linguistic concession, the Pearson regime directed the federal civil service to launch an ambitious French- and English-language training program. Further gestures were made to Quebec. It was allowed to opt out of the 1964 Canada Pension Plan, retaining control of pension funds as part of the Quiet Revolution's strategy of economic development and empowerment. (By 2002 the resulting Caisse de dépôt et placement du Québec controlled a $133-billion pool of capital, Canada's biggest stock and bond portfolio manager.) The decision was also taken to drop the Red Ensign in favour of the present flag.

Armed with these moves and amid a growing uneasiness and anger among traditional English Canadians, Pearson, more desperate than hopeful that he would receive a majority, called an election in 1965. The "three wise men" from Quebec agreed to run and were promised cabinet posts. Pearson asked Canadians to give him the majority mandate he needed to finish the tasks he had begun, both in reforming and expanding social programs and in resolving the Quebec problem. The Quebec electorate responded, giving him 56 of 75 seats. But the response was not enthusiastic — the Liberal popular vote in Quebec remained unchanged at 46 per cent. It was clear that in Quebec Pearson was regarded as the lesser of two evils, not as a reformer. In English Canada the results were much less gratifying; Pearson won only 75 of the 190 remaining seats, 51 of them in Ontario, and he faced almost a total shutout in the West (only 9 of 70 seats). So while Pearson had the lukewarm support of Central and Atlantic Canada — 107 of 160 seats in Quebec and Ontario; 20 of 33 seats in Atlantic Canada — the largest of the two great English-Canadian peripheries had refused to embrace him.

Undaunted, the Pearson government continued completing the construction of the welfare state, under prodding from the NDP, by proceeding to a national medicare program and announcing a war on poverty. Further concessions were made to Quebec with Pearson's 1966 policy of equality of treatment for francophone and anglophone applicants for jobs in the federal bureaucracy, supplemented by a bilingualism bonus for those in the lower levels of the civil service who worked in both languages. This was the carrot. The stick was the new justice minister, Pierre Trudeau, who began a sustained ideological offensive against Québécois nationalism, particularly its tendencies toward separatism. In the 1966 Quebec provincial election, this separatist tendency in Québécois nationalism became explicit for the first time.

The 1966 defeat of the Lesage government and the re-election of the Union Nationale were largely attributed at the time to a feeling among the Québécois that things were going too quickly and that it was time to slow down and return to the safe embrace of conservative nationalism. A close examination of the results, however, suggests otherwise. Two separatist parties ran candidates in the election. The right-wing Ralliement National (RN), which favoured associate state status for Quebec, won about 4 per cent of the Québécois vote (3.1 per cent overall). On the left, the socialist and separatist Rassemblement pour l'Indépendance Nationale (RIN) won about 7 per cent of the Québécois vote (5.6 per cent overall). The RIN vote hurt the Liberals badly and helped defeat the Lesage government. The RIN ran in just over two-thirds of the seats, focusing on metropolitan Montreal and other major urban centres. They won about 11 per cent of the Québécois vote in metropolitan Montreal and between 8 and 12 per cent in places like Trois-Rivières, St. Jérôme, Hull and Shawinigan. More significant, perhaps, was the fact that the RIN attracted very strong support among Québécois between the ages eighteen and twenty-five where the party presented candidates. At the time, the spectacular and unexpected defeat of the Lesage government overshadowed this much more significant development. The separatist option in Quebec had sufficient electoral support that it now had to be taken seriously, even if only because it could act as a spoiler. Only six seats separated the victorious Union Nationale from the defeated Liberals, and thirteen of the Union Nationale victories had occurred because the RIN had pulled sufficient votes from the Liberals. The real message of the election then was not to slow down the process of change, but to speed it up by becoming more assertive in advancing the claims of the Québécois nation.

If the size of the separatist vote was disturbing, the demographics were doubly so. The size of the vote suggested that the left-wing RIN had broken out of the student and New Left ghetto where it had got its start six brief years before. The separatist option received its strongest support among young people. In addition, intellectuals in cultural areas — teachers and professors, artists, actors, writers, musicians — were tilting more and more to independence, as were the new generation of Quebec professionals, white- and blue-collar workers and small-business people, who were all rankling at the system of English privilege. Significant inroads were made in working-class districts, particularly among young workers. These demographics could only be interpreted to mean that the electoral future of the separatist option in Quebec was one of growth, particularly if a party presented itself in which the electorate had confidence. Though the RIN was clearly not yet that party, the support it had won on a shoestring budget, with a chaotic organization and in spite of the excessive abuse heaped upon it suggested the political situation for independence was ripening. If nothing else, the 1966 election made separatism, in a non-terrorist and democratic expression, an option to be debated and voted on, rather than simply an option to be discussed on the intellectual sidelines and political fringes of Québécois nationalism. The lid of Pandora's box was off, and it has remained off.

Events in Quebec accelerated incredibly between 1966 and 1970, and many thought the trajectory was toward separation. René Lévesque, who more than any other single figure embodied the ultimate aspirations of the Quiet Revolution, appealed to the Quebec Liberal Party in 1967 to adopt his idea of "sovereignty association." The idea was seductively simple: Quebec would become a sovereign nation but maintain a close economic association with Canada. Indeed, the associative bonds could be extended into other areas, as long as Quebec's sovereignty and equality as a nation were the first premise of negotiations and agreements.

Lévesque's proposal was soundly rejected, as everyone expected, whereupon he split from the Liberals and founded Le Mouvement souveraineté-association (MSA). Within months, buoyed by the support he found in Quebec and the surprisingly high levels of sympathy he galvanized in English Canada, Lévesque was confidently predicting Quebec's independence in two to five years. French president General Charles de Gaulle had lent considerable credence to the separatist option with his provocative declaration in July 1967 from the balcony of Montreal's Hôtel de Ville, "*Vive le Québec Libre!*" While the call palpably electrified the huge listening crowd, it also created a major diplomatic furor that resulted in de Gaulle's premature departure from Canada. The French government heaped insult on Canadian injury by providing quasi-official welcomes for visiting separatists from Quebec, like RIN leader Pierre Bourgault and MSA leader Lévesque, that gave considerable international legitimacy to the movement.

Unity negotiations between the RIN, MSA and RN led to the 1968 founding of the Parti Québécois, under Lévesque's charismatic leadership. It had the declared and prescient intent of winning at least one in four Quebec votes in the next provincial election, expected in 1970. The major Quebec trade union federations moved toward the explicit endorsation of independence, as did the nationalist, popular mass organization, La Société Saint-Jean-Baptiste. All of these events were sharply punctuated by the FLQ's apparently unstoppable symbolic bombing campaign.

While René Lévesque was rising to political leadership of the Québécois nation on this wave of separatist sentiment, Pierre Trudeau was rising in the federal system on the inevitable countervailing wave of anti-separatist sentiment both in English Canada and among the still powerful federalists in Quebec. Trudeau was the perfect foil for English Canada in general, and Quebec federalists in particular, in the struggle against Québécois nationalism and separatism. Urbane, witty, highly educated, independently wealthy and unsullied by past associations with the old Liberal Party, Trudeau was seen as a fresh force in national politics. Despite his previous lack of involvement in electoral politics, he had strong, if unusual, political credentials. He had fought Duplessis and supported the unions during their darker days. He had flirted with the NDP but never embraced the party. He had publicly denounced the Liberals for accepting U.S. nuclear weapons on Canadian soil. More importantly, Trudeau was a firm and dedicated opponent of Québécois nationalism and had been throughout his adult life. The son of a French-English marriage, he was fluently bilingual. For many he embodied the ideal of the new Canada — at ease in both languages and cultures but emotionally committed to neither. He presented himself as the rational, sophisticated, bilingual model of the new unhyphenated Canadian. Given his roots in Quebec, Trudeau was able to denounce Québécois nationalism and, even more severely, separatism with a contempt and arrogance that would have provoked mass indignation among Québécois had his statements come from an English-Canadian politician. Having failed in four elections, Pearson decided to step down. His invitation to Trudeau and the other two wise men from Quebec to join his government, and Trudeau's immediate elevation to the role of justice minister, amounted to a "laying on of hands." Trudeau was clearly the leadership choice of the prime minister and most in the Liberal establishment.

At a key federal-provincial constitutional conference in February 1968 Trudeau boldly faced down Union Nationale premier Daniel Johnson, refusing to recognize Quebec's special status as a province containing one of the two founding nations. Rather, Trudeau laid out the doctrine that would more or less guide his years in power: a binding national Charter of Rights; the constitutional equality of provinces in a co-operative federal system orchestrated by the senior government at Ottawa; determining the character of any new federalism not by negotiation between English Canada, represented by Ottawa, and Quebec, but by negotiations between all eleven governments. At its root, of course, was Trudeau's conception of a dominating unhyphenated Canadian nationalism, nourished and sustained at the federal level. His vision was, in fact, not much different from Diefenbaker's, and it was no less offensive to Québécois nationalists.

Perceived as the one candidate who would not only stand up for Canada but also effectively keep Quebec in line, Trudeau easily won the leadership. Immediately thereafter, on 20 April 1968, he was sworn in as prime minister. Three days later he dissolved Parliament and called an election for 25 June. The campaign was dominated by the Quebec question. The choice was clear: who could deal best with Quebec? The accommodating Robert Stanfield, willing to take seriously the two-nations concept, or Pierre Trudeau, who would make no such accommodation with Québécois nationalism?

Trudeau's victory was sealed on 24 June 1968 during the Saint-Jean-Baptiste Day parade in Montreal. Separatists chose the occasion to demonstrate against Trudeau, denouncing him as a traitor. Riot police moved in, and the scene beneath Trudeau's reviewing stand became an ugly and violent confrontation, as police bludgeoned and arrested demonstrators, who responded with bottles, bricks and attacks on police vehicles. A few of the missiles were hurled in Trudeau's direction. The prime minister's bodyguard tried to convince him to leave the stand for his safety. Trudeau refused and even physically resisted his protectors' efforts to pull him from the stand. All this occurred in front of television cameras and was instantly broadcast across the nation. The next day, as Canadians went to the polls, the news coverage on radio and television and the laudatory front-page stories in daily newspapers across the country left no doubt that this was a prime minister who would face down the separatists. Trudeau won a convincing victory, the first for a prime minister in a decade, taking 154 of 264 seats, including 7 of 32 Atlantic seats, 56 of 74 Quebec seats, 63 of 88 Ontario seats, 27 of 68 Western seats, and the seat for Yukon and the Northwest Territories.

During this same period, the B and B Commission continued its quiet work. Volume I of the report, *The Official Languages*, released in 1967, had concluded that the Québécois constituted a "distinct society" with control over key features of their collective life. This reality, the report suggested, should be confirmed at the federal level by legally adopting French and English as equal official languages of Canada and appointing a regulatory mechanism to enforce the language law. Provincial governments were similarly called upon to adopt the two official languages. Volume II, *Education*, was issued the next year. It sought to placate the fearful by suggesting that parents be allowed to educate their children in the official language of their choice and that educational choice be provided across the country for speakers of the minority official language. One of the Trudeau government's first acts was to accept the recommendations of Volume I by introducing the 1969 *Official*

Languages Act, which granted equal status to French and English in federal institutions, guaranteed federal services in both languages across the country and established the Office of the Commissioner of Official Languages to police implementation.

Under the constitution, the Volume II proposals on education required provincial action. The language of education was a key issue in Quebec. The English minority in Quebec had long enjoyed access to their own cultural institutions, including a well-funded school system from kindergarten to university. Meanwhile, francophone minorities in English Canada enjoyed no such special consideration, even when numbers made it feasible. Indeed, what few rights to French-language use and education francophones possessed had been unconstitutionally snatched from them. Only in locales in English Canada where there were large concentrations of French speakers, such as St. Boniface in Manitoba, Gravelbourg in Saskatchewan and major portions of New Brunswick, had francophones managed to maintain a toehold against hostility and pressure, often having to create an elaborate community conspiracy to circumvent provincial laws designed to suppress the French language. Though long since resigned to the obliteration of French in English Canada for all practical purposes, a key feature of the Québécois nationalist consensus was that French had to be well protected in Quebec. A combination of assertive self-confidence deriving from the Quiet Revolution and the growing demographic changes led inevitably to confrontation on the language question. As the Québécois birth rate fell and immigration into Quebec increased, the Québécois share of Quebec's population declined. In the Montreal area, this decline was quite sharp. Assuring the future of the Québécois meant ensuring the integration of immigrants to the French-speaking majority rather than to the English minority. Yet immigrants realized that the gateway to success in Quebec and to easy mobility across the rest of Canada was integration with the English minority and the adoption of English as the language of education and work. This meant that, where possible, immigrants wanted to educate their children in the English school system.

Matters came to a head on 27 June 1968, just two days after Trudeau's election. The local school board in the Montreal suburb of St. Léonard moved to limit the language of instruction in all grade-one classes in the coming school year to French. There was no doubt that this was a step toward imposing French as the sole official language of the province. There was even less doubt that this was an attack on the English minority; it struck at one of the most important roots of any cultural community's self-perpetuation and social reproduction — schooling in that culture's language. And there was also no doubt that this was potentially a first step in dismantling the English minority's structure of privilege in Quebec.

The St. Léonard board was, in fact, doing nothing different from what had been done to the French minority elsewhere from the Conquest on. Receiving a taste of its own medicine, English Canada reacted with indignation, demanding rights for itself in Quebec that it had refused to give to French speakers in the rest of Canada — preferred language protection, including the right to education in English at the state's expense. The St. Léonard crisis, involving demonstrations, counter-demonstrations and even violence and rioting, rocked the nation.

Again, English Canada, and most importantly the English minority in Quebec, won the confrontation. In 1969 the Union Nationale government, in a spirit of concession to the B and B Commission's recommendations and reeling from the intensity of the language conflict, introduced and finally adopted Bill 63, *An Act to promote the French language in Quebec*. This outraged Québécois nationalists. They saw it as a profound humiliation and a sign of defeat by, and surrender to, English power and influence. Where was the legislation to promote English in Ontario or Saskatchewan? More than that, despite the bill's small but significant efforts to enhance French and to assure some knowledge of French by all, it actually caved in to the pro-English lobby both by giving all parents the freedom to choose the language of instruction for their children and by obliging school boards to establish and fund programs of instruction according to those choices. The bill was a total capitulation to English Canada. It provoked mass protests in Quebec that involved tens of thousands as well as serious rioting during a strike by Montreal police, and troops had to be called in to maintain order and protect property. As a concession to this popular opposition, and in an effort to defuse it, the Union Nationale government established the Gendron Commission to make a full inquiry into the language issue.

The St. Léonard crisis and Bill 63's passage presented English Canada with a perfect opportunity to make amends for the past and work toward a more amicable future by imitating the generosity of the bill, by, in fact and in spirit, heeding the call of the B and B Commission. Two actions on the part of the English-Canadian provinces would have indicated good faith; guaranteeing the right of French-speaking minorities to educate their children in French and declaring French and English to be equal official languages in each province. In other words, measures were required to give to francophones across Canada what English Canada was determined the English minority should have in Quebec. English Canada missed another opportunity.

Only New Brunswick, with its large Acadian minority, responded by adopting French and English as official languages of equal status. No other English-Canadian province followed suit. Some small concessions were made: amendments to education leg-islation to allow the use of French as a language of instruction under highly controlled and limited conditions; promises to pro-vide some provincial services in French where numbers warranted and when feasible; the Ontario legislature agreeing to permit mem-bers to speak on the record in either language; and so on. These gestures were not enough. Indeed, they were so slight that they seemed more like insults. Québécois nationalists used the gestures to full advantage to expose English-Canadian hypocrisy, bad faith and lack of generosity. For federalists in Quebec, and in Ottawa, the sheer stinginess of English Canada's response was a profound embarrassment.

The B and B Commission lobbed a further bombshell with the 1969 publication of Volume III, *The Work World*. This report doc-umented the yawning economic chasm between the Québécois majority and the English minority in Quebec. It was common knowledge that the English minority enjoyed considerable eco-nomic privileges, but they had never been so thoroughly revealed. Nor had the gap between French and English ever been so clearly set out. When the cultural and linguistic privileges enjoyed by the English minority were combined with their considerable eco-nomic benefits, the political impact was incendiary.

The B and B Report was relentless and microscopic. The average English male in the labour force earned just under 50 per cent more than the average Québécois male. The commission's researchers controlled for all factors relevant to income earning ability and found that about 80 per cent of the difference could be explained only by the Québécois/English ethnic difference. But it was more than just income inequality; it was everything else. The English were over-represented, and the Québécois under-repre-sented, in the better occupations; while the reverse was true in the unskilled labour categories. The upper management of most firms was English, while the Québécois took the lower and poorer-paid jobs. Large business concerns tended to be English; the small ones tended to be Québecois. Even the skilled and better-paid working-class occupations were dominated by English workers. English engineers, architects, lawyers and physicians earned more than their Québecois counterparts. The most privileged group in all of Canada was located in Quebec: unilingual anglophone males. The aptness of the colonial analogy struck a now deeper chord — you did not even have to speak the language of the majority to hold, enjoy and retain your privileges. And the very real economic reasons why immigrants to Quebec yearned to integrate to the English minority rather than the French majority were made crystal clear by the B and B data. Italians in Quebec did much better than those in Ontario. The only place in all of Canada where a salary earner of Ukrainian origin exceeded the national average income was in Quebec, again ahead of the Québecois average. The B and B report also detailed that English was not only the language of work but also of promotion and career opportunity. To be successful a Québecois had to be fluent in English, slamming the door of opportunity on the overwhelming majority of Québecois who were unilingual. Furthermore, the report noted that the economic status of the Québecois, compared to the English minority, had actually worsened since 1930.

Needless to say, this volume of the B and B Report was considerably more popular among Québecois nationalists than others because it lent all the weight of a federal royal commission to their claims that Quebec languished in a colonial situation. Lévesque and Bourgault never tired of quoting from *The Work World*. Journalists pored over the data and generated countless articles in the popular press, while scholars crunched and re-crunched the numbers which, though generated by a royal commission to save Canada, appeared to contradict the arguments about the economic benefits of Confederation for the Québecois. Any new deal for Quebec in Confederation was going to have to address the touchy issues of making French the language of work and of closing the economic gap between the Québecois and the English minority. Behind the language issue, therefore, lurked the deeper structural issue of the transfer of real economic power, opportunity and privilege. If English Canada and the English minority in Quebec had shown a lack of generosity on language and education issues, on the economic issue Québecois nationalists expected even fewer concessions.

In such circumstances, the election of 29 April 1970 was a

significant test of the mood of the Québécois. Was Lévesque's prediction of a 25 per cent vote for sovereignty correct? Was the Trudeau formula of bilingualism, French power in Ottawa, greater economic opportunities for the Québécois, all delivered in a context of hard-nosed federalism, winning favour? A Gallup poll in 1968, using a toughly-worded question on support for separation in Quebec, found 11 per cent in favour, 71 per cent opposed and 18 per cent undecided. Yet, in 1969, when Gallup asked people in Quebec about the breakup of Confederation, 47 per cent thought it would occur, 25 per cent thought not and 28 per cent remained undecided. With Lévesque asking for support for something non-threatening and vague like "sovereignty-association," all bets were off and English Canadians, especially in Quebec and Ottawa, became increasingly worried about the outcome, especially when Lévesque's Parti Québécois campaign seemed to catch fire.

The Union Nationale government was thoroughly discredited as a result of the Bill 63 fiasco. The Liberal Party, now led by Robert Bourassa, had just come through a divisive leadership race. The Créditistes decided to shift from their exclusive focus on the federal arena to run provincially. In such a four-way fight, the outcome was highly uncertain, and many in English Canada and in federalist circles feared that the charismatic Lévesque could conceivably win. So the dirty tricks and fear campaign began. Federalists in Quebec and Ottawa claimed that the Québécois would experience an overnight drop of 35 per cent in their standard of living if Lévesque and the PQ were elected. Plants would shut down, unemployment would spiral and savings and investments would be put at risk. Potential investors would panic and refuse to risk their capital. Worse, there would be a massive flight of capital out of the province.

This point of view seemed confirmed by the events of early Sunday 27 April, two days before the election. That morning, nine Brinks armoured trucks pulled up to the front door of the Royal Trust building on Dorchester Boulevard. This in itself was unusual, not only because it was Sunday morning but also because Brinks typically used the garage entrance, for obvious security reasons. Despite the early morning hour, photographers from the Montreal *Gazette* were on hand to get some front-page pictures. The trucks were ostentatiously loaded with boxes of "fleeing capital" in the form of what were claimed to be "securities" and were driven toward the Ontario border. Their route conveniently took them past waiting television camera crews, who duly recorded this tangible evidence of a "flight of capital," which was then broadcast and rebroadcast for the next two days to counterpoint the newspaper pictures and headlines and hysterical interviews with representatives of the business lobby and responsible Quebec politicians, like premier-in-waiting Bourassa. The event had been elaborately staged, requiring the co-operation of the media, Royal Trust and the Brinks Company. It was just one more incident in a campaign of hysteria and fear, which Lévesque denounced as "economic terrorism."

Lévesque and the PQ were temporarily stopped on 29 April 1970. The PQ won 24 per cent of the vote but took only 7 of 108 seats in the National Assembly. The Liberals took seventy-two seats with 44 per cent of the vote, winning a comfortable majority government. The Union Nationale won eighteen seats with 20 per cent, while the Créditistes took twelve seats with 11 per cent. The English minority voted en bloc for the Liberal Party, while the Québécois were deeply divided. But a close analysis of the results was deeply disquieting for the federalist victors. About one Québécois in three had voted for the PQ. Again, like the RIN before it, the PQ did best among the groups that owned the future: the young, the educated, and cultural workers. When one also considers that the conservative nationalists in the Union Nationale (UN) won 20 per cent of the vote, the political message was not reassuring. Though Lévesque personally went down to defeat and it retained the status of official Opposition, there was little doubt that the UN was in its death throes and that the real opposition and alternative in Quebec had become the PQ. For this reason the PQ election-night rally had all the characteristics of a victory party, and one can understand why Lévesque's statement "this is a defeat which feels like a victory" brought the PQ partisans to their feet, cheering. A PQ victory appeared as close as the next election if the Quiet Revolution continued to unfold as it had since 1960. For the first time since 1837 a sovereign future for the Québécois seemed a real possibility. The events of October 1970 were, however, to result in a brief but painful delay.

On 5 October 1970 the Quiet Revolution ended, the gloves came off and the apparently irresistible democratic trajectory of the Québécois toward some form of sovereignty was derailed by political violence, both the illegal political violence of the FLQ and the legal state violence of Ottawa. Early that morning, the FLQ escalated its terrorist tactics by kidnapping the British trade commissioner in Montreal, James Cross. Threatening to kill Cross, the FLQ gave authorities forty-eight hours to meet seven demands: the cessation of police actions to find the abductors and Cross; the broadcast of the FLQ manifesto on prime-time television over the CBC and its affiliates across Quebec, and its front-page publication in the major Quebec newspapers; the "liberation" of twenty-three "political prisoners"; a plane to take the freed FLQ cadres to Algeria or Cuba; the re-employment of the "Lapalme boys" by Canada Post; the payment of "a voluntary tax of $500,000 in gold bullion" to be placed on the plane; and the release of the name and picture of the latest police informer in the FLQ.

Not unexpectedly, the Quebec and Ottawa governments initially refused all the demands and took considerable pains to reject the FLQ's allegations about the twenty-three "political prisoners." These were FLQ activists convicted of terrorist actions: mainly armed robbery and bombings. A few had also been convicted of murder when deaths had occurred during the commission of the offences. They had, of course, been convicted of violations of the Criminal Code, although their crimes were politically motivated by the romantic vision of the terrorist hero who courageously confronts the state and, by example, hopes to inspire more and more among the population to do likewise. The FLQ had also begun to win some public sympathy because of their treatment by the criminal justice system: two members had been held for more than three years with neither bail nor trial; those convicted, often first offenders and certainly not criminals in the normal sense, received sentences unprecedented in length; FLQ members who were charged were routinely denied bail; one of the prisoners had been sentenced to 126 terms of perpetual confinement; and many of the twenty-three claimed to have been beaten and tortured. Under the circumstances, it appeared that FLQ activists, when convicted, were treated much more harshly precisely because their crimes were politically motivated. This issue of the "political prisoners" became the source of a temporary split between Trudeau in Ottawa and Bourassa in Quebec.

In retrospect, Ottawa and Quebec then made a serious political miscalculation. Having initially rejected all seven demands, the authorities relented and, as an act of good faith, agreed to broadcast and print the FLQ manifesto. The 1970 manifesto was a much better polemic than the more tedious academic version of 1964. It was full of the immediacy of recent political events, made free use of the vernacular, reiterated many widely held grievances and was salted with irreverence and contempt for key authority figures ("Drapeau the dog, Bourassa the Simard side-kick, Trudeau the queer, the sub-ape Robert Shaw"). It made good use of the distortions of the earlier election, especially the electoral maldistribution that gave the PQ less than 7 per cent of the seats despite their winning 24 per cent of the vote and what it called "the Brinks show."

It is not clear why the decision was taken to permit the broadcast. Perhaps it was seen as the most innocuous of the demands, involving no compromises of the state's authority. Perhaps the authorities believed that the tone and content of the manifesto would alienate ordinary Québécois and that the excessive political rhetoric would leave them unmoved. Perhaps they just hoped to buy a few days' time, during which the police effort would successfully uncover the location of Cross and his abductors. Whatever the official reasoning behind the decision, the impact of the manifesto on the Québécois population was entirely unexpected. Everywhere people from all walks of life — priests from the Gaspé, students and professors, trade unionists, randomly selected "person in the street" TV interviewees — began to draw a clear and sophisticated distinction that was very unsettling to the authorities. They liked the FLQ's analysis and political message but disliked their terrorist tactics. There followed a flowering not only of an intense media discussion and debate of the issues but arguments and discussions on street corners, in taverns and in classrooms. Background articles on Québécois grievances appeared in newspapers both in Quebec and across English Canada. Though the authorities had bought some time with the broadcast, that time was taking events in an unexpected political direction and appeared only to make the climate of opinion increasingly favourable to the FLQ. The public reaction was not what the authorities had had in mind. Indeed, the ensuing political debates were deflecting attention away from the central issue from the perspective of the governments in Ottawa and Quebec — the kidnapping and threatened "execution" of Cross. Public fear began to ebb during the next few days, as the FLQ kept cancelling and reissuing new execution deadlines while demanding negotiations. Increasingly the view was that the FLQ were not really serious about the threat to kill Cross. On the sixth day, 10 October, Quebec justice minister Choquette issued a joint declaration on behalf of the governments of Ottawa and Quebec stating that the broadcast was it; that is, there would be no deals and no further concessions on the seven demands.

No one expected the FLQ's reply, perhaps anticipating only another ultimatum. Instead, later that same day the FLQ kidnapped Quebec labour minister Pierre Laporte, a further escalation of the confrontation and a stunning blow to the hard-liners in government circles. It was one thing to kidnap a foreign diplomat, a symbol of the British tradition. It was a more serious matter to directly attack the state by abducting and threatening the "execution" of a cabinet minister. The former unity of position that had characterized the Ottawa, Quebec and Montreal governments finally cracked and then collapsed completely under a growing demand that negotiations be opened with the FLQ in order to save the lives of Cross and Laporte.

The day after Laporte's abduction, Premier Bourassa broke ranks, partly as a result of a sad and disturbing letter from Laporte begging that he and Cross be exchanged for the FLQ "political prisoners." In his statement, Bourassa offered to open official negotiations with the FLQ regarding what amounted to an exchange of Cross and Laporte for the liberation of imprisoned FLQ members. The Quebec government appointed lawyer Robert Demers, and the FLQ named Robert Lemieux, who had represented FLQ members in court. In an effort to encourage Bourassa in his decision to open negotiations, sixteen prominent Québécois leaders, including Lévesque, the leaders of the major trade union federations, the leader of the Catholic Farmers' Union and the editor of *Le Devoir*, issued a statement declaring that this was a Quebec crisis to be solved by the Québécois, concluding "we most urgently recommend negotiations to exchange the two hostages for political prisoners — these negotiations must be made in the teeth of all objections from those outside Quebec." Meanwhile, junior college and university student activists were organizing meetings to discuss the FLQ manifesto and to consider a student strike in support of the document's program. This process culminated in a huge and boisterous rally on 15 October in Montreal's Paul Sauvé Arena at which the crowd demonstrated its wholehearted support for the FLQ's manifesto. During the rally the Quebec government announced its final offer: the release of five of the FLQ prisoners in exchange for Cross and Laporte.

Two days earlier Trudeau had made clear his opposition to Bourassa's decision to negotiate with the FLQ and to accept the term "political prisoners"; for him, the FLQers were in fact, and in law, nothing more than "criminals," "bandits" and "outlaws." During a famous confrontation with TV journalist Tim Ralfe on the steps of Parliament, Trudeau justified his initial deployment of troops in Ottawa and Montreal to guard public buildings and public officials with repeated references to the threat posed by a "parallel power." He said, "Society must take means to prevent the emergence of a parallel power which defies the elected power," even if such harsh measures offended the "bleeding hearts" and "weak-kneed." As far as Trudeau was concerned, such people could "go on and bleed." When asked by Ralfe how far he would go, his answer left no room for doubt: "Just watch me…I think that goes to any distance." Trudeau was clearly convinced that any concessions to the FLQ would amount to a total capitulation to an illegal power derived from the kidnappings and execution threats. But his comment was also directed at the group of sixteen who were presenting themselves as advisers to Bourassa in the midst of crisis and instability. His greatest fury, however, was reserved for Bourassa's capitulation, which he saw as the first step in what could be the collapse of the Bourassa government's resolve to stand firm. Such a collapse, particularly in the context of growing popular support for the aims of the FLQ, could set the stage for a more general political crisis.

Furthermore, Bourassa's decision to break with Ottawa and the declaration of the sixteen, essentially telling Ottawa not to meddle, amounted to a demand that Ottawa cease acting as an effective federal government with the overriding constitutional power to ensure "peace, order and good government" in Canada. Trudeau had no doubt that such a course would accelerate Quebec's path toward separation and transform Lévesque from premier-in-waiting to de facto premier. However one assesses Trudeau's subsequent actions, his political analysis of the crisis the federal government faced was brutally sound. Had he not acted decisively, Trudeau's worst fears might well have been quickly realized given the tempo of events in Quebec. That he went much further than was necessary in the circumstances is without question. Trudeau was never one to take half or quarter measures when it came to exploiting an opportunity to squash or to humble Québécois nationalism, for which he had nothing but contempt.

On 14 October troops were sent into Ottawa. On 15 October troops began to position themselves in Quebec, especially in Montreal. At 4 a.m. on 16 October, Trudeau and his cabinet invoked the *War Measures Act* (WMA), making Canada the only western democracy to use war powers during peacetime. Ottawa declared that Quebec was in a state of "apprehended insurrection," citing letters from Premier Bourassa, Mayor Drapeau and the Montreal police chief. Over 5,000 troops were deployed in Quebec. The FLQ was outlawed and membership became a retroactive crime, without an opportunity to recant, punishable by five years in prison. Even having associated with a member of the FLQ became a crime, as did giving assistance to the FLQ or making statements that appeared to advocate the aims of the FLQ, all similarly punishable by a prison term of five years. Again, quite unlike previous invocations of the law during wartime, no opportunity was provided to anyone suspected to renounce association with the FLQ. All civil rights and liberties across Canada were technically suspended: a person could be arrested without charge, held incommunicado and without bail for twenty-one days and without trial for ninety days. Since it was a federal statute, the proclamation, though focused on Quebec, extended to all of Canada. The WMA gave the government dictatorial powers over virtually every aspect of Canadian life. The immediate public reaction, particularly in English Canada, was massive support for Trudeau: a poll days after the proclamation found that 87 per cent of Canadians supported the move. Three days after proclamation the government asked for the support of the House of Commons. NDP leader Tommy Douglas, in what was his finest hour in federal politics, stood alone, together with fifteen members of his caucus, to oppose the government, likening the invocation of the WMA to using "a sledgehammer to smash a peanut."

As soon as the WMA was proclaimed, the arrests in Quebec began. Before the sun came up 242 people had been arrested, fifty of whom had run for the PQ in the April election and two of whom were candidates opposed to Mayor Drapeau's Civic Party in the coming 25 October Montreal municipal election. Those arrested, besides the core leadership of local PQ associations, also included not only those suspected of FLQ sympathy, very broadly defined, but labour leaders, community activists and organizers, separatists of all types and those known for effective opposition to any of the three levels of government. By the end of the arrests some days later, 465 had been arrested, their homes and offices ransacked and searched and their families and neighbours terrorized. Of these, 403 were eventually freed without charge. Most were not even subjected to any kind of interrogation. Of the remaining sixty-two, thirty-two were charged, but the government decided not to prosecute. At the end of the day, only eighteen were convicted of minor offences, such as complicity, or of being accessories after the fact. Leaders of the police units trying to crack the case later revealed that the invocation of the WMA provided no help in the investigations that finally solved the case. Indeed, not a single FLQ member involved was caught in the WMA arrest net. Nor did the WMA and the 5,000 troops provide any help in finding the hostages. The case was finally solved using normal painstaking police investigative procedures. The people arrested were victims of state violence: often arrested in the dead of night; not allowed to inform family, friends or employers about what had happened; and held without charges or bail. Some lost jobs; others claim to have been verbally and/or physically abused by police and prison guards; and all most certainly would have experienced terror, degradation and humiliation.

But the person who paid the highest price was Pierre Laporte. The day after the WMA was proclaimed Laporte's body was found in the trunk of a car in the parking lot of a small military airfield on the outskirts of Montreal. The FLQ communiqué announcing Laporte's "execution" suggested the act was a cold-blooded response to the harsh actions of the authorities. The condition of the body (many cuts and bruises), the results of the autopsy and various statements by officials and the accused, in subsequent interviews and at trials, suggest the murder of Laporte was not coldly calculated.

The best reconstruction of his death appears to have been as follows. The FLQ cell holding Laporte panicked when the WMA was proclaimed. Laporte, already in a very fragile emotional state as revealed in his earlier letter to the premier, also understandably panicked, fearing that his abductors might carry out their threats. While temporarily left alone in the bedroom where he was held, Laporte either freed himself from any bonds restraining his wrists or made his escape attempt despite the bonds and threw himself through a window. His abductors, hearing the noise, raced into the room, saw Laporte part-way out the window, and pulled him back inside. In the ensuing struggle, Laporte was strangled by the chain holding the religious medal he wore around his neck. If it happened that way, it was certainly murder. But was it a cold-blooded, deliberate execution? Or was it the action of frightened, violent and fanatical young men who suddenly realized the enormity of the consequences of what they had done? Many questions remain. Did they really intend to murder Laporte? If so, why did the FLQ cell holding Cross not follow suit? Though Laporte was the victim of FLQ political violence, in another sense he was the inadvertent victim of state violence. The unanswered question that will always plague reflections on the October Crisis remains: had Ottawa not proclaimed the WMA and sent in the troops, would Laporte, like Cross, be alive today? There is no doubt about the criminal responsibility for Laporte's death, and those responsible were tried, found guilty and sentenced. But a large share of the moral and political responsibility for his death must be assigned to Trudeau, Bourassa, Drapeau and all those Canadians who cheered and applauded the harsh measures. Laporte's life was sacrificed to protect the integrity of state power. The state wanted more, however. His family, against their inclinations, were pressured into allowing officials to put on an elaborate state funeral at which Trudeau, Drapeau and Bourassa sought public justification for their actions. It was one of the most grotesque and maudlin events in Canadian history.

But Laporte's kidnappers were not the only ones to react with fear and panic. Fear, panic and hysteria became general, affecting the whole country, touching down here and there with sometimes comic, other times malevolent, results. Much of this mood resulted from a deliberately orchestrated campaign by the governments involved to justify their actions. The really serious fear campaign began with the imposition of the WMA and intensified with Laporte's death. Claims were made that the FLQ had infiltrated all key institutions of Quebec, that three thousand armed FLQ terrorists were ready to begin an insurrection, that the FLQ had a "hit list" of two hundred Quebec leaders marked for assassination, that the kidnappings were just the first step in a revolutionary plan and that mass meetings, then a massive bombing campaign, then a bloodbath of executions, cumulating with the installation of a provisional government, would follow. No scenario was too fantastic, no tactic too bizarre, to be blurted out by one prominent politician or another. The media, which had been somewhat balanced, though sensationalist, before the imposition of the WMA, got clearly on the government's side after the proclamation, reporting as fact every wild exaggeration and every fantastic notion.

English Canada was not left unscathed by the hysteria and fear. The B.C. cabinet passed an order-in-council requiring the instant dismissal of teachers or professors who, in the opinion of the police, advocated the policies of the FLQ. Seven members of the Vancouver Liberation Front, a student-based radical group, were arrested without charge and held over a weekend by Vancouver police. The mayor of Vancouver threatened to use WMA powers to clean his city of hippies and transients. A student at Carleton University had his home searched in the first hour; nothing was found but he was taken to jail and held incommunicado for six days. A student at Ottawa University was arrested and held for four days because he happened to be called Bernard Lortie, the name of a known member of the FLQ. The editors of several university newspapers across Canada were visited by police and threatened because of their intention to print the FLQ manifesto. Former brigadier and then Regina Chamber of Commerce president Orris Keehr advocated strengthening the militia by giving employees time off with pay for training so that Canada could better defend itself against a "bunch of kooks who think they can actually take over this country."

Then there was the extensive self-censorship by the media, often more vigorous than any government-appointed censor would have dared. Toronto's CHAN Television abruptly stopped a 60-minute taped interview show when it realized that the guest was a prominent Quebec labour leader who had been arrested in the first hours of the WMA. National CBC radio cancelled the broadcast of a Max Ferguson skit satirizing the WMA with a routine where Trudeau has been mistakenly arrested and held incommunicado. The CBC sent out a directive to all producers and directors ordering them to get on side with the government during the crisis. Government censors in Alberta banned the film *Red*, which featured a Métis who goes to Montreal. The airing of a TV documentary on Lenin, the Russian revolutionary leader, was cancelled. Mayor Drapeau told Quebec film censors to order the withdrawal of the film *Quiet Days in Clichy* from two Montreal theatres, or he would have the theatres raided and arrest everyone seeing the film, as well as the censors themselves. (The film was pulled.) Virtually every journalist and commentator active at the time in Quebec, as well as elsewhere in Canada, is full of stories of how censorship was imposed on his or her work during the crisis.

The fearsome icing on this cake of hysteria for all of Canada was Créditiste leader Réal Caouette's 18 October 1970 call for the summary execution by firing squad of all FLQ leaders. Despite continuing support for Trudeau's actions, enthusiasm waned and doubts about the wisdom and necessity of the state's measures increased. Even Trudeau himself had warned of the inherent dangers of such an authoritarian approach when he proclaimed the act.

The situation was salvaged when the crisis more or less ended with the arrests of those responsible for Laporte's kidnapping and murder in November, followed quickly by the discovery of the location where Cross was held. Negotiations resulted in Cross's release in exchange for safe passage to Cuba for his kidnappers.

The immediate political effect of the October Crisis no doubt fulfilled many of the expectations and intentions of Ottawa. The FLQ was utterly destroyed. The confusion and vacillation of the Bourassa government was abruptly halted. The popular mobilization was stopped dead, and we will never know what might have been the final outcome. Mayor Drapeau won a 92 per cent victory in the Montreal civic election. The WMA clearly played no role in the final resolution of the kidnappings and the murder of Laporte, and the trials and convictions went forward through the criminal justice system. And that system, to its credit, did not reflect the hysterical mood at the height of the crisis. All those convicted were out of prison, either on parole or with sentences completed, in eleven years or fewer and have since "gone straight." A few have written books about their experiences. Most have remained politically inactive and silent about the October events, often as a condition of parole. Efforts to get the full story have been unsuccessful — the Quebec Keable Commission to inquire into police wrongdoing in Quebec was stopped by Ottawa's refusal to co-operate and finally by court injunction. The 1980 McDonald Royal Commission on the Security Service examined a great deal of the evidence, but key parts of the report have been kept secret.

Despite this veil of official secrecy around the October events, enough has leaked out over the years to suggest that at least some aspects of the crisis were deliberately orchestrated by authorities in an effort to provoke polarization, perhaps as part of a campaign to discredit the democratic separatist option by linking it in the public mind with extremism and terrorism. At the public political level, this was very clear at the time — there was no "apprehended insurrection," no uprising of three thousand armed FLQers, no systematic assassinations and no widespread and focused bombing campaign. Nor did the authorities find any physical evidence of such plans as a result of the searches and arrests under the WMA. But there was also a great deal going on at the level of the clandestine state. Prior to the kidnappings, both the Montreal police and the RCMP security service knew a great deal about the FLQ, as did many journalists who covered FLQ activities and the trials of FLQers. An hour after the Cross kidnapping, *La Presse* correctly named one of those involved.

The fingerprint of another prominent and well-known FLQer was found on a FLQ communiqué after Laporte's kidnapping. Most of the FLQ militants involved in the kidnappings were routinely followed by undercover police long before the October events. Some were even followed during the crisis! The police actually had photos of FLQ members stalking Cross in the days before his abduction. One of the kidnappers had been linked earlier that year to FLQ kidnap plans. He had been arrested in February 1970 in a panel truck on his way to kidnap the Israeli consul. In the truck police found a sawed-off shotgun, a ransom note and a wicker basket large enough to hold a man. He was merely charged with possession of the illegal shotgun and released on bail. In June 1970 a police raid on an FLQ safehouse in the Laurentians scotched a plan to kidnap the U.S. consul. In that raid the police found weapons and 250 copies of the manifesto that was later read over the air. In the circumstances, why did the authorities claim they knew nothing and were completely baffled by the October kidnappings? One of the kidnappers later complained that he feels he was manipulated and that the authorities could have prevented the whole thing, given the extent of their knowledge at the time. He is convinced that for some reason the authorities wanted the plans to go ahead.

When these scattered facts are put together with later admissions of illegal and provocative activities by members of the RCMP security service, the scenario gets shadowy. RCMP security service agents have admitted to stealing dynamite; setting off bombs; writing FLQ communiqués; breaking into a left-wing news agency's office; breaking into the PQ office to steal membership lists and financial information; opening mail; routinely gaining access to confidential medical files; committing arson to destabilize the FLQ; and using kidnapping, unlawful confinement and threats of violence to frighten FLQ members and associates to become informants. Suddenly, some FLQ claims that they didn't set off all the bombs or write all the political communiqués attributed to them in the 1960s become more believable. The claim by former FLQ intellectual Pierre Vallières that the communiqué written announcing Laporte's murder was not written by a Québécois no longer seems just paranoid fantasy. One obvious possibility is that the security forces sought to get maximum public impact from the panic slaying of Laporte and put the car there themselves. The FLQ allegedly left Laporte's body in a car parked in the parking lot of a military airfield, adjacent to the military's Mobile Command headquarters. Therefore, by some means, the FLQ killers, well known and sought by every military and law enforcement agency in the province, managed to drive a car carrying Laporte's body in the trunk through a series of two or three roadblocks in broad daylight in order to reach the parking lot. This is difficult to believe.

Some have suggested the RCMP security agents acted on their own in an excess of zeal. That is unbelievable. Security agents do not engage in such domestic activities without clearance and orders from the highest political level. The hints and pieces of the October puzzle are tantalizing and suggestive but incomplete. Too many gaps have to be filled by conjecture and hypothesis. But we do know that politicians in power and clandestine security forces joined together to obscure the facts and to manipulate the Canadian people in October 1970. And only those directly involved have been brought to justice. The veil of secrecy must be lifted so the full facts can be disclosed and those responsible can be called to the bar, if not of justice, then at least of history and public opinion. Until that happens, the 1970 October Crisis remains unfinished business.

In English Canada support for Trudeau's use of the WMA was very high, in some quarters almost obscenely enthusiastic. Many in English Canada believed the October events marked the effective end of Lévesque and the PQ because, upon sober reflection on the implications of separation, the Québécois would wake up to the folly of that option. Indeed, many in English Canada believed that merely advocating separation by democratic means amounted to treason and ought to be treated as such. For those, the whole repressive episode, as long as it remained confined to Quebec, was a necessary and long overdue tonic to shock ordinary Québécois and to deflect them from the separatist course. Many, many in English Canada shared the view that the events had hopelessly compromised Lévesque and the PQ, and that political support for separatism in Quebec would begin to melt away.

If it is true that one of the long-range political goals of the authorities in using the WMA was to link terrorism and the PQ's democratic separatist option, thereby discrediting the latter, the effort failed. Lévesque emerged from the crisis looking good. He had tried to save lives by calling for negotiations. He had denounced Bourassa's weakness and vacillation vis-à-vis Ottawa. He had warned Trudeau not to try to turn Quebec into a prison by imposing collective repression. He declared that he and the PQ would fight if Trudeau tried "to tie up Quebec in impotence." And he had movingly and repeatedly denounced terrorism at every turn.

Perhaps the October events slowed down the PQ's momentum to some extent, but there was no fundamental reversal. In the February 1971 by-election to fill Laporte's seat, the PQ vote held at the level of April 1970. And in the provincial election of 1973 the PQ vote grew to 30 per cent, though it still won only 6 of 110 seats. Though the PQ was now the official Opposition, Lévesque, who again failed to win personal election, and the PQ had believed they would win. There is little doubt that residual fear from October 1970 played a role in postponing the PQ's victory. In fact, the electoral fall-out from October 1970 seemed also to hurt Trudeau. In the 1972 federal election Trudeau was humbled by the English Canada he had served so well. In Quebec, support for Trudeau faltered only slightly, falling by 4.5 per cent but still delivering 56 of 74 seats. But in English Canada Trudeau won only 53 of 190 seats with 34.5 per cent of the vote. It appeared that though English Canadians had cheered him in 1970, they had very serious reservations about the concessions he continued to insist on making to Quebec.

Indeed, that was the nub of the problem. The WMA and the troops, though provoking temporary fear and hesitation, could not hope, in the long run, to win the hearts and minds of the Québécois. And English Canada yearned for a final settlement. At the end of the Quiet Revolution, the choices for the Québécois were clarified, and they were now reflected in the National Assembly: they could either remain in a Canada that accorded Quebec a place of cultural security and dignity or adopt some variation on the theme of independence. For English Canada that meant recognizing that there could be no going back to the good old days of English-Canadian certainties. In fact, concessions would have to be made; the structures of English privilege in Quebec would either have to be greatly modified or disappear altogether. Even in the midst of the October Crisis, on 18 October 1970, the National Assembly voted unanimously to abolish Article 80 of the *BNA Act*, which guaranteed the boundaries of what were originally seventeen English provincial constituencies. The boundaries of these protected constituencies could not have been changed without the consent of a majority of the MNAs occupying them. Though most of the constituencies had become largely Québécois, it was the end of yet another piece of the elaborate structure of English privilege in Quebec. To win and keep Quebec for Canada, many more concessions would be necessary.

* * *

The Quiet Revolution, ending so dramatically and abruptly with the October Crisis, permanently transformed politics in Quebec and, by extension, in English Canada. A political process was begun in Quebec that posed sharp questions that could not and cannot be avoided. Nor can the process be reversed. The trajectory was set and the choices for the Québécois were clear: continue in a satisfactorily reformed Canadian federation or embark on the path to sovereignty. The former path requires structural concessions from English Canada sufficient to satisfy the Québécois nation's sense of injustice from the past and anxieties about the future. The latter path requires the consent of a majority of Québécois, a consent they have been reluctant to grant. Still, support for sovereignty among the Québécois continued, despite ebbs and flows, to grow.

Lévesque, the Referendum
and Patriation

On 15 November 1976, René Lévesque and the Parti Québécois won a convincing victory: 71 of 110 seats with 42 per cent of the popular vote. Lévesque had not expected to win, anticipating only a significant breakthrough, including personal victory for himself and a very strong PQ Opposition. He certainly never expected the opportunity to govern with a comfortable majority. The Liberal collapse was so thorough that even Premier Bourassa was defeated, ironically at the hands of poet and journalist Gérald Godin, who had been arrested under the *War Measures Act* in 1970. The Québécois, or at least PQ supporters, were jubilant and began an exhilarating all-night celebration in the streets of Montreal that took some of them to Westmount where their celebrations rubbed salt into English wounds.

English Canada's initial reaction was one of shock, anger and incredulity. Despite the concessions, despite the October Crisis and the troops, despite yet more concessions, the Québécois weren't satisfied. Their demands were endless and unreasonable, went the dominant English-Canadian view. With an avowedly separatist party now in power in Quebec, what had been a perceived but distant threat of the breakup of Canada suddenly became real and palpable. English Canada, therefore, braced itself for the beginning of a process that might well have ended with the separation of Quebec. And nothing English Canada had done to placate Quebec had been sufficient to postpone this awful final moment of decision.

Indeed, from English Canada's point of view, great strides had been taken since October 1970 to accommodate Québécois aspirations. Constitutional renewal, including patriation, a language charter, an amending formula and an opting-out provision were offered at Victoria in 1971. At first, Premier Bourassa agreed to this Victoria Charter, but after a brief sampling of opinion back home, alive with negative opinions, fears and reservations about the deal, Bourassa withdrew his agreement with a great deal of egg on his face. The charter had failed to come to grips with the constitutional bottom line of Québécois nationalism; that is, special status for Quebec, a new division of powers and a guaranteed Quebec veto. Meanwhile, Trudeau pursued his strategy of federal bilingualism and French power in Ottawa, while flatly rejecting any notion of special status for Quebec. Furthermore, Trudeau turned up the heat on Québécois nationalism. He instituted an aggressive multiculturalism policy, partly in an effort to reduce the centrality of the French/English polarization, and insisted on the constitutional doctrine of the equality of provinces, in an effort to forestall Québécois insistence that the matter ought to be resolved through bilateral negotiations between Ottawa and Quebec.

While they created many career and business opportunities for a significant number of Québécois, federal bilingualism and French power in Ottawa did nothing to relieve the language tensions in Quebec. In Quebec, the language issue remained a matter of making French the language not only of day-to-day life and work but also of economic decision-making and career opportunity. The Gendron Commission, appointed by the Union Nationale government in 1969 to defuse the St. Léonard crisis, issued its report in 1972. The report included extensive research studies on the language of work and economic opportunity and again confirmed, in more detail, the dramatic economic disadvantages experienced by the Québécois compelled to use English as the language of work, especially as they moved up the occupational hierarchy. Comparisons with the past again indicated that the Québécois were not progressing very rapidly in closing the gap with English Canadians in Quebec. The evidence showed that language was the key to dismantling English privilege and unlocking economic opportunity for the Québécois.

As a result, the Gendron Commission recommended that French become Quebec's official language, though English would continue to enjoy the status of a national language in the province. Under growing pressure, in 1974 the Bourassa government introduced and passed Bill 22, *The Official Languages Act*, which declared French the province's official language in all key areas: business, labour, education, selected professions, public administration and so on. Further, an implementation program and a regulatory system were put in place to enforce the new law. An important escape hatch was left open, however. Those who wished to educate their children in English could choose to submit their children to testing to ensure their knowledge of English. If they failed to demonstrate such knowledge, they would be enrolled in the French-language system.

Predictably, English Canadians were not happy with this development. While English Canada was reluctantly embracing official federal bilingualism, Quebec was apparently marching towards French unilingualism. Though this sentiment overlooked the fact that all provinces but New Brunswick continued to embrace English unilingualism, English Canada's capacity for upholding a linguistic double standard remained unchallenged.

Bill 22 particularly angered the English minority in Quebec. The law compelled them to make profound linguistic adjustments in all spheres of life. Furthermore, the language test for education inevitably began to divert immigrant enrolments from the English to the French school system. Yet the Québécois nationalists were still not satisfied. The law did not go far enough or fast enough in making Quebec a thoroughly French-speaking province. The language test still allowed access to the English school system to those willing to go to the expense and effort of tutoring their children. At the end of the day, Bill 22 was a political disaster for Bourassa; it won the premier no friends and created new enemies, particularly among the English minority and immigrants.

Any political good that bilingualism may have done among the Québécois during the early 1970s was at least temporarily wiped out by the dispute over the language of air traffic control at Quebec airports. Québécois pilots and air traffic controllers resented being compelled to use English, even at Quebec airports. English-Canadian pilots and controllers insisted that English was the language of international aviation, and that, for safety reasons, it ought to continue to be the uniform language in Quebec. In 1973 Ottawa created a task force to look into the matter, and in 1975 its report recommended that both French and English be allowed at five Quebec airports.

English-Canadian air traffic controllers went on strike to express their opposition, and English-Canadian pilots supported them, creating major national disruptions in air service. Meanwhile, Québécois air traffic controllers and pilots split off to form their own organization, Les Gens de l'Air, to press the case for bilingualism in air traffic control. When Ottawa caved in to the

English air traffic controllers and settled the strike by allowing them a veto over the use of bilingualism in the air, there were angry convulsions in Quebec. Although the crisis was finally resolved in stages by a commission of inquiry between 1976 and 1979, and bilingualism was extended to all airports in Quebec, the immediate political damage in Quebec was considerable.

To the Québécois, English Canada appeared unyielding and arrogant, willing to permit only a restricted use of French, a sort of bilingualism by English permission. At the same time, English Canadians took the view that the Québécois were again being hypersensitive and unreasonable in pressing the language issue in ways that jeopardized air safety. In retrospect, it was another unnecessary and gratuitous language dispute provoked by English Canada. But it struck at the very heart of the language issue in Quebec. If French was to become the language of work, it had to be the language of work in all spheres, not just in those conceded by English Canada. And if Canada truly embraced official bilingualism in the federal sphere, then it had to be nothing less than a real, day-to-day bilingualism, not a bilingualism based on English-Canadian sufferance.

Despite these continuing confrontations, the Québécois remained ambivalent about the stark choices before them, which explains why the same electorate could strongly support the implacable federalism of Trudeau in 1974 and yet elect the separatist Lévesque in 1976. The Québécois had indeed made significant gains since the Quiet Revolution. French was gradually becoming the dominant language in Quebec; federal politicians and senior civil servants from Quebec played leading roles at the highest levels in Ottawa; the system of English privilege in Quebec was either being actively dismantled step-by-step or was under serious seige. In 1961, an English male in the Quebec labour force earned, on average, just under 50 per cent more than his Québécois counterpart. By 1970 this income lead had been narrowed to about 33 per cent. In 1961 unilingual English males in Quebec comprised the most privileged group in Canada. By the mid-1970s, the most privileged group was made up of bilingual English males in Quebec. Still, the upper ranges of the occupational hierarchy remained beyond the reach of most Québécois. The English minority was still heavily over-represented at the top. For English Canadians, however, the change was sufficient evidence that real structural transformation was indeed occurring and would continue. For the Québécois, it was happening much too slowly, and their impatience was growing.

Clearly, this mood of exasperation had finally grown sufficiently to express itself electorally in Lévesque's victory. Fearing
the worst, English Canada made great efforts to remind the PQ
government of the limits of its mandate. Editorialists and commentators in English Canada, and Trudeau himself, pointed out
that the PQ had no mandate to move toward sovereignty. Only 42
per cent of the electorate had given Lévesque his majority. Just
two years previously 54 per cent of the same electorate had supported Trudeau and the federalist Liberals. The Quebec electorate
had simply voted out a bad government in the hopes that
Lévesque and the PQ would bring good government. The Québécois had perhaps voted for change. But they had not voted for
independence. Further evidence of this position was provided by
a Gallup poll held just a few months after Lévesque's victory.
Only 22 per cent in Quebec favoured the hard separatist option.
While this figure was certainly ominous — it had doubled since
1968, and the question was on separation not sovereignty-association — it revealed no mandate in Quebec public opinion to
pursue separation.

English Canada began to relax as the intentions of the PQ
government became clearer. Though many in English Canada did
not realize it at the time, Lévesque and the PQ had long before
separated the election of the PQ to provincial power from the
achievement of Quebec sovereignty. Even if a PQ government
were elected, there would be a separate referendum on sovereignty. This commitment was made in the 1973 election, and it
was made even more clearly in the 1976 campaign. The moderate architects of this strategy contended that without promising a
separate referendum on sovereignty, the PQ could never hope to
win election. Their position seemed to be confirmed by the 1976
results. Yet, had the PQ government wished to, it could have
made building toward a referendum a central thrust of the work
of both party and government from the outset. But it did not,
since the PQ had also promised to move to a referendum only
after making an effort to achieve a negotiated settlement with
Ottawa. As a result, both sovereignty and the referendum were,
for all practical political purposes, put on the back burner during
the PQ's first three years in power.

Lévesque's careful, non-inflammatory approach to the sovereignty issue was indicated in his decision regarding the Bourassa
government's Centre d'Archives et de Documentation (CAD).
CAD, composed of bureaucrats at the highest level in the Pre-

mier's Office, was established in 1971 in the aftermath of the October Crisis, and it was assigned the task of collecting clandestine political information in co-operation with federal and provincial police agencies as well as the Privy Council Office in Ottawa. When Lévesque took over as premier in 1976, CAD had assembled confidential files on 30,000 people and 6,000 organizations in the province. Lévesque chose not to expose the situation by establishing a commission of inquiry to uncover just how far the political spying had gone. It would have been particularly significant to reveal whether laws had been broken and civil rights violated, whether the active infiltration of organizations had been carried out and whether efforts to destabilize organizations and discredit selected activists had been undertaken. Lévesque simply disbanded CAD and ordered the files destroyed. In the context of the dirty tricks of 1970 and after, a thorough public exposure of CAD and its activities might have proven a potentially potent weapon in mobilizing the population more quickly in the direction of sovereignty. As an act of statesmanship, Lévesque chose not to do so.

But the PQ's moderation extended beyond its approach to sovereignty. Given the Quebec state's key role during the Quiet Revolution and given the PQ's view, held since its founding, that the provincial state had to be used aggressively to empower the Québécois nation in its march toward self-determination, there was a general expectation that under the PQ the provincial government would become more intrusive in the economy and act as a more aggressive instrument for attacking both English privilege within the province and English Canada's external influence. Except in the areas of auto insurance and asbestos, this did not occur. The PQ government was careful and prudent. It made no large, dramatic strides in expanding the role of the state. This was the source of some comfort in English Canada, since the doctrines of the new Québécois nationalism pointed strongly in the direction of an expanded and more powerful provincial state.

The PQ government did move, however, on a series of social measures in accord with its social democratic program, making it the most progressive provincial government in Canada, far ahead of Allan Blakeney's NDP regime in Saskatchewan. Anti-scab legislation was passed, restricting the use of "replacement workers" during strikes to essential activities and property protection. The regressive sales tax on shoes, clothing and furniture was removed, a benefit to those with lower incomes. The minimum wage became the highest in Canada and was indexed to the cost of living. More generous income supports were provided to the poor. Quebec became the national leader in programs designed to support the family and working women. Income tax rates were indexed to the cost of living for those earning less than $30,000 annually, a real boon to ordinary wage and salary earners. Children under sixteen got free dental care, while senior citizens got free prescription drugs. And there were many other such measures, few of which received attention in English Canada.

Overall the PQ approach was one of *étapisme* — a gradual step-by-step approach to ultimate sovereignty. Having unexpectedly won power, the PQ, the argument went, must first prove that it was a competent, prudent and responsible government. Above all, it must not rush off in too many directions and initiate drastic changes that might worry the population, arouse the business lobby or fail abysmally. Reforms must be carried out, but only those the people strongly supported and only those the PQ government could be certain would have positive outcomes. Most important, the PQ must reassure internal and external investors by proceeding cautiously in the sensitive area of the economy. Lévesque did not need to be reminded about how well-orchestrated economic fear campaigns had been used against the PQ from the outset. The issue of sovereignty was to be postponed while the PQ government carried out this program of reassurance. No hasty moves would be taken; no abrupt changes in the course of the government would occur. Except for the PQ's ultimate commitment to sovereignty, which for English Canada hung ominously in the air, Canadian political life went on much as before and the initial fears provoked by the PQ victory ebbed among English Canadians.

Though many in English Canada were pleasantly surprised by the PQ's moderation, close PQ watchers were not. In fact, Lévesque and Claude Morin, minister of intergovernmental affairs, had fought the *étapisme* strategy through the structures of the PQ only with great difficulty, opposed at every step by party activists and significant elements of the top leadership. Lévesque, it must not be forgotten, had been a late and reluctant recruit to sovereignty. He was never committed to independence in its fullest sense, and he was uncomfortable with and suspicious of those, like the RIN, who were. Lévesque was a bit of an anglophile in that he did not want to sever links with English Canada, hence his concept of sovereignty-association, and he was a vigorous champion within his party and his government of the rights of the English minority in Quebec. In retrospect, if there ever was a Quebec separatist leader with whom English Canada could have made an excellent, workable deal, Lévesque was that leader. From founding the PQ, which at Lévesque's insistence had only officially included the MSA and the right-wing RN (the RIN dissolved itself and advised its members to join the PQ), the marriage between Lévesque and determined separatists was uneasy. Lévesque needed the talent and energy of the *indépendantiste* movement, and the movement needed Lévesque's popularity and credibility. Though they agreed sufficiently to work for sovereignty, there were constant sharp disagreements on strategy and tactics. Lévesque and his MSA group refused to conceive of a sovereign Quebec in the absence of an economic association with Canada, while the *indépendantistes* saw sovereignty as the priority, untied to any conditions about association.

Lévesque was aided immeasurably in his battle for a moderate, *à petites étapes* approach to sovereignty by Claude Morin, whose decision to join the PQ in 1972 had been a major coup for the party. His decision came as a surprise to many, since Morin was widely known for his self-interested caution, particularly when it came to career decisions. Morin had been a central figure in the Lesage government, first as its key economic adviser then as the first deputy minister of intergovernmental affairs. He was widely recognized as the most significant adviser during both the Liberal and UN periods in office. After his resignation he wrote a book, *Le pouvoir Québécois...en négociation*, lamenting the fact that Quebec always lost out in federal-provincial negotiations, something the PQ liked to hear from a man of his experience.

It was not therefore unexpected when Lévesque catapulted Morin into a leadership role second only to his own. Morin became the key architect and engineer of the PQ's *étapiste* referendum strategy. Prior to the 1973 election, PQ policy called for a referendum solely to accept or to reject a proposed constitution for an independent Quebec. During the 1973 election campaign, the PQ promised that independence would result only after a separate referendum on the issue. This arbitrary policy change in the heat of an election was later confirmed as party policy. But Morin added a further twist. Such a referendum would occur only after efforts to negotiate sovereignty-association with Ottawa had failed. After the 1976 victory, Morin added a further modification to the referendum commitment by indicating that the PQ government would begin to negotiate sovereignty-association for Quebec only *after* winning a referendum.

Morin also played a central role in successfully advocating another significant modification to the PQ's sovereignty strategy: as long as Quebec remained in Confederation, a PQ government would participate fully in federal-provincial negotiations in order to win more concessions for Quebec within the federal system.

An additional feature of PQ policy had to do with the concept of "sovereignty-association" itself. Was the emphasis to be first on winning sovereignty, then on negotiating association? Or was there a hyphen between the two words? With a hyphen, the concept "sovereignty-association" was a package whereby winning sovereignty depended on winning association. Morin came down heavily on the side of the hyphen. This may sound like a petty, pedantic issue, merely a question of quibbling about punctuation. But it was absolutely central to the PQ's approach. Clearly the strategy for winning sovereignty first and then negotiating some form of association would differ markedly from one used to win sovereignty and association at the same time. What if Ottawa and the other provinces spoke loudly with one voice saying there can never be any form of economic association between an independent Quebec and the rest of Canada? The debate raged in the party until October 1978, when Lévesque, speaking in the National Assembly as premier, clearly placed the hyphen in the phrase and said Quebec aspired to sovereignty-association, which would be the basis of any referendum question. Morin proceeded to work on the wording of the future referendum question with a focus on seeking the public's authorization to negotiate sovereignty-association rather than on its support for sovereignty.

The overall impact of the Lévesque-Morin *étapiste* strategy was to defuse the sovereignty issue in the short and medium term by postponing the day of the hard final question into the relatively distant future: first, there would be a referendum seeking permission to try to negotiate sovereignty-association; if the referendum were successful, the PQ government would then enter what might be fairly lengthy negotiations; if those were not successful, then there would be another referendum on some sort of declaration of sovereignty. Furthermore, by focusing on providing a good, moderate, business-like day-to-day provincial government, the PQ administration was increasingly caught up in the detail of running the province and carrying out those reforms constitutionally possible under the *BNA Act*. Finally, by deciding to participate fully in federal-provincial negotiations, the PQ government was drawn into federal-provincial gamesmanship, slipping deeper and deeper into the give-and-take of Canadian federalism. Such an approach had the clear advantage of easing fears and quieting nerves.

But the approach also carried with it serious political risks. First, by defusing the sovereignty issue and postponing the final decision into the distant future, the PQ's raison d'être was compromised. Second, a good, fair, reform-minded provincial government might deliver enough to make leaving Canada less and less attractive to the average Québécois. Third, by seeking to appease investors and the business lobby, especially those from English Canada and the United States, the PQ inadvertently delivered the message that perhaps there were serious economic risks and sacrifices attached to sovereignty after all. Fourth, an aggressive participation in federal-provincial negotiations might prove sufficiently successful in winning significant constitutional concessions that the need for sovereignty might appear much less urgent to many Québécois. And finally, a soft question that asked only for a mandate to negotiate sovereignty-association might lead many to believe the PQ, behind its bold facade, really had cold feet about the whole project and was just using the threat as a means to squeeze more out of English Canada. This last opinion was widely held in English Canada and served to stiffen resistance to Quebec's demands.

Language, however, was one issue on which the PQ government did not dare be moderate and compromising. And despite Lévesque's hesitations and reservations, the PQ government made rapid, irreversible progress on the francization process in Quebec. Bill 101, *La Charte de la langue française*, was introduced and passed in 1978 and completed the work started by Bourassa's Bill 22. In effect, French, already the official language of Quebec in most crucial spheres, became the official language in all areas of life. There was no way to avoid it: if you wanted to live and work in Quebec, you had to speak French. Only those parents who had obtained an English-language education in Quebec could enrol their children in the English school system. All others, immigrants as well as English Canadians from outside Quebec, were compelled to enrol their children in the French system. The testing escape hatch was closed. Companies with fifty or more employees had to embark on a compulsory and regulated francization program. Significantly, as a gesture of goodwill to non-Québécois and to business, the law backed away from compelling a Québécois quota among those employed. The focus remained on language skills in French, regardless of ethnic origin. English Canada was not pleased. Many English Canadians in Quebec, faced with the daunting prospect of achieving fluency in French, chose to leave. Amid much publicity the century-old Sun Life Insurance company announced the move of its head office from Montreal to Toronto as a result of Bill 101. Québécois were bitterly angry at Sun Life, and Ottawa was profoundly embarrassed. Sun Life's departure had been preceded in 1976 by the move of important sections of Prudential's head office operations from Montreal. Subsequently, there was a haemorrhage of English head offices leaving Quebec in the ensuing years, including, according to a survey by Quebec's organized business lobby, 629 firms between 1979 and 1982 alone.

Bill 101 was a clear declaration to all of Canada. No provincial political party in Quebec would survive if it dared to compromise the essential features of the bill. Many English Canadians outside Quebec were outraged by the law, and provincial politicians in English Canada frequently attacked it to pander to anti-Quebec sentiments. But the wise and the prudent among English Canadians, both within and outside Quebec, knew the francization process was irreversible and represented the linguistic minimum that the Québécois would accept in the Canadian federation. Quebec was demanding for itself neither less nor more than English Canada had long since imposed, often unconstitutionally, in the other nine provinces. At least Quebec could point with justified pride to how well it treated its established English-Canadian minority — the children of those educated in Quebec in English could enjoy the same privilege.

Despite the initial attention focused by the election of the PQ in 1976, punctuated by the Bill 101 furor, English Canadians understandably were equally, if not more, preoccupied with other issues that affected them more directly throughout the 1970s. Quebec was not the only crisis afflicting the federation in that eventful decade. Confederation's other problem child, the West, again began demanding redress of its historic grievances. Relatively quiescent since the clashing battles of Alberta's William Aberhart and Saskatchewan's Tommy Douglas in the 1930s and 1940s, the West roused itself to demand an improved place in the federation.

From Riel onwards, the West, particularly the Prairie West, had resented both its economic place in Confederation as resource hinterland and captive market and its lack of real political clout in determining national policies. Though westerners largely joined Ontario in the commitment to keep the West English and Protestant and in articulating a fundamental hostility to Quebec, they resented the region's status as a dependent investment frontier and captive market for Ontario capitalists. While the West's agitations had won many concessions, these included neither additional constitutional powers nor a basic redesign of national economic policies to its benefit. The concessions were, however, enough to quiet the West during the period of post-war prosperity, and it was even initially prepared to accept concessions to Quebec during the Pearson and early Trudeau years, particularly when those concessions cost them nothing and were made in the context of the general expansion of federal spending programs.

But in the late 1960s and early 1970s when prosperity ended and recession struck the entire region, the West began again to express aggressive anger about its place in Confederation. The first obvious evidence of western arousal led to dramatic changes in government in all four western provinces with the common denominator of dissatisfaction with the resource strategies of the 1950s and 1960s. Everyone in the West wanted economic diversification, new development, secure jobs and prosperity, but they began to question the price. Clearly, resource development by external, largely foreign, capital was not doing the job. Other than expanding the list of resources being extracted, real economic diversification to ease the booms and busts of a resource economy had not occurred. What little industrial development had taken place in the West in industries related to the natural products of the region, like milling and meat-packing, was closing down as the magic of the market, improvements in transportation and technological innovation led to increasing centralization closer to the large markets of Central Canada. In different ways, the new western provincial governments all said the western provinces should control resource development so that westerners would retain more benefits and revenues. The industrial spinoffs of resource extraction, including inputs and value-added processing, should be located in the West. And more and more revenue from the extraction of non-renewable resources for export had to be reinvested in the region to assure its economic future.

The election of the four new regimes marked a new era in the West's struggle for a place in the sun in Confederation and in the national economy. Just as the great social powers conferred on the provinces by the *BNA Act* had allowed earlier western movements to push for the construction of the welfare state in the era following the Great Depression and World War II, the provinces' control of natural resources could be used to push for a better economic and constitutional deal for the West. The West, therefore, began to use its resource wealth as a bargaining chip in the constitutional debate. If Quebec could use its hefty political clout to gain constitutional concessions, perhaps the West could use its resource clout in a like manner. More and more, the constitutional debate, formerly seen in the West as an arcane, technical process largely between Quebec and Ottawa, came to be seen as an arena to push for a western breakthrough. What was sauce for the goose could be sauce for the gander — if Quebec needed constitutional concessions to deal with its linguistic and cultural concerns, could not the West make some kind of trade and obtain constitutional concessions to empower the region in the control of resources?

Trudeau's obsession with Quebec nationalism and separatism, his clumsy agricultural policy initiatives in the West, his imposition of a bilingualism that made no sense to many westerners and his lack of sympathy for western concerns about resource development began the process of western political estrangement that saw the western Liberal Party, federally and provincially, virtually annihilated in a decade. Trudeau's conviction that a large part of the Quebec problem, indeed of the growing crisis of Confederation, had to do with an excessively weak federal government and his commitment to strengthen it ensured further confrontations with the West. The West was happy enough to see Trudeau flex federal muscles against the Québécois, as he had during the October Crisis, but it did not appreciate a similar flexing against the West on the issue of resources.

Two contradictory forces ensured a confrontation: the growing determination in the West that provincial powers should be used aggressively to maximize provincial benefits from resource development, and a growing conviction on the part of the Trudeau regime that federal power, atrophied by lack of use during the Diefenbaker and Pearson years, had to be reasserted. Ottawa found itself fighting on two fronts: to the East, separatism in Quebec, and to the West, the growing assertion of provincial powers over natural resources.

In the early 1970s the world's oil-supplying countries organized themselves into a cartel, the Organization of Petroleum Exporting Countries (OPEC), determined to reap a greater share of revenue. Sporadic pressure to increase the world price continued until 1973, when OPEC began a series of unilateral moves that doubled, tripled and finally quadrupled world oil prices. The "energy crisis" was upon us, creating a bonanza for oil-producing countries and for major international oil companies. The crisis was a disaster for oil-consuming countries. The industrial sectors of the advanced countries, including Canada, deeply dependent on cheap oil, found themselves in a crunch. The costs of home heating and auto fuel cut deeply into the disposable incomes of families, while spiralling inflation related to oil prices and interest rates further contracted incomes and jeopardized industries. In Canada the energy crisis added a new dimension to the Confederation crisis.

The western energy provinces moved to capture the windfall profits associated with the oil price rise. The federal government also moved aggressively. Ottawa imposed an oil price freeze in the fall of 1973, slapped on a federal oil export tax to capture increased revenues and decided to deny resource companies the right to deduct provincial royalty charges before they computed federal taxes. All these moves markedly diminished the extent to which the energy provinces could capture the windfall. They were supplemented by a 1974 law granting Ottawa the power to fix oil prices. Furthermore, Ottawa threatened to impose a federal tax on natural gas exports and resisted dramatic increases in natural gas prices in Canada.

Alberta and Saskatchewan responded by revising their royalty schedules upward and, in the case of Saskatchewan, by taking into public ownership all non-Crown oil and gas rights and imposing a surcharge on oil production (the surcharge was later ruled ultra vires). Alberta similarly moved to establish technical public ownership rights over its oil, though it hesitated to go as far as Saskatchewan, by creating a marketing commission mechanism and by declaring that the royalty share of oil going through the marketing commission was publicly owned. These legislative moves, and a host of other technical enactments and regulations, were designed to buttress provincial constitutional control over all aspects of oil and gas development: production, marketing and pricing. By asserting ownership rights over oil and gas after they were out of the ground, the provinces were less likely to be seen as interfering with trade and commerce, an area of clear federal constitutional jurisdiction.

By 1975, an impasse was reached with both levels of government sharing the wealth with the industry in an atmosphere of hostility and confrontation. As the 1970s unfolded, Allan Blakeney and Peter Lougheed won renewed and convincing mandates from their electorates by declaring their intention to continue to fight for provincial control of resources against the arrogant intrusions of the federal government. And for his part, Trudeau repeated that he had no intention of letting the western provinces hold the nation to ransom over energy pricing.

The West had a strong case. Resources came under exclusive provincial jurisdiction. Yet when the *BNA Act* was drafted, its authors had in mind such resources as timber, land and the less significant mining sector. They saw resources as incidental to the great effort of nation-building and the construction of an East-West economy where the wealth to be made chiefly lay in commerce and manufacturing. As the new resource wealth of the West developed, most of it was for export, and federal powers over trade and commerce easily contained the situation. However, the western provinces' efforts in the 1970s to extend their control over resources involved aggressive new departures. No longer simply content to sell the rights to exploit resources to investors and then to collect royalties as the resources were extracted and exported, the provinces were now trying to control the whole process in an effort to capture this new wealth as a basis for economic diversification as well as for revenues.

Ottawa also had a strong case. The oil crisis had driven up the price for oil to the point where Central and Atlantic Canada were in deep trouble. Forced to pay burgeoning world prices for much of Canada's needs in the East, the federal government tried to soften the impact by enforcing a low domestic price. The difference between the world price paid and the administered domestic price had to be made up, the federal government argued, at least partly by the greatly expanded revenues being earned by western exports of oil and natural gas. By 1975, Canada was in a serious deficit position in the oil trade as its imports of oil at world prices outpaced the revenues from exports of western oil. The resulting dislocation and inflation would be a disaster for the national economy. Furthermore, the rise in oil prices had worsened the growing crisis in Central Canadian industry, which required cheaper than world-price energy sources in order to sustain its competitiveness. Therefore, the federal government argued that it was in the interest of the national economy, in this case the industrial heartland of the nation, to establish energy-pricing policies that would protect Canada's manufacturing sector.

The western provinces largely agreed with such arguments in principle. The debate centred on how much of the bonanza the West ought to give up in the national interest. Westerners complained that it was not fair that they should again be called upon exclusively to bear the full cost of Canadian nationhood. The 1896 Wheat Boom in the West had set the stage for the realization of a viable East-West economy cementing the Dominion. The West had largely paid, through land grants, mineral rights and a period of monopoly, for the railway that first bound Canada together. The West's tariff-captive market had helped make Central Canada's industries successful. Now, once again, Canada was calling on the West to give up the profits of the energy boom to help salvage the nation. Many in the West felt that too much had been asked in the past and that too much was being asked again.

After endless negotiations, the federal and provincial governments agreed on a policy of a gradual upward movement of oil prices, though the federal government refused in principle a commitment to a rapid move to world prices. A complex formula for federal-provincial-industry revenue-sharing was negotiated. There was also an agreement providing for federal-provincial-industry involvement in the development of unconventional oil such as the tar sands, heavy oil upgraders, the offshore and the northern frontier. The compromise was completely unsatisfactory to the West, which continued to insist that the region was being asked to surrender too much of the boom to aid the nation. Anger at Ottawa and a pervading sense of bitterness increased in the West.

In the federal election of 27 May 1979, the West got its revenge on Trudeau, with a little help from Ontario, when Joe Clark won the largest bloc of seats in the House of Commons and became the prime minister of a minority Tory government. After the acrimony of the energy wars and Trudeau's heavy federal hand, the West liked Clark's vision of Confederation as a "community of communities," giving him 57 of 77 seats. Atlantic Canada, as usual, hedged its bets, but it still gave Clark the edge with 18 of 32 seats. Though tempered by a dependence on its expensive imported oil, many of the resource concerns of the Western provinces were shared in Atlantic Canada, which looked with hope at the future promise of offshore oil and gas development. Ontario, disturbed by the energy conflict, a developing industrial crisis and the continuing Quebec problems, and deeply aware that eleven years of Trudeau had seemed to deepen the strains on Confederation (which was, after all, originally largely Ontario's creation), reluctantly shifted into the Tory column 57 of 95 seats, ending seventeen years of Liberal hegemony in Ottawa. If Trudeau's tough federalism had only served to increase separatist support in Quebec and begun to drive the West into another episode of fury, then perhaps Clark's commitment to reason, compromise and decentralization deserved a try.

Quebec, on the other hand, stayed with Trudeau, giving him the strongest support ever with 67 of 75 seats and 62 per cent of the popular vote. As a result of this loyalty, Clark was denied a majority. The irony of Quebec's electorate voting heavily for Trudeau's strong centralist federalism just two-and-a-half years after electing Lévesque was not lost in English Canada, especially among those who were annoyed and uneasy that Clark had won such a tenuous victory. The result was, however, cause for elation in the PQ government; it gave them a window of political opportunity. Fighting a referendum campaign in Quebec just shortly after Trudeau had refreshed a strong mandate for federalism, including incontestable support in Quebec, was an unhappy prospect for Lévesque and the PQ. Now, however, they had the best of all worlds: Trudeau, the champion of Quebec, laid low by English Canada; an English-Canadian prime minister in power with virtually no support in Quebec; and finally, and perhaps best of all, a prime minister committed to decentralization and ideologically disinclined to make heavy-handed use of federal power. Lévesque wasted no time. Just a month after Clark's victory, he announced that the referendum on sovereignty-association would be held in the spring of 1980. Trudeau's decision to resign from politics in November 1979 seemed to mark the end of one of the most tumultuous eras in Canadian politics, and many greeted the event without regret.

As it turned out, both the West and Lévesque were to be profoundly disappointed by Joe Clark. At first, things went well for the West. In the late 1979 budget, the Clark government gave the West major concessions on energy with a four-dollar-a-barrel increase in oil prices in 1980 (something Trudeau had only promised over two years) followed by equally dramatic increases projected into future years. The overall objective was to move by stages, but at considerable speed, to the world oil price. This represented a potential windfall for the West, especially Alberta. But this measure was received with little enthusiasm in Ontario and Quebec, both staggering under the blows inflicted by the energy crisis. Atlantic Canada was also unenthusiastic, though Newfoundland's Brian Peckford was placated by Clark's promise that coastal provinces would enjoy substantial control of offshore energy developments, something Trudeau had flatly refused to concede. In other words, Clark had set himself up to become the lightning rod for the deep divisions between energy-consuming and -producing provinces with Tory Ontario and Tory Alberta pulling him in opposite directions. Convinced that the leaderless Liberals would be hesitant to force an election for some time, Clark had also set himself up for a fall by announcing early in his mandate an intention to govern as if he enjoyed a majority, probably one of the most suicidal positions a leader of a minority government can take. Inevitably, Joe Clark's seven-month-old government was defeated in the House of Commons on 13 December 1979. With visions of Diefenbaker's 1957 and 1958 performance dancing in his head, Clark set the election date for 18 February 1980. Three days later, phoenix-like, Trudeau announced he had reconsidered his resignation and would fight the election as Liberal leader.

Clark's defeat was a foregone conclusion. On the energy issue the West was isolated, finding little support or sympathy in Central and Atlantic Canada. The energy-consuming regions wanted lower than world energy prices and generally supported federal initiatives under Trudeau to regulate energy prices and to share out the costs of the crisis on a fair, national basis. Clark was perceived as weak and as having gone far too far in serving the West's sectional interests to the detriment of the general good of the nation. Given the evident elation of the PQ in Quebec upon Clark's election, and the alacrity with which Lévesque had moved on the referendum after Trudeau's defeat, more and more Canadians were concerned about whether Clark could adequately represent the federalist option in the coming referendum debate.

Trudeau won his majority in February 1980, and his victory can be almost solely attributed to his promise to Central and Atlantic Canada that he would resist the West's demands for unreasonable increases in oil prices and for provincial jurisdiction over energy resources unimpeded by federal authority. Trudeau simply wrote off the West. The results confirmed the effectiveness of his strategy: 19 of 32 seats in Atlantic Canada, 74 of 75 seats in Quebec and 52 of 95 seats in Ontario. In the West, the Liberals won only two seats and both of these were in Manitoba. Despite later myths in the West that blamed Quebec for Clark's defeat, what won the election for Trudeau was the shift in Ontario, largely based on Trudeau's energy promise and on the support of Ontario's Tory premier, desperate for cheap energy. Ontario once again favoured a strong central government in which Ontario would play its proper and decisive role, something denied the province by Clark.

Now unimpeded by any obligation to the West, Trudeau proceeded to impose the National Energy Program, taking for Ottawa authority over energy resources by establishing new price- and revenue-sharing regimes without western consent. The regulated domestic oil price would never be allowed to go above 85 per cent of the world price. The new revenue-sharing regime more than doubled the amount going to Ottawa, while sharply cutting the shares for the producing provinces and the industry. The program also involved a strong push for the Canadianization of ownership of the energy industry, incentives for nonconventional development and frontier exploration, and a bigger direct federal role in energy development through PetroCan. The reaction in the West, especially in Alberta, was unconcealed fury. It provoked the rise of western separatist sentiment and eventually led Alberta's Lougheed to do the unthinkable by staging in two cuts of 5 per cent each in the flow of oil eastward.

Immediately after his victory, however, the bulk of Trudeau's attention was devoted to the referendum campaign in Quebec, set for 20 May, just three months after his victory. Fresh from his biggest victory ever in Quebec and armed with a series of polls taken by the Clark government, Trudeau was confident that the No side would carry the day, assuming it had an effective campaign.

In retrospect, a number of things stand out in the referendum campaign that have coloured Quebec politics up to the present. One was the incredible economic fear campaign mounted by the No side. Another was Trudeau's sneering contempt for Québécois nationalism, a contempt that had obviously deepened over the years and that he made no effort to conceal. Yet another was the contrasting crowd scenes conveyed on national television after the results were in (60 per cent No; 40 per cent Yes). At the Paul Sauvé Arena in Montreal, there were thousands of Yes supporters singing, hugging and openly crying as Lévesque spoke and promised "*á la prochaine.*" At the No headquarters, there were only a few hundred, subdued in their victory, as if they had just participated in something distasteful in which they could take little pride. Was it another defeat for the PQ that had all the taste and appearance of a victory?

More significant were the demographics of the Yes and No votes. The No vote included overwhelming support from both the anglophone and the ethnic vote, in the neighbourhood of 90 per cent. The Québécois vote had split down the middle: about half voted No, half Yes. Québécois No voters tended to be older (over 50) and more affluent, those for whom Confederation had not been such a bad deal and who feared change the most. And fear was the biggest part of the No campaign; fear of change, fear of separatism, fear of the future, fear of losing old-age pensions and family allowances, fear of a fall in standard of living and so on. Québécois Yes voters, on the other hand, tended to be younger and somewhat less affluent as a whole. Students, for example, overwhelmingly voted Yes, as did those aged eighteen to twenty-five. Even the working class was split between young and old, although the major trade union centrals publicly endorsed a Yes vote and thus trade union activists were largely pro-Yes. Those working in Québécois cultural areas, journalists, teachers, professors, artists, writers, actors, the human professions and so on, tended to go with the Yes option. In other words, the demographics of the Yes vote left considerable room for optimism for the future, suggesting the pro-sovereignty forces would grow quickly in the absence of an acceptable renewal of federalism.

In fact, among the militants and activists on the Yes side there was much disappointment, but no sense of a permanent defeat. There was little demoralization. They believed that the future was theirs. Their arguments made some sense. The hysteria of the No campaign had actually hardened up Yes support just as much as it frightened away the uncertain. The 40 per cent Yes vote was basically, therefore, a bedrock pro-independence vote. Convinced that English Canada could not and would not give Quebec what it wanted and needed to embrace a renewed federalism, they argued that all Lévesque had to do was to go to the conferences and let the English-Canadian premiers and Ottawa fight among themselves. They argued that if a constitutional change package was developed that won the agreement of all, or even the majority, of English-Canadian premiers, it would be so trivial that it would be offensive to the Québécois. In other words, their view was that the referendum campaign was just another step toward ultimate independence. In that context, the 40 per cent result was hardly cause for despair. This was advice, however, that Lévesque rejected, a perspective he declined to share.

Of greatest significance for what was to come in the following months and years was Trudeau's promise in his final speech of the campaign, just days before the vote, that a vote for the No side would be taken as a clear mandate "to change the constitution, to renew federalism." This, Trudeau declared, was a "most solemn commitment." The speech was vintage Trudeau. In the context of the referendum campaign, such a promise implied constitutional renewal that would address Quebec's concerns, concerns on which a consensus had developed among the Québécois since the Quiet Revolution: some kind of special status; a provision for opting-out of federal programs with compensation; an acceptable amending formula that included a Quebec veto in some form, at least in highly sensitive areas (e.g., federal institutions, language, culture, immigration, etc.). Trudeau had never believed in yielding such concessions in the past and had no intention of doing so now — it would negate his whole political raison d'être. On the other hand, many believed that this vital vote on sovereignty-association, the first test of popular support among the Québécois for federalism, had perhaps shifted the ground beneath Trudeau enough that he might be willing to yield something.

A variation on this same promise was made not only by Quebec federalists but by federal and provincial English-Canadian politicians throughout the campaign. Saskatchewan's Blakeney came to Quebec with a speech making just such a promise. That was the soft side of English Canada's response. The hard side was a declaration that if Quebec moved to sovereignty, it should not expect association. The message from English Canada to the Québécois was arrogant: this referendum asking for a mandate to negotiate sovereignty-association is a waste of time because we will never enter into such negotiations. But if you vote No, and express this one last time your commitment to federalism, we solemnly promise that a renewed federalism will be the first order of business for all of Canada.

As in the past, however, English Canada proved to have a short memory when it came to promises to Quebec. English Canada interpreted the 60 per cent No victory with a singular lack of grace, exulting in the defeat of Lévesque and sovereignty-association. The fact that 40 per cent of Quebec voters had supported the Yes side — in itself an ominous and riveting fact — was swept under the carpet of English-Canadian consciousness as if it were of no consequence. For many, if not most, in English Canada, the Quebec issue was now more or less dead, finished, and it was back to business as usual.

Trudeau, however, saw it differently. Now having a strong double mandate from Quebec, with 68 per cent in the February election and 60 per cent in the referendum, he was in a position to realize his dream of patriation of the constitution with a Charter of Rights and Freedoms forever enshrining individual rights and defending them from the collective assaults of Québécois nationalism. This, however, would also realize the greatest fears of Québécois nationalists of all varieties, sovereigntist and federalist alike, that Trudeau's brand of federalism, so widely supported in English Canada and so deeply hostile to Québécois nationalism, would be entrenched in the constitution with a charter and an amending formula forever immune to Quebec's desire for constitutional change. In Quebec it was widely believed that this would not only forever shackle the Québécois nation but also deprive it of the means to defend itself from gradual assimilation. Lévesque and a majority of Québécois knew that Trudeau's patriation formula would never include those things Quebec had been demanding since the Quiet Revolution — a Quebec veto, an acceptable amending formula, opting-out rights with financial compensation, a new division of powers to give Quebec the tools needed to defend and empower the Québécois nation. Coming so quickly on the heels of his promise during the referendum battle of a renewed federalism that would address Québécois concerns, Trudeau's determination to proceed unilaterally by exercising ultimate federal powers was seen in Quebec as a profound betrayal.

With little owed to the West, Trudeau believed he was in a position to proceed unilaterally and without provincial consent if necessary. If anything, this determination angered the West as much as it angered Quebec; they both viewed it as a blatant attempt to increase federal powers at the expense of the provinces. It was a widely held view in the West that the Trudeau government was determined to get through naked power what it couldn't get through negotiation; control of western resources and a growing share of the wealth from those resources. Premiers Lougheed and Blakeney, supported by other provincial premiers, made it clear that no formula for patriation and constitutional amendment that did not both enhance and enshrine provincial control of resources and provide an acceptable amending mechanism could win their support. Lévesque, in an act of singular generosity and eager for allies, leapt to the West's defence, accusing Ottawa of having "ravaged Alberta's resources." Only Ontario and New Brunswick supported Trudeau from the outset. Ontario wanted to preserve a strong central government able and prepared to assert a national will, a will that Ontario had always played a major role in shaping. New Brunswick felt the need to reaffirm its support for Trudeau's bilingualism strategy and, like others among the poorer provinces, worried about the loss of a strong federal government.

Constitutional opinion was divided, but many experts took the view that Trudeau could not hope to gain the patriation and significant constitutional amendment with the consent of only two of ten provinces. There was no consensus in appeal court decisions on the issue in Quebec, Manitoba and Newfoundland. Ottawa referred the matter to the Supreme Court, which further confused the issue by ruling that unilateral patriation without provincial consent would violate the federal principle and that "substantial" provincial consent was required by convention but not by law. Therefore, Trudeau could act legally in a unilateral fashion, but such action would be conventionally improper. A committee of the British Parliament, which technically had to approve Trudeau's request, had already recommended that unilateral patriation not be granted. And hiding in the shadows, waiting to ambush Trudeau, was Quebec with its veto. Though never legally tested, on constitutional matters Canada had always accepted the convention that Quebec had veto rights over constitutional changes (later the Supreme Court was to find that Quebec never had a veto in any legal, constitutional sense).

In Quebec, Trudeau's determination to act unilaterally perhaps saved the PQ from electoral defeat. After the referendum defeat, many expected that the PQ, discredited and humbled, would lose the next election and go though a period of reassessment. Lévesque, not unexpectedly, denounced Trudeau's patriation plan as treachery, as a betrayal of his promises to Quebec. Having promised that sovereignty would not be an issue in the next provincial election and seeking a common front with the seven English-Canadian provinces opposed to unilateral patriation, Lévesque handily won re-election in April 1981 with almost 50 per cent of the vote, proving that Trudeau was not the only political leader capable of rising phoenix-like from the ashes of defeat. The stage was, however, set for yet another humiliating betrayal, the worst in Lévesque's political life.

Part of Claude Morin's *étapiste* strategy had included the undertaking that as long as Quebec remained in Confederation, the province would participate in the federal-provincial negotiating process. With sovereignty-association defeated and Trudeau determined to patriate the constitution with a charter, Morin became the architect of a further refinement of that strategy to deal with the current crisis, proposing that Lévesque join with the other seven dissenting premiers in a common front against Ottawa, something Morin had always previously opposed. As Morin himself conceded, it was one thing for Quebec simply to participate in federal-provincial meetings; it was quite another to submerge Quebec as one member in an anti-Ottawa coalition of eight provinces that included seven English-Canadian ones. Not only could Quebec's distinctive position get lost in such a coalition, but also, given the historical record, Quebec had no reason to expect the English provinces would stick with Quebec to the end. Yet the urgency of stopping unilateral patriation seemed to justify an exceptional and risky effort.

The agreement binding the Gang of Eight, as they came to be known, was clear. They would support Trudeau's patriation of the constitution if the amending formula for future changes required the agreement of Ottawa and at least seven provinces containing no less than half the population of Canada, and if any province could opt out of such future constitutional changes and/or federal programs with equivalent financial compensation. The dissenting premiers also opposed Trudeau's proposal to enshrine a Charter of Rights and Freedoms. In exchange, Lévesque agreed to relinquish Quebec's veto, since the opting-out/financial compensation clause would protect Quebec from future unacceptable changes. This accord was Lévesque's bottom line on agreeing to patriation, a bottom line he believed he now shared with the other seven premiers.

In the meantime, Trudeau hesitated. The Supreme Court decision was a legal victory but a profound political defeat. Trudeau could act legally in a unilateral fashion, but such action would be conventionally improper. In order to obtain patriation and constitutional amendment without more deeply dividing the nation, Trudeau needed to win some of the eight dissenting premiers over. It would be seriously divisive if all the provinces of one region, like the West, continued in opposition and forced Ottawa to walk over them. Ottawa looked for a crack in the common front, putting out feelers to Alberta's Lougheed and Saskatchewan's Blakeney and Romanow, and urging the isolation of Quebec on the grounds that Lévesque didn't want any kind of deal and was just using the other seven provinces to scuttle the process.

The western premiers, especially Lougheed and Blakeney, were deeply worried about developing western separatist sentiment. A continued impasse followed by Ottawa taking measures to force the issue would only deepen western disaffection, which was beginning to include attacks on the western premiers for being too soft and ineffectual in the battle with Ottawa. Lougheed's Rambo decision to turn down the flow of oil eastward had led him to the precipice: if he continued the shutdown, Ottawa could eventually assert federal constitutional power to stop him, perhaps taking over the regulation of the oil and gas industry entirely on the grounds of defending the national interest from sectional sabotage. Such an event would lose the gains Alberta had made and provide an incredible stimulus to separatist sentiment. Lougheed needed a way out, or he risked disaster. So, too, did Blakeney, who feared the uncertain outcome of a continuing federal-provincial log-jam. Therefore, the needs of these two premiers, on the one hand, and the prime minister, on the other, came together, setting the stage for a compromise on energy policy and the constitution, a compromise that both sides could claim as a victory. Trudeau wanted to patriate the constitution, with a Charter and an amending formula, in ways that would give no concessions to Québécois nationalism. The energy-producing premiers, including those with offshore potential, such as British Columbia, Newfoundland and Nova Scotia, wanted strong constitutional protection of provincial control of resources and an amending formula that would secure the regions' interests in the future. They also wanted a higher price for oil and gas and a better revenue-sharing deal. The premiers were, in fact, for sale. And Ottawa was in the market for as many premiers as it could buy.

A deal was struck. Ottawa would yield to Alberta and the other energy-producing provinces higher oil and gas prices and a larger share of revenues. Furthermore, Ottawa agreed to consider seriously a stronger constitutional provision guaranteeing provincial control of resources and an amending formula similar to that already acceptable to the Gang of Eight. This formula effectively gave both Western Canada and Atlantic Canada a regional veto by stipulating that no constitutional change could occur if all four western provinces or all four Atlantic provinces united in opposition. In exchange, the premiers would have to abandon Lévesque by dropping the opting-out and financial compensation elements of the premiers' accord. They would also have to yield on the question of the Charter.

These were the essential elements, with some fine-tuning, of the final agreement reached in November 1981 at the first ministers' meeting in Ottawa. That many informal meetings and consultations had occurred without Lévesque's knowledge in the months before was obvious in the slick way events unfolded. Final wording of the agreement was initiated by Blakeney, then hammered out by Romanow, Ontario's Roy McMurtry and Ottawa's Chrétien, and finally approved at an all-night meeting of the dissenting English-Canadian premiers, a meeting to which Lévesque was not invited. It was a sordid episode in Canadian constitutional history. The key players, Blakeney, Romanow, McMurtry and Chrétien, did not just betray Lévesque; they also jeopardized Canada's future by excluding and isolating Quebec.

The premiers sprung their betrayal on Lévesque at a breakfast meeting on 5 November 1981. The package contained a Charter of Rights and Freedoms (but at the insistence of the western premiers it allowed a notwithstanding override for certain key sections) and minority-language law, no provision for opting-out and financial compensation, and a mobility clause that might interfere with Quebec's interventions in the labour market. There was not a crumb for Quebec. None of Quebec's concerns had been addressed. Indeed, the opposite was the case — the whole package seemed anti-Quebec. The West and Atlantic Canada, however, got not only a regional veto but also a strong, though still imperfect, resource-control clause. Lévesque was shocked and profoundly humiliated, initially and uncharacteristically at a loss for words. But upon his return to Quebec, he found the words and did not hesitate to use them — "shameful betrayal, deceit, stab in the back, night of the long knives, treachery, political sluts." No word or phrase was strong enough to convey his harsh anger and cold fury. With some prescience, though he was not to live to see it, he warned English Canada that this betrayal and humiliation of Quebec would have "incalculable consequences."

Lévesque's anger and humiliation at the time had another more private dimension. Just the month before the 1981 first ministers' meeting Lévesque had been informed that Claude Morin, his minister of intergovernmental affairs, was an informer for the RCMP Security Service. Loraine Lagacé, the representative of the Quebec government in Ottawa, presented Lévesque with incontrovertible evidence that Morin was a mole. Lévesque confronted Morin, who admitted it was true, and Lévesque demanded his resignation. Though it was agreed that the resignation would be delayed until after the first ministers' meeting and take effect quietly in the new year, Lévesque must have been devastated.

It wasn't until 1992 that the whole sordid story came out. The most influential adviser to every premier of Quebec regardless of party since Jean Lesage, deputy minister of intergovernmental affairs from 1963 to 1971 and then PQ minister of intergovernmental affairs from 1976 until his resignation, Morin became an informer for the RCMP in the early 1960s and was paid as much as six thousand dollars a month for his services. He was widely known to have been the central influence in developing the PQ's moderate course, including the referendum strategy, the decision to place the hyphen in "sovereignty-association," the decision to participate fully in federal-provincial meetings and the fateful decision to join the common front with the seven dissenting English-Canadian premiers. During all this time, he was secretly meeting his RCMP handlers, who had given him the code names "Q1" before the PQ victory and "French Minuet" afterwards.

It is not clear how much Morin admitted to Lévesque in 1981, and even in 1992 Morin confirmed only the essentials of the story, finally denying wrongdoing and protesting his innocence in a book published in 1994. But Lévesque's understandable bitterness about, and hostility to, the anti-PQ tactics of the RCMP Security Service are well known. During the trial of one RCMP agent for illegal activities, Lévesque lost his cool in the National Assembly, saying, "The agents of the RCMP are caught in a trial for illegal acts and they are like fish that eject a sticky, dirty liquid to hide themselves." As a result of his outburst, the judge declared a mistrial.

The as-yet unanswered questions about Morin's role as an informer and mole in the PQ cabinet, especially given his power and influence over the government's policy direction, are obvious. Did the RCMP direct Morin to resign his job in 1971, to join the PQ, and to seek prominence in the party? Did Morin's information-gathering mandate include details about the political discussions and the debates about policy options in the cabinet? Was Morin directed by Ottawa to push for the major shifts in PQ policy, shifts that deeply divided the party and that proved so politically disastrous for Lévesque? Clearly, the RCMP Security Service does not pay six thousand dollars a month for casual conversations in Le Concorde hotel in Quebec City merely as a diverting entertainment. Why did Morin, already long an informant for the RCMP, and not at all known as a partisan for sovereignty, suddenly quit his high-ranking post in 1971 and join the PQ?

The importance a spy agency attaches to a "source" can usually be judged by the rank and ability of those assigned as "handlers." If this is the case, Morin was viewed as a very, very important source indeed. In the June 1992 *Canadian Forum*, Richard Cleroux, a journalist specializing in Canada's secret police, reported that Morin's handlers were the very best the RCMP Security Service had to offer; all of them rose to very high ranks in either the RCMP or, later, the civilian Canadian Security Intelligence Service (CSIS). Morin's handlers included Raymond Parent, later to become the RCMP's assistant commissioner, and Leo Fontaine, later the deputy director general of CSIS in Montreal, directing security operations in Quebec. A third figure, to whom Fontaine reported, was Jean-Louis Gagnon, in 1992 the director of CSIS for Quebec. Gagnon is well known for his political talents and played a role of major importance in the 1980 referendum. Parent was assigned to "D Branch," the RCMP's separatist hunters working on a cabinet order signed by Prime Minister Trudeau that directed the infiltration and destabilization of separatist organizations. He also worked closely with "G Branch," which was assigned dirty tricks and illegal activities, with his signature appearing on the order directing the theft of PQ membership lists. In other words, Morin was handled by three top operatives — Cleroux describes Parent as "one of the toughest anti-separatist spymasters," Fontaine as "a brilliant spy handler" and Gagnon as "a cultured, educated man...the ideal man to plot the moves."

Morin's claims that he gave away nothing and in fact got more information from his handlers than they got from him is simply not believable. Furthermore, evidence presented to the McDonald Commission, a royal commission established in 1977 to inquire into the RCMP's secret "dirty tricks" campaign against separation in Quebec, revealed the high quality of the information obtained by the RCMP from "paid sources in the PQ," including "the annual budget of the PQ, a project for an independent Quebec, a possible Quebec cabinet shuffle, the legislative priorities of the Quebec government, a proposed federal-provincial agreement between a federal and a provincial cabinet minister, and the instructions from a Quebec cabinet minister to Quebec public servants on how they could use federal funds abroad to promote Quebec interests." In the political chess game between Quebec and Ottawa from 1976 to 1980–81, such information, and probably much more besides, would have been vitally useful as Ottawa plotted its moves and countermoves. Even more useful would have been having a key Quebec cabinet minister proposing measures that would weaken the PQ's drive toward sovereignty.

Despite his continuing denials and assertions of innocence, everything Morin touched is now tainted by the probability that, as a paid informer, he was acting under the political direction of Ottawa. The fact that every major shift he advocated not only deeply divided the party but also proved to be a serious miscalculation can only serve to heighten such reasonable suspicions. Indeed, such a possibility may have upset Lévesque as much as hearing that Morin was an informer. It must have created for Lévesque a moment of terrible, sickening self-doubt to have learned that the man who had appeared most closely to share his own tactical approach to sovereignty turned out to be the lowest form of political life, an informer for Ottawa's secret police.

Lévesque's subsequent decline can be dated from this double betrayal: the one a public spectacle of humiliation that he could neither forgive nor forget; the other a private assault on his own political judgement in trusting Morin so completely. His behaviour during this last, painful period of his career, until his retirement in September 1985, became erratic and unpredictable, estranging and driving out of the cabinet almost all of his loyal old *indépendantiste* colleagues and raising widespread public speculation about his stability and health. In some of his speeches at public events and in the National Assembly he became rambling and incoherent, often losing his train of thought and making inappropriate remarks.

Within the party his sudden political shifts created upheaval and division. Immediately after the first ministers' meeting, his anger was so intense and his passionate defence of independence for Quebec so eloquent that PQ delegates responded at the December 1981 convention by deleting "association" from the term "sovereignty-association," declaring that the next election would be a straight fight over sovereignty. This declaration seemed to fit with Lévesque's imposition of a total boycott on Quebec's attendance at all federal-provincial conferences announced just days after the November meeting. But Lévesque still opposed the pure sovereignty option, threatened to resign and forced a plebiscite in the party. And he finally won overwhelming support. But there was a cost associated with this kind of confrontation and uncertainty: PQ membership numbers went into a nosedive from a high of 300,000 in 1980 to just over 200,000 during the internal plebiscite. At first, Lévesque threatened to take the PQ directly into federal politics, whereupon the PQ council voted to do so in June 1982, but then four months later the council deferred the question because Lévesque did another flip-flop. The next year, despite Lévesque's profound hesitations, the PQ decided to support a new federal party, Le Parti Nationaliste, a farcical paper creation of a small number of PQ activists. Meanwhile, Lévesque busily offended his former friends in the trade union movement by voiding collective agreements, reneging on negotiated increases, legislating strikers back to work and taking a hard line in collective bargaining. The PQ vote in three 1983 by-elections collapsed by more than 80 per cent in one and 60 per cent in the other two. The PQ's membership in 1984 fell to one-half the 1980 figure.

By far the biggest crisis was provoked by Lévesque's *beau*

risque strategy during the months just prior to his retirement. When Trudeau announced his decision to step down after his famous walk in the snow on 29 February 1984 and was replaced by John Turner in June, Lévesque recognized an excellent opportunity to help defeat the federal Liberals. Joe Clark's replacement by Brian Mulroney as Tory leader had given the Tories a fluently bilingual leader with some hope of success in Quebec. When Prime Minister Turner called the federal election for 4 September 1984, Lévesque seized the opportunity. Relegating the Parti Nationaliste to the sidelines, much of the PQ infrastructure, responding to clear signals from Lévesque, threw in with the federal Tories at the local level. PQ members joined the federal Tory party, sought nominations and put their well-developed electoral machinery into high gear to help Mulroney. When Mulroney promised "a new era of federal-provincial co-operation" and pledged to bring Quebec into the constitutional fold "with honour and enthusiasm," Lévesque publicly indicated that he endorsed Mulroney, further distancing himself from the Parti Nationaliste.

Mulroney's enormous victory, including 58 of 75 Quebec seats with 50 per cent of the vote, provided Lévesque with what he saw as an opening to Ottawa, a chance both to erase the 1981 humiliation and to address at least some of Quebec's lingering constitutional grievances. As a sign of good faith, Lévesque immediately ended Quebec's boycott of federal-provincial meetings. Mulroney, stinging from attacks that he had made a deal with separatism, called upon the PQ to show Canada signs of good faith as a prelude to healing the constitutional wounds. In response, Lévesque accelerated the process, underway since 1981, of distancing the PQ from its commitment both to sovereignty and to the left-wing social democratic elements of its original program, laying out his proposal to seek a rapprochement with the federal Tory government, a gamble he called *le beau risque*.

If *le beau risque* were accepted, Lévesque proposed, the PQ had to abandon its central commitment to sovereignty and postpone it into the distant future, though the ultimate commitment to sovereignty would remain in the background as a sort of "insurance policy." Then the PQ government would seek a deal with Mulroney. Lévesque proceeded to implement this strategy by making a public commitment that the next provincial election would not be fought on the PQ's traditional commitment to sovereignty. This unilateral action provoked the resignation of seven prominent cabinet ministers, including Jacques Parizeau, and a special convention was held to decide the issue. There was never any doubt that Lévesque would win the debate, as he had always won every debate within the party in the past. Parizeau and others warned that Lévesque's about-face on sovereignty and the increasing conservatization of the party's policy would lead to political decline and ultimate disaster. These warnings fell on deaf ears.

As far as Lévesque and what was left of the PQ parliamentary caucus and party membership were concerned, the decks had been cleared in preparation for a renewal of constitutional talks with Ottawa. Mulroney, however, remained noncommittal regarding a timetable, preferring to mark time until the Quebec provincial election, due in 1985 or 1986. The PQ appeared to be on the ropes, and Bourassa, now reborn as Quebec Liberal leader, could well become the new premier. From Ottawa's point of view, a constitutional deal negotiated with a Bourassa Liberal government rather than the PQ government would be infinitely easier to sell in English Canada. Not only that, but the continuing carping criticism that Mulroney had climbed into bed with the Quebec separatists in order to get elected was so close to the truth that almost any deal struck with the PQ, no matter how modest, would be tainted and thus a likely candidate for automatic rejection in English Canada.

Lévesque's turn to *le beau risque* deeply damaged the PQ. Unable to deflect him from his course, a course largely determined by a desire to make up for his failure in 1981, and unable to defeat him, the strong *indépendantiste* wing of the PQ withdrew to the sidelines. Pierre-Marc Johnson, the leader of the *le beau risque*/conservative faction of the PQ, increasingly obtained Lévesque's ear, rising to prominence in the vacuum created by the exit of Parizeau and other key figures in the cabinet. But Johnson did not play the role of loyal dauphin to Lévesque. Rather, he was more like Iago, encouraging Lévesque to abandon his principles and turn his back on his old colleagues. The polls continued to suggest that Lévesque faced certain defeat in the next election, and they indicated the PQ would do better under Johnson. Johnson and his faction urged Lévesque to retire rather than face defeat. Finally Lévesque agreed, and on 29 September 1985 he was replaced as premier by Johnson.

As PQ leader and, briefly, as premier, Pierre-Marc Johnson was convinced that a sharper right turn on social and economic issues, the substitution of a vague notion of "national affirmation" for sovereignty-association and the pursuit of *le beau risque* with Mulroney's brand of federalism would all lead to victory, so he called an election for 7 December 1985. He couldn't have been more wrong. The PQ was crushed by Bourassa's Liberals, taking only twenty-three seats with 37 per cent of the vote, while the Liberals took ninety-nine seats with 58 per cent. The Québécois obviously decided that if Quebec were to abandon the sovereignty option and pursue *le beau risque* with Tory Ottawa, they might as well elect a real Québécois federalist party to do it, rather than the sanitized retread of the Union Nationale the PQ was becoming under Johnson.

* * *

The defeat of the PQ and Quebec's return to the safe federalist embrace of Bourassa's Liberals seemed to confirm that one of the most tumultuous chapters in Canadian political history had ended with a whimper. Trudeau was gone, or so Canadians thought. Lévesque was gone. Not only was there a new prime minister with a fresh and strong mandate, but there were also new premiers leading most of the provinces. The Quebec separatist threat appeared doubly dead, for not only had the PQ under Johnson decisively turned its back on sovereignty-association, the party had also been badly defeated. English Canadians therefore relaxed about the Quebec question, though it still simmered on the back burner since Quebec remained a non-signatory to the new constitution, itself an irrelevant legal fact but nevertheless a very significant political reality.

6

The Meech Lake Accord

As a result of his de facto pact with Québécois nationalism and separatism, Prime Minister Brian Mulroney had pulled off something of a coup in Canadian history. He was the first Tory leader to sweep Quebec since Diefenbaker in 1958 and Sir John A. Macdonald in 1882. Very much aware of how quickly Diefenbaker's support in Quebec had dissipated, Mulroney was driven by the need to deliver something tangible to Quebec on its constitutional grievances quickly if he hoped to win a second mandate in 1988 or 1989. But in order to deliver to Quebec, Mulroney recognized that he had to give something in exchange to gain the support and acquiescence of the other regions. Since he was elected on a decentralist, "provincial rights" platform, this proved an easy task.

Soon after Mulroney's election a metamorphosis occurred in federal-provincial relations. Although things got off to a rocky start over the usual divisive issues and Canadians settled into their favourite sport after hockey — watching Ottawa and the provinces fight it out — reason and contentment soon reigned. Individual premiers would race angrily down to Ottawa to confront Mulroney but come away happy, apparently putty in the new prime minister's hands. Suddenly Canada's ten provincial premiers had become a remarkably tame bunch. No prime minister in modern times had enjoyed such support from Canada's premiers. The premiers had made life hell for Diefenbaker and Pearson, while Trudeau positively enjoyed his years of strife with them. Joe Clark's brief two-hundred-day Camelot left him shredded by Alberta's Lougheed and Ontario's Davis over the energy issue. Yet, harsh words and expressions of angry resolve seemed to evaporate quickly from the premiers' lips after a little private stroking by

Mulroney. It appeared that Mulroney actually had delivered on his promise of "a new era of federal-provincial co-operation." In early September 1987, Gallup found that 53 per cent of Canadians agreed that since the Mulroney government's election in 1984, Ottawa and the provinces were getting on better than before, including 62 per cent of those in Quebec. Furthermore, Gallup found that almost one-half of Canadians shared the perception that Quebec was now more satisfied with its place in Canada.

It soon became obvious why federal-provincial peace and harmony began to prevail, and it had little to do with Mulroney's political artistry or social skills. As Trudeau had often sarcastically noted, the one sure way for Ottawa to get harmonious support from the premiers was to give them everything they wanted. Mulroney didn't quite give them everything, but he came close. To the Atlantic provinces Mulroney gave everything they asked for to increase provincial control of, and benefits from, offshore energy development. While much of the activity was then mothballed as a result of low world oil prices, it was a boom waiting to happen. To the western energy provinces he also gave everything they wanted on oil and gas policy, such as a free market, deregulation, unrestricted exports, the world price and an end to intrusive federal taxation. By promising to build on existing economic strengths in federal economic development policy while not tampering with the market, Mulroney reassured Ontario that its special place as the industrial centre of the nation would not be put at risk by federal initiatives. But the main dish served up at this provincial banquet was the Meech Lake Accord, which promised powers for provinces that no premier had ever dreamed possible. The Accord assured the premiers that they would finally be relieved of their subordinate status, mounting the Canadian political stage as nothing less than associate prime ministers of ten associate states.

The roots of the Meech Lake Accord lay in the five conditions the new Bourassa government established as Quebec's minimum requirements for constitutional reconciliation with the rest of Canada. They included the recognition of Quebec as a "distinct society" in the preamble of the constitution, an equal say on immigration into Quebec, a right to participate in selecting judges from Quebec for appointment to the Supreme Court, limits on the federal spending power requiring provincial consent for spending in areas of provincial jurisdiction, either a general veto for Quebec on all constitutional changes or opting-out and financial compensation rights in cases of transfers of provincial powers to Ottawa, combined with a Quebec veto on changes in federal structures and the creation of new provinces. Compared to what had been demanded since the Quiet Revolution, these were modest demands for Quebec, so modest that the PQ ridiculed them. But the defeat of the PQ and the election of Mulroney had opened a door: Quebec was in a mood to settle for a minimum, and English Canada yearned to put the constitutional battle with Quebec to rest. On the basis of these demands Mulroney was able to convince a 1986 first minsters' meeting to enter into a negotiating process focusing exclusively on Quebec's proposals.

On 30 April 1987 Mulroney met with the ten premiers at Meech Lake in an attempt to win their final approval for constitutional changes designed to overcome Quebec's objections to the 1982 pact. Here and in later meetings in Ottawa, agreement was reached on a series of proposals. Although Bourassa agreed to many changes that seriously weakened Quebec's five conditions in order to secure support from the other premiers, the essentials of the principles remained intact. The most surprising thing about the agreement was that what had been billed as a "Quebec round" of constitutional negotiations, focusing exclusively on Quebec's concerns, had in fact become a radical proposal to transform Canada fundamentally. In an effort to placate the English-Canadian provinces, which continued to insist that all provinces were equal and must be treated the same, Mulroney managed to grant Quebec's minimum demands for signing on to the constitution only by giving the same powers to all other provinces. Quebec was granted a veto, but so was every other province. Quebec was conceded significant powers on immigration matters, but so was every other province. The same held true for the other features of the Meech Lake Accord: opting-out rights and a say on Supreme Court and Senate appointments. The only unique feature of Meech for Quebec was the distinct society clause. In other words, in exchange for allowing Mulroney to slip the distinct society clause into the Accord to win Quebec, the other nine provinces obtained enormous new powers.

Canadians had been told repeatedly since the Quiet Revolution that giving in to Quebec's demands for some form of special status with special powers would weaken Canada's federal system to the point of rendering Ottawa ineffectual as a national government. Suddenly, as a result of a quickly and secretly concluded agreement, Canadians were now being told that national unity was best served by giving all ten provinces special status and special powers, abruptly transforming Canada's federal system into an agreement among increasingly autonomous associate mini-states, more like ten fiefdoms or satrapies held together by the largesse of Ottawa's taxing and spending powers. Even Joe Clark's idea of a decentralized Confederation as a "community of communities," which Trudeau had ridiculed with heavy sarcasm as a federation of shopping malls, had never dared go so far. Mulroney's Meech agreement seemed more inspired by an extension of Lévesque's notion of sovereignty-association to all ten provinces; growing political autonomy for ever more powerful provinces involved in an economic association overseen by Ottawa.

After the agreement at Meech Lake, which was finalized at a first ministers' conference in early June, there was enormous pressure on all Canadians to get on side. Those who hesitated to provide instant and uncritical support were accused of sabotage, of threatening national unity. It became the *sine qua non* of politically correct thinking in Canada; all reasonable Canadians devoted to keeping the country together were expected to support Meech. Enormous pressure was put on all political parties in the House of Commons and in the provincial legislatures to make the deal unanimous and to refrain from partisan posturing over the Accord, pressure that was largely successful in the House of Commons but unsuccessful in some of the provincial legislatures. Even the PQ was restrained in its criticisms, recognizing that the Meech Accord, which clearly went some modest distance in enhancing Quebec's powers while reducing Ottawa's, could be of use to a future PQ government in a drive for sovereignty.

A three-year deadline for approval commenced when Quebec's National Assembly approved Meech on 23 June 1987. During 1987 it appeared that Meech approval was a foregone conclusion as speedy passage was obtained in the Saskatchewan and Alberta legislatures and in the House of Commons. In early June 1987 Gallup found that 56 per cent of Canadians thought the deal was good for Canada, while at the same time 58 per cent admitted they knew little or nothing about it. Regarding the main details of the Accord, however, they were deeply divided, with 25 per cent believing too much power was being turned over to the provinces and 40 per cent expressing disapproval of the distinct society clause. From the outset the deal was, then, on thin ice. It won initial popular acceptance as an act of blind faith in what the premiers and the prime minister had accomplished in secret. Yet on the two central features of Meech, enhanced powers for the provinces and distinct society, there was deep public unease.

The greatest unease, of course, revolved around the distinct society clause, the one thing Meech gave Quebec that it did not give to all provinces. Much of the concern had to do with the meaning and significance of the term and the contrasting meanings given in Quebec and English Canada by politicians. In Quebec, Bourassa and Mulroney insisted the clause was very significant. In English Canada, the premiers and Mulroney insisted the clause was largely symbolic and that English Canada had nothing to worry about. In Quebec, popular unease had to do with whether the clause had as much meaning as they were assured, while in English Canada it had to do with whether the clause was really as innocuous as suggested. And it didn't help to calm matters that constitutional experts were divided on the issue and that each side marshalled expert testimony to buttress its case.

It was during this period that one of those colossal collective misperceptions occurred that sometimes change the course of history. Thinking the Quebec question was now more or less settled, English Canada fell asleep. It became something of a cliché among the press and politicians in English Canada that Québécois nationalism, especially in its separatist expression, was a spent force. Even Québécois nationalists agreed to a degree, though as PQ MNA Godin preferred to put it, Québécois nationalism was only "hibernating." On the surface, there appeared to be sufficient reason to reach this conclusion, particularly in the political realm.

Many young Québécois took the view that the great nationalist battle had been more or less both won and lost. It was won because French had become more secure as the language of life and work in the province. It was won because Meech had unprecedently secured unanimous approval from both English Canada and Quebec. It was won because the "privilege gap" between English Canadians in Quebec and the Québécois continued to close.

The battle was also lost. The loss of the referendum and Lévesque, and the PQ's turn away from sovereignty-association, led to the popular abandonment of the dream of an independent Quebec, at least for the time being. All of this was grist for the English-Canadian media, which reported avidly and endlessly on the decline of Québécois nationalism. We were told that the new Québécois generation was tired of politics, eager to learn English, determined to get ahead, and largely uninterested in the clash of great principles.

But those closely watching Quebec noted that some of the old nationalist spirit was still present. The odd small bomb went off and the odd brick was hurled through plate glass windows over the language issue. Premier Bourassa's incomprehensible (for English Canadians) unwillingness to make significant concessions to the English-Canadian minority in Quebec over the issue of permitting bilingual signs, despite the fact that his party policy explicitly promised such a concession, should have been a signal. His calm words, heavy with meaning, in justifying his stubbornness, "*Il y a le programme du party, mais tout chef politique doit tenir compte de la paix sociale,*" should have been another signal. In other words, despite this apparent wintertime of Québécois nationalism, there remained everywhere the sense that another explosion awaited if nationalist sensibilities were seriously affronted. It was a measure of just how fragile the nationalist peace was that even Bourassa felt the apparently minor slight of bilingual signs could have been enough to cause an eruption. It may have been winter, and Québécois nationalism may have been hibernating, but spring could come quickly and Québécois nationalism could reawaken hungry and cranky.

Two major events occurred in the fall of 1987 that should have shaken English Canada out of its slumber. The first event of that momentous autumn was the sudden death by heart attack of René Lévesque on 1 November. His death revived, at least briefly, the nationalist yearnings for independence among many Québécois. More than 100,000 Québécois in Montreal and Quebec City lined up to weep over his body while it lay in state, more than 10,000 attended his funeral in Quebec City, and many hundreds more wept daily at his graveside in subsequent weeks and months in an outpouring of genuine sorrow no English-Canadian politician's death has ever provoked. It was deeply moving, almost unsettling, to witness. One had the impression that a national hero, not just a politician, had died. Moreover, as all flags flew at half-mast and as one witnessed the grand spectacle of a state funeral, the symbolism was obvious: Quebec buried René Lévesque as if he had succeeded in becoming the president of the independent democratic Quebec republic of his dreams. The distasteful memory of his last few years in power and his turn away from sovereignty were forgotten and his actions forgiven. Québécois nationalism no longer appeared quite so dormant. More than that, the belief that somehow the gulf between the two solitudes had disappeared was called into question by the differing reactions to Lévesque's death in the English and French press. *The Globe and Mail* felt it necessary to qualify English Canada's tributes to Lévesque in ways the Québécois found patronizing. The Montreal *Gazette*'s main headline on 3 November, "Lévesque had earlier attacks: M.D.," contrasted sharply with those of *Le Devoir*, "*Deuil national au Québec*," and of *Le Soleil*, "*Le Québec en deuil de René Lévesque: Drapeaux en berne et funérailles nationales.*" The two solitudes remained, even in the grief expressed upon the death of René Lévesque.

The second event that should have awakened English Canada was the fall of PQ leader Pierre-Marc Johnson in the wake of Lévesque's death. Many English-Canadian analysts saw a cause-effect relationship — the emotional catharsis and the brief resurgence of separatist sentiment drove Johnson to resign. The truth was more prosaic. Johnson's fate was sealed long before Lévesque's death, and if the death had any effect, it was simply to speed up Johnson's own recognition that he was finished, especially without Lévesque's personal support. The crucial events leading to Johnson's fall all occurred before Lévesque's heart attack: Parizeau's denunciation of Johnson for abandoning the party's twin pillars of independence and social democracy; Godin's brutal attack on Johnson, saying, "under Johnson the party is going nowhere, except perhaps to its death"; regular meetings of the *indépendantiste* ex-cabinet ministers, led by Parizeau, who had been plotting Johnson's fall for many months.

The reason for their move against Johnson was simple and political: he had failed dismally. First, there was the catastrophic defeat of 1985. Then there was Johnson's lacklustre performance in the Assembly against Bourassa. Finally, there was the September 1987 by-election in Notre Dame de Grâce. Though an 80 per cent non-Québécois riding and a Liberal seat since 1939, the results were disturbing. The PQ vote was cut in half, while the provincial NDP tripled its vote, taking second spot away from the PQ. An earlier province-wide poll saw the PQ's support fall to 26 per cent, while the NDP's shot up to 23 per cent. Another poll just weeks later put the NDP one point ahead of the PQ. Other polls showed the PQ regaining lost ground if Johnson were dumped and replaced by Parizeau. When it became clear that the Quebec NDP was seriously threatening to replace the PQ as the alternative to Bourassa, the knives came out.

Certainly the aftermath of Lévesque's death played a role, but only that of convincing Johnson not to resist. Johnson was remembered by PQ stalwarts, perhaps unfairly, as the man whose counsel led to Lévesque's about-face on independence, whose promise of victory led to the 1985 débâcle, and whose continuing leadership promised an even darker future at the hands of the NDP. Lévesque's death reminded people of his inspirational dream, not his post-1981 betrayal of that dream. Johnson, more than any other prominent figure in the PQ, symbolized not the early audacious dream of Lévesque, but the later sad, even pathetic retreat. Lévesque's death helped crystallize the moment and the decision: Johnson had to go. The PQ had to re-embrace its raison d'être, sovereignty. And the new leader, Jacques Parizeau, made it immediately clear that the PQ stood for "sovereignty, first, last and always." Sovereignty was again a political option for the Québécois. In the fall of 1987, Québécois nationalism may have been sleeping, but it was an increasingly restless sleep. The death of Meech was to awaken it sharply.

The Meech Lake Accord simultaneously unravelled at the top and at the bottom, and as a result its demise became inevitable. At the top, Pierre Trudeau briefly came out of retirement from public life and issued an op-ed article attacking Meech that was featured in newspapers across Canada. Three months later, he reiterated his attack before the Joint Senate-Commons Committee on the Accord. Trudeau's criticism that the Accord disastrously weakened the federal government by enhancing provincial powers struck a popular chord, confirming the fears of many. However, his attack on the distinct society clause, which struck an even deeper chord in English Canada, on the grounds that it would undermine bilingualism was a bit dishonest. The truth was that English Canada had never embraced true bilingualism and there was no reason to expect it ever would. Indeed, English Canada's grudging acceptance of Trudeau's forced bilingualism at the federal level was often used as a club to demand bilingualism in Quebec, while at the same time refusing to endorse bilingualism in English-Canadian provinces. However, the impact of Trudeau's intervention was considerable, serving to galvanize general opposition to the Accord in English Canada, while stiffening the backbones of many in the Liberal Party to begin a campaign of resistance. In October 1987 New Brunswick premier Richard Hatfield, a staunch Meech supporter, was swept from office by Liberal Frank McKenna, a critic of the Accord. In the spring of 1988, the Accord suffered additional blows. A reluctant friend of Meech, Manitoba's NDP premier Howard Pawley was defeated and replaced by a Tory minority government led by Gary Filmon. Filmon was a mild supporter of Meech, but he faced a strong opposition led by Liberal Sharon Carstairs, a fierce opponent of the Accord. After holding hearings, the Senate roused itself from its torpor, approved a basketful of amendments and sent the Accord back to the Commons, forcing the Commons to override the Senate. Despite the fact that in 1988 five more provinces, Nova Scotia, Prince Edward Island, Ontario, Newfoundland and British Columbia, ratified the Accord, leaving only New Brunswick and Manitoba, the Accord was losing support at the top. The final blow occurred the next year when Liberal Clyde Wells, a harsh critic of Meech, became Newfoundland premier. A year later the New-foundland legislature withdrew its approval of the Accord.

The Meech Accord was also unravelling at the bottom. The ini-tial popular support for the agreement had been rooted in ignorance and trust, a dangerous combination in democratic politics. That support eroded very quickly as anti-Meech popular agitations swept the country. Women's groups complained that the Meech Accord would freeze the status quo, preventing future improve-ments in women's constitutional status with reference to gender equality guarantees. Still bitter about their failure to win constitu-tional recognition of the rights to aboriginal self-government, aboriginal organizations were particularly critical, resenting the successful constitutional fast-track for Quebec's concerns while aboriginal concerns had been dismissed so cavalierly. Furthermore, Meech provisions would freeze aboriginals out of future changes in the constitution because of the universal provincial veto. Angry that the Meech Accord granted each province a veto on the estab-lishment of new provinces, people in Yukon and the Northwest Territories were deeply fearful that such a provision foreclosed the possibility of future provinces in the North. Trade unions and vari-ous non-governmental organizations began to complain loudly about the weakening of federal powers and the resulting end to future national social programs characterized by national stan-dards. The charge was made that, had Meech been in place, medicare, old age pensions, the Canadian Pension Plan and the unemployment insurance program would never have been adopted. English Canadians began to complain that the distinct society clause gave Quebec too much and made the English-Canadian provinces second-class constitutional creatures. The NDP began a public and divisive debate over the pros and cons of the Accord. Legal and academic experts lined up on both sides of the issue, giv-ing equally learned but completely contradictory interpretations of the meaning of the legal text. It was not surprising, therefore, that popular support for Meech collapsed.

In 1988 and 1989, Mulroney was faced with demands both

from premiers and from various popular organizations for a reopening of the Accord. He refused, fearing the agreement would unravel and offend Quebec. As opposition grew and dissenting premiers felt compelled to use hard-ball tactics to get some changes, the Mulroney government at first refused to consider a parallel accord addressing the desire for changes, then suggested the door might be open to a parallel accord after all. Mulroney established a special Commons committee, chaired by Jean Charest, to hold hearings and to make recommendations for add-ons to Meech. The Charest Committee suggested a series of changes and additions designed to defuse opposition in English Canada. These additions angered Quebec, where they were seen as the beginning of another gang-up, a prelude to yet another betrayal. Mulroney's friend and protégé Lucien Bouchard resigned in protest.

The final death scene of Meech occurred in June 1990. It began with a secret first ministers' meeting called to hammer out a way to salvage the Accord. Prior to that meeting Premier Clyde Wells had offered to submit any revised Meech Accord to a referendum in Newfoundland and to abide by the results. When this proved impossible because of time constraints, Wells offered a free vote in the legislature. New Brunswick's Frank McKenna had offered to approve Meech if his concerns were even partially addressed. Manitoba's premier Gary Filmon promised to fast-track approval of Meech if his concerns were met half-way. Bourassa indicated that, though he was prepared to consider reasonable change, he could not participate in any tampering with the distinct society clause. There was, therefore, considerable tense optimism as the first ministers met from 4 to 9 June 1990, when an agreement to a modified Meech was finally reached, hinging only on the conclusion of a fast-track approval process in Manitoba and a referendum or free vote in Newfoundland.

Then certain key players made some astonishing revelations about what had gone on behind the closed doors. Filmon complained that the feds had engaged in electronic eavesdropping on his cellular phone conversations with Opposition leader Carstairs and NDP leader Gary Doer. Wells complained of "nastiness" and "threats," claiming that if the public knew what was being said behind those closed doors, it would be outraged. Then Carstairs declared that "ethics were absent" during the negotiations, that Ottawa "tried to destroy opponents of Meech" and that the "fear of retribution" was the only reason she finally supported Premier Filmon's decision to sign the agreement.

The Accord collapsed when Prime Minister Mulroney bragged about his "roll of the dice" and about how he had treated the final Meech negotiations just like an election campaign, deliberately delaying convening the premiers in order to put maximum pressure on the dissenters by creating a crisis atmosphere as well as by preventing Wells from holding a referendum in Newfoundland. This roll-of-the-dice confession perfectly echoed the Mulroney of the 1984 election campaign, who bragged openly about his post-election patronage intentions, saying "Ya dance with the lady what brung ya." The spectacle of the occupant of the highest office in the land bragging about his brazen tactics was the last straw or, as Premier Wells put it, "the final manipulation." Meech was dead, though it took MLA Elijah Harper's refusal to permit fast-tracking through the Manitoba legislature to deliver the final *coup de grâce*. And it was self-evident to everyone but the prime minister that Meech died largely because he had spoken out a few days too soon. According to the prime minister, however, Meech was dead because of Clyde Wells, who was subsequently publicly punished when Ottawa initially refused to sign the Hibernia agreement and who to this day remains Mulroney's preferred scapegoat for the death of Meech.

Brian Mulroney certainly bore the tactical responsibility for the death of Meech, and to some extent the moral responsibility, not only for his manipulative tactics but also for his effort to slip an accommodation of Quebec by English Canadians unnoticed and without their express approval. Yet the more basic historical reasons for the death of Meech were English Canada's continuing hypocrisy about, and hostility to, the aspirations of Québécois nationalism. Mulroney might have pulled it off if certain events hadn't intervened at just the wrong moment, events that once again polarized English Canada and Quebec and forced Mulroney to fall between the stools of the two solitudes.

In February 1988 the Supreme Court ruled that section 110 of the 1885 *Northwest Territories Act*, which guaranteed francophone rights to trials in French, the publication of French law texts and the status of French as an official language in the legislature, did not cease to have validity when Saskatchewan and Alberta were established as provinces in 1905. In other words, French-language rights had been illegally and unconstitutionally extinguished in the two provinces. These provinces were and remained constitutionally committed to official bilingualism. However, the Court further ruled that section 110 was not entrenched in the Canadian constitution;

therefore, both Saskatchewan and Alberta had to decide quickly whether they wanted to proceed with what was now a requirement for bilingualism or wished to adopt English unilingualism by statute. Here was a clear opportunity for Alberta and Saskatchewan, both of which had ratified Meech just months before, to live up to its spirit. Both provinces quickly and with a certain meanness of spirit decided not to do so, adopting draconian legislation annulling French-language rights. Saskatchewan premier Grant Devine was quite frank about the matter: "This has been very hard. Put yourself in the place of a premier of a province where 97 per cent of the people speak English." Indeed, he went on to assert in an interview with *Le Devoir* that the 97 per cent of Saskatchewan population that spoke English opposed the Meech Accord and was against the use of French in the province in any official capacity. For the Québécois, it was just another outrage to add to a long list. It also left them wondering why a similar justification for French unilingualism in Quebec was unacceptable in English Canada. The Québécois did not get demonstrably angry about this further suppression of French, since the francophone diaspora had been long ago abandoned by the Québécois to its fate in English Canada, but the event did serve to make the passage of Meech seem increasingly vital in Quebec. English Canadians might be speaking soothing words, but their actions on the bottom line of language issues remained the same as always, mean and nasty.

The November 1988 free trade election also served to drive a wedge between English Canada and Quebec, elevating hostility levels among many English Canadians against the Québécois. In one of the most bitterly fought elections in Canadian history, characterized by a huge expenditure of funds by the pro-free trade business lobby, Brian Mulroney won a second term with a comfortable majority. Many in English Canada opposed to free trade irrationally blamed the Québécois for Mulroney's victory and his securing of free trade, pointing to the fact that without his Quebec seats, Mulroney would have failed. It is true that Bourassa strongly and publicly supported the free trade deal. It is also true that Québécois nationalists either supported free trade or refrained from active opposition. Their arguments were subtle and nuanced. Recalling how economic fear had been repeatedly used against the PQ, and most heavily during the referendum, Québécois nationalists suggested that free trade, which would result in strengthening north-south and weakening east-west trade flows, would remove economic fear as a trump card that English Canada could use in a future referendum. If the Canadian federation ceased to exist as a viable east-west economy, the arguments about the economic advantages of Confederation would be compromised. Furthermore, a future independent Quebec would benefit from strong, pre-existing trade links with the United States. Finally, English Canada's fear of cultural domination by the United States was understandable, particularly given the weakness of indigenous English-Canadian culture. The Québécois did not, however, share these cultural fears. Québécois culture, they alleged, was vital and, thanks to its linguistic distinctiveness, had nothing to fear from strong American trade links.

Yet those who blamed the Québécois for Mulroney's free trade victory overlooked the anti-free trade agitations carried out by Québécois farmers and workers. It is doubtful that the Québécois voted for Mulroney primarily because of free trade. It is much more likely the Québécois voted for him because of Meech Lake, which Mulroney was trying to salvage from English-Canadian carping. It may have been true that the Québécois supported free trade in exchange for Meech and distinct society, but that was the best deal ever offered by any prime minister in Canadian history. Unfortunately, many opposed to free trade in English Canada were also initially most sympathetic to the Québécois nation's aspirations. Bitter at the Mulroney victory, many turned their backs on Quebec at this crucial time, depriving Quebec of an important lobby in English Canada. "Why should I support Meech as a gesture of reconciliation when Quebec has stabbed us in the back on free trade?" became a commonly expressed sentiment among many who ordinarily might have supported the distinct society concession to Quebec.

If it had not had such disastrous consequences and if English Canada had not seized upon the issue to berate Quebec, the public signage and commercial advertising decision of the Supreme Court and Bourassa's subsequent actions might have become a ludicrous historical curiosity. Section 58 of Quebec's Bill 101, *La Charte de la langue française*, required that public signs, including commercial signs, be rendered in French only. This law had been challenged in Quebec courts in 1985 and finally percolated up through the system to the Supreme Court. On 15 October 1989 the Supreme Court found that the sign law violated Quebec's own human rights charter, pointing to the predominance of French in bilingual signs as a means of avoiding a charter violation. Unhappy with the decision, cognizant of the explosiveness of the language issue and aware that the Québécois were determined that Montreal remain a French city, yet also sensitive to the English-Canadian minority in Quebec, Bourassa tried to effect a compromise. First, he introduced Bill 178 to amend Bill 101, requiring that outside signs be in French only, while signs inside businesses could be bilingual if French predominated. Then he invoked the notwithstanding clause of both the Quebec Charter and the Canadian Charter of Rights and Freedoms in order to protect the law from further court challenges.

The reaction in English Canada to these events was hypocritical and vastly out of proportion to what had actually occurred. Looking for a way to tap the traditional and now-growing anti-Quebec mood in his province and party, Manitoba premier Gary Filmon used Quebec's actions as an excuse to withdraw the Meech Accord from the legislature. To suggest, as Filmon did, that Canada now faced a constitutional crisis of the first order as a result of Quebec's sign law was a gross exaggeration. It says a great deal about the mood of the time that Filmon would dare make the language of signs a major constitutional crisis. It says even more that the English-Canadian media took it with the utmost seriousness, rather than with the sarcasm and ridicule it deserved.

The notwithstanding clause was originally placed in the Canadian constitution, not at the insistence of Quebec which, after all, had nothing to do with the new constitution, but at the insistence of the English-Canadian premiers, especially Saskatchewan's Blakeney. Forgetting all this, the premiers and the prime minister himself demanded that the notwithstanding clause be removed. The clause had been put in the constitution for precisely this kind of situation; that is, for situations when the courts interpret the constitution in ways that defy the democratic political will of the population as expressed through elected legislators. There had been no outcry back in 1982 when the Lévesque government passed a law providing for the blanket application of the notwithstanding clause to all provincial statutes. There had been no outcry when Saskatchewan premier Grant Devine invoked the notwithstanding clause to order public employees who had not yet gone on strike to stop striking and to get back to the work they had not yet stopped doing. Nor had there been a hue and cry when Saskatchewan and Alberta abruptly revoked French-language rights. But for English Canada, the Quebec sign issue became a pretext for letting loose the pent-up anti-Quebec spleen held in check during the first steps of the Meech process. The language of signs in Quebec was so fundamental a principle, for English Canada, that it was worth putting

Canada at risk. If it were not so sad, if the subsequent events were not so divisive, the whole episode would be laughable.

The manipulation of the signs issue by some English-Canadian politicians and the anti-Quebec response of some English-Canadian media provoked a knee-jerk reaction across the country. A series of Gallup polls in the weeks and months following the eruption of the signage issue revealed an unprecedented level of English-Canadian hostility to Quebec. Fully 59 per cent of English-speaking Canadians disapproved of Meech's distinct society provision, while 58 per cent of French-speaking Canadians approved. When asked to balance the rights of English-speaking Quebeckers to have freedom of speech against the right of the Québécois to preserve their culture, 72 per cent of English-speaking Canadians opted for freedom of speech over cultural protection, while 78 per cent of French-speaking Canadians felt the opposite. And while 96 per cent of English-speaking Canadians supported bilingual commercial signs in Quebec, fully 38 per cent of French-speaking Canadians rejected the Supreme Court's suggested compromise. Astonishingly, 30 per cent of English-speaking Canadians actually supported English-only signs in Quebec, while 95 per cent of French-speaking Canadians rejected such a provocative proposition.

In the aftermath of the signs brouhaha, a petition calling for the declaration of official English unilingualism in British Columbia signed by ten thousand people in the greater Victoria area was presented to the legislature. The signatures included five of six Esquimault councillors, one of whom said, "Bilingualism just shouldn't be here. I'm afraid the French lost it on the Plains of Abraham and we're catering to a minority. I'm sick of it." These were extreme words and actions. Like the incident in Brockville, Ontario, when a group of English Canadians expressed their feelings about Quebec's aspirations by wiping their feet on the Quebec flag, like the scores of local governments across English Canada that declared themselves unilingual English and like Preston Manning's "love it or leave it" challenge to Quebec, they reflected a hostility that seemed to be growing.

As the months passed, English-Canadian anger over the signage issue spilled over to infect their attitudes toward the entire effort to achieve a constitutional reconciliation with Quebec. Another series of Gallup polls made it evident that there could be no deal and that the two solitudes were retreating further from any hope of reconciliation.

The reaction in Quebec in response to the sign controversy

and the final death of Meech was electric, catching many English Canadians off-guard. Not unexpectedly, Premier Bourassa withdrew from constitutional negotiations, saying that in the future he would engage solely in bilateral negotiations with Ottawa or one-on-one negotiations with each province as necessary. Mulroney's friend and protégé Lucien Bouchard quit over Mulroney's compromise on distinct society in the late-stage efforts to salvage Meech and founded the Bloc Québécois. The Bloc's numbers grew to nine MPs, who declared their intention to work for Quebec's sovereignty in the House of Commons — an unprecedented development. In August, the Bloc won a smashing by-election victory in a Quebec riding.

* * *

Separatist sentiment grew dramatically in Quebec. In 1979, the year before the referendum, separatist support stood at only 18 per cent. From 1989 to 1992, that figure had fluctuated between 30 and 40 per cent. On the softer sovereignty-association question, Quebec support fluctuated between 50 and 60 per cent. More worrisome, however, was the deep support for sovereignty-association among Québécois business leaders. A 1991 survey of 3,000 Québécois business leaders found 72 per cent not only favourable to sovereignty-association but also convinced that sovereignty-association would be a long-term economic benefit to the Quebec economy. Given the key role economic fear and uncertainty played in the 1980 referendum, the fact that important elements of Quebec's business elite were moving to sovereignty-association suggested that the economic tactic was less likely to succeed in future. Quebec's major trade union centrals once again declared their enthusiastic support for sovereignty. This trend was earlier reflected in the 1989 Quebec election which, although resulting in the re-election of Bourassa, reflected a surge in support for the PQ under Parizeau, campaigning openly on sovereignty. Polls after the failure of Meech put the PQ significantly ahead of the Liberals. The failure of Trudeau's bilingualism flagship was duly recorded in the post-Meech polls; 64 per cent of Canadians believed the program had failed completely. It appears that Trudeau, having helped to destroy Meech, had also inadvertently destroyed the credibility of bilingualism as the preferred alternative strategy for English and French living together in the bosom of a single state.

7

The Charlottetown Referendum

After the death of the Meech Lake Accord in June 1990, Canada was engaged in a constitutional dance that increasingly appeared out of control. Both Bourassa and Mulroney were unavoidably committed to carrying on the process of constitutional negotiations. In fact, the political survival of both depended on salvaging something from the wreckage. Both Bourassa's own Liberal Party, through the Allaire Report, and Quebec's National Assembly, through the Bélanger-Campeau Commission, committed Quebec to a referendum in October 1992 on either sovereignty or an acceptable offer of a renewed federalism from Ottawa. Though both reports demanded sweeping powers for Quebec that left English Canadians speechless, Bourassa asserted that his government's bottom line was an offer that addressed the five elements of the Meech Accord in a way that was acceptable to Quebec. Bourassa's political future in the next provincial election and the future of a continuing, viable federalist option in Quebec depended on Ottawa making such an offer before the expiry of the referendum deadline. Having signed on to Meech, widely seen in Quebec as a set of minimal conditions, and having been humiliated as deeply as Lévesque had been in 1981, Bourassa could do nothing less. The PQ and Parizeau waited in the wings, eager to accept the challenge of leading Quebec to sovereignty.

Mulroney also had no choice. The two towering accomplishments that helped his re-election in 1988, Meech Lake and free trade, had come badly unstuck. As a result, Mulroney's popularity had sunk to a low point never before experienced by an incumbent prime minister. For Mulroney to have even a remote possibility of political survival, he would have to salvage something from the Meech débâcle. If no reasonable offer were made to Quebec, the Bloc Québécois was poised to sweep the Tories from Quebec's electoral map.

When constitutional negotiations reopened in 1991, Canadians were assured that the intention was to develop a package that would not simply be a Meech Lake Accord Part II. This round was to be a "Canada Round" and an attempt to address all the issues that helped unravel Meech. It was to be a wide-open, democratic and public process with no more secret deals cobbled together in private. As discussions took place, they indeed appeared to be wide open, and no issue was unwelcome on the table. The process was long, exhausting and stressful, involving a joint Commons and Senate committee road-show that heard from seven hundred people and was deluged by 3,000 written submissions, a series of six televised and carefully staged national conferences from coast to coast, many top-level secret multilateral meetings over countless days, interminable discussions both within and between the delegations representing each key player and countless private phone calls to Bourassa and his team, who refused to participate. In addition, there was the very profligate public expenditure of more than twenty-two million dollars by the Spicer Commission. The pace of the process was frenetic, sometimes appearing to border on panic, because the urgency of the process was very clearly established by Quebec's absence from the table and the need to make an offer of renewed federalism to Quebec before the referendum deadline. Clearly, the process had to address the two most controversial features of Meech that had led to its failure in popular support: distinct society for Quebec and weakening the federal government's power. Most urgently, Quebec's disaffection and sense of betrayal had to be overcome. The constitutional concerns of Canada's aboriginal people also had to have some priority.

On 8 July 1992, the premiers of the nine English-Canadian provinces announced an agreement on constitutional changes after a lengthy and secret meeting. The first draft of the Charlottetown Agreement was thus produced. It was, for all intents and purposes, a Meech Lake Accord Part II. Like Meech, the Premiers' Accord proposed the irrevocable transformation of the fundamental character of Canada. Provincial powers were to be increased dramatically, while the central government was to be weakened beyond any reasonable capacity to provide coherent national leadership. In addition, the Accord included the abolition of all existing unambiguous federal powers to override provincial legislation. The premiers proposed to pick the federal carcass nearly clean, a carcass Joe Clark and Brian Mulroney willingly yielded up to them. And, though Quebec was granted distinct society status in the proposed "Canada clause," this concession was dramatically offset by commitments to the "equality of provinces" and to Canada's "linguistic duality" in the same clause. Furthermore, the equality-of-provinces doctrine was given dramatic effect in a proposal for a new, very powerful Triple-E Senate. Finally, the Premiers' Accord proposed to entrench the inherent right of aboriginal self-government in the constitution.

Reactions to the Premiers' Accord were mixed. Prime Minister Mulroney, who had reportedly expected the premiers to fail, initially expressed cautious and uneasy support. This response was not surprising. Since Mulroney's election in 1984, he had reduced the power and effectiveness of the central government, while giving the provinces much of what they demanded. Even Mulroney, however, may not have contemplated stripping Ottawa of so much power. He was particularly concerned about the Senate proposals. In the West and Newfoundland, partisans of the Triple-E Senate were elated at winning such a complete and stunning victory. Although Premier Bourassa typically neither rejected nor accepted the Accord, opinion in Quebec was uniformly negative, uniting federalist and separatist alike. Quebec could never accept losing so much power at the centre in the proposed Senate.

For a time, it appeared that the Premiers' Accord would unravel, forcing Ottawa to act unilaterally through the House of Commons in order to make an offer to Quebec before the October deadline. But a unilateral offer from Ottawa, without the provincial consent needed to effect constitutional changes, would have been a nearly meaningless gesture. And given the enormous pressure on Bourassa to proceed with a referendum on either sovereignty or an offer of renewed federalism, there would have been little opportunity to put together an alternative package in time. Furthermore, the nine English-Canadian premiers, having reached a consensus on a package that delivered so much to the provinces, were eager to see it accepted as well. Aboriginal leaders, having won the unexpected unanimous consent of the nine premiers and Ottawa to the constitutional entrenchment of the right of aboriginal self-government, were also eager to rescue the agreement.

Desperate for some kind of saleable deal, Premier Bourassa agreed to return to the table at a formal first ministers' meeting if Quebec's three major concerns with the premiers' package could be acceptably addressed. First, Quebec could not sanction the reduction in the province's power that would occur if the proposed Triple-E Senate were accepted. Substantial changes would be required in that area. Second, Quebec might accept the constitutional entrenchment of aboriginal self-government as long as such entrenchment could not be used in the courts to extend aboriginal land claims or to establish complete immunity from provincial law. Third, Quebec required some additional movement on the federal-provincial division of powers. Reassured that Ottawa, the premiers of English Canada and the aboriginal leaders were open to such discussions and possible substantial concessions, Bourassa agreed to return to the table.

Accordingly, following two preliminary meetings at Harrington Lake, an agreement was hammered out at a first ministers' meeting from 18 to 22 August 1992. The July Premiers' Accord more or less remained, despite some significant changes to the Senate and the House of Commons. The agreement was fine-tuned at a final first ministers' meeting in Charlottetown on 28 August 1992. (See Appendix I).

After finalizing the text of the Charlottetown Agreement, the first ministers spent most of their time at Charlottetown discussing a formal approval mechanism. Above all, they were determined to avoid a long, drawn-out process, like Meech, during which support for the Agreement could wither and die. Furthermore, as a result of the collapse of Meech, all first ministers had publicly promised that no more constitutional deals would be approved in secret without public, democratic consultation. In fact, some of the premiers owed their elections at least partly to public disgust with their predecessors over Meech. British Columbia and Alberta had passed legislation requiring a referendum on any constitutional amendment. Mulroney had promised "national consultation" in his 1991 Throne Speech. In the October 1991 Saskatchewan election, voters had overwhelmingly endorsed their right to be consulted by plebiscite on future constitutional changes. Both Manitoba and Newfoundland were committed by statute to a rather complicated process of public consultation before they could approve constitutional changes. And, of course, Quebec was irreversibly committed to a referendum.

Anticipating probable failure by the premiers to agree on constitutional changes, the Mulroney government had earlier introduced legislation to allow a national referendum supervised by Ottawa. Above all, the approval process had to deal with Quebec's already-established referendum date of 26 October 1992. Clearly, the wisest course was to agree on one question to be put to all the people of English Canada on the same day, allowing Quebec to pose the same question in French according to rules already established there for the 1980 referendum. There was some debate about whether to put just one question on the ballot, in which the public would be asked to accept or reject the entire package as a so-called "seamless web," or, as Newfoundland's premier Clyde Wells wanted, separate questions on each major item in the Agreement. The problem with Wells's proposal was that the electorate could then support only those items that were popular, such as aboriginal self-government, while rejecting the more controversial items such as the new Senate or distinct society. Mulroney argued strongly against the proposal, suggesting the question should be the simple and stark equivalent of "Are you for this deal or are you for the breakup of Canada?" The first ministers agreed to this course, although Wells remained reluctant. The final wording adopted was: "Do you agree that the Constitution of Canada should be renewed on the basis of the agreement reached on August 28, 1992?"

The first ministers also agreed that Ottawa would hold a federal referendum in every province but Quebec. Quebec would ask the same question in French, but carry out the referendum under Quebec law. Finally, Quebec's referendum date of 26 October 1992 was accepted. Formal public announcement of these decisions was delayed as a courtesy to Bourassa so he could first meet and persuade his caucus in the National Assembly, as well as the delegates at the already-scheduled convention of the Quebec Liberal Party. To have announced these decisions immediately would have left Bourassa open to charges in Quebec of being a prisoner of an agenda and a process imposed by English Canada. Assuming public approval in the referendum, the House of Commons, the Senate and the various provincial and territorial legislatures would then proceed to speed passage of the required formal legal texts. In this way, it was believed that the pitfalls of Meech would be avoided: rather than secret deals, there would be a public campaign culminating in an expression of the popular will by ballot; rather than a painful, lengthy process of squabbling and nit-picking, there would be a rapid and clear popular decision. The public approval process would be over and settled in two months. Although that would not prevent critics of the deal from attacking it in the House of Commons and the legislatures, any future effort to derail legislative approval after a victorious referendum outcome would have little political legitimacy.

Still, in spite of the apparently impeccable logic behind holding a referendum, there was profound unease among the political leaders. Both Mulroney and Clark had serious reservations about the idea, as did most of the premiers. In June 1992, government house leader Harvie Andre had warned, "I hope we don't have a referendum. A referendum will be a terrible bloody thing." The two major referendums of the century had been deeply damaging and inconclusive. Mackenzie King's 1942 vote on conscription had cleaved English Canada and Quebec more deeply than anyone expected. The result was so politically unacceptable, and the passions aroused on both sides so angry and volatile, that King was forced to retreat from fully implementing conscription. In retrospect, Ottawa would have been wiser not to have held the vote and to have proceeded with more aggressively persuasive voluntary recruitment, especially in Quebec. The 1980 Quebec referendum had created deep and bitter divisions in that province and arguably set in motion the process that led finally to the Meech disaster. In a sense, the first ministers at Charlottetown were, in fact, reaping what had been sown in the referendum on sovereignty-association. Although 60 per cent were against a mandate to negotiate sovereignty in that referendum, it had settled nothing. In both cases, the referendums made the controversies they were intended to resolve deeper and more damaging. There was no reason to expect that this referendum would be any different. Yet, despite these reservations, the government appeared unavoidably committed.

To allay these fears, strategists pointed out that the juggernaut of support for the Yes side seemed irresistible. In favour were all the premiers and territorial leaders; the prime minister and his entire cabinet, the House of Commons and all federal party leaders; the Senate; the most prominent aboriginal leaders; the top leadership of organized labour and the established business lobby (although it was split in Quebec). How could such unanimity at the top not persuade the public to get on side? Still, the referendum was a huge gamble that, if unsuccessful, could worsen the situation. What if English Canada voted Yes and Quebec voted No? What if two or three western provinces voted No along with Quebec? What if the result was so close as to be politically insignificant one way or the other, merely confirming that the Canadian public was more or less equally polarized?

In answer to such gloomy questions, eager proponents of the referendum strategy pointed to polls that suggested Canadians were tired of the reform process, wanted the constitutional issue resolved as soon as possible and would support their leaders. An early September Angus Reid poll seemed to confirm this view: in English Canada 61 per cent would vote Yes and 20 per cent No, with 18 per cent undecided; in Quebec Yes had the edge at 44 to 42 per cent, with 14 per cent undecided. These numbers suggested a strong Yes in English Canada and a close Yes in Quebec — a more than sufficient mandate to adopt the Charlottetown Agreement. Still, nothing could be certain. Up until the moment the referendum writ was dropped, Canada's united political elite more or less controlled the agenda, stage-managed the process and paced the debate. After the writ was dropped, control would slip from their grasp and anything could happen. And given the political volatility of Canadians over the preceding decade and their contempt for their political leaders, there was no guarantee that they would give the political elite the clear and unequivocal Yes that it so eagerly wanted.

As a result, the cards were stacked to give the Yes option the edge. The question itself was carefully constructed to encourage an affirmative response. The use of the word *renewed*, rather than the more neutral words *adopted* or *approved*, was a clear effort to link the question to the promise made by Trudeau and the English-Canadian premiers to the Québécois during the 1980 sovereignty-association referendum. "Renewal" of the constitution had been promised in exchange for an affirmation of federalism, but no renewal had occurred — at least not one with which the Québécois had agreed.

The federal referendum law, in marked contrast to that in Quebec, neither established real spending limits nor provided access to government funds to ensure fair balance in the debate between the Yes and No forces. The formidable Yes forces in English Canada could thereby establish as many Yes committees as they wished and put on a massive propaganda effort with no real limits on spending, as each and every committee could spend up to $7.5 million. This opened the door to an uncontrolled effort to buy a Yes vote through advertising in print and on the airwaves. The No forces in English Canada could never hope to match the spending potential of the Yes side. In addition, the absence of government subsidies virtually ensured that the No side would be shut out of comparable access to the expensive and effective airwaves. The last barrier to unlimited spending in the referendum campaign was removed when the Canadian Radio-television and Telecommunications Commission (CRTC) lifted all advertising restrictions by ruling that partisan referendum advertising would be considered programming rather than political advertising. The effect of the CRTC decision was to allow unlimited partisan spending during the referendum on TV and FM radio. (Restrictions on AM radio had been dropped in 1985.)

In contrast, the Quebec referendum law was much fairer. The referendum was overseen by a panel of judges. The Yes and No sides were required to organize themselves into two umbrella organizations, each chaired by a member of the National Assembly. Each committee could spend only one dollar per voter to a maximum of $4.7 million for each of the two committees. Third-party advertising was strictly forbidden. Each side received the same subsidy from provincial coffers. Bloc Québécois efforts to obtain similar rules to govern the federal referendum were stonewalled in the House of Commons.

To reinforce the Yes side's advantage, Ottawa released a multi-million dollar blizzard of ads celebrating Canada's 125th "birthday" and providing information on the Charlottetown Agreement, all thanks to the taxpayers. These ads called out for a Yes vote, without explicitly saying so, by appealing to our patriotism and by applauding Charlottetown. The advantage of these ads was that not only were they paid for by the Ottawa government, but they could also be played and printed in Quebec, thus getting around Quebec's referendum law.

Delaying the actual legal text was another tactic the Yes side used. After the Charlottetown Agreement was finalized in August, Canadians were told a full legal text would be available very soon. Then they were told it would be available midway in the referendum campaign. Then they were told by Clark that the public did not really need a legal text to judge the Agreement. Then there were hints that the legal text might not be ready until very close to voting day and perhaps not until after the vote. It was unclear whether the delays represented an honest difficulty in rendering the Agreement into complicated legalese, whether last-minute behind-the-scenes negotiations were still going on or whether the Yes side was deliberately delaying, or even denying, access to the text until the vote was over. Whatever the reasons, it was very risky.

One had only to recall that when the Meech Lake Accord was issued in legalese, its decline began. While it was merely vague principles and propositions, Meech supporters could defend it in platitudes and generalities, and easily dismiss opponents. But once the legal text was on the table and the experts began to interpret the meaning and implications of the legal language, it soon became clear that there were deep, honest divisions in the opinions of the experts. Ordinary citizens reasoned that if the experts could not agree, how could they be expected to agree? The early debates on Charlottetown suggested that expert opinion on the meaning of the legal text would be similarly divided. Deliberately delaying the legal text, or even denying access until the vote was over, was attractive to Ottawa. By denying the No side something definitive to attack, the Yes side could easily dismiss the opponents of the Agreement. On the other hand, Canadians might feel manipulated or insulted. It would also be unprecedented in democratic tradition to ask an electorate to approve a constitution before the final legal text was a matter of public record.

The final tactic for ensuring the success of the Agreement was the formation and launch of the Canada Yes Committee. The committee was composed of several prominent, non-partisan Canadians as national co-chairs and boasted the membership of three former premiers, two former national political party leaders and prominent personalities in law, business, religion, education, science and the arts and letters. The Charlottetown Agreement was still vulnerable: it had originated in secret meetings among the nine English-Canadian premiers and had been finally approved in further secret meetings with Bourassa and the prime minister. Given the public's suspicion of politicians, it was crucial to present the Charlottetown Agreement as now outside the grimy world of horse-trading, deal-making backroom politics. Given the record of public anger over Meech and its failure, the appeal to Canadians had to come from a more neutral source. Though the Canada Yes Committee received the explicit endorsement of the three federal party leaders, all the premiers and territorial leaders and the national aboriginal leadership, its makeup was clearly designed to keep active partisan politicians at arm's length. At its kickoff, the Canada Yes Committee told Canadians that a Yes was not merely an approval of constitutional changes, but a vote for everything that was good, prosperous and hopeful about Canada, including "a promising, certain future for our young people; the acceptance of a good compromise that has been worked out with intelligence and honour; good news for the economy; an affirmation of the values and the diversity of our country." By extension, a No vote was not just a rejection of a proposed constitutional amendment; it was reckless and irresponsible; it jeopardized our children's future, threatened to wreck the economy and repudiated Canadian values. The gloves were off at the outset.

Prime Minister Mulroney had signalled this tough campaign line earlier when, upon announcing the successful conclusion of the Charlottetown Agreement, he had harshly said, "I know there will be fights...And I know that the enemies of Canada will...be out in full force. They will encounter me and my fellow first ministers...fighting for Canada." Although Mulroney quickly backed off from his explicit "enemies of Canada" line, the basic theme remained that those who opposed the Agreement would help destroy Canada. The referendum was not just about an agreement; it was about Canada. The answer on October 26 was a Yes or a No to Canada.

Another theme favoured by the prime minister was economic fear. Polls had repeatedly revealed that Canadians were deeply anxious and insecure about the economy. Clearly, if economic recovery, stability and well-being could be linked in the minds of Canadians to approval of the Charlottetown Agreement, the initial Yes lead might be consolidated and increased. The prime minister hammered home this point relentlessly. A No would lead to "political instability...[which] gives rise to economic uncertainty [and]...the loss of economic opportunity...First and foremost, investors flee political uncertainty." A Yes, on the other hand, would "reduce uncertainty, increase stability and re-invigorate the economy," and bring "good news for the economy." The Yes team across Canada repeated such arguments. With remarkable unanimity, they insisted that a Yes would be an incredible tonic for a beleaguered economy.

Constitutional affairs minister Joe Clark was assigned the task of carrying messages of political instability. In a set speech repeated at meetings across Canada, he warned that "if we reject this agreement...this country would begin to crumble."

Almost as soon as the referendum campaign began, popular support for the Yes side started to drop. By the third week of September, an Angus Reid poll reported that, on a national basis, the Yes and No options were tied in popular support. The No option was leading in Quebec by 45 to 38 per cent and in British Columbia and Alberta by 50 to 34 per cent. The Yes lead in Saskatchewan and Manitoba was cut to a dangerous 41 to 40 per cent. Yes was enjoying a comfortable lead only in Ontario and Atlantic Canada. A Léger et Léger poll in Quebec told an even worse story: 41 to 30.5 per cent for No over Yes, with 28.5 per cent undecided. As a result, in what he later described as a deliberate "tactical counter-attack," the prime minister took a desperate and risky step by escalating his attack on the No side during a speech at Sherbrooke, Quebec, on Monday, 28 September. Indeed, in retrospect, the prime minister's escalation was clearly co-ordinated with a number of events the previous weekend in an effort to increase the level of economic anxiety among Canadians.

On Friday, 25 September, Royal Bank chair Allan Taylor released a forty-seven-page report, "Unity or Disunity: An Economic Analysis of the Benefits and Costs," at a press conference where he strongly endorsed the Yes side. The report was premised on the worst-case scenario of Quebec's separation — namely, no economic association and hostile polarization — but the timing of its release and Taylor's remarks made it clear that, according to the bank, Quebec's separation might follow a No vote. According to the report, economic and population growth in Canada would grind to a halt and then fall sharply, per capita income would collapse by 15 per cent and thousands would rush to emigrate from Canada to the United States.

On Sunday, 27 September, speaking to the Canadian Chamber of Commerce in Victoria, Al Flood, chair of the Canadian Imperial Bank of Commerce, provoked dramatic headlines across Canada. The following day, the Regina *Leader Post*'s front page captured the essence of his claims: "Yes side says No is chaos." Clumsily combining the themes of economic and political instability, Flood said, "The slightest hint of instability can send global financial markets into disarray. We have seen these things happen to other countries…and there is no reason why they cannot happen here if the international investment community concludes that we are politically unsound."

On Monday, 28 September, during that speech at Sherbrooke, Quebec, Mulroney dramatically ripped up a copy of the Charlottetown Agreement for the benefit of the television cameras. He went even further than the bankers. Picking up on the warnings of Taylor and Flood, Mulroney declared voting No "means a direct contribution to separatism…the second-to-last step before separation [which] would plunge us into the unknown, into political instability and economic insecurity." No, according to the prime minister, amounted to nothing less than "the beginning of the process of dismantling Canada." Premier Bourassa agreed: "A No vote could mean a possible breakup of the federation."

Economic scare tactics had worked well for hard-line federalists

against Lévesque and the PQ during the 1970 and 1973 Quebec
election campaigns, and even more effectively during the 1980 sovereignty-association referendum. But in those campaigns, the costs
of separation were defensible arguments, since the independence of
Quebec was clearly on the table. Even hard-line separatists and
moderate sovereigntists concede that there are economic costs associated with Quebec's independence, although nowhere near as high
as federalists allege. Had the 1992 referendum been on Quebec
independence, the economic fear campaign would have had a big
impact, perhaps even a decisive one. But the referendum was not on
separation, and the efforts of the Yes side to emphasize this issue
failed utterly. The Canadian people refused to buy the argument, and
the Yes team and the business community themselves were deeply
divided on the political and economic consequences of a No vote.

Many Yes team members, including Canadian Labour Congress
president Bob White, NDP leader Audrey McLaughlin, Newfoundland premier Clyde Wells and social activist June Callwood,
publicly and firmly rebuked the banks and the prime minister for
their scare tactics. Although many among the business lobby continued to issue warnings, business opinion was divided. Some business
experts cautioned Canadians not to panic but to ride out what was a
temporary blip. Many money market brokers, particularly in the
United States and Japan, predicted that interest rates in Canada
would fall after the referendum regardless of the outcome simply
because the Canadian economy was too fragile to sustain high interest rates. They contended that Canada's economic difficulties had to
do with the economy itself: nearly negligible growth, little prospect
for an upturn and Canada's structural captivity by the weak U.S.
economy, Canada's biggest market. With such conflicting messages
coming from the business lobby, it is not surprising that the effort to
generate economic hysteria in order to extract a Yes vote fizzled
quickly. Although the dual themes of the negative political and economic consequences of a No vote remained cornerstones of the Yes
campaign, the tone in which the messages were delivered changed
quickly from breathless hysteria to persistent moderation.

While it was true that support for Meech had simultaneously
unravelled at the top and at the bottom, support for Charlottetown
unravelled almost exclusively at the bottom. Thus, though the
political, labour and business elites remained united in favour of
the Agreement, the constituencies they hoped to deliver began to
march out of control. This move to a No in English Canada was
assisted by the interventions of three prominent Canadians, each

representing significant if contradictory political tendencies. Former prime minister Trudeau, Judy Rebick of the National Action Committee on the Status of Women (NAC) and Reform party leader Manning all came down dramatically on the No side. Their support was a blow to the Yes campaign and helped to derail the initial strategy of insisting that a No vote was not only unthinkable but illegitimate. By their very different interventions, and for very different reasons, each gave many Canadians a rationale for voting No. Most important, each gave a No vote public legitimacy.

Manning did not declare his decision to campaign for a No until 10 September 1992, almost two weeks after the finalization of the Charlottetown Agreement. At first, he briefly toyed with supporting the deal or adopting a stance of neutrality. However, his advisors, middle-level leadership and the Reform rank-and-file made it clear that he had no choice but to come out strongly against Charlottetown.

Manning restricted his No campaign to a few major themes. He argued the Agreement would lead to almost-interminable constitutional negotiations; he complained that it committed Ottawa to heavy social spending, meaning the government would have difficulty balancing the budget; he stated the amending formula would make the deal irreversible, thereby depriving future generations of the means to fix the constitution; and he insisted the Agreement failed to provide "effective regional representation," the closest he came to embracing the explicit role of champion of western alienation. Given the cauldron of anger bubbling among the Reform rank-and-file, his campaign was remarkably low-key.

While Manning's position on the Agreement was perhaps predictable, NAC's active opposition to Charlottetown caught many observers off guard. They had expected the organization either to sign on to the Yes side, stay silent or perhaps simply issue a critical press release. Instead, the NAC executive committed the organization and its president, Judy Rebick, to an active campaign for a No vote.

NAC's opposition to Charlottetown was based on three central concerns. First, Rebick declared solidarity with the Native Women's Association of Canada (NWAC), arguing that the aboriginal self-government proposal failed to provide aboriginal women with adequate equality guarantees. Second, she argued that the Canada clause jeopardized the gender equality rights that women had already won in the 1982 constitution. Finally, she warned that the Agreement might jeopardize existing social programs and make it impossible to develop future social programs with national standards. Rebick became a tireless and effective campaigner for the No side, and as the campaign progressed, she increasingly spoke not only for Canada's organized feminist lobby, but also for the rank-and-file trade unionists and New Democrats who felt that they had been abandoned by their own leaderships.

Trudeau had played a significant role in the death of the Meech Accord, and it was universally expected he would pass judgement on the Charlottetown Agreement as well. His intervention in the campaign came in two salvos. The first was a scathing and contemptuous denunciation of Québécois nationalists in the 28 September 1992 issue of *Maclean's*; then he offered a detailed critical analysis of the agreement in a speech on 1 October 1992. In it, he developed five substantive arguments for voting No. First, he attacked the use of political and economic terrorism by the Yes side: "politicians — and politicians in high places, and even bankers in high places — are trying to make us think, make us believe, that a Yes is a yes to Canada, and a No is a no to Canada. This is a lie that must be denounced." Second, he noted that a Yes would not bring constitutional peace but endless bickering and that "the blackmail would continue." Third, Trudeau noted that the Charlottetown amending formula ensured the Agreement would be irreversible. Fourth, he argued that the proposed Canada clause undermined the individual rights enshrined in the Charter, creating a "hierarchy of classes of citizens," thereby threatening minorities, especially official-language minorities. Fifth, he said the Charlottetown Agreement seriously weakened the federal government and jeopardized social programs, especially those in the poor provinces. In other words, Trudeau declared, the Charlottetown Agreement was a "mess that deserves a big No."

With these two interventions, Trudeau crystallized significant currents of opposition to the Agreement, appealing simultaneously to anti-Quebec bigots in English Canada, official-language minorities in every province, Canadians who cherished the primacy of the Charter's individual rights over collective rights, those who feared the excessive devolution of federal powers and those who were concerned about protecting existing social programs and developing new ones. Perhaps of greatest importance in the heat of the referendum campaign was Trudeau's blunt condemnation of the scare tactics of the Yes side, thereby giving many Canadians the courage to contemplate a No vote. "The question of Yes or No is," Trudeau reminded Canadians, "yes or no, do you want us to reform, or amend, the Constitution on the basis of the so-called consensus of Charlottetown?" Trudeau's pivotal role in stopping the Yes team's scare campaign in its tracks should not be underestimated.

The unravelling of popular support for Charlottetown cannot be explained alone by these interventions by Manning, Rebick and Trudeau. They simply helped, giving diverse groups of Canadians intellectual and political hooks on which to hang their relatively spontaneous sense of opposition. It appears that the largely ignored Spicer Commission report of June 1991 had been more on the mark than anyone anticipated: it had warned of the popular "fury in the land" against politicians and that Canadians had "lost faith" in "the political process and their political leaders." While the Reform party and NAC had considerable influence, they were no match for the Yes side's potential. And, of course, Trudeau only had influence at an aloof distance. He did not actively campaign, nor did he have an organization with troops to deliver a No vote. Theoretically and on paper, the Yes side had a formidable organization. By the end of the campaign, 191 Yes committees and only thirty-four No committees had been officially registered with Canada's Chief Electoral Officer. The central Yes campaign in English Canada had an estimated media budget of more than five million dollars, and countless local Yes committees had ample funds to put out their message in local media and local daily newspapers. Maclean Hunter registered itself as a Yes committee in order to run legal pro-Yes ads at its own expense in *Maclean's*, *The Financial Post* and the *Sun* daily newspaper group (in Toronto, Ottawa, Calgary and Edmonton). Provincial governments were free to spend as well and did so. The editorial consensus of English Canada's daily newspapers was unprecedented, and they did not hesitate to push the Yes message.

The No campaign in English Canada had virtually no money, relying for national mass exposure on its half share of the ninety minutes of free network time provided under referendum campaign regulations. Since this was a campaign that involved convincing, identifying and delivering the vote, the Yes side theoretically had the enormous advantage of the support of the entire campaign infrastructures of the three major political parties. The three-party alliance worked reasonably effectively at the top — the three parties' top media and campaign strategists worked for the Yes team — but it was soon discovered they could not deliver the troops on the ground. Efforts to build joint constituency organizations to go door to door, to put up signs, to check off Yes supporters on the voters' list and to prepare to get out the vote all failed. Not only did the elites of the three parties find that they could not deliver their activist troops to campaign, they found they could not deliver their supporters to vote Yes.

Although the Liberal Party in English Canada was officially in favour of Charlottetown, Jean Chrétien did as little campaigning as possible, and his defence of the Agreement was neither passionate nor convincing. Trudeau's interventions had the biggest impact among Liberals in English Canada and among English-Canadian Liberals in Quebec. In addition, a number of other prominent party members, such as constitutional lawyer Deborah Coyne and Liberal leaders Sharon Carstairs of Manitoba and Gordon Wilson of British Columbia, came out strongly against the agreement.

Except for Mulroney and a few high-profile cabinet ministers, most Tory MPs either ran for cover or did as little unenthusiastic campaigning as they could. Given the low levels of Tory popular support and the profound unpopularity of Mulroney, this approach was understandable. Indeed, too much aggressive campaigning by Tory MPs might have hurt rather than helped the Yes side. Tory premiers hardly threw themselves energetically into the battle, at least not until the very end.

In supporting Charlottetown, the three NDP premiers and national leader Audrey McLaughlin abandoned the central tenets of NDP policy, disillusioning many NDP supporters in the process. First there was their support of the new Senate, probably the most appalling *volte face* in Canadian political history. From its founding in 1935, the CCF/NDP has always favoured Senate abolition. Second, McLaughlin's participation in such a transparent provincial-rights grab was inexplicable to many party members. Traditionally, the NDP had opposed the devolution of too much power to the provinces. Third, with the deal, the leaders of the NDP relinquished their willingness to concede special status to Quebec, joining the English-Canadian effort to impose a fundamentally unacceptable constitutional solution upon Quebec. Finally, many NDPers were outraged that their leaders had participated in an effort to constitutionalize one of the major items of the neo-conservative agenda of the preceding decade — to weaken and render impotent the central government. In exchange for a meaningless and toothless Social Charter, the NDP leadership had largely bargained away the most important tool Canadians have had to fight for reform and change, namely, the instrumentality of a strong central government. The NDP leadership, therefore, found that it was not only unable to deliver its electoral base to the Yes side, but also failed to deliver its party membership en masse.

The top leadership of the Canadian Labour Congress (CLC), with its 2.3 million members, faced the same problems as the NDP leadership, largely for the same reasons. Despite formal support for the agreement by the CLC's Executive Council, the rank-and-file of the labour movement remained largely unconvinced. Two major national unions, the Canadian Union of Postal Workers and the Public Service Alliance of Canada, publicly broke with the CLC and formally endorsed the No side, largely over the same issues as NAC. And, of course, the Quebec Federation of Labour was overwhelmingly against Charlottetown, like all other Quebec labour organizations. Ed Finn, a longtime labour activist and retired research director of CUPE, spoke for many in labour when he called the agreement a "legalistic monstrosity...far better consigned to the garbage dump than enshrined in the Constitution."

The English-Canadian business lobby was solidly on the Yes side, particularly at the top corporate level and among the organized Chamber of Commerce sector. But there were some important cracks. Although the influential Canadian Federation of Independent Business came out strongly in favour of Charlottetown, its leadership admitted that a large portion of its membership was against it. The powerful British Columbia Employers' Council faced such division that it decided to stay neutral. Eric Kierans, one of the most respected English-Canadian business leaders, at first declared himself in favour of the Agreement and then announced, as he left for vacation, that he had changed his mind and had voted No in an advance poll. In Quebec, the business lobby was deeply fractured. The most powerful and influential business organization, l'Association des manufacturiers du Québec, which includes such members as Alcan, Northern Telecom and IBM Canada, decided to stay neutral while at the same time describing the Agreement as "disappointing." André Bérard, chair of the National Bank of Canada, formerly seen as a loyal federalist, also declared neutrality. Finally, in a significant setback for the Yes team, the 61,000-member Chambre de Commerce du Québec opted for neutrality. These decisions may have had something to do with the hostility faced by the Royal Bank in Quebec following its intervention on the Yes side. Many customers in Quebec closed their accounts in protest, *Non* stickers were plastered on many branches, and *Non* campaign leader Parizeau accused the bank of profiting by secretly speculating on the sharp decline in the Canadian dollar that the bank had helped to provoke.

But the most irreparable damage to the Yes campaign was the

unravelling of support for the aboriginal self-government aspect of Charlottetown among some First Nations. The most positive feature of the Charlottetown Agreement for English Canadians and Québécois alike was the commitment to the inherent right to aboriginal self-government. Many in English Canada were inclined to support the deal just to affirm that right. From the outset, however, NWAC had strongly opposed the deal on the grounds that not only were aboriginal women excluded from the negotiating table, but also that the clause of the Agreement giving aboriginal culture and traditions primacy might prevail over gender equality rights.

NWAC was not the only organization in the aboriginal community to have doubts about the Agreement. By late September, the Council of Crees of Quebec and the Mohawks were both proposing a boycott of the referendum, as were thirty First Nations in Alberta. Then the Manitoba chiefs began to express doubts. And there were rumours that the Union of B.C. Chiefs was moving toward support for a No. Elijah Harper also refused to endorse the deal. He indicated that if he had to vote, he would vote No, but it was better for aboriginals to boycott the referendum.

The chiefs' concerns were of fundamental importance. First, there was a fear that the Agreement might erode treaty rights as a result of constitutionalizing them. Second, there was a related concern that the devolution of power both to the provinces and to aboriginal governments might also weaken existing Crown treaty obligations and Ottawa's responsibility for them. Third, there was a growing apprehension that the "peace, order, and good government" concession to Quebec made the aboriginal self-government clause meaningless. Fourth, among treaty Indians there was some concern about the inclusion of the Inuit and the Métis in the aboriginal self-government clause. What impact would the inclusion of these groups have on the existing and future rights of status Indians? Where would the money for self-government come from? Finally, there was a feeling that too much power had been granted to Quebec and that the aboriginal people in Quebec needed stronger assurances. Among many chiefs, especially the Mohawks, there was also a principled rejection of the whole process on the grounds that they already enjoyed self-government on aboriginal lands, and always had. There was a final effort to secure the chiefs' endorsement, but many remained unconvinced. Despite the fact that Ovide Mercredi and other aboriginal leaders continued to campaign for a Yes, the failure of the Assembly of First Nations to endorse Charlottetown was a mortal blow to the Yes campaign in English Canada.

There were a series of other events that nipped at the heels of the Yes campaign, undermining its credibility. There were the absentee premiers who failed to go on the campaign trail. Premier Clyde Wells of Newfoundland initially refused to campaign actively outside his own province and only agreed to do so later when he was satisfied that the legal text was acceptable. Premier Don Getty of Alberta had announced his retirement from politics right after the Agreement and did not take a particularly active part in the campaign, even in Alberta. Premier Gary Filmon of Manitoba failed to become active until late in the campaign. Premier Mike Harcourt of British Columbia spent so much of his time repairing the personal political damage he suffered as a result of the Agreement that he did not campaign outside the province. Premier Roy Romanow of Saskatchewan only made obligatory appearances and speeches. In the early phase of the campaign, the premiers' absenteeism had to do with overconfidence. Later, as the Yes campaign faltered, eagerness to campaign was tempered by memories of how the public had punished many of the incumbent politicians involved in Meech, also known as the "Peterson factor." Then there was the "Mulroney factor." If a large part of the reason that support was slipping for the Agreement had to do with Mulroney's unpopularity, the premiers doubted the wisdom of linking themselves too closely with the prime minister, who had largely seized for himself centre stage in the national Yes campaign.

Then there was the controversy over the legal text. While it was true that there would not be an enormous demand for a legal text among Canadians in general, those with a special interest required one as soon as possible, if only to confirm that the legalese faithfully replicated the Agreement in letter and spirit. As September came to an end and there was still no legal text, criticism mounted. Finally, at the end of September, Premier Wells of Newfoundland, Deputy Premier Horsman of Alberta and Justice Minister McCrae of Manitoba clearly stated that a legal text was needed or their provinces would reconsider their support for the deal. The Agreement was finally published in all daily newspapers on 3 October 1992, and Clark announced that the legal text would be available by mid-October.

By the time the legal text was generally available to the public, however, there were only ten or eleven days left in the campaign. Yet the release of the text did not lay suspicions to rest. It was, after all, entitled "Draft Legal Text" and described only as "a best efforts text." Furthermore, there were some significant and controversial changes to the original Agreement in the legal text. The democracy guarantees of the Charter were not to apply to aboriginal governments. Only the appointment of the governor of the Bank of Canada was definitely to be subject to Senate ratification, rather than the heads of all federal regulatory agencies and cultural institutions. Electrical power was added to natural resources as subject to Senate defeat. The double-majority requirement in the Senate on matters of French language and culture was now defined in terms of a majority of all senators and of all "French-speaking" senators rather than all "francophone" senators. Thus, the presumed veto of Quebec's six senators was now dubious. Finally, the concession Wells wanted — that Senate laws defeated in the House of Commons would go to a joint sitting — was included. These were all serious last-minute changes and further undermined public confidence in the Agreement.

A further problem of credibility for the Yes campaign related to the very different versions of the meaning of the Agreement that were presented in Quebec and in English Canada. Every time Mulroney bragged loudly in Quebec about all the gains made for the province, the Yes campaign was hurt in English Canada. Yet when English-Canadian politicians told English Canadians that the deal gave Quebec very little, the Yes side was damaged in Quebec. When Premier Wells told a Calgary audience on 7 October 1992 that the Charlottetown Agreement was an improvement on Meech because it had put a "fence" around distinct society, giving it a more limited meaning than in Meech, the *Le Devoir* headline was "*Wells: le Québec s'est satisfait de moins que Meech,*" and another nail was hammered into the coffin of the Yes campaign in Quebec. The same was true when B.C. intergovernmental affairs minister Moe Sihota explained in Quesnel, British Columbia, on 6 October 1992 that Bourassa had "lost" and had run into a "brick wall" on "special status." The same was true on 14 October 1992 when Manitoba premier Filmon told a farm and business audience in Russell, Manitoba, "When Quebec said, 'We want all those other powers,' we said: ... 'No. This is as far as we'll go.'" Clearly, Wells, Sihota and Filmon were trying to persuade English Canadians to support the deal on the grounds that Quebec had received comparatively little. Yet every such argument made in English Canada echoed back in Quebec and served to undermine the Yes side there. And such arguments did not finally help in English Canada because Mulroney continued to tell the Québécois about their thirty-one gains, the best deal for

Quebec in 125 years. Thus, the Yes side faced a serious credibility gap in both Quebec and English Canada.

In an unforeseen irony, the Yes campaign's overwhelming superiority in media access turned into a liability. With its multi-million-dollar media budget, the Yes side, in ordinary politics, should have been a steamroller. With ample enough resources to insert one- and two-page spreads in all major dailies on at least two occasions, as well as to expose every Canadian television viewer to thirteen pro-Yes ads each week throughout October, the Yes side was confident. In addition, huge Yes billboards dotted Canada from coast to coast, Yes lawn signs sprang up and stood out sharply if only because of the near total absence of No signs everywhere but in Quebec, and pamphlets appeared in every single mailbox, all providing the Yes message with constant daily reinforcement. But the Yes propaganda campaign failed.

Many of the ads were misleading. Some ads claimed the new Senate was Triple-E. It was not, and only the ignorant or dishonest could claim otherwise. Others implied that the Social Charter clause provided clear protection to ordinary Canadians. It did not. Others boasted that the Agreement brought Canada an effective economic union. It did not. Many Canadians found the television commercials insulting. Yet the Yes campaign stubbornly persisted in playing these ads despite clear evidence they were counter-productive. The widely shared perception that Ottawa was misusing taxpayers' dollars to influence their votes in what was supposed to be a fair and democratic referendum process did not help the Yes side either.

The battle in Quebec was a separate, almost internal, event. Once again, the Québécois debated among themselves whether their vision of Quebec as one of two founding nations could be reconciled with English Canada's latest version of federalism. It was significant that Ottawa was conducting a referendum in the nine English-Canadian provinces under federal law, while Quebec was holding a separate vote under Quebec law. This difference was more than a matter of symbolism. The rules governing the referendum in Quebec were much fairer. While in English Canada the disparate, poorly organized No side seemed badly outmatched by the well-oiled Yes machine, in Quebec both sides were more evenly matched. As Mulroney declared, in Quebec he expected a "bare-knuckled fight." On the Yes side was the Bourassa government and the Quebec Liberal Party, the preponderance of the business lobby and, at least initially, the formerly formidable federalist forces. On the No side were the sovereigntists, supported by between 30 and 40 per cent of the population and very well organized in the PQ and Bloc, a significant portion of the business lobby and organized labour. As the campaign unfolded, the No side also picked up elements of the nationalist wing of the Liberal party and even a significant share of Trudeau federalists. While the first post-Charlottetown polls gave the Yes side a large forty-one point lead in English Canada, in Quebec the Yes lead was a mere two points. At first, it was assumed that whichever side won in Quebec, it was going to be a close call, decided by a few percentage points. But then the Yes campaign in Quebec began to unravel.

The biggest problem was the Agreement itself. The Québécois had been prepared for some kind of serious resolution after Meech and were awaiting a referendum on renewed federalism or sovereignty. During the year prior to Charlottetown, more than 500,000 Québécois had signed a petition insisting that Bourassa hold such a referendum as promised. Thanks to the Allaire and Bélanger-Campeau reports, the Québécois had very definite ideas about what acceptable renewed federalism entailed, ideas that bordered on a popular consensus. When Bourassa agreed to go back to the table to negotiate the Charlottetown Agreement and then announced success, there was an initial misperception on the part of many Québécois. Obviously, they reasoned, Bourassa must have obtained something significant in the Agreement. Hence, the early September polls showed that slight two-point lead in public support in Quebec. But as soon as the Agreement was subjected to analysis, support began to collapse. The distinct society clause in the Charlottetown Agreement was weaker than it had been in the Meech Lake Accord. The Senate was still unacceptable. There was no new division of powers acceptable to Quebec. There was no clear veto, especially over the creation of new provinces.

As well, Bourassa's arguments for the deal were half-hearted and defensive. On one occasion he compared the deal to a lottery consolation prize: "*L'entente est comme un prix de consolation, acceptez-la et prenez des billets pour le prochain tirage.*" Or, he argued, it was better to accept the deal than to fight on: "*Ce n'est pas la perfection. Mais, c'est mieux que l'affrontement, les tensions et le recul.*" Or, as he once conceded in English, "It is not an absolutely extraordinary deal," though "there are substantial gains there for Quebec." Even the Yes slogan in Quebec suggested satisfactory resolution was put off for now: "*L'avenir commence par un Oui.*" Certainly, Bourassa participated in Clark and Mulroney's

The Charlottetown Referendum 161

scare tactics. Yet, his active defence of the deal itself was clearly tempered by the deal's self-evident flaws from the point of view of the Québécois.

The No campaign in Quebec was determined to make the deal itself the battleground and resisted all efforts to shift the terrain to other issues such as the contention that a No vote equalled a vote for sovereignty or that the political and economic consequences of a No vote would be disastrous. At one point, Parizeau said, "I won't discuss sovereignty. I'm discussing the constitutional proposal we have before us." The No slogan also zeroed in on the deal: "*A ce prix-là, c'est Non!*" The No side's approach was to lay the Charlottetown Agreement out like a corpse on a slab and to engage in a clinical dissection in full public view. Significantly, the first copies the Québécois received of a full text were distributed by the No campaign machine, with critical comments and remarks written on the margins throughout. From the outset, the No campaign saw the deal as its biggest asset and insisted on keeping the public's attention focused on the details.

Events at the Quebec Liberal convention on 29 August 1992 only confirmed the flaws in the Agreement. The resolution approved by the convention clearly damned the deal with faint praise: "That the Quebec Liberal Party recognizes that…the agreement…while beneath the party's program, represents a genuine progress that is concurrent with Quebec's traditional demands." The convention, which was open to all individual Liberals who happened to show up, was stacked with busloads of loyalists, including many non-francophone Québécois. It was widely acknowledged that there had been a brisk last-minute sale of memberships in the party. In protest, Mario Dumont, the leader of the Liberal youth wing, walked out of the convention and was followed by a few dozen youth delegates. Only later was it clear that he indeed represented the overwhelming majority sentiment among Quebec's young people. And when Jean Allaire, the author of the famous party report on the constitution, voted against the resolution and then later formally joined the No side, a large bloc of Quebec nationalist Liberals joined him. By the time Allaire had finished his quiet but lethally effective No campaign within the Liberal party, more than seventy local executive members had resigned. When Allaire earnestly said, "the offers…received amount to nothing less than a surrender by Quebec," people who would not give Parizeau or Bouchard the time of day listened.

The impact of close public scrutiny of the deal and the events at the Liberal convention were enough to turn the tide against it. In the early polls, there had been a large bloc of undecideds, but in the ensuing weeks, the undecideds began to break for the No side as the Yes campaign in Quebec stumbled from one disaster to another.

One of the disasters was *l'affaire Wilhelmy*, which dominated the campaign in Quebec for a crucial period and lingered like a bad aftertaste until voting day. The controversy helped kill any hope the Yes forces had of rallying its rapidly dwindling public support in a final push. At the centre was a tape of an electronically intercepted cellular telephone conversation between Diane Wilhelmy, Quebec's Deputy Minister of Intergovernmental Affairs, and André Tremblay, Bourassa's top constitutional advisor. Wilhelmy had been absent from the Charlottetown negotiations due to ill health, while Tremblay had attended.

Intercepted just days after the Agreement was concluded, the call caught Quebec's two top constitutional advisors commiserating with each other about the deal. They agreed it was a disaster for Quebec and that Bourassa had been an ineffective and weak negotiator, abandoning Quebec's traditional demands, collapsing under the relentless pressure from the English-Canadian delegations and finally settling for far less than was defensible. In the course of the negotiations, Bourassa had ignored all the advice given him and agreed to a flawed package for no other reason than he was desperate to obtain a deal to present to the people of Quebec.

Though the economic scare tactics of the prime minister at Sherbrooke were at least partly designed to divert attention from *l'affaire Wilhelmy* and to stop the slide in the polls for the Yes side, Trudeau's 1 October intervention was more effective than anyone expected. But in Quebec, where Trudeau's constitutional views were old news, the biggest impact of his speech was not his detailed analysis of the deal but rather his attack on the economic scare tactics. For a former prime minister of some stature, and one who himself had not hesitated to raise the economic issue when debating Quebec's sovereignty, to stand up in public and call the prime minister and the leading bankers of Canada liars was a strong antidote. The Yes team had anticipated Trudeau's constitutional criticisms, were prepared for them and answered them quickly. But they did not expect that Trudeau would sandbag them with such a frank and frontal assault on the economic scare theme, a theme they had intended to make a central focus of their campaign.

The final blow was delivered in the 16 October edition of *L'Actualité*, which obtained, from an unnamed source, a collection of Quebec government briefing documents for the Ottawa and Charlottetown meetings. These documents were highly confidential, normally secured in a locked safe. The documents filled in all the details and dramatically confirmed the earlier tantalizingly scant, but highly suggestive, telephone conversation between Wilhelmy and Tremblay. Bourassa had agreed to a deal that both surrendered Quebec's historical demands and succumbed to "domineering federalism." The deal repudiated Quebec as one of Canada's founding nations, shackled Quebec with the equality-of-provinces provision and denied Quebec any form of special status. The deal contained far less than Meech, since the distinct society clause had been made trivial and virtually useless legally. The deal allowed even more intrusions by Ottawa into Quebec's affairs via the many administrative agreements to be negotiated under the Charlottetown Agreement. The documents revealed a certain envy that English Canada, with Bourassa's agreement, had allowed the aboriginal people to make great gains in achieving many of Quebec's basic constitutional objectives, including a clearly demarcated order of government with special status and a clear veto over constitutional changes affecting them. Since it was a province, therefore subject to the equality-of-provinces doctrine, and with the diminished distinct society clause, Quebec was denied these gains. The documents advised that the Agreement would lead to "perpetual negotiations." Finally, it was confirmed that Bourassa's minimal demands for additional powers had been flatly rejected by the English-Canadian first ministers, reinforcing the statements made by Wells, Sihota and Filmon.

The effect was devastating. Despite efforts by Bourassa to dismiss the documents as "anonymous allegations," and Mulroney to rant about "idiocies and absurdities regarding certain negotiations" while defending Bourassa as "a remarkable Premier," the blow was fatal. Given the previous high levels of No support, defeat of the Agreement in Quebec was already virtually assured. The publication of the documents in *L'Actualité* simply removed any hope of a comeback for the Yes side. Gallup carried out its last pre-vote poll from 15 to 19 October. Not only did the poll suggest the Agreement was going down to heavy defeat in the West, but Yes and No were also tied in Ontario. Only Atlantic Canada remained firmly Yes. In Quebec, the No side was leading by an astonishing twenty-eight points (58 to 30 per cent) with only 12 per cent undecided.

On 26 October 1992, 75 per cent of Canada's 18.5 million eligible voters rendered their final judgement on the Charlottetown Agreement, including 83 per cent of Quebec's 4.9 million voters. Turnout in English Canada ranged from a low of 54 per cent in Newfoundland to a high of 76 per cent in British Columbia. Nationally, it was a decisive No victory, 55 to 45 per cent, excluding spoiled ballots. In Quebec, the No victory, at 57 to 43 per cent, was substantial but failed to exceed the strongest No votes in English Canada. In British Columbia, No carried 68 per cent, in Manitoba 62 per cent and in Alberta 60 per cent. The No side carried six provinces, including the four western provinces, Quebec, and, by a narrow margin, Nova Scotia (51 to 49 per cent). The Yes carried four provinces. The deal was given strong approval in Newfoundland (63 per cent), Prince Edward Island (74 per cent) and New Brunswick (62 per cent), and was passed by a narrow margin in Ontario — a mere 12,000 votes of the 4.8 million cast. The North was split, with the Yukon voting No and the Northwest Territories voting Yes. It was a decisive, irreversible defeat of the Agreement, forcing the Yes team to abandon the last hope of some premiers for salvaging parts of the deal under the 7/50 rule. If Yes had won in seven provinces, representing more than 50 per cent of the population, those elements of the agreement not requiring unanimity could be passed. The magnitude of the defeat firmly foreclosed such a controversial temptation.

For a large group of Canadians the No vote was a vote *for* the Charter and the protections it provides individual Canadians. For another large group of Canadians the No vote was a vote *for* a strong central government, *for* national social programs with national standards and *against* the devolution of too much power to the provinces. Together these two groups probably accounted for the biggest single bloc of No voters in English Canada with as many as 37 per cent of English Canadians voting No, according to the Decima poll done on voting day. The Charter and the strong central government and social programs arguments had been central to the failure of Meech.

The Charlottetown Agreement was presented to the Québécois as English Canada's final offer of renewed federalism. Bourassa, Mulroney and Clark, together with the English-Canadian premiers, made that repeatedly clear. If the Québécois rejected the deal, they were warned, there would be no repetition, and no return to the table, and the thirty-one gains for Quebec would be lost. It was a dangerous and risky game — final-offer politics always is — because there was no fallback position. When the Québécois answered with, as Parizeau described it, "the No that ends all Nos," it was for very clearly stated reasons. The final offer was not good enough. The Agreement was a poor deal because Quebec did not obtain the minimum the Québécois demanded in order to secure their nation. As Allaire put it on 26 October 1992, "We know what we want, so stop trying to sell us something else."

A disturbingly significant portion of the No vote in English Canada was clearly a vote against Quebec. Throughout the campaign this was clear, particularly in the West, and most especially in British Columbia and Alberta. A poll conducted by Angus Reid/Southam in mid-October found that 40 per cent of English Canadians believed Quebec got too much, registering strong opposition to "too much power" for Quebec, the 25 per cent seat guarantee and distinct society status. Eighty-one per cent believed that if they voted Yes, Quebec would proceed to escalate its demands. Polling in British Columbia found the same attitudes, even more strongly expressed. Polls also found strong currents of western anger over the perception that the western premiers had betrayed their commitment to a truly Triple-E Senate by yielding to Quebec's sabotage. Much of this, quite simply, was rooted in bigotry and ignorance. After campaigning in the West, Mulroney's government house leader, Harvie Andre, expressed surprise at how many people he found who "hate French and French-Canadians," and that he found "more bigotry and hatred than I thought existed." A significant portion of the No vote in English Canada, then, was opposed to any concessions to Quebec, regardless of the consequences. And now that stream of English-Canadian politics had a political vehicle in the Reform Party and had been legitimized as never before as a result of the referendum.

* * *

The day after the results were in, Parizeau claimed the No vote in Quebec meant that the Québécois had returned, after a detour, to the "highway to sovereignty." He went on, "Canadian politicians tried to reconcile the irreconcilable, and it didn't work. And from both sides we told them it will never work." Bouchard said, perhaps more hopefully, "There were two roads for Quebeckers before the referendum — profoundly renewed federalism and sovereignty. These two options must now find a convergence."

8

The 1993 Federal Election

The defeat of the Charlottetown Agreement ruined a variety of individual political careers and contributed to the collapse of both the Tories and New Democrats federally. The referendum battle catapulted the Reform party in the West and the Bloc Québécois in Quebec into regional and thus national prominence, transforming Preston Manning overnight from a right-wing crank into a self-styled contender for prime minister and Lucien Bouchard from a relatively unknown cabinet minister into a central actor shaping the future of Canada. Ironically, a large role in shaping the destiny of Canada was thereby placed in the hands of two political leaders both hostile to what Canada had become, with contradictory views on the place of Quebec in Confederation. Preston Manning's "New Canada" had no place for a "special status" Quebec; Manning insisted that Quebec submit to the equality-of-provinces doctrine. Lucien Bouchard saw no future for Quebec in Canada in the absence of some kind of "sovereignty/new partnership" formula.

The first and most prominent casualty of Charlottetown was the prime minister. Though Brian Mulroney's support had collapsed long before the Charlottetown vote and his personal unpopularity helped ensure the Agreement's defeat, his fate, like that of Quebec premier Robert Bourassa, was inextricably linked to a resolution of the Quebec question. Mulroney's promise to bring Quebec back into the Canadian constitutional fold with "honour and enthusiasm" had set the stage for the de facto alliance with Québécois nationalists in his 1984 sweep. Furthermore, his efforts to salvage Meech won the continuing support of Québécois nationalists in 1988, an election he would have lost without Quebec. Although the Québécois nationalist pillar of Mulroney's unprecedented electoral alliance had begun to crumble, first with the defection of Bouchard and then very quickly with the failure of Meech, the success of Charlottetown remained his last desperate hope.

And it was certainly a desperate hope. Mulroney's determination to cling to office despite plummeting support became increasingly pathetic. He clearly waited to be driven out by negative public opinion. By the time Mulroney announced his resignation on 24 February 1993, his approval rating had remained at or below 21 per cent for three full years before it fell like a stone to 14 per cent after Charlottetown. No incumbent prime minister had been so reviled in Canadian history. By 1991, Tory support in Quebec had sunk to 16 per cent according to Gallup, while Bouchard's Bloc Québécois had reached 42 per cent. And while Mulroney's Quebec supporters were defecting and stampeding to the Bloc, his support among Tory westerners, the other pillar of his electoral alliance, also fell, though not as precipitously; much of it went to Preston Manning and the Reform party.

Canadians turned against Brian Mulroney because of his policies and their effect on Canada. His loyal efforts to implement a corporate agenda were disastrous. His attacks on social spending placed Canada's social, education and health infrastructures at serious risk and established in their stead a harsh, social Darwinist, two-tiered system of access: one for the rich and another for the poor. His programs of privatization and deregulation crippled the national transportation system and put the public at risk in the air, while loosening the legislated bonds of social responsibility on corporate behaviour in a variety of areas, from drugs to the environment to advertising. Tax relief for both the rich and the corporate sectors, combined with his regressive taxation attack on ordinary Canadians dependent on wages and salaries, embittered middle Canada and set the stage for a mass, anti-government tax revolt carefully orchestrated by the business lobby. The free trade initiatives, which had only marginal public support, were economically catastrophic for the Canadian economy and Canadian wage earners, sending the country into a downward spiral of accelerating de-industrialization. In addition, Mulroney's clumsy constitutional initiatives deepened the chasm between English Canada and Quebec and led to the emergence of the Bloc Québécois. He deliberately weakened federal power, encouraged the centrifugal assertion of provincial rights and left Canada with a federal government incapable of governing, thus depriving the people of the instrumentality of a democratic state that could defend them from unrestrained corporate power in an unregulated global market. Victory in the Charlottetown referendum would not have saved Mulroney, but its defeat made his departure from politics before another federal election a foregone conclusion.

The late Robert Bourassa might have stayed on as Quebec premier after Charlottetown to seek vindication had he not been diagnosed with skin cancer in 1990. Bourassa's declining health led to his decision to leave politics, a decision he did not announce until 14 September 1993 in the midst of the federal election campaign. Yet the evidence is clear that even the old master, now federalist/ now nationalist Bourassa, would have had to overcome enormous obstacles in order to win another term in the wake of Charlottetown. The image of the premier caving in to federal pressure, selling out Quebec's historic demands and desperate for any deal in order to avoid a referendum on sovereignty left a bad aftertaste in Quebec. The Quebec Liberals were trailing behind the Parti Québécois in the polls. The nationalist members of the Liberal Party had either left to fight the Charlottetown Agreement or had been ejected from any positions of influence. The two most influential disaffected nationalist Liberals, Jean Allaire and Mario Dumont, had declared their intention to launch a new political movement, which was formally registered with Quebec's Chief Electoral Officer on 19 January 1994 as l'Action démocratique du Québec. The Bourassa government had adopted Bill 86 legalizing bilingual commercial signs in June 1993, amid growing concerns about the security of the French language, which, when combined with the government's notorious failure to enforce existing language laws vigorously, made the government increasingly vulnerable to attacks by the Parti Québécois. Events since the Quebec Liberal convention to approve the Charlottetown Agreement had placed the hard federalist wing firmly in charge of the party and the government. Consequently, in the next Quebec election the Liberal government would be forced to champion existing federal arrangements with no clear alternative. In such a context, Bourassa's typical equivocation on the national question, his maybe-yes maybe-no approach to Quebec and the constitution, was unlikely to succeed. Had Bourassa been healthy, it is hard to imagine a scenario in which he could have won another term.

The true extent of the deep malaise of the Quebec Liberal Party became clear after Bourassa's resignation. No one wanted the job of premier except Daniel Johnson, destined to repeat the fate of his brother, Pierre-Marc Johnson; that is, a brief career as unelected premier followed by defeat at the polls. This reluctance was understandable. The Liberals continued to trail the PQ in the polls, especially among francophone Québécois voters. Two-thirds of voters were dissatisfied with the Bourassa government's perform-ance. One-half the cabinet and many backbenchers declared an intention to leave politics. As a result of Charlottetown's failure, the Quebec Liberal Party had no clearly defined election platform and no constitutional package to replace the defeated Agreement. The absence of the usually vigorous nationalist wing left the party stag-nant and bereft of ideas. Even Johnson's over-eagerness for the post failed to flush out an alternative, despite the fact that he had run a poor third out of three when he last went for the leadership in 1983 and was widely seen as anti-labour, pro-big business, strongly in favour of status quo federalism and harshly neo-conservative. In addition to these weaknesses, Johnson lacked basic political skills, suggesting that the party had already resigned itself to defeat in the next election and could not, therefore, find another candidate as an alternative. Consequently, there was no leadership contest and Daniel Johnson was quietly acclaimed as Quebec Liberal leader at a party executive meeting on 14 December 1993. On 11 January 1994, with only eight months remaining in his mandate, he was sworn in as premier of Quebec.

No one had anticipated the extent of the negative conse-quences of the referendum loss in the upcoming federal election, constitutionally required in the fall of 1993. The federal Liberals remained somewhat immune from these negative consequences, except in Quebec, largely because neither the Liberals nor their leader, Jean Chrétien, had played a central role in Charlottetown. In addition, many prominent Liberals, such as Pierre Trudeau and those who followed his lead, had attacked Charlottetown and urged a No vote. But the chief political architects of the Agree-ment, the Tories and the New Democrats, suffered terribly.

Granted, long before the Charlottetown referendum, the Tory ship of state was foundering, clearly a defeated government going through the motions, clinging to office to the end of its constitu-tional mandate, driven on by a desperate prime minister. The top Tories in the government knew this best of all — all the polls, both private internal polls and very public polls, carried the same mes-sage of a terrible, unavoidable defeat. The Charlottetown referendum transformed certain humiliation into virtual annihila-tion. The extent to which Tory insiders expected defeat was clear from the moment Mulroney announced his resignation. Not a single front-bencher wanted his job, and even experienced ministers in the second row ran for cover. Mulroney himself, having already promoted Kim Campbell's candidacy, begged a number of prominent cabinet colleagues to run, without success. Having failed in the obvious choices, Mulroney then pleaded with Bernard Valcourt and Jean Charest. He failed to convince Valcourt, and it took two hours of charming wheedling at 24 Sussex Drive to persuade Charest; the clinching argument was Charest's future ambition. By the end of Mulroney's efforts, only two cabinet ministers and three back-benchers had agreed to stand. This was not the leadership race one would have expected in a party that believed that there was the slightest chance of victory.

The leading contender, Defence Minister Kim Campbell, was indecorous in her hunger for higher office and blithely unaware she was about to share the fate of her former colleague Rita Johnson (who was devoured at the polls in 1991 for B.C. premier Bill Vander Zalm's sins). Campbell's record inspired little confidence, although desperation among Tories and copy hunger among journalists gave her a brief boost. Campbell had been in public office since 1980, when she secured a seat on the Vancouver Public School Board as part of a right-wing slate. In the 1987 provincial election she won a seat in the Legislature but Premier Vander Zalm placed her firmly on the back benches where she languished only briefly. Campbell then secured the Tory nomination for Vancouver Centre and won a close victory in 1988. From there she caught the prime minister's favourable notice and glided easily to prominence, starting out as junior minister for Indian affairs, then justice minister and finally defence minister. Her record in the cabinet was not impressive. Her shifty position on negotiating Indian land claims, which was opposed in British Columbia and supported in Ottawa, undermined her credibility. As justice minister she executed a number of astonishing policy reversals. A self-declared pro-choicer, she tried to recriminalize abortion. After the Montreal massacre of fourteen female university students in 1989, she became a passionate public advocate of gun control, while privately caving into the right-wing gun lobby by producing a law that was mostly public relations fluff. But perhaps the greatest disappointment was Campbell's record in defence, which alone should have barred the road to the prime ministership. After the loss of the Soviet menace and calls on all sides for a peace agenda involving deep reductions in military spending, Campbell became one of the new warhawks (carefully coached and tutored by senior military officers). At first she favoured spending billions on military helicopters; then, as a candidate facing public crankiness about such profligacy in hard times, she discovered reasons to rethink the helicopters, finally cutting seven at a savings of a billion dollars. In addition, her clumsy handling of the cover-ups in Somalia where Canadian soldiers were accused of homicide raised doubts about her fitness for high office.

Nipping at Campbell's heels, Jean Charest hoped to convince Canadians that his main claims to fame were youthful exuberance and fluent bilingualism. First elected in 1984 at the age of twenty-five, he was elevated to the safe post of minister of youth and sport in 1986, giving him a lot of politically neutral public exposure. Charest's first misstep was telephoning a Quebec Superior Court judge. Unfortunately, the judge was about to render a decision in a case of a track-and-field coach who had been cashiered from Team Canada and was suing for reinstatement. The judge wisely refused to talk to the brash upstart and blew the whistle. Charest at first denied any wrongdoing. Only after a heart-to-heart with his mentor, Brian Mulroney, did he admit a serious violation of the cabinet's code of conduct. Cabinet ministers are not supposed to interfere in judicial proceedings. In January 1990, Charest resigned in disgrace.

In April 1990, Mulroney gave Charest a chance at redemption, naming him to chair the special Commons committee to save the tattered Meech Lake Accord. The committee's hearings exploded in Charest's face in Saskatchewan when some members accused him of weeding out and harassing Meech opponents trying to appear before the committee in public sessions. When Charest presented his hurried report on 16 May 1990, Meech began its final unravelling. Charest proposed a series of additions to the Accord, which satisfied few in English Canada but deeply angered many Québécois due to a weakening of the distinct society clause. The day after the report was tabled, a Quebec Tory MP quit the caucus in disgust. The next day, Quebec premier Bourassa flatly rejected the proposals. On the fifth day, Lucien Bouchard, then still Mulroney's Quebec protégé and lieutenant, resigned from cabinet and, on the sixth day, from the Tory caucus. By the end of June 1990, eight Tory MPs had quit over Charest's compromise. The next month the Bloc Québécois was founded. Charest's role in these events had largely disappeared from public view, to his evident relief. He was, however, rewarded by Mulroney, who welcomed him back in the cabinet as minister of the environment. Nevertheless, it is clear that Charest shares in the dubious honour of having played a key role in provoking the chain of events that led to the emergence of the Bloc Québécois, the first Quebec separatist party successful in federal politics in Canadian history.

Given the records of the two top contenders for leadership of the Conservatives, it was clear why Chrétien kept smiling even as the interest in the Tory race created upward blips in the polls. The Liberal machine, in the House and on the hustings, would eat the lightweight Kim Campbell or Jean Charest for breakfast. Nevertheless, some Tories were hopeful that Campbell — a fresh face, a woman, a westerner, a relative outsider rather than a member of the elite old guard — could turn things around. By April 1993, Tory support, though still seven points behind the Liberals, had reached its highest point in four years, with all other parties down significantly. Forty-four per cent of Canadians now believed Campbell would make the best prime minister, twice the percentage that supported Jean Chrétien.

It was these polls, as well as a series of internal polls and encounter group results, that persuaded delegates to select Campbell as leader at the June 1993 convention. Campbell, the early darling of the media and the prime minister himself, spent more than four million dollars to win the leadership (twice the amount spent by Charest). Even so, as a result of a poor performance in her speeches at the convention and growing doubts about her ability and depth among many, she was almost defeated by Charest.

The federal NDP's fall from grace began with the Charlottetown Agreement. Despite ranging in the polls from 20 to 40 per cent from 1984 to 1992 and doing very well in 1988, the federal NDP effectively committed political suicide by supporting rather than opposing the Agreement. In June 1992, Gallup reported the federal NDP enjoyed the support of 21 per cent of voters. By October 1992, that figure had fallen to 18 per cent and by the next month, to 14 per cent. By April 1993, the NDP appeared to have bottomed out at 13 per cent, still a respectable number and still well ahead of Reform. But the federal NDP also had to contend with the growing disappointment with the social and fiscal policies of the three NDP provincial governments which, when combined with disillusionment over Charlottetown, was undermining the party alarmingly. All three NDP governments — Rae in Ontario, Harcourt in British Columbia and Romanow in Saskatchewan — had been explicitly elected on platform promises to combat and reverse the neo-conservative agenda. All three failed to do so, instead joining the neo-conservative consensus and insisting that debt and deficit reduction and program cuts, rather than economic stimulation, tax reform and an expansion of the social security net, were essential. As a result, all three provincial NDP governments lost significant support, especially the Rae government in Ontario where the NDP quickly fell to third place in the polls.

Federal NDP leader Audrey McLaughlin then compounded this loss by making another serious error. On 29 April 1993, McLaughlin fired Ontario NDP MP Steven Langdon as House finance critic when he publicly criticized the Rae government's draconian attack on the deficit and the debt with massive cuts in spending on public sector programs and jobs. Langdon, acutely aware of the collapse of NDP support, realized some distance was needed between the federal party and the NDP premiers. His criticisms were not the uncontrolled outburst of a wounded ideologue. Rather, they constituted an astute effort to salvage the party's future in the looming federal election. As point man taking the flak, he provided McLaughlin a perfect opportunity to step in as federal leader to place a more diplomatic version of the same message at the centre of Canada's political debate. Langdon's public intervention, which understandably angered premiers Rae, Romanow and Harcourt, provided McLaughlin with an opportunity to strut her prime-ministerial stuff. She could have swivelled her guns on the Mulroney/Campbell government, denouncing Ottawa for forcing the provinces to the wall by cuts in federal funding. She could have commiserated with the NDP premiers, the junior partners in a Tory-driven executive federalism, who did not have the fiscal and economic powers needed to do what social democrats would like to do and would do when federal power was won. She could have complained that, while she didn't much like what the NDP premiers were doing and she certainly wouldn't take any cues from them as prime minister, she understood why they might feel forced to do such distasteful things under fiscal pressure from Tory Ottawa. She did none of these things. Instead, McLaughlin blasted Langdon, sided firmly with the NDP premiers, and once again, just as during the Charlottetown debate, exposed herself as a captive of her party's provincial premiers. McLaughlin stumbled badly, forgetting that all Canadians — even Canadians who support social democracy — expect federal leaders aspiring to the highest office in the land to speak for all of Canada, not to be, or even to appear to be, captives of provincial politicians.

Justifying Langdon's firing on 29 April 1993, McLaughlin said, "I don't think there's anyone in Canada, in any province, in any territory, or indeed federally, who doesn't believe that we have to be conservative in the sense of addressing the budget and the deficit." Her observation gave aid and comfort to the NDP's business enemies. The NDP's major roadblock in its drive for electoral success had always been a public perception of the party as ineffective managers of the economy, a perception created and sustained by the business lobby and the media. By firing Langdon and by her fateful words, McLaughlin inadvertently fed that perception. The business lobby and its loyal columnists delighted in suggesting the episode again revealed the NDP as woolly-headed and idealistic in opposition, while facing internal difficulty doing the right and necessary thing in power. Therefore, the media suggested the Langdon/Rae/McLaughlin episode revealed the reality and discipline of power rather than emphasizing the fundamental differences either in federal/provincial powers or between social democracy and neo-conservatism. Thus, the attention of the media and the public was effectively deflected from the federal NDP's strong economic policies, unveiled in February 1993, involving massive taxation reform, deep cuts in defence spending and an ambitious job-creation program in both public and private sectors through a national investment fund and public infrastructure renewal. Instead, the message to an already cynical and disillusioned public was and remained that there was no alternative and the business lobby was in command, even if the NDP won power. Had Audrey McLaughlin and her federal caucus stood up to the three NDP premiers during Charlottetown and said No, had she moved behind Langdon both to put his comments in the context of federal/provincial differences in power and to distinguish herself from the fiscal neo-conservatism of the NDP premiers, the federal NDP's standing in the polls might have been very different in the spring, summer and fall of 1993. But she did not, and as a result support for the federal NDP collapsed to 8 per cent, threatening the party with its worst defeat since the Diefenbaker sweep of 1958.

On 8 September, when Prime Minister Campbell finally set the date for 25 October 1993, there began, in effect, two election campaigns, one in English Canada and one in Quebec. While English Canada debated the record of the Mulroney years and argued about who would be the best prime minister and which party would be the best for government, the people of Quebec argued about whether it was worth sending anyone but sovereigntists to Ottawa to represent their interests to prepare the ground for Quebec's final future exit from Canada. Initial theories that voters in Quebec were just "parking" their votes with the Bloc very quickly evaporated as support for that party not only held firm but increased as the campaign unfolded.

The day Campbell called the election, an Environics poll reported that the Tories and Liberals were virtually tied. That poll was the peak for the Tories; afterward it was all downhill. Campbell became a loose cannon whose verbal gaffes destroyed the Tory campaign from the outset. Despite the fact that 71 per cent of Canadians saw job creation as more important than the deficit, Campbell relentlessly made deficit reduction the major focus of her campaign, promising to get it to zero in five years, a truly astonishing goal. Pressed for details on how this was to be done, especially on the costs of cuts in government spending, Campbell insisted she was "showing reality to the country." When pressed to respond to Canadian anxieties about unemployment and jobs, she bluntly declared that there were bleak prospects for any improvement in unemployment until the next century. As a result, she came across as arrogant, harsh and uncaring.

As the campaign continued, Campbell was repeatedly questioned about the link between possible cuts to social programs and deficit reduction. In exasperation she blurted out the words that were to become fatal for her campaign: "You can't have a debate on such a key issue as the modernization of social programs in forty-seven days," referring to the election campaign's duration. When further pressed for details, she began to get visibly annoyed and accused the media of badgering her and failing to deliver her real campaign messages clearly and fairly. "I'll throw myself across the railway tracks to protect the system [of social programs]," she insisted.

The final blow to her campaign was the decision to use ads that attacked Chrétien personally, making fun of his appearance and speech and asking Canadians if they wanted such a man as their prime minister. Campbell denied knowledge of the ads before they were broadcast and pulled them off the air immediately, apologizing, but it was too late. Her "doing politics differently" claim became a public joke, and more and more references linked her to Mulroney and his style and record.

Allan Gregg, the Tory pollster, reported that in the week after the social policy blunder their rolling polls recorded a twelve-point drop and that the day the attack ads were broadcast was followed by the Tories' worst night in the polls. By late September, the Tories were behind the Liberals by seven points, by mid-October by eighteen points and by 21 October, four days before the election, by twenty-eight points. Early talk of a minority government had given way to talk of a Liberal majority and concerns about whether the Tories would hold the twelve seats necessary to retain party status in the House of Commons.

The Liberals were able to manipulate events to their advantage during the campaign. Having read the polls carefully, the party tailored its campaign to address Canadians' economic anxieties and anger about Mulroney's neo-conservative agenda and its consequences. The Liberals' Red Book carried messages of hope, of turning the corner, of reversing the neo-conservative agenda and of returning to a strong, caring and interventionist central government. This persuasive package of promises was summed up in the Red Book as follows: "For far too many Canadians, after nine years of Conservative government, [the Canadian] dream has turned into a nightmare. Our economy is in disarray....Over a million Canadian children live in poverty. Many of our national institutions have been shaken. Our cultural and social fabric has been weakened....[H]ope for tomorrow has turned into fear of the future....For Canadians, the next election is about one simple question: what kind of country do we want for ourselves and our children?"

Everywhere Chrétien went he waved the Red Book and repeated its promises, which had been carefully crafted to be vague and general. But the Liberals did not need to stick to their script, as Campbell's campaign gaffes gave them all the ammunition they needed. As Chrétien quipped when asked how late he had to stay up at night to prepare for the following day's campaign events, "I just go to bed and have a good night's sleep. Then I read the paper in the morning about Ms. Campbell and I have enough for the whole day." When pressed on the deficit, Chrétien attacked the Tory numbers and said he was also concerned about the deficit and would address it in a careful and responsible way, but creating jobs and turning the economy around were more important and would be the best thing for the deficit in the long run. In response to Campbell's social policy blunder, Chrétien exploited the opening to the hilt: "It's unbelievable that she doesn't want to discuss the serious issues of the nation during the election. Tell me when we would be able to discuss it? What is the hidden agenda?" When told about Campbell's remark about throwing herself on the tracks to save social programs, Chrétien retorted that such a promise was "very easy when you have closed down all the railways." On free trade, which a strong majority of Canadians still opposed, he promised renegotiation and a refusal to sign the North American Free Trade Agreement (NAFTA) unless significant changes were made. He would get rid of the GST and bring in a fair tax system. In fact, just as Trudeau had in 1968 and 1974, Chrétien shrewdly wrote off the right, over which the Tories and Reformers were fighting, and went after the traditional Liberal centrist base, sidling left to woo the NDP's electoral base. For forty-seven days, Jean Chrétien sounded like a moderate and committed social democrat, slightly to the left of Bob Rae and Roy Romanow, with no hint that after the election he would become a passionate advocate of the neo-conservative business agenda.

The NDP was squeezed out in the election. The party's position on Charlottetown and the record of the three NDP premiers resulted in a sense of betrayal among supporters. The party couldn't get the troops out and money was hard to come by. It was squeezed by the Liberals, who had quickly occupied traditional NDP territory, stealing much of the rhetoric of the NDP's February 1993 economic program and presenting themselves as front-line fighters against the neo-conservative agenda. And it was squeezed by the Reform party, which had replaced the NDP for many westerners as the region's defender and champion in national affairs. Even at the start of the campaign, the NDP had bottomed out at 8 per cent, falling further to 7 per cent in the last poll before the election. McLaughlin's campaign was like a funeral procession; few came to meetings, the media lost interest, the door-to-door canvass faltered and the NDP had largely ceased to be a factor in the national election. One reporter complained that covering the party was "like watching a dog die." In response to the crisis, the entire NDP campaign was devoted to holding enough of its traditional seats in order to cling to party status in the House. To do this McLaughlin embarked on a last-minute effort to beg for support in order to keep a Liberal majority government honest, focusing exclusively on saving medicare and fighting free trade.

The Reform party had been on a roll since the Charlottetown referendum, and that roll continued throughout the election campaign. Starting the campaign in September with 13 per cent of decided voters, Reform finished four days before the election with 19 per cent, still largely concentrated in Alberta and B.C. Reform's campaign focused on increasing the western right-wing base that the party had already stolen from the Tories. Reform proposed draconian measures to reduce the deficit to zero in three years and to enact punitive and conservative social policy reform. The party struggled to maintain its breakthrough as the champion of the West and of common sense, with its widespread use of shallow populist rhetoric and appeals to break with the "old line" parties, which now included the NDP. Reform, unfettered by running candidates in Quebec, also continued to appeal to the anti-Quebec stream in English-Canadian politics. It attacked bilingualism, condemned the separatists in Quebec, repeatedly and ominously raised Chrétien's Quebec roots and warned that only a large group of Reform MPs could prevent the Bloc and the Liberals under Chrétien from negotiating a new pro-Quebec constitutional package or developing unfair programs to again pander to Quebec, Confederation's "spoiled child."

The 1993 federal election in Quebec seemed eerily unaffected by the campaign in English Canada. The basic issue was whether Quebec representatives in Ottawa should continue to participate seriously in governing the federation or should work diligently to accelerate separation. Ever since the separatist/sovereigntist option successfully emerged in 1966 as a serious democratic choice in Quebec, it had been clear that to be taken seriously politically and constitutionally, sovereigntists must win significant support in federal elections. The contradiction of electing sovereigntists in provincial elections and strong federalists in federal elections, which had characterized the Lévesque/Trudeau era, had to be resolved. There had been many calls during the years for a revival of a nationalist/sovereigntist federal option in Quebec, inspired by the Bloc Populaire. Many adherents of the Rassemblement pour l'indépendance nationale (RIN) had repeatedly advocated contesting federal elections. After the formation of the PQ, such advocacy increased in intensity, ebbing and flowing with signals from Lévesque and the PQ leadership. One such stillborn effort was the Union Populaire, which gained only a handful of votes in the 1979 and 1980 elections. Immediately after the "night of the long knives" in 1981, Lévesque and the PQ officially supported the formation of the Parti Nationaliste to challenge federal elections. Very soon thereafter, however, Lévesque reversed himself and embarked on *le beau risque* with Mulroney and the Tories. As a result, when Bouchard founded the Bloc Québécois in the wake of the Meech disaster, the political ground was well tilled, the theoretical principles had been repeatedly debated and the tactical and strategic necessity of such an eventual move was widely accepted by sovereigntist intellectuals and activists. Furthermore, when the Bloc began to organize, it already had the PQ's political base and organizational infrastructure, making it possible, almost overnight, to move from a small group of MPs in the House of Commons to a mass party with mass support. Additionally, with support for sovereignty in Quebec soaring in the aftermath of Meech, the Quebec electorate was eager to embrace the sovereigntist option in federal elections.

The reaction of many in English Canada to the founding of the Bloc was often outright hostility and anger. This only served to solidify Bloc support among the Québécois. There was a lot of nonsense about loyalty and disloyalty, particularly when the Bloc dismissed as a technicality the oath newly elected MPs must take in order to take their seats: "I do swear that I will be faithful and bear true allegiance to Her Majesty Queen Elizabeth the Second." Suddenly, the House of Commons and the ranks of newspaper columnists were full of instant constitutional experts insisting that it was not possible for a separatist to take a seat in the House of Commons because an honest separatist could not take such an oath. Reform party MP Deborah Grey led the charge, and many commentators picked it up. One Ottawa historian insisted, "One cannot profess to serve the state while trying to dismantle the state — it is a contradiction." Liberal MP John Nunziata had already set the tone by accusing Bouchard of being a "traitor" and many Reform MPs echoed the sentiment, some even suggesting Bloc MPs should be tried for treason.

Such facile and erroneous opinions only served to inflame the situation while purveying abysmal ignorance about the Canadian parliamentary system. The oath to the Queen, as head of state, implies neither an absolute personal loyalty to her or the Crown, nor an unqualified loyalty to the policies and arrangements of the existing state she symbolizes. Rather, the oath is a declaration that the elected person, on behalf of those he or she represents, will dutifully advise the Queen, and the state she represents, regarding policies to be pursued.[1]

When the election was called, Bloc support in Quebec stood at 45 per cent. In the last poll, four days before the election, that support climbed to 50 per cent. All parties except the Bloc avoided too much talk about constitutional renewal and the problems of national unity. They had surveyed the wreckage of Meech and Charlottetown, seen the polls suggesting the electorate wasn't interested in talk about constitutions, and were aware of the growing anger among a significant minority of English Canadians toward Quebec, an anger fanned repeatedly by the Reform party. Nothing was on offer to Quebec except administrative arrangements and vague promises of general decentralization. Having said loudly that Charlottetown was the final "take it or leave it" offer, the three major parties had no room to manoeuvre. For its part, the Reform party had always staked out the position that Quebec should take or leave the pre-Charlottetown status quo; Reform's "New Canada" involved dismantling many of the concessions made to Quebec and francophones since the Quiet Revolution. As a result, the Bloc had no competition on constitutional matters. The party's message was clear and simple, and the Québécois were receptive. The old domineering federalism hadn't worked for Quebec, and English Canada was not willing to offer any substantial concessions. Therefore, sovereignty and a new negotiated post-sovereignty partnership was the only road open. Bloc MPs would represent and defend Quebec's interests in the Canadian federation while undertaking to work toward a sovereign Quebec.

On other issues the Bloc took positions similar to the NDP and echoed many positions taken by Chrétien and the Liberals: reducing defence spending; protecting social programs, especially medicare and unemployment insurance; and reforming the tax system to make it more just. On economic matters, the Bloc endorsed free trade and advocated a more interventionist role for the government via public investment to create jobs, lower interest rates to stimulate the economy, and programs to enhance competitiveness. On the debt and the deficit, the Bloc agreed on the necessity for reduction, but opposed severe measures that threatened social and health programs, arguing that only a sovereign Quebec would have the tools to deal effectively with the debt and the deficit. On the creation of a strong, globally competitive Quebec economy, the Bloc insisted that sovereignty would lead to a better economic future, freeing Quebec from the shackles of both a dying federalism and a series of disastrously ineffectual national economic strategies.

The alleged merits of sovereignty led to some sharp exchanges during the French-language leaders' debate. Campbell said to Bouchard, "You say you are a separatist. [It's] unacceptable that you should run as a candidate in a federal election." This left an opening for Bouchard that went down well in Quebec: "You're going to refuse to receive Bloc Québécois members in Parliament? Are you going to reject the democratic will expressed by Quebeckers?" In response to Bouchard's attacks on Chrétien's legitimacy as a Quebec leader given Chrétien's record of "betrayals," Chrétien, who was already very low in the polls in Quebec, rose to the bait: "I'm a proud francophone. I'm a proud Quebecker. I'm a proud Canadian. Does this indicate the level of intolerance that would exist in an independent Quebec?" The comment was well-received in English Canada, especially among English Canadians and strong federalists in Quebec, but did little to help Chrétien among the plurality of Quebec voters. The attitudes Chrétien expressed were considered passé within Quebec sovereigntist and nationalist circles. Though the debates had little effect on the overall campaign, within Quebec public perceptions of Bouchard as the "best prime minister" doubled after the debate. By the end of the campaign it was clear that earlier federalist expectations that Bouchard and the Bloc did not have staying power were without foundation.

In March 1993, Gallup had reported that 52 per cent of Canadians wanted a majority government in Ottawa, but 54 per cent anticipated a minority government, most expecting a Liberal minority. Perhaps here we can find part of the reason for the unusual outcome of the 1993 election. Polling figures during the campaign, if projected based on past results, would indeed have produced a Liberal minority. There was clear evidence that the Reform party would do well in the West. As a result of the NDP and the Tories' collapse, the party did even better than expected, winning 24 of 32 seats in British Columbia with 36 per cent of the vote, 22 of 26 seats in Alberta with 52 per cent, and 4 of 14 seats in Saskatchewan with 27 per cent. Reform also picked up one seat in Manitoba and one in Ontario. Particularly gratifying for Reform was their popular vote in Ontario (20 per cent), which suggested they had come within a whisker of breaking out of their western ghetto. Nevertheless, with 51 of 52 seats, and 58 per cent of their total vote concentrated in the four western provinces, the Reform party remained, in reality, a regional protest party. The Bloc also did better than expected in Quebec, winning 54 of 75 seats with just over 49 per cent of the vote, ironically winning the role of Her Majesty's Loyal Opposition in the House of Commons.

The collapse of the Tories and the NDP was worse than expected. The Tories were reduced to two seats, one in New Brunswick and the other in Quebec, and 16 per cent of the national popular vote, the worst defeat of a governing party in Commonwealth history. The NDP, though reduced to 7 per cent of the vote, was able to capture nine seats because its vote was effectively concentrated in the West with one seat in Manitoba, five seats in Saskatchewan, two in British Columbia, and McLaughlin winning her Yukon seat. The collapse of NDP support in British Columbia was spectacular: there the party fell from 37 per cent and nineteen seats in 1988 to 16 per cent and two seats in 1993. The results in Ontario were also crushing: the NDP fell from 20 per cent of the vote and ten seats in 1988 to 6 per cent and no seats in 1993. Significantly, the NDP candidate who did best in Ontario was Steve Langdon, fired by McLaughlin in April for criticizing the Rae government. He won 28 per cent of the vote in his Essex-Windsor seat, outstripping candidates in seats where the NDP vote was traditionally stronger.

The 1993 election is notable for two reasons other than the collapse of the Tories and New Democrats and the rise of Reform and the Bloc. First, the undemocratic nature of Canada's parliamentary system became grotesquely clear. Though winning 16 per cent of the vote, the Tories, with two seats, won less than 1 per cent of seats, rather than a representative share of fifty-one seats (based on assigning seats according to provincial shares of the popular vote). The Bloc, with 13.5 per cent of the vote, should have won thirty-seven seats in a fair and representative system rather than fifty-four. The NDP should have won twenty-eight seats rather than nine with its 7 per cent. Only Reform came close to a representative share of seats, winning 19 per cent of the vote, which should have delivered fifty-four seats rather than the actual fifty-two won by Reform. The clear beneficiaries of Canada's "first past the post" system were Chrétien and the Liberals with 41 per cent of the vote and 177 seats, giving them 60 per cent of the seats and a comfortable majority government (in a fair system the Liberals should have won 124 seats). According to the polls such distortions convinced 45 per cent of Canadians that Canada should move to a proportional system. There was clearly something wrong with an electoral system in which it took an average of 31,000 votes to elect a Liberal MP and more than a million votes to elect a Tory MP, or where a similar level of support led to a triumphant electoral breakthrough for the Bloc and Reform, and near annihilation of the Tories.

The 1993 election is also notable for being arguably the most effective case of spontaneous strategic voting by an electorate in Canadian history. Indeed, this strategic voting helps explain the regional electoral behaviour that contributed to the undemocratic distortions noted above. Prior to the election, Gallup had found that Canadians wanted a majority government, and a month after the election Gallup found that 64 per cent were happy with the result. An examination of the results suggests that many Canadian voters did what they could to give Chrétien and the Liberals a majority. They were aware, and worried, that the Bloc was winning in Quebec and that Reform was doing the same in the West, as well as attracting much of the right-wing, anti-Quebec Tory vote in English Canada generally. Voters in Ontario and Atlantic Canada, in particular, abandoned their traditional electoral loyalties in droves in order to ensure a Liberal victory. Only spontaneous, strategic voting on a mass level can explain the anomaly of the Liberals winning 98 of 99 seats in Ontario with 53 per cent of the vote, and 31 of 32 seats in Atlantic Canada with 57 per cent. Indeed, concerns about a hung parliament, with the Bloc and Reform tearing each other apart, contributed to a Liberal breakthrough in the West — 27 of 86 seats with more than 30 per cent of the vote, an unprecedented result in more than thirty years. Hence, a significant part of the collapse of both the NDP and the Tories, especially in Ontario and the West, can be explained by the migration of large numbers of their traditional supporters to the Liberal Party to ensure a majority government in response to the dual threat posed by the Bloc and Reform.

The Quebec results, however, were of most significance for the future of Canada. A sovereigntist party — with almost 50 per cent of the vote and 54 of 75 seats in Quebec — now represented the Québécois in the House of Commons. The Liberals won nineteen seats with 33 per cent, and the Tories won one seat (Jean Charest) with 13.5 per cent. The Bloc won smashing victories in most seats in which francophones were a strong majority — frequently with majorities of between 55 and 65 per cent. Fourteen of the nineteen Liberal seats were won on the Island of Montreal, resulting from overwhelming support for the Liberals among anglophones and allophones (people whose first language is neither English nor French), often with huge majorities (83 per cent in Mont Royal, 71 per cent in Notre Dame de Grâce, 61 per cent in St. Léonard; and 65 per cent in Pierrefonds-Dollard, for example). In the five Liberal seats won off the Island of Montreal, two were in strong federalist territory (Gatineau-La Lièvre and Hull-Aylmer), one was the prime minister's seat and the other two were tight races with the Bloc. And, of course, Jean Charest easily won his Sherbrooke seat. Bouchard had no doubt about the significance of the Bloc's victory when he said, "A new chapter has been opened. We are going to Ottawa to build something new, something that will prove beneficial to both nations." Other sovereigntists were more blunt. PQ leader Parizeau declared, "Two-thirds of Quebec MPs will now say in unison: 'We want our own country.'...In two years, Quebec will have its own country, Quebec will be sovereign, Quebec will be independent."

English Canadians were generally less than gracious in their response to the Bloc's success, with 56 per cent believing the

Bloc should be denied status as official Opposition in Ottawa (including more than 60 per cent in the West and almost 90 per cent of those who voted Reform). Ontario premier Bob Rae vowed to confront Bouchard: "Here's a guy who wants to break up the country....I think his policies should be confronted at every level. I think he's deluding himself if he thinks that the rest of the country is going to sort of sit back...and accept the breakup of the country. I don't intend to." Rae's comments signalled a series of hostile comments from the premiers of English Canada, most notably the NDP premiers. Such angry reactions, as well as continued sniping about the "treason" of Bouchard and the Bloc, could not, however, erase the ominous significance of the result. Trudeau was well aware of that significance when he said, after voting in an advance poll before leaving for travels in the Far East, "If you weaken the government of Canada, which Bouchard intends [to do], you do no favour to Canadians; you do a favour to those who believe in separatism....Bouchard represents the disintegration of Canada. If that's what they want, they can vote for him." With the election of the Bloc, sovereigntists could now claim to have an overwhelming democratic and constitutional mandate to speak for the people of Quebec in the House of Commons. Success for the PQ in the coming provincial election and a majority vote in a future sovereignty referendum could set the stage for the democratic, peaceful and orderly exit of Quebec from Canada. This was the most significant reality to emerge from the 1993 election — it gave Quebec sovereigntists the biggest positive push in the history of their struggle on the trajectory toward successful separation.

Notes

1. The Magna Carta of 1215 first affirmed that loyalty to the Crown was not unqualified and that the Crown, or the state, was required to abide by the law. The Bill of Rights of 1689, after a bloody civil war, established the supremacy of Parliament over the Crown or the state, leading finally to our form of fully responsible and democratic government. The Queen is head of state and appoints her representative, the Governor General. The cabinet comprises the Governor General's closest advisers and, though technically appointed by him or her, must be nominated by the prime minister and have the confidence of the House of Commons. The House of Commons as a body advises the head of state through the cabi-

net and prime minister. Elected members are obliged to proffer their best advice according to their conscience to ensure good government. The practical reality, by constitutional custom, is that the prime minister is the de facto head of state. The prime minister selects the Governor General, the cabinet and senators. But the prime minister must answer to the House of Commons and, at least every five years, to the people. To say that the MP's oath is an expression of loyalty to the state is in fact to say that the oath is an expression of loyalty to the current prime minister. In a democracy, this is patently untenable, since the prime minister holds office at the pleasure of the House of Commons and, ultimately, the people. Again, we are back to 1689 when, in the aftermath of a civil war and the execution of a king by Parliament, the British Crown itself clearly existed (and exists) at the pleasure of Parliament — Parliament was and is, within the constitution and the common law, supreme. Therefore, when a person is elected a member of Parliament or a provincial legislator, and takes the prescribed oath, he or she merely affirms that he or she will support the constitution and the laws. But in that constitution and in those laws, as well as in the theory and practice of democracy itself, are the necessary mechanisms for change — whether it be a minor amendment to a law, a revolutionary change in constitutional arrangements or the very dismantling of the state itself. The limits on an MP's actions are the same as on the rest of us — they must be lawful actions. Furthermore, an MP can be removed from his or her seat only by the House of Commons itself, as occurred with Louis Riel, or by the voters in a general election. The problem with a complex federal democracy such as Canada is that loyalty is inevitably divisible. Each of us, in one way or another, divides our loyalties according to gender, family, class, ideology, ethnicity, region and nation. The secret of Canada's success has always been rooted in a commitment to recognize, to accept and to reconcile our divided loyalties. Words such as "disloyalty" and "treason" and calls for an indivisible loyalty to the state destroy that process of reconciliation. People who use such words are neither friends of democracy nor of Canada.

9

The 1994 Quebec Election

The next phase in the struggle, the Quebec provincial election, was set for 12 September 1994 and campaigning began on the heels of the federal election, heating up when Johnson was sworn in as premier in January 1994. Though a provincial election, it was a national event of great significance, hence a number of premiers, business leaders and federal politicians participated.

If the PQ won, Parizeau promised a speedy sovereignty referendum on a clear question. If the PQ lost there would be no referendum and sovereignty would be delayed until another provincial election, sapping the movement's momentum and leaving the Bloc to linger in Ottawa through another federal election. It was a tough fight, from the point of view of federalists. Bourassa and the Liberals, and then Johnson and the Liberals, were trailing the PQ in the polls. Bouchard and the Bloc had just won a smashing victory. Public support for sovereignty in Quebec was on the upswing. English Canada was cranky and appeared unwilling to offer a new constitutional deal to Quebec. Even if such a willingness could have been cultivated, there was a lack of political will among English-Canadian leaders to do so. Johnson and the Liberals would face the Quebec electorate with nothing but the status quo on offer.

In Ottawa, Bouchard and Chrétien competed for the hearts and minds of the Québécois, while Chrétien walked a trembling tightrope in English Canada between the contradictory demands and expectations of the general public and the neo-conservative business lobby. Chrétien initially made a few gestures based on his Red Book promises by cutting the controversial helicopter purchase, reversing the Tory-initiated privatization of Pearson International Airport, reducing defence spending, eliminating some unpopular tax advantages for the privileged and the corporate sector and creating jobs through an infrastructure program. But finance minister Paul Martin insisted on pursuing the neo-conservative agenda of attacking the deficit and debt through cuts in government spending. A few gestures were also made in this direction: reductions in unemployment insurance benefits, a clawback of income tax credits for seniors with incomes higher than $49,000 and a public-sector wage freeze. Granted, this represented mere nibbling at the edges of the neo-conservative agenda and Martin promised the complaining business lobby that harsher deficit reduction measures were yet to come. Human Resources Minister Lloyd Axworthy was assigned the job of reviewing not only the entire unemployment insurance program but also all social programs, with a view to rationalization and cost savings. The signals were clear, as Martin kept reiterating, that big cuts were coming and everyone knew they were put on hold due to the coming Quebec election.

The scene in Ottawa was dramatic and symbolic, especially for the Québécois. Here was a prime minister from Quebec, a committed federalist with approval ratings across English Canada that were so high they were unprecedented, but with much lower ratings in Quebec. There, across the floor in the House of Commons as leader of the Official Opposition, was Bouchard, a committed sovereigntist, commanding support in Quebec and levels of public trust and adulation unknown since Lévesque. On constitutional issues, Bouchard and Chrétien agreed: neither wanted to talk very much about them, but for very different reasons. Chrétien, looking over his shoulder at the ugly mood in English Canada and the wreckage of Meech and Charlottetown, was trapped. To discuss the constitution in any way that appeared to re-open the negotiations or that appeared to offer Quebec concessions would be pounced on by the Reform party and the largely francophobic English-Canadian media. Bouchard did not want to talk about the constitution because he believed that era was over. The only option to be discussed was sovereignty and a new partnership between two sovereign nations, perhaps modelled on the European Union. Bouchard did not, however, hesitate to extol sovereignty and attack Chrétien as the architect of Quebec's 1982 humiliation and as Trudeau's puppet. As the Liberals moved toward and then hesitated on cutting and restructuring social programs, Bouchard attacked, declaring himself the defender of Canada's social safety net, saying, "It's a strange paradox that a sovereigntist party from Quebec will be the only party fighting to preserve the main value of Canada....The signals are quite clear. [The Chrétien government] will attack social programs." Bouchard also used his position as leader of the Opposition to raise his status as a statesman internally and externally, carrying the sovereignty message to Europe, the United States and Western Canada. With the PQ well ahead of the Quebec Liberals in the polls, and with Bouchard carrying his "good news" messages about inevitable sovereignty across the country and around the world, Chrétien's strategy of non-interference in Quebec's election and his avoidance of the separatist issue seemed more and more risky, something Preston Manning never tired of pointing out.

During May and June 1994, in a move allegedly orchestrated by Chrétien and Ottawa, federal Indian affairs minister Ron Irwin and premiers Romanow of Saskatchewan and Harcourt of British Columbia commenced a series of harsh attacks on the idea of Quebec sovereignty and on Parizeau and Bouchard personally. Given the brouhaha that developed over the subsequent days and weeks, it is difficult not to believe that Irwin, a minister in Chrétien's cabinet, and Romanow, a close confidant of Chrétien's, were acting as stalking horses (with the prime minister's approval) to test the effects of a hard line. On 16 May 1994, Harcourt expressed some harsh views on Quebec separatism, views very similar to those of Reform leader Manning: "If [the Québécois] decided to separate...we'd be the worst of enemies. The anger...felt by British Columbians...would be immense." He went on to suggest Quebec couldn't count on leaving with its present borders intact. "It's you're in or you're out...it's much, much clearer." He accused Bouchard and Parizeau of misleading the Québécois by suggesting that Quebec's separation would be amicable. "Oh, it would be terrible consequences for everybody....[Bouchard and Parizeau] think it's going to be logical and civilized. Forget it, it won't be. There will be great bitterness and a nasty split. And they'll suffer, not just economically but they'll suffer every which way, the people of Quebec."

The following day in an address at a two-day meeting on self-government between Quebec aboriginal leaders and federal and provincial officials in Quebec City, Irwin promised that Quebec's aboriginal people could choose to remain part of Canada in the event of separation. He also insisted that Quebec was not a nation and had no legal claim to sovereignty. This was followed on 18 and 19 May by a series of personal attacks on Bouchard and Parizeau. During a meeting of the four western premiers in Gimli, Manitoba, Romanow accused Bouchard and Parizeau of being the "master illusionists of Quebec politics...advancing a con job...about separation. They say it's inevitable — that's a con job. That it's going to be easy — that's a con job. That there's going to be some economic association thereafter — that's a con job." Romanow explained that he was provoked into commenting by "the spectacle of Her Majesty's Loyal Opposition travelling to Washington and Paris and other parts of the country preaching the virtues and inevitability of Quebec separation." Harcourt and Romanow were unable to persuade their two Tory colleagues, Gary Filmon of Manitoba and Ralph Klein of Alberta, to put together a joint public response to the separatist threat. By that time, Preston Manning had joined in the war of words: "An example of a nonsensical statement is Mr. Bouchard saying the boundaries of Quebec are inviolate but the boundaries of Canada are not. Either they're both inviolate or they're both subject to negotiation." Despite such a strange bedfellow, Romanow and Harcourt refused to back off from their comments; indeed, Romanow escalated the confrontation in late May by insisting that a Yes vote on sovereignty in a Quebec referendum was not sufficient grounds for separation and that the constitution contained no mechanism for separation. And a few days later, Romanow attacked Bouchard again, saying his actions were "malicious" and "contributing to economic uncertainty," and his role was "fundamentally flawed and…illogical." Even Prime Minister Chrétien, who had insisted on staying out of Quebec's debate on separatism because it was a "hypothetical" question, was drawn briefly into the fray when he said, "The best protection…for Quebec's territory is to stay within Canada." Later he also reiterated that he had no intention of discussing separatism prior to a referendum should the PQ win the coming election, but nevertheless took the opportunity to suggest that the sovereigntists would mislead the people of Quebec: "If [the PQ] win the election and hold a referendum I hope they will not try to hide their real option. They have to say that it's separation that they want. They call themselves sovereigntists and it's not even a French word. It's not in the dictionary."

The reaction in Quebec to these comments — especially those on territory — was as predictable as it was instantaneous and unanimous. Parizeau restated his 1991 position that Quebec's borders "are what they are….There's no way the federal government will say…we are going to carve out pieces of you. Nobody does that in a country where the rule of law applies." Accusing the federal government and the premiers of using aboriginal people as pawns in a cynical anti-separatist campaign, he said, "As the sovereignty of Quebec becomes more probable, they are angry....I've got to say periodically, 'Pipe down...a great deal of your ill will, of your hollering, has absolutely no legal or constitutional basis. And, therefore, as ministers or premiers, keep your shirt on.'" Bouchard was also blunt, declaring that any attempt to re-draw a sovereign Quebec's borders would unite all francophones: "If there is one thing sacred in Quebec, as in any other country, it is territory....Even Robert Bourassa would get angry." Finally, given the reaction in the province, Quebec premier Johnson made a solemn declaration in the National Assembly: "We will defend Quebec's territory no matter what happens."

In the midst of this war of words, Johnson asked politicians outside the province to keep their noses out of Quebec politics. "We're not in a mode where we're into scare tactics or scenarios now. We want to keep the temperature down." Only Preston Manning ignored this advice, despite a specific request from Liberal strategists who told him his meddling would only help Parizeau. This advice was understandable: every outburst from outside had been met head-on by sovereigntist leaders whose stature among the Québécois was thereby elevated as defenders of Quebec. Federalists in Quebec and experienced analysts of Quebec politics warned that such attacks, threats and warnings by English Canadians from outside Quebec only inflamed passions and made the sovereigntists' job easier. A successful attack on sovereignty must come from within Quebec from federalists and non-separatist Québécois nationalists. The prime minister also intervened, suggesting that everyone, especially his own ministers, should stop responding to hypothetical questions about the future of Quebec and get on with the real, pressing work they had to do. That the premiers took this to heart became clear in the remaining months prior to the election as the rhetoric was toned down, if for no other reason than it clearly didn't help Johnson and only boosted the popularity of Bouchard and Parizeau among the Québécois. The premiers became so disciplined that at their annual premiers' conference, held in Toronto at the height of the Quebec election late in August, they even refrained from blasting Ottawa for fear of helping elect Parizeau and went out of their way to praise Johnson. Only New Brunswick premier Frank McKenna broke ranks and put his foot in his mouth, saying, "If we end up with a separatist government in Quebec, there's no interest in solutions. What they want is to establish a separate country and throw all of us into a vortex of debt and despair."

This war of words, provoked by English-Canadian politicians

and responded to with such enthusiasm and alacrity by Bouchard and Parizeau, raised a number of important issues and intensified the polarization between English Canada and Quebec. Romanow and Harcourt's comments, in particular, gave credence to the dreary stream of dangerous nonsense that had emanated from English-Canadian extremists ever since the collapse of Meech. Groups such as the right-wing Alliance for the Preservation of English in Canada and many in the Reform party, to which the Alliance was closely linked, talked loosely of the use of military action to support the establishment of non-francophone ethnic enclaves in west Montreal and the North, to force a territorial corridor through a sovereign Quebec to link Ontario and Atlantic Canada and even to suppress the move to sovereignty as treason. Comments such as those of Romanow and Harcourt tended to add considerable weight and credibility to such extreme and dangerous talk. Raising the territorial question in that context was extremely provocative. It was also dishonest. Regardless of the history of Quebec's boundaries, particularly the lands transferred to Quebec by federal statute in 1898 and 1920, the Canadian constitution stipulates that a province's borders cannot be changed without the province's consent. Hence, Quebec's boundaries must remain intact until the moment of sovereignty, at which point territory and boundaries become a matter, among many others, for negotiation. The PQ's 1994 sovereignty program, while making the case for Quebec's territorial integrity after sovereignty, proposed that "the framework for questions of [Quebec's] territorial integrity will be international law," thus presumably making a commitment to submit such issues to arbitration by the UN's International Court of Justice in the case of an impasse. Threats to Quebec's territory thus were not only premature but were bellicose posturing of the most dangerous kind, given the role territory has played in provoking strife in world history.

The manipulation of the aboriginal issue was also questionable. Granted, most aboriginal nations in Quebec, with the exception of the Huron, understandably have grave concerns about their future rights and entitlements in a sovereign Quebec and have consistently opposed Quebec sovereignty. Despite reassurances by Bouchard and Parizeau, despite the relatively good record (compared to English Canada) Quebec had had prior to Oka and despite the 1975 James Bay Agreement, aboriginal leaders want the matter resolved and do not want to separate. Sovereigntists would be compelled to deal with aboriginal rights and to do so under close international scrutiny. Yet for English Canada to use the aboriginal issue as a trump against Quebec sovereignty smacked of hypocrisy, given its own record of treatment of aboriginal people, and it was clearly seen as such both by the aboriginal communities and by the Québécois.

Taken together, and putting the best possible light on them, these episodes in the campaign were serious errors in judgement. Putting the worst possible light on the situation, it was a deliberate effort to test the effectiveness of scare tactics in persuading the Québécois to step back from the precipice of sovereignty. If scare-mongering was the intent, the episode provided an opportunity to assess the political effects and consequences of English Canada's use of threats on a sovereign Quebec's territory. The evidence was clear. Such an approach was counter-productive, and served only to exacerbate the fear and anger of those opposed to separation, to stiffen the resolve of those committed to separation and to compel those in Quebec who struggle diligently to reconcile federalism and Québécois nationalism to walk a tightrope from which they inevitably fall.

Although the economic costs of separation continued to be raised throughout this war of words, Quebec sovereigntist leaders, perhaps having learned from two decades of confronting economic fear campaigns, met the negative claims head-on, just as they had during the Charlottetown referendum campaign. The soil for a successful economic fear campaign was certainly not as rich as it had been in the past. The free trade agreements had their expected effects, as Quebec trade shifted more and more southward and as economic links to Canada became less and less important. A study conducted for the Caisse de dépôt found that Quebec exports to the United States between 1988 and 1992 had surged in all economic sectors, and this growth had been significantly greater than that experienced by Canada as a whole. Another study found that between 1981 and 1995 Quebec's exports to the rest of Canada grew by 67 per cent, while international exports grew by 208 per cent. This changing economic reality was accompanied by a shift in public opinion. In January 1994, Gallup found that, although 53 per cent of Québécois believed the Canadian economy would be worse off without Quebec, opinion regarding the province was almost equally divided, with 35 per cent of Québécois believing their economy would be better off and 37 per cent believing it would be worse off. Meanwhile, 74 per cent of Canadians outside the province believed the Quebec economy would be worse off, another example of the two solitudes. The depth of this economic disagreement was confirmed when a poll found that 60 per cent of non-francophones blamed Montreal's high unemployment levels on the sovereignty debate, while only 28 per cent of Québécois shared that view.

Further evidence that federalism and bilingualism may not have delivered economic justice to francophones was reported by *The Globe and Mail* using hitherto unpublished data from Statistics Canada that showed that between 1977 and 1991 the income gap between individual francophones and anglophones in Canada had more than doubled, while among francophone and anglophone families the gap had grown by 50 per cent. In Quebec, francophone incomes had reached the level of anglophone incomes in 1992. Indeed, in the case of men, francophone incomes had edged ahead of those of anglophones, although a large part of the explanation lay in the decline of anglophone incomes, on the average, between 1977 and 1992 as a result of the flight of head offices and higher-income anglophones from the province in the wake of the 1976 PQ victory and the new, tough language laws. In fact, the anglophone share of Quebec's population fell from 13 per cent in 1971 to 9 per cent in 1991; in absolute numbers, from 789,000 to 626,000. It was not surprising, therefore, when Gallup reported once again, just as it had in three previous polls since Meech, that 54 per cent of Canadians believed that the federal bilingualism policy package had failed, including 61 per cent of Québécois and 58 per cent of all francophones in Canada.

Unlike Lévesque and earlier sovereigntist leaders, Parizeau and Bouchard were not at all defensive about the economic issue. On the contrary, both leaders aggressively insisted that both Canada and Quebec would benefit economically in the long run from Quebec separation. Parizeau, a distinguished economist, a top-level career civil servant and academic, and a member of the economic elite himself, was particularly confident in his knowledge and experience and dealt easily with complex economic issues, preferring to attack federalism as a drag on Quebec's economy rather than apologizing for sovereignty or agreeing there might be large costs involved. Indeed, Parizeau consistently blamed federalism and the constitutional deadlock for Quebec's stagnant economy and high unemployment and poverty figures. Parizeau also insisted on keeping the politics of sovereignty separate from business issues, continually reassuring the business community that economic life in Quebec, especially secure and profitable investment, would not be jeopardized by sovereignty. Whenever prominent business leaders or financial institutions warned about the heavy costs of sovereignty, Parizeau and Bouchard were both quick to rap their knuckles for "fear-mongering." As Parizeau said in June 1994 in response to a negative comment by Canada's banking regulator, superintendent of financial institutions Michael Mackenzie, "Why don't you handle the money and we will handle politics? Whenever they start playing the political game, someone must step on their toes and say, 'Watch Out.'" In response to a claim by the Bank of Montreal's chief economist that a PQ win on the proposed sovereignty program would "create a great deal of fear" in financial markets, Parizeau counter-attacked vigorously: "Some of [the bankers] have tried to frighten Quebeckers. I will always be on the side of Quebeckers. I will always defend them." When the Royal Bank joined the doomsayers, Parizeau accused Canadian banks of using Québécois money to finance a fear campaign against the PQ and of using Québécois savings to finance a Liberal victory indirectly: "Some Canadian financial institutions are trying to play politics with our own money. Fair enough, but we don't have to believe them....It will pass in a few weeks like it has passed for thirty years." Parizeau and PQ candidate Daniel Paillé implied that banks, brokerage houses and other financial institutions that persisted in such economic fear tactics in the run-up to the Quebec election would pay a price after a PQ victory in lost business. The result was fewer negative interventions from the business community.

The 1994 election was unprecedented because it presented the Québécois with a stark and clear choice: status quo federalism or sovereignty. Johnson was the first Quebec premier since the Quiet Revolution to wrap himself in the Canadian flag as an unambiguous champion of Canada and federalism. And Parizeau was the first sovereigntist leader to be unapologetic and determined in his absolute devotion to separatism "first, last, and always," even unafraid of embracing the term "separatist," offering nothing but a quick referendum on sovereignty and, of course, better government than the Liberal "clowns" provided. Throughout the campaign, the PQ maintained its lead in the polls, just as they had since Charlottetown, beginning in the third week of July with 51 per cent and ending a week before the vote with 49 per cent, while the Liberals fell from 44 per cent to 38 per cent. Parizeau also consistently outscored Johnson on issues relating to leadership competence. This was the obvious reason Johnson agreed to the 29 August televised debate with Parizeau, the first since 1962 when Johnson's father, Union Nationale premier Daniel Johnson Sr., lost to Liberal leader Jean Lesage. History repeated itself when, according to the post-debate polls, Parizeau easily won.

Johnson and the Liberals decided to make independence the central issue of the election. A vote for the PQ was a vote "to initiate the process toward sovereignty and independence....We will be at a turning point....There would be eight, ten, twelve, or even fifteen months of uncertainty and constitutional turmoil...a fate worse than recession." Johnson also hammered away at the economic problems posed by the PQ's obsessive pursuit of sovereignty, noting that the choice was between "the strengthening on the one hand and the rupture and division on the other of the Canadian economic and political union," warning that "the economic recovery is really here...in spite of a certain fragility." In response, Parizeau and the PQ embraced the sovereignty issue and turned it back on the Liberals, reminding voters that the election was not really about sovereignty because that would be decided in a referendum in less than a year; nevertheless sovereignty was Quebec's "destiny," was achievable and would turn the economy around. At every opportunity, Parizeau flaunted his commitment to sovereignty, puzzling Liberal strategists, because they expected to put the PQ on the defensive by making independence the central issue. From time to time expressing exasperation at the media's insistence on pursuing the sovereignty issue relentlessly, Parizeau nonetheless never once deviated from his confident, pro-sovereignty message, despite always reminding voters that the final decision was theirs to make in a separate referendum. In the last half of the campaign, Bouchard intervened to help the PQ by warning the Québécois that the election of Johnson and the Liberals would lead to the submission of Quebec to Ottawa. "Elect Johnson and that's handing the destiny of Quebec to Jean Chrétien," said Bouchard, making it clear that the battle was not just between the PQ and the provincial Liberals but between Quebec and English Canada. Polls continued to show that the Liberal effort to make the election a vote on separation failed and continued to fail throughout the campaign — the Quebec electorate wanted to toss the Liberals out and their first purpose in voting was to get change and good government.

Late in the campaign, facing certain defeat, Johnson broke his own taboo by raising constitutional matters. He criticized Bourassa's strategy for seeking constitutional change, which had ended in Meech and Charlottetown, and he distanced himself

from Trudeau's vision, saying he would push for greater autonomy for Quebec as well as accelerated decentralization. "All my
political career is based on a defence of Quebec's interests," he
said, though his basic "constitutional policy is to provide job
opportunities for Quebeckers." In late August, he stated that Quebec's position with him as premier would remain to "exercise our
own jurisdiction with more and more autonomy, that the federal
government gets out of the way...and that we make sure [the federal system] is as efficient for the taxpayer as possible."

Then, in early September, still facing defeat, Johnson appeared
to convert to Québécois nationalism when he reversed his earlier
Canada-first defence of federalism. Speaking to the Quebec City
Chamber of Commerce, Johnson said that he could conceive of
being a Québécois without being a Canadian, but not of being a
Canadian without being a Québécois. He went on to describe himself as a Québécois above all, dismissing his earlier comment about
being a Canadian first as an "unfortunate use of words." Delighted,
Parizeau described Johnson's late conversion as "revolting," attacking him on two fronts: first, for being opportunistic enough to adopt
"any position...to be popular at any time," and second, for continuing the confused and indecisive ambiguity for which Quebec
federalists had become famous.

Virtually ignored by the media in English Canada, the nationalists who had abandoned Bourassa over Charlottetown and founded
the ADQ campaigned hard. Led by the prominent Jean Allaire and
the former Young Liberal leader Mario Dumont, the ADQ ran eighty
candidates in the election. Allaire and Dumont, who at twenty-four
became the youngest leader of a credible registered political party
in Quebec history, were uncomfortable with Parizeau's hard line
on sovereignty, preferring Lévesque's earlier, softer "sovereignty-
association" approach. As Dumont put it, "I think we can be
sovereigntist without being separatist. I'm certainly a sovereigntist in
the sense that I want Quebec to have its powers. But I'm not a separatist because I believe in a new partnership with the rest of Canada."
Not unlike Bouchard, he pointed to the supranational parliament of
the European Union as a model. Rather than seeing a successful referendum on sovereignty as a final decision, Dumont believed it
would provide Quebec the political clout to persuade Canada to
negotiate a new partnership. If Canada refused to negotiate, however, he believed Quebec would separate. The ADQ was seen as a
minor spoiler, but its support grew from 3 per cent at the beginning
of the campaign to 9 per cent a week before the election.

On 12 September 1994, Parizeau and the PQ won 77 of 125 seats with 44.8 per cent of the vote, while the Liberals, gaining significantly in the last days of the campaign, took forty-seven seats with 44.4 per cent. The big surprise of the election was the election of Dumont in his seat and the ADQ's 6.5 per cent of the popular vote. Though less than 1 per cent separated the PQ and the Liberals, the wins for the PQ were spread primarily among the francophone population, whereas the Liberals' vote tended to be largely concentrated in anglophone and allophone seats, where Liberal candidates won by large majorities but the overall vote did not translate into a fair share of seats. The results suggested that Johnson's tactics of trying to turn the election into a vote on independence, to worry voters about the PQ's sovereignty process upon victory and to raise the economic uncertainty issue had closed the gap with the PQ. But most of the votes that had been scared off the PQ had gone to Dumont and the ADQ, not to the Liberals.

* * *

Many in English Canada refused to recognize the significance of the results, responding to the outcome with equal measures of ill grace and wilful blindness. Indeed, many English-Canadian politicians and commentators embarked on a systematic and creative reinterpretation of the outcome. The result was not a vote for sovereignty, they maintained, just one for change and good government. Of course, Parizeau and the PQ had never claimed the provincial vote was on sovereignty, even though Johnson had done so repeatedly. Furthermore, English Canada, by and large, continued to ignore the very real fact that Parizeau presented his priority commitment to sovereignty frequently, firmly and with candour. Hence, he clearly had a mandate to establish the agenda and to set the process in motion, with the clear democratic blessing of the Quebec electorate, which had granted him all the power of the Quebec state to do so. The election result was a moral defeat for the PQ, some commentators crowed, because the popular vote was so close. Whether we like it or not, the objective in a parliamentary democracy is to win seats, and here the PQ's victory was decisive. Furthermore, English-Canadian commentators tended systematically to overlook the 6.5 per cent of the vote won by the ADQ and deliberately to ignore the fact that Dumont ran on a sovereignty-association platform. Hence, the pro-sovereignty vote had been over 51 per cent of the electorate, nearly the percentage the PQ had at the beginning of the campaign. Hence pro-sovereignty support in the election was hardly at a level to inspire confidence in the outcome of the looming referendum. Yet many English-Canadians began expressing an ungrounded confidence that, given the closeness of the vote, the approaching sovereignty referendum was doomed to defeat. English Canada's capacity for self-serving delusional thinking on the Quebec question again seemed remarkably immune from repeated doses of reality.

10

The 1995 Sovereignty Referendum

Immediately following the election in Quebec, the major players began to position themselves for the coming referendum. Initially, there was an effort by English Canada's premiers and federal politicians to warn Parizeau that, given his narrow win, he did not have a mandate to pursue his sovereignty agenda. The usual economic debate emerged, focused on the heavy costs to Quebec of separation, the terrible effects of economic uncertainty on the entire economy and the benefits of federalism for Quebec. One study suggested the minimum annual cost to Quebec of sovereignty would be $3.4 billion, but these costs would begin to decline after the first three years. The PQ government released confidential economic studies done by the Johnson and Bourassa governments, alleging the federal system cost Quebec three billion dollars a year. Federalists countered with statistics that proved Quebec benefited from federalism to the tune of six billion dollars a year. Pro-federalist business leaders indicated that though they had been relatively silent during the election, they would campaign very actively in any future referendum. Chrétien tried to bait the PQ into an early date for the referendum but the PQ declined. At first, the party held to Parizeau's ten-month timetable, but later modified it to twelve to fifteen months, after an intervention by Bouchard. Parizeau rejected Dumont's suggestion that a referendum be put off until Quebec's economic house was in order. Johnson, the Opposition leader and official leader of the No campaign, called for modifications to the federal system, noting that a vote against sovereignty was not a vote for the status quo. He insisted that Ottawa would eventually renew federalism and "adjust the constitutional framework."

Undeterred, Parizeau and the PQ adhered to their promised timetable. In early December 1994, the premier tabled a draft bill on sovereignty in the National Assembly that opened with a declaration that "Quebec is a sovereign country." In brief and clear terms, the bill laid out the PQ's plan for achieving sovereignty. It also provided assurances by authorizing the government to seek an economic association with Canada, guaranteeing the rights and freedoms of anglophone and aboriginal citizens and proposing an orderly transition plan. After lengthy debate and public consultations, the bill would eventually be amended and approved by the National Assembly, but would not come into force until "one year after its approval in a referendum." This referendum, to be successful, would require a majority of votes cast in favour of the following question: "Are you in favour of the Act passed by the National Assembly declaring the sovereignty of Quebec?" This was clearly a very different question from the one asked in 1980, which had been long, convoluted and confused, and had asked only for a mandate to negotiate sovereignty-association. If successful, the referendum would have the effect of triggering sovereignty within one year. In a sense it was a unilateral declaration of independence by referendum.

Not unexpectedly, the bill was roundly condemned by federalists across Canada and by aboriginal leaders in Quebec. It was described as "not democratic," "a scam," "flawed" and "dishonest" by the prime minister; "a unilateral denial of all aboriginal and Cree rights" by Matthew Coon Come, leader of the northern Cree; and "a fraud" by deputy prime minister Sheila Copps. "Parizeau has broken his word," intoned Romanow; "trickery," ventured McKenna; "illegitimate" and "propaganda," declared No leader Johnson. Parizeau's response was blunt, "Quebec is on the fast track to sovereignty and there is nothing the rest of Canada can do to stop it....You're a Canadian or you're not....This thing has to be settled." The issue for Quebec sovereigntists was clear: "The more time goes by, the more the Canadian majority is determined to act as though there is but one nation in Canada, as though all provinces are equal. This is the Canada of tomorrow. Do we want to be part of it? Absolutely not."

The Quebec referendum campaign had four phases. The first phase was the early stage of preparations and positioning for the referendum, during which Parizeau was the key leader. Bouchard was absent from the scene due to his near-fatal bout with "flesh-eating disease" (necrotizing fasciitis) that kept him sidelined until late February 1995. The second phase was the period of confusion and disagreement in the ranks of the sovereigntists, which was not resolved until April 1995. The third phase was the period with Parizeau leading the Yes campaign, including its formal launch, until Bouchard took over the de facto leadership of the campaign on 9 October 1995. Finally, the fourth phase was the period with Bouchard at the helm, during which support for the Yes side began to grow and panic set in among the No forces.

During the first phase, Parizeau and the PQ government put the process in motion. Fifteen regional commissions were established to hold public hearings throughout Quebec in order to get feedback and proposals for modifications to the sovereignty agenda. At first, Johnson refused to participate and suggested that federalists boycott the commissions since they were just a propaganda exercise. Very quickly, however, he changed his mind when it became clear that people were taking the consultation process very seriously and intended to participate (more than 53,000 would take part by the end). Parizeau and the PQ focused their strategy on winning over the "soft nationalists." In the months leading up to the actual campaign, the media were full of claims and counter-claims: debates among legal experts about constitutional matters; warnings of the dire consequences of separation by some economic experts and by others, reassurances that the economic impacts would be insignificant; proposals that a Yes vote be denied recognition; debates about whether 50 per cent plus one vote is enough to break up a country; and arguments over sharing the debt and dividing up federal assets. As one would expect, for every claim or threat made by federalists, there was a counterclaim and a response by sovereigntists in this tit-for-tat battle for the hearts and minds of the soft nationalists. By late February 1995, when Bouchard returned from his convalescence, Yes support was stuck at 45 per cent, with 55 per cent for the No side. Though this was an improvement on Lévesque's 1980 showing, polls clearly indicated that the No side was coasting to an easy win.

The problem was Parizeau's hard line and his insistence on a clear, tough question. Determined not to give English Canada the means to interfere directly in the Quebec debate (as Lévesque had done with his mandate to negotiate and his hyphen in sovereignty-association), Parizeau was making it very difficult for the soft nationalists to move his way. These were the sovereigntists who feared a rupture that might be messy and difficult, who still wanted links with Canada and who wanted any breakup to be amicable. Sovereigntist arguments that these links would be inevitable after a Yes vote and that most English Canadians wanted some association with a sovereign Quebec did not provide this group with enough reassurance, particularly in the face of repeated threats and warnings from English Canada. Parizeau appeared willing to fight on, hoping that by the end of the day the sheer weight and passion of the arguments for sovereignty, combined with the pro-sovereignty momentum since Meech, would be enough to succeed. Nevertheless, continuing resistance from aboriginals in Quebec, dire economic predictions, harsh comments from English Canadians and the prospect of endless turmoil and uncertainty were all taking their toll by keeping the soft vote from embracing Parizeau's sovereignty project in the numbers he needed.

On 19 February, in the first interview after his surgery, Bouchard suggested that the referendum question be modified in order to find a question a majority of Québécois could embrace with some comfort. During March and April, Bouchard amplified his remarks by suggesting the question be changed to include some reference to political and economic association. He made it clear that he was not happy with the proposed tough question, and he had grave concerns that the referendum would be lost. Dumont agreed and insisted, as he always had, that some form of political and economic association be clearly tied to sovereignty. There was even some talk that the referendum be delayed until a more auspicious time. Ever hopeful, English-Canadian media analysts and politicians did not hide their delight at this rupture in sovereigntist ranks, painting it as a power struggle between the PQ and the Bloc (a rather silly idea, given that the two parties had virtually the same membership). In reality, the disagreement was about tactics and strategy, a disagreement as old as the sovereignty movement itself. Parizeau took the harder line, as he had since he broke with Lévesque and led the undoing of Pierre-Marc Johnson. He continued to insist that Quebec opt clearly and unambiguously for sovereignty. If a sovereign Quebec then opted for an association, Parizeau would not be opposed; indeed, he would favour such an arrangement. But after 1980, he refused to make Quebec sovereignty contingent in any way on English Canada's willingness to agree to an association. Bouchard, for his part, did not want to hold a referendum unless victory was reasonably certain, and he was willing to toy with the concept of linking association in some way to sovereignty. Bouchard believed that a referendum victory on a softer version of sovereignty was preferable to a defeat on a hard question.

Both men had strong cases that were doubtless argued out thoroughly in private. Parizeau could point to four polls taken since the election that gave Yes 45 per cent and No 55 per cent. Hence support for the Yes side had stabilized at 45 per cent, not an insignificant level with which to go into a referendum campaign. Furthermore, polls had shown that party preference had shifted significantly against federalist forces: the PQ had remained stable at 45 per cent; the Liberals had dropped eight points to 35 per cent; Dumont's ADQ had jumped to more than 17 per cent. These figures suggested that the momentum for sovereignty was building and gave Parizeau a reasonable argument that a clear question could win.

Bouchard could point to the same numbers, arguing that victory on a soft question was assured, given that more than 60 per cent of Quebec voters preferred one of the two sovereigntist parties. Defeat on a hard question could set the movement back a decade, while victory on a soft question would be better for the momentum of the movement, even if the result would be more ambiguous. What gave Bouchard the argument was that without Dumont, defeat was certain. Dumont must be brought clearly on side with the Yes team if there was to be any hope of victory. The clinching argument was the results from the fifteen commissions: they indicated that tying sovereignty to some form of association or new partnership was essential for victory. Faced with such pressure, Parizeau relented and agreed to link sovereignty to some form of association in the question, but refused absolutely to delay the referendum beyond 1995, which was something Bouchard and Dumont were prepared to consider. Polls in late April helped buttress Parizeau's decision. One poll showed that if sovereignty were linked to association with Canada, Yes support would rise to 53 per cent and No would fall to 47 per cent, whereas a question just on sovereignty would lose 44 per cent Yes to 56 per cent No. Suggestive of things yet to come was another poll that found that with Bouchard leading the Yes team, support increased to 46 per cent for Yes to 42 per cent for No, regardless of the question; with Parizeau at the helm, the Yes side enjoyed only 36 per cent compared to 52 per cent for the No side.

The new agreement among the three sovereigntist leaders was laid out in formal terms and signed with great fanfare on 12 June 1995. The new question, which was later tabled in the National Assembly, was much fuzzier than Parizeau's original one: "Do you agree that Quebec should become sovereign, after having made a formal offer to Canada for a new Economic and Political Partnership, within the scope of the Bill respecting the future of Quebec and the agreement signed on 12 June 1995?" In practical terms, the question made little real difference because if Canada refused to negotiate such a deal Quebec would become sovereign on 30 October 1996. It was still a unilateral declaration of independence by referendum. Furthermore, the English-Canadian premiers and the prime minister had repeatedly stated that there would be no such offer from Canada. Nevertheless, the question contained the required reference to sovereignty in the context of a commitment to forge new links, or associations, with Canada. And, as had been clear in 1980, no matter what question was posed, the No side would campaign as if a Yes vote meant an automatic, dangerous, immediate and messy separation. Politically speaking, the debate remained clearly about sovereignty.

The campaign was officially launched on 11 September with voting day set for 30 October. During this period, the debate became much more bitter. Though most federalists were confident, especially after a late June poll put the Yes for sovereignty with association at 48 per cent and the No at 52 per cent, some warned of overconfidence given the shift in the pro-sovereignty balance of forces since 1980. Claude Ryan, the leader of the No side in 1980, warned that the referendum would be difficult to win without a commitment to return the veto to Quebec. Former prime minister Joe Clark warned that the polls were so close that the Yes might win and he feared that the federalists were fumbling the ball. With the addition of association to the question, the gloves came off as federalists warned that a Yes meant separation and there would, in fact, be no association. Saskatchewan premier Romanow asserted Quebec would be "a foreign country with no special treatment"; at a meeting in St. John's, the premiers said a sovereign Quebec could not expect to continue with existing trade links with the rest of Canada; Johnson, the leader of the No side in Quebec, declared a clear Yes or No on sovereignty was required, because "separation means borders"; Manitoba premier Filmon flatly stated there would be no negotiations on association; Finance Minister Martin said there would be "no economic partnership…no favours….Quebec would be just another country"; Prime Minister Chrétien repeatedly stated the only issue up for discussion was "the separation of Quebec"; Alberta premier Klein joined the chorus, as did Premier Harris of Ontario, saying there would be no ties with Quebec if the Yes side won. This response was part of the federal strategy to counter the sovereigntists' agreement to include a reference to association in the question; the intent was to make it unmistakably clear to the people of Quebec that there would be no discussion of association after a Yes victory and that a Yes vote meant separation, complete and unqualified: "A one-way ticket to separation" was the way the prime minister put it.

This campaign of political refusal was supplemented by the usual economic fear campaign, especially after the kickoff of the official campaign. The Chamber of Commerce warned that a Yes victory would put 470,000 jobs at risk. The federal finance minister warned that a Yes outcome would jack up interest rates and cause the dollar to collapse. Johnson claimed that a Yes win would lead to average tax increases of three thousand dollars a year and a sixteen-billion-dollar deficit. Later he claimed it would lead to an immediate loss of 92,000 jobs, with more to follow. As federal concerns rose, the claims became more fantastic. By 17 October, Martin warned that a Yes victory would put one million jobs at risk. Again, the sovereigntists' response was to release contrary figures and studies to bolster their claims that there would be no dire economic consequences and that Quebec would benefit economically from sovereignty. The sovereigntists also accused big business and the federalists of trying to destroy Quebec's sovereigntist and social democratic experiment and warned that the federal government would begin cutting the social safety net right after a No victory. On the practical side, the Quebec government bought up hundreds of millions of Canadian dollars in the midst of the campaign to prevent a sharp fall in the dollar, which they expected to be engineered by federalist forces in an effort to frighten the Québécois.

The business lobby did not participate as directly in this campaign as it had in the past. Indeed, much of the Charlottetown economic fear campaign had been carried out by members of the business elite, and it had failed. Furthermore, some, such as the Royal Bank, had paid a price in lost business in Quebec as a result of a boycott because of the economic fear document released by the bank during Charlottetown. Many business leaders, therefore, stayed silent. In the previous year's election, Parizeau had warned financial institutions that they would lose business if they interfered. This warning carried over into the referendum, such as when Standard Life Assurance's Claude Garcia called on the Québécois to "crush" the separatists in the referendum in order to put the sovereignty issue permanently to rest. After that intervention, the PQ government opened up bids for the $11.5 million insurance contract formerly held exclusively by Standard Life and stripped Garcia of his duties as chairman of the board of the University of Quebec at

Montreal. Furthermore, the business lobby was deeply divided, as indicated by the very prominent business leaders now in the ranks of the PQ government, such as Jean Campeau, former head of the Caisse de dépôt, Daniel Paillé, a top executive with Québecor Inc., and Richard Le Hir, former leader of the Quebec Manufacturers' Association. (Le Hir, sidelined by Parizeau due to a patronage scandal, renounced his sovereigntist past in September 1996 and began seeking a federal Liberal nomination.) In addition, the public was suspicious of negative economic preaching by business leaders as a result of Charlottetown; companies were concerned about losing business if they offended an aggressive government quite prepared to use its power against its political adversaries; and there was a desire not to give Bouchard and Parizeau any highly visible big business targets for emotional attacks. The overall result was that the business lobby stayed largely out of the public fray and worked behind the scenes by contributing financial and personnel resources to the No campaign.

By early October, it was clear the campaign was not going well for the Yes side. ADQ leader Dumont complained publicly of the "loser mentality" rampant among the Yes forces. This was confirmed in the polls: on 30 September, Yes had 46.8 per cent and No, 53.2 per cent; on 6 October it was Yes at 47 per cent and No at 53 per cent. Though an improvement over the stalemate prior to linking sovereignty to association, it was still not enough to win. On 9 October, Parizeau named Bouchard to be "chief negotiator" for Quebec sovereignty after a Yes victory and Bouchard assumed the effective helm of the Yes campaign. By 12 October, Bouchard had redefined the meaning of a Yes vote to include a strong mandate for him to negotiate with Canada. This mandate became one focus of the Yes campaign from then on: if the Québécois gave Bouchard a strong hand to negotiate, the new economic realities would force Canada to the table. Another focus remained independence and sovereignty, including a continuing hard line from Parizeau. Thus, during the last phase of the referendum campaign, the Yes side gave the Québécois mixed messages from which to choose. There was Bouchard at the helm playing soft cop, and Parizeau, still the official leader of the Yes team, playing hard cop. The effectiveness, partly due to the softened message, partly due to the trust and affection enjoyed by Bouchard and partly due to the ineptitude of the No team, had a dramatic impact as Yes fortunes began slowly to turn around: on 14 October, it was Yes at 49.2 per cent and No 50.8 per cent; on 20 October, Yes had 50.2 per cent and No, 49.8 per cent;

on 28 October, Yes and No were tied at 50 per cent each. The referendum had been transformed from a certain defeat for the Yes to a dead heat.

English Canada, after a deluge of propaganda that the No side would win easily, was ill-prepared for the sudden prospect of a Yes victory. Indeed, leaders of the No forces, especially those in Ottawa and most particularly the prime minister himself, reacted with poorly concealed panic. As Canada tottered on the edge of the abyss, federalist arrogance was now coupled with near begging as English Canada tried to pull the Québécois back from what was repeatedly described as a final-and irreversible decision to separate. Although the dual No campaign of refusing any association whatsoever after a Yes outcome and fostering a climate of economic fear had an effect in Quebec (for example, polls revealed that approximately 66 per cent of voters in Quebec would easily say Yes to sovereignty if Ottawa and the nine English-Canadian provinces promised association), it seemed to have more effect in English Canada. Indeed, English Canada had convinced itself with its own propaganda that a Yes vote would be an economic catastrophe and reacted shrilly when a Yes victory became a real possibility.

After the 20 October poll put Yes ahead at 50.2 per cent to 49.8 per cent, the No message became decidedly mixed: there were promises of love and big changes if Quebec voted to stay; threats of the dire consequences of a Yes vote. Finance Minister Martin promised a No vote would bring significant changes to the federal system to address Quebec's concerns. After some open begging by No leader Johnson, the prime minister first rejected and then three days later declared his support for recognizing Quebec as a distinct society and for a qualified constitutional veto for Quebec. This was followed by a nationwide television appeal by a visibly shaken prime minister pleading with Quebec to stay in Canada. On 27 October the No campaign engineered a large unity rally in Montreal's Canada Place, using subsidized bus and airline tickets to bring in Canadians from all over English Canada. Participants in the rally declared their love for Quebec and urged the people to vote No and stay in Canada. At the same time, the prime minister warned Quebec of the ugly mood in the rest of the country in the event of a Yes vote and of how the Québécois may lose their pensions, currency (putting their savings at risk) and passports. Furthermore, he again suggested that a narrow victory for the Yes side would not be enough to break up the country. In the midst of this crisis atmosphere, a mood deliberately orchestrated by the No campaign, the results of referendums held by the Cree and the Innu on sovereignty were announced — a massive vote for a No. Meanwhile, hundreds lined up at the Montreal passport office to get their passports before the vote. In response to this growing federalist panic, Bouchard and Parizeau held firm, appealing finally to the national pride and confidence of the Québécois. As Bouchard put it in one of his last speeches of the campaign, "Seize it and vote Yes...say Yes to ourselves. Say Yes to the people of Quebec."

On 30 October, the Quebec electorate narrowly voted against sovereignty as 94 per cent of the eligible voters trooped to the polls. The final tally was 50.6 per cent for No against 49.4 per cent for Yes. Only 53,000 votes separated the Yes and the No. Opinion remains divided on what finally saved federalism in Quebec: some point to the unity rally (later found by Quebec's Chief Electoral Officer to be a flagrant violation of Quebec's referendum law on spending limits); others to Daniel Johnson's eleventh-hour plea for a commitment to grant Quebec distinct status and a veto, first refused and then embraced by the prime minister; others to simple fear of the unknown and the unpredictable in the midst of a contrived crisis atmosphere. Efforts have also been made to reinterpret the Yes vote in ways other than a vote for sovereignty: it was a vote for change, a vote to give Bouchard a strong hand in negotiations with Ottawa and the rest of Canada, a vote for sovereignty-association, a vote against English-Canadian bullying and intransigence or a vote to affirm Québécois nationalism in the face of English-Canadian attempts to deny the existence of the Québécois nation. All of these, of course, contain some truth: the Québécois wanted change, chose to assert their pride, wanted association with Canada and resented bullying and threats. But all this rationalization does not erase the enormous democratic political significance of the vote. The fact remains that 60 per cent of Quebec's francophones voted for sovereignty in a political context that had demonstrably hardened and clarified the choice. Had the percentage of Yes voters been slightly higher, given the PQ government in Quebec City and the Bloc's prominence in the House of Commons, Quebec would have been on an irreversible trajectory to separation, especially if English Canada had continued its refusal to negotiate association.

In his address to the Yes rally on the night of 30 October, Premier Parizeau expressed his sadness and frustration at the result with some ill-chosen and inflammatory remarks: "It's true we have been defeated, but basically by what? By money and the ethnic vote. All it means is that next time round, instead of us [francophone

Québécois] being 60 or 61 per cent in favour, we'll be 63 or 64 per cent." Almost as soon as the words escaped from his mouth, Parizeau was subjected to a barrage of criticism from all sides. Montreal's ethnic leaders accused him of racism, while many sovereigntists described his words as unfortunate and unacceptable. The remarks, however, were consistent both with Parizeau's previous bluntness and with certain political and sociological truths. The PQ's efforts at a breakthrough in winning support among the so-called "ethnic," or allophone, communities had failed consistently to climb much beyond 10 per cent. The PQ had only slightly better success among the anglophone minority.

That the anglophone and allophone votes go en bloc to federalists during elections and to the No side during referendums remains an axiom of Quebec politics. This should not be surprising. Indeed, a massive vote by anglophones and allophones for sovereignty would have settled the question for sovereignty back in 1980. Given these groups' anti-sovereignty sentiments, and older francophone Québécois' reluctance to risk sovereignty, the question had always been whether the sovereigntists could ever hope to achieve the nearly 65 per cent required among francophone Québécois to win a referendum.

After an analysis of the results of the Charlottetown referendum, Parizeau had announced to a PQ national council meeting in January 1993 that sovereignty could be achieved without the support of allophones and anglophones. The implication was clear: the sovereigntists should give priority to developing support among francophones and worry less about pursuing an unattainable breakthrough among non-francophones.

Efforts by English-Canadian political leaders and commentators to use the "ethnic" issue to smear Quebec sovereigntists reflect another dimension of the hypocrisy and double standard so common in English-Canadian reactions to Québécois nationalism. Recent federalist strategy in Quebec has been built on the cornerstones of "ethnic politics" and bloc voting, as have historical English-Canadian efforts to erase or contain the French fact from the Conquest onward. In recent Canadian history it was the Liberal party, commencing most notably with Clifford Sifton's immigration policies in the West, that used "ethnic" or "recent immigrant" politics to help secure its domination of federal politics from 1896 onward. The use of ethnic politics was also evident in federalist actions in the 1995 referendum, although it was barely mentioned in the English-Canadian media, leaving most Canadians in ignorance. For the first time in history, in the run-up to the referendum vote during the autumn of 1995, Ottawa cut red tape to facilitate the rapid creation of 15,000 new voting citizens in Quebec prior to 30 October. Ottawa's immigration and citizenship department distributed information to new citizens explaining voter registration procedures, and official newsletters to recent citizens instructed them that they had a duty to fight for a strong and united Canada. In the spring of 1995, a former MP and Liberal party organizer in Quebec publicly requested the re-establishment of deportation laws targeted at refugees and immigrants who supported sovereignty, taking aim directly at Bloc MP Osvaldo Nunez, who had escaped from Pinochet's Chile. In the days preceding the referendum, leaders of various ethnic communities in Quebec correctly bragged that 90 per cent of their communities would vote No. Furthermore, Prime Minister Chrétien's warnings about the loss of passports, pensions and currency, Finance Minister Martin's hyperbole about the loss of one million jobs, and repeated warnings from English-Canadian politicians and the media about chaos and instability were clearly aimed at the ethnic and recent immigrant vote. While Canadians of long standing in Quebec and the rest of Canada could laugh at such outrageous claims, immigrants and refugees in Quebec, many of whom had fled countries and regions characterized by serious economic and political instability, would understandably be deeply affected, perhaps even frightened.

The dangers of manipulating ethnic politics in Quebec were obvious. The federalist strategy of using the ethnic vote as a reliable pawn opened the door to scapegoating by Québécois nationalists. Sovereigntist failures to break the allophone and anglophone bloc vote led to an exclusive focus on developing the francophone bloc vote, a dangerous "us against them" scenario, as suggested by Parizeau's comments after Charlottetown and as stated explicitly in his 30 October speech. Parizeau's remarks encouraged such scapegoating and smeared the ethnic communities as the saboteurs of Québécois aspirations. This position was dangerous and irresponsible. Obviously, in his speech Parizeau could have mentioned the many other reasons for the referendum's defeat: the 40 per cent of francophones who voted No; the 85 to 90 per cent of anglophones who voted No; the Cree and Innu who voted No. An analysis of how the resistance of these social elements to sovereignty could be overcome, how future reassurances and guarantees would have to be more effectively developed, and so on, would have transformed his speech from an inflammatory and irresponsible bombshell into a thoughtful political analysis. Instead, it gave aid and comfort to the racist and xenophobic extremists among Québécois nationalists, provided federalists with brickbats to hurl at sovereignty and Québécois nationalism and discredited the sovereignty movement at a crucial moment when the world's attention was focused on it.

On 31 October 1995, Premier Parizeau resigned, expressing regret for his "harsh comments" and repeating his disappointment at the failure of the sovereigntists to win more ethnic voters to their cause. He insisted that "the words were too strong but the reality doesn't change." While it was evident that the storm over his comments had accelerated the timetable, Parizeau insisted he had always intended to resign quickly if the Yes side failed and had, in fact, announced earlier that even if the Yes side won he would stay on only long enough to see the sovereignty negotiation process through to a conclusion, insisting that at age sixty-five he shouldn't outstay his welcome. As expected, Bouchard was crowned as uncontested PQ leader and sworn in as premier of Quebec in January 1996. Once described by Lévesque as a "Napoleonic strategist," Parizeau had served sovereignty well, bringing the PQ back from post-Lévesque oblivion, reasserting the PQ's central commitment to sovereignty, masterminding the 1992 Charlottetown campaign, playing a key role in the Bloc's 1993 victory, securing the PQ's re-election in 1994 on a hard sovereignty position and bringing the movement to the threshold of victory in the 1995 referendum. His intellectual distance and arrogance and his undisguised wealth and privileged background were forgiven due to his political commitment and principled adherence to sovereignty, allowing him to win the respect of the Québécois, but never their affection. According to some Quebec commentators, his successor, Lucien Bouchard, came close to combining the best elements of the political persona of Lévesque and Parizeau. Like Lévesque, Bouchard enjoyed the affection of the Québécois, rivalled Lévesque's charisma and inspiration in public oratory, and, like Parizeau, was reputed to be a shrewd tactician and strategist. Most believed that Bouchard's accession as premier, barring an unprecedented catastrophe for the sovereigntists, assured the PQ's re-election, making another sovereignty referendum likely after the next Quebec election.

11

Ottawa's Plan B

Many on both sides of the sovereignty debate inside and outside Quebec greeted the referendum result with relief and naive expectations that the narrow victory for Canada would lead to dialogue, change and renewal. After all, this was what the federalists had promised in the panic stage of the referendum campaign and what Bouchard's repeated emphasis on the concept of a new partnership seemed to call for. A significant portion of sovereigntists expressed relief that the result had not been reversed, giving the Yes side a narrow victory, particularly as revelations emerged about the many No votes that had been designated as "spoiled" by overzealous pro-Yes officials at the polls in some of the strong pro-federalist ridings. Many federalists were disturbed by the failure of Chrétien to read the situation correctly, pointing to his unfounded overconfidence until the last ten days of the campaign; they expressed doubt that the "take it or leave it, no concessions, no negotiations" approach had been the wisest course.

The hope that the referendum would lead to rational dialogue and reasonable negotiations proved to be wishful thinking. The public mood in English Canada had little sympathy for Québécois aspirations, as polls revealed deep opposition to distinct society and a veto for Quebec. Meanwhile, in Quebec, polls found that the Québécois wanted significant changes in Quebec's place in Canada but had no confidence in Chrétien's willingness to negotiate "real change." Dramatic confirmation of this unwillingness came in December 1995 when the Chrétien government "delivered" on the prime minister's referendum promises of distinct society and a constitutional veto for Quebec: passing a resolution in the House of Commons that recognized Quebec as a distinct society, and Bill C-110, which guaranteed the federal government would not initiate amendments to the constitution without the approval of Canada's five regions. Largely symbolic and constitutionally meaningless, these gestures were viewed by Québécois nationalists as an insult. Chrétien declared his referendum commitments to the people of Quebec fully discharged and got even tougher with the sovereigntists. In this exercise in duplicity and aggressive posturing the prime minister was not alone. Indeed, he was carrying out the wishes of English Canada, which elected him in 1993 and, according to the polls, would re-elect him as long as he remained a faithful servant of the interests of English Canada vis à vis Québécois nationalism.

Days after the referendum, the "provincial rights" premiers began to circle the barely resuscitated federal corpse. At an early November 1995 meeting in Yorkton, Saskatchewan, the four western premiers once again tried to exploit the urgent need to provide constitutional accommodation to Quebec. The western premiers proposed to eliminate an effective central government in Ottawa as the price for accommodating Quebec. To save the Canadian federation, they proposed to destroy it. Combining effrontery and bad faith, given the negative catharsis Canadians had just experienced, the western premiers proposed to convene a first ministers' meeting without the prime minister. There, Canada's federal powers would be dispersed to the provinces. Echoing the process that brought Charlottetown, the western premiers, hungry for power, appeared prepared to sandbag the discredited federal government while presenting themselves as the saviours of the federation.

Manning and the Reform party began to provoke the Québécois sovereigntists in an effort to sustain the anti-Quebec anger in English Canada that had served them so well in 1993. In December 1995, the party released *Twenty Realities of Secession*, laying out harsh terms for Quebec's departure: redrawing borders to accommodate partition for anglophone, allophone and aboriginal minorities; denial of dual citizenship; a corridor through Quebec to Atlantic Canada; and preparations for violence. Manning proposed measures to impeach Chrétien as prime minister should a Yes vote win, since a prime minister from Quebec could not be trusted to negotiate for Canada. References to Quebec sovereigntists as traitors continued to be commonplace in Reform rhetoric. During six federal by-elections on 26 March 1996, the Reform party campaigned on the slogan "Boot the Bloc," unsuccessfully appealing to voters to help remove the Bloc as Official Opposition. Such provocations only increased support for sovereignty in Quebec. As Tory leader Jean Charest put it: "Manning is planning Canada's funeral…vying for the position of Canada's number-one undertaker." Manning's likely motives were clarified by Tom Flanagan, Reform's former chief strategist, in his book, *Waiting for the Wave*, noting the likeliest scenario for Manning's ascension to the prime ministership involved exploiting the crisis provoked by Quebec's separation.

The Chrétien government, stinging from Reform's criticisms that the government was weak, proceeded to get tough. In 1996, Ottawa began a two-track approach to fighting Quebec sovereignty, widely touted as Plan A and Plan B. Plan A, the carrot, involved carrying the good news about federalism to the Québécois via a massive propaganda effort. In 1996 the Canada Information Office (CIO) was established with a dual mandate: to counter pro-sovereignty arguments and to raise Ottawa's visibility in Quebec. The CIO was given an annual budget of $20 million (plus $23 million extra in the first year to distribute free Canadian flags). Additionally, Public Works Canada was given an annual budget of $50 million to spend on a sponsorship program to raise Ottawa's profile at sporting and cultural events all over Quebec. Between 1996 and 2003 Ottawa spent almost half a billion dollars, over and above that routinely spent on various information campaigns across Canada and aired in Quebec, on federal propaganda in Quebec to win hearts and minds.

The passage of the distinct society resolution and the veto bill, as well as the administrative devolution of power for employment training programs with the promise of more such devolution in future, were also part of this soft approach to win hearts and minds. Furthermore, Chrétien used the March 1996 by-elections, three of which were in Quebec, to bring into his cabinet "two wise men" from Quebec, Stéphane Dion and Pierre Pettigrew, to spearhead the fight against sovereignty and to enhance the weight of Quebec francophones in Chrétien's cabinet. Efforts to get more prominent and respected non-sovereigntist Québec nationalists to run had failed and neither new minister had a significant political following in francophone Quebec. Such were the elements of Plan A: a massive, pro-federalist propaganda campaign; a House resolution on distinct society; a bill on a veto; some minor administrative devolution; and the appointment of two new, strongly anti-nationalist Québécois cabinet ministers with little political credibility in Quebec. Nothing else was on offer to Bouchard's Quebec. But the message to the people of Quebec and the Quebec business community was repeated relentlessly: greater largesse to Quebec was blocked by Bouchard and the PQ government.

Plan B, the stick, was chock-full of aggressive measures to bully Quebec. All these measures involved threats to use superior federal powers to interfere in the referendum process, to deny Quebec the right to act upon the result if there were a sovereigntist victory and to tamper with Quebec's borders in the event of separation, including the partition of Quebec in support of minority claims. The most provocative were Ottawa's threats to Quebec's post-sovereignty territorial integrity. The government also asserted that any move to sovereignty if a referendum were successful was unconstitutional and therefore legally foreclosed.

Ottawa escalated its attack by joining Jean-Guy Bertrand's legal challenge of the constitutionality of Quebec's sovereignty plans. Bertrand, a former PQ cabinet minister turned born-again federalist, unsuccessfully attempted to obtain an injunction against the 30 October referendum. The judge ruled that any attempt to secede was indeed unconstitutional, but refused to stop the referendum on the grounds that democratic principles insist that the Quebec people had a right to be consulted in a referendum. After the referendum Bertrand launched another suit to stop future referendums on sovereignty, to declare Quebec's right to self-determination stops short of any right to secede, and to rule that unilateral secession would be unconstitutional. With Ottawa's intervention, the stakes were raised since a victory would provide the legal pretext for Ottawa to intervene with a heavy hand in the next referendum. Bouchard initially reacted by threatening to call a quick election and referendum, but then backed off. The situation was defused when both Ottawa and Quebec withdrew from the Bertrand case. And the Bertrand case was put on hold when Ottawa decided in September 1996 to refer the whole issue to the Supreme Court for a final determination of the legal and constitutional issues raised by Quebec's drive to sovereignty.

Ottawa's legal challenge was a political provocation, an explicit threat both to the Quebec government and to those in Quebec contemplating voting for sovereignty. Ottawa had commenced a political fear campaign. Challenges to the legality of a successful referendum, and warnings about partitioning and/or constricting Quebec's territory, implied a willingness to use force against the democratic will of a people. Similarly, to declare support for the right of minorities to partition Quebec after a Yes vote, as both Chrétien and Dion had done, implied a willingness to use force to impose the will of the minorities on the majority in Quebec. Perhaps it is naive not to assume that Ottawa has a Plan Z sitting in a safe in the Privy Council Office, a plan for sending military forces into a separating Quebec, as well as the political and administrative measures necessary for such an event to occur: the suspension of the Quebec government and the National Assembly; the arrest and detention of Bloc MPs and PQ MNAs; the disarming of military and police units of questionable federalist sympathies; and the necessary plans and personnel to take over the political administration of Quebec. All these things can be lawfully done with the maximum powers granted to Ottawa in the constitution, provided the support of the House of Commons is sustained. All this seems bizarre and far-fetched, particularly given the Chrétien government's assurances that Quebec would never be kept in Canada against the will of the people. Nevertheless, Ottawa's rhetoric and actions in the post-referendum period led logically to a final resort to legal force, and at the very least constituted an effort to strike fear in the hearts and minds of the Québécois, who retained vivid memories of the recent imposition of the *War Measures Act* and the cruel repressions of 1837–38.

The escalation of Ottawa's rhetoric gave aid and comfort to anti-Québécois extremists, encouraging the growing acceptability of public expressions of hatred against sovereigntists. As a result, views that were formerly limited to the cranks of the Reform party, or a few of the English-Canadian extremists in Quebec, became commonplace in public discourse. In the 22 July 1996 issue of *Maclean's*, Diane Francis felt free to write inflammatory exaggerations about the "seditious behaviour by separatists regarding our military" and "separatist attempts to get military personnel to defect." She called for a witch-hunt against pro-sovereigntists in the military and the expulsion of Bloc defence critic Jean-Marc Jacob from the House of Commons. *Saturday Night*'s headline in the July/August 1996 edition was inexcusably irresponsible: "The writing's on the wall: Things are not getting better in Quebec. They're getting worse, and fast. Chaos, terrorism and violence are now a safe bet." The partitionist movement became more aggressive in its rhetoric, aggravating the issue of commercial signage in an effort to polarize Montreal, all with the public endorsement of the prime minister. Liberal MP Anna Terrana said to a *Vancouver Sun* journalist, "What is happening now is what happened before the war in Germany...First [the Nazis] founded the party, then they got hold of the institutions, including the unions. They got themselves a charismatic leader. And now, they're going through ethnic cleansing...The PQ has the same strategy of trying to get rid of those who are not *pur laine*." She refused to withdraw her remarks until after a gentle prime ministerial rebuke, issuing a heavily qualified retraction: "I may be definitely wrong, but there is a similarity." Deeper down in the foul muck of hate politics lurked the Anglophone Assault Group, which issued death threats against Bouchard and his two sons and declared its intention to use violence to win Montreal's secession from a sovereign Quebec.

English Canadians outside Quebec were thereby conditioned to begin to see the province through the extremists' eyes and to believe that the situation was volatile, unstable and moving toward violence. As extremist views gained routine expression in the mainstream media and among politicians seen as moderate, all with the apparent blessing of the Chrétien government, it became easier to persuade English Canadians outside Quebec to give unquestioning support to harsh methods and believe every exaggerated and nonsensical claim made by anti-sovereigntist extremists. At the worst, the soil was tilled for legal violence and civil war; at best, the chasm between the two solitudes widened and reasoned dialogue became futile.

Reactions in Quebec to Ottawa's hard line were drearily predictable: in January 1996 support for a Yes vote in a sovereignty referendum stood at 52.4 per cent; by July 1996 it had increased to 53 per cent. In 1996, 75 per cent of Québécois expected a sovereign Quebec in the future, 60 per cent in the next ten years and more than 47 per cent in the next five years. PQ support rose to 50.5 per cent, Quebec Liberal support fell to 29.7 per cent and ADQ support rose to 9.4 per cent, giving pro-sovereignty parties 59.9 per cent in total. Bloc support stayed in the forties, despite Bouchard's departure as leader, while support for Chrétien's Liberals in Quebec hovered around 30 per cent. As premier, Bouchard promised to focus his government's efforts on jobs, the economy and deficit reduction; he held out olive branches to Quebec's minorities and suggested the sovereignty issue be debated with reason. To facilitate this, the Bouchard government began to prepare a more elaborate draft of its 1995 partnership proposal, now described as "a new Canadian union" based on a two-nation partnership. Bouchard hoped this would win hearts and minds in English Canada. The PQ hoped that by proposing a radical decentralization of federal powers, involving the premiers directly in the discussions from the outset and advocating an autonomous provincial presence in the structures of the new partnership, there was a slim chance of winning over the "provincial rights" premiers in a grotesque and desperate alliance against Ottawa.

Quebec politicians responded aggressively to Ottawa's provocations. Speaking to Chrétien's threat to use disallowance powers, Bouchard said, "He must be desperate to say such an enormity. I can't understand why a man who knows politics and is supposedly a democrat would resort to the grandmother of the *War Measures Act* to stop Quebec." Bouchard sharply attacked Ron Irwin, the Indian affairs minister, when he speculated about aboriginal land not being included in a sovereign Quebec and the possibilities of post-sovereignty violence against aboriginals in an independent Quebec; he called Irwin "an imbecile, an idiot, a perfect idiot." Responding to Ottawa's constant musings about setting the required vote for a Yes victory at 55 to 66 per cent and about partition and changing borders, Bouchard declaimed, "If the federal government and federalists continue to attack the territorial integrity of Quebec, they will provoke…an extraordinary unity and solidarity that will trigger support for sovereignty above the levels they will have set in order to stop it." Bouchard also expressed surprise at the "audacity" of Chrétien's "encroachments on democracy" in encouraging partition. Bouchard appealed to Ottawa to cease provoking "a dangerous debate" and to desist from its "intimidation, provocations and scare-mongering tactics"; he warned that such an approach would "backfire" and lead to a growth in support for sovereignty and Quebec's accelerated departure from Canada. In the midst of this brouhaha, ADQ leader Dumont appealed to the rest of Canada, saying he had an "open mind" about proposals for reforming Canadian federalism, but that any change must be "deep, serious and rapid," sadly expressing the view that there appeared to be "no real hope" for gaining even Quebec's minimum expectations from Ottawa.

Federalists in Quebec found themselves mercilessly squeezed. Liberal leader Johnson, under attack by Ottawa federalists for his inadequacies as the No leader, in turn attacked Ottawa for its failure to promise constitutional change on distinct society and a veto until defeat became nearly certain. Furthermore, Johnson distanced himself from Ottawa's position, declaring his support for the right of Quebec to self-determination and telling Chrétien to stop discussing the illegality of separation and unilateral declarations of independence. "Trying to stop Quebec from separating after a Yes vote would be like ordering a man who has jumped off a bridge to fall back up," Johnson observed. The best way to avoid another referendum, Johnson reminded Chrétien, was to meet Quebec's constitutional minimum of distinct society and a veto. In response to attacks from federalists in Ottawa, Johnson declared that he wouldn't be "a valet, an echo, a loudspeaker" for Ottawa's views and that his "preoccupation [was] the interests of Quebeckers." Even the dying Robert Bourassa was pulled into the debate, insisting that native lands would clearly fall under the jurisdiction of an independent Quebec, since control of the lands had been settled in the 1975 James Bay Agreement. Bourassa also spoke out against partitionist rhetoric, insisting that "partition is nonsense legally and administratively." It appeared that Ottawa's tough stance was singularly unsuccessful in Quebec, provoking a polarization that favoured sovereigntists. Indeed, Ottawa's political base in Quebec, according to the polls, was shrinking as francophone Québécois were pushed to support sovereignty in response to Ottawa's bullying. Ottawa also seemed to be either pushing soft nationalists into the arms of the sovereigntists, or driving them out of active politics in despair.

Chrétien was determined to stay the course and settle for nothing less than the defeat of Bouchard and the newly resurgent sovereignty movement. From Ottawa's perspective the threat was unprecedented, and it was, at this moment in history, embodied in Lucien Bouchard. Bouchard, with a little help from Manning and the Reform party, had virtually single-handedly destroyed the Mulroney government, created the Bloc Québécois and brought it to the status of Official Opposition in the House of Commons, and intervened at the eleventh hour in the 1995 sovereignty referendum, coming within a whisker of victory. Now Bouchard was premier of Quebec, enormously popular and threatening to sweep Quebec for a personal mandate as premier, followed by another referendum. From Chrétien's point of view, the traditional middle-way represented by the soft nationalist element in the Quebec Liberal party had no chance against Bouchard. Bouchard had to be discredited, his charisma at least tarnished and his government undermined and destabilized. The soft nationalist leadership of the Quebec Liberal party had to be driven into the political wilderness, at least temporarily. And all of this, if the federal strategy was to work, had to happen before two looming and unavoidable political tests: a federal election in 1997 or 1998, and a provincial election in Quebec in 1998 or 1999.

By the late fall of 1996, the Chrétien government's strategy was clear. It was a monumental gamble, a "roll of the dice" for much higher stakes than Mulroney's gamble over Meech, involving a gamble with the survival of the Canadian federation itself.

If it backfired, as some early indications suggested it might, the strategy would increase Bouchard's popularity, drive the soft nationalists into the arms of the sovereigntists and set the stage for a victorious sovereignty referendum. The strategy was Plan B all the way, one very much in the legacy of Trudeau's approach to Québécois nationalism and separatism — no negotiations, no concessions, expressions of contempt for Québécois nationalism and individual sovereigntists and continued threats of asserting superior federal powers to forestall separation.

The strategy evolved as the drama unfolded, beginning with four central elements. The first was destabilization. By forcing the Bouchard government to continue dealing with crises provoked by threats from Ottawa and internal challenges from partitionists and English language rights groups, the strategy deflected the PQ from providing orderly, good government and from getting on with, and receiving credit for, the practical agenda of dealing with the economy and the deficit. Maintaining a crisis atmosphere destabilized the economy by reinforcing business jitters, by discouraging new investment and by encouraging established firms to leave Quebec, put off expansion plans or expand capacity elsewhere. Furthermore, such provocations went down well on Main Street in English Canada, undermined the Reform party and solidified English-Canadian support for the Chrétien government.

The second element was polarization. Polarizing the situation in Quebec maintained a crisis atmosphere and hampered the Bouchard government's efforts to return to normalcy, to succeed with initiatives to reassure Quebec's minorities and calm business fears. This polarization gave further encouragement to the anti-sovereignty movement, including extremist elements, to keep up the pressure on the Bouchard government. Furthermore, maintaining a crisis atmosphere in Quebec kept English Canadians on side, forcing them to choose between a strong, majority Liberal government and chaos. The instability would deny the Bouchard government an opportunity to present its proposed partnership to English Canada in an atmosphere of reason and compromise. As well, the constant crises kept international opinion uncertain, warning off countries to which the sovereigntists typically appealed for support and sympathy, most notably France and the United States.

The third element in the strategy, and perhaps most risky for the Chrétien government, was effectively writing off Quebec for the purposes of the next federal election, focusing on appeals to English Canada. Though this would certainly result in the re-election of the Bloc as the dominant party representing Quebec in the House of Commons, it would nevertheless reveal the bedrock of hard federalist support in Quebec on which to build for the next election.

The fourth element was targeted at the business community. Through judicious high-profile business patronage, Ottawa underlined the tangible rewards of supporting federalism by rewarding the business friends of federalism and punishing the business friends of sovereignty. The message was clear: those business leaders who publicly fought sovereignty could expect federal largesse, those federalist business leaders who had remained largely silent during the referendum should re-examine their position, and those business leaders who embraced sovereignty could expect nothing from Ottawa. Coming on the eve of Premier Bouchard's tri-partite economic summit with business and labour leaders to seek co-operation in developing an economic plan for Quebec, Ottawa's message was not lost, and those business leaders willing to exchange economic co-operation with Bouchard for an abandonment of sovereignty were emboldened to increase the pressure. Meanwhile, PQ and labour activists were increasingly angry at Bouchard's willingness to embrace an approach to deficit and debt reduction involving large cuts in social, health and education spending. These combined pressures began to create a political crisis within the sovereignty movement, as the proposed spending and tax cuts and the downplaying of sovereignty demanded by the more aggressive among the business lobby as the price for tackling Quebec's debt, high unemployment and stagnant economy began to provoke sharp resistance from former premier Parizeau and the more militant sovereigntists and social democrats in the PQ. Ottawa's fondest hope was that this process would both deeply divide the sovereignty movement and begin to destroy Bouchard's charisma, undermining his personal popularity. Hopefully, the federalists reasoned, such outcomes would make Bouchard's almost certain re-election in 1998 or 1999 something less than a popular coronation, and Bouchard himself might begin to reconsider plans for another referendum in 2000 or 2001.

The first test of Ottawa's strategy occurred during the federal election of 2 June 1997. In many ways the election was a replay of 1993, when Chrétien warned of the threats to unity posed by the Reform party in the West and the Bloc in Quebec, implying that a minority government would see the country fall into disarray due to these contradictory regional stresses. By late May, the national unity issue had inevitably come to dominate the campaign with Tory leader Jean Charest emerging as the self-proclaimed new conciliator of the Canadian federation, attacking both Reform and the PQ, while insisting that the Chrétien approach was failing. The big question for Ottawa and Chrétien was clear. Was Plan B working well enough in English Canada to keep the solid support in Ontario necessary for a majority government? Was Plan B working well enough in Quebec that the tough line would rally federalist forces sufficiently to reduce the Bloc's hold on Quebec's seats and increase the number of Liberals elected in Quebec?

Chrétien was vindicated, narrowly winning a majority government with 155 of 301 seats and 38 per cent of the popular vote, down from 41 per cent in 1993. Chrétien was able to win 101 of Ontario's 103 seats, 6 of 14 seats in Manitoba, and 6 of 34 seats in British Columbia. In Quebec, Chrétien managed to make something of a comeback, almost matching the Bloc in popular vote (36 to 38 per cent), while winning twenty-six seats to the Bloc's forty-four. The Liberals racked up huge victories in the Montreal-area seats with large anglophone and allophone populations, victories that translated into fewer seats. Meanwhile, the Bloc held sway in those seats that were overwhelmingly francophone. Tory leader Charest brought the Tories back from near oblivion, winning twenty seats, including five in Quebec. The Reform party failed to make an Ontario breakthrough, but won sixty seats in the four western provinces, thus replacing the Bloc as Official Opposition.

The outcome was troublesome, particularly given the huge gamble Chrétien had embarked upon. Throughout the campaign it was never clear that the Liberals would emerge with a majority, as late polls indicated support below 40 per cent. Then there was the growing evidence of a resurgence of NDP and Tory fortunes (in the end the Tories won 20 seats and the NDP won 21). Further, the evidence was clear that the Liberal vote was collapsing in Atlantic Canada where they won only 11 of 32 seats compared to the 31 won in 1993. The resurgence of the NDP and the Tories, and the Liberal collapse in Atlantic Canada, reflected the growing public disaffection with Chrétien's betrayal on the question of social spending and program cuts. This bitterness over the Liberal conversion to savage fiscal conservatism, one that made Mulroney beam with "I told you so" self-vindication, suggested that the national unity card was no longer, in itself, enough to keep English Canada on side in the fight against the sovereigntists. But Ontario saved the day, voting strategically to give the Liberals a narrow four-seat majority.

While these results were far from a ringing endorsement of

Chrétien's first term, they clearly reflected the short-term electoral effectiveness of his tough line on Quebec combined with appeals to English Canada to keep a strong majority government in office in the interests of national unity. Furthermore, the results in Quebec surprised many, suggesting that Chrétien's tough approach had indeed consolidated the federalist vote, while the polarization had apparently driven many federalist voters to Charest as the self-proclaimed new voice of conciliation in the national unity debate. The sovereigntist movement, by 1997, was clearly in some disarray and losing momentum. Accordingly, Ottawa pressed ahead. Armed now with clear evidence, Chrétien could more confidently dismiss those who continued to argue that tough tactics would backfire and play into sovereigntist hands.

One of the least savory aspects of Ottawa's Plan B was the increasingly focussed, virulent and relentless personal attacks on Bouchard's motives and character, which began to increase in intensity after the successful 1997 federal election as part of the run-up to the looming Quebec election. Led by Intergovernmental Affairs Minister Stéphane Dion, described by one journalist as the "spear carrier" for federalism in Quebec but perhaps more accurately described as the pit bull of federalism, this campaign was given extensive play by the English-Canadian and pro-federalist media. Dion's campaign was a relentless attack on the flaws and contradictions in the sovereignty cause, buttressed by accusations that Bouchard and the sovereigntists were undemocratic, hypocritical, irrational and dangerous. By supporting the idea of partitioning Quebec to save minorities, in the name of self-determination and democracy, from the authoritarian imposition of sovereignty, and by insisting that super-majorities were essential in a sovereignty referendum just to begin the negotiation process, Dion successfully threw Bouchard and his ministers off-guard and provoked often spluttering emotional responses. Such an atmosphere of personal vendetta, deliberately created by Dion and frequently sustained by Bouchard's responses, set the context for one of the most egregious efforts at character assassination in Canadian political history. Liberal MP John Godfrey commissioned psychiatrist Vivian Rakoff to do an analysis of Bouchard. That analysis, entitled "The Mystical Unity of a Folk Identity" and duly released to the media in August 1997, was little more than a politically motivated character assassination in which the psychiatrist implied that the Quebec nationalist movement had fascist and racist tendencies, and that Bouchard was vain, narcissistic and quick to change loyalties due to an "aesthetic character disorder." While most commentators found the whole episode offensive and distasteful, *The Globe and Mail* supported the analysis editorially (26 August 1997). The smear of psychiatric instability had been successfully applied in a very public way to Bouchard and thus the damage was done. While it simply tended to confirm many of the existing prejudices against Bouchard among English Canadians, it cannot have had anything but a damaging effect on Bouchard's general political reputation, with some inevitable consequences in Quebec.

Besides this personal vendetta against Bouchard, there was a campaign of collective vilification directed at the PQ, the sovereignty movement and, frequently, francophone Quebeckers as a national group. The Jewish lobby in Montreal complained incessantly that among large numbers of the adherents of the sovereignty movement lurked dangerously anti-Semitic attitudes. The anglophone lobby, frequently backed up by the English-Canadian press, suggested there were terrifying xenophobic, racist and authoritarian tendencies among large swaths of the sovereignty movement. The campaign was relentless and never-ending, and continues to this day. Even in the aftermath of 11 September 2001, sovereigntists were frequently smeared as terrorist sympathizers — the prime minister himself put this tag on the Bloc during a debate in the House of Commons. This amounted to nothing less than the character assassination of a whole people, and many Québécois were deeply hurt by these smears.

With Chrétien safely returned to power, the premiers joined Ottawa's Plan B efforts by meeting in Calgary in September 1997 and reworking the ideas initially discussed by the four western premiers at Yorkton in 1995. From the moment of its release the Calgary Declaration was on the fast track to failure, but there was a conspiracy in English Canada to continue insisting that it remained an English-Canadian olive branch offered to Quebec sovereigntists. The attitudes behind the document were well expressed by Ontario premier Mike Harris when he said, "The federal government should simply announce the country is indivisible and get on with it," and by Saskatchewan premier Roy Romanow when he said, "Ever since I've been premier I've been telling the people of Quebec that if there's separation there will be dire consequences." The proposal, in fact, hammered Québécois nationalism in three unacceptable ways. First, it trivialized Québécois nationalist aspirations, which lie at the root of the sovereignty movement, by reducing them to merely a question of language. Second, it again trumpeted the equality-of-provinces constitutional doctrine, an idea with little support among serious democrats and virtually none among the Québécois. Third, it heaped injury on the Meech and Charlottetown insults by proffering recognition of "the unique character of Quebec society," generally viewed in Quebec as a bargain-basement, nearly meaningless version of the earlier inadequate "distinct society" offer. As a result, the Calgary Declaration immediately went down in flames in Quebec, a fact discretely ignored by the nine premiers and the prime minister. In Quebec, the Declaration was a public joke, described variously by Bouchard as a "pitiful spectacle" and "an empty shell," reducing Quebec, by its insulting promise of "uniqueness," to a "political eunuch." Bouchard dismissed the document by saying, "Never has English Canada tried to convince Quebec with so little." Both hard and soft nationalists among francophone Québécois viewed the initiative as yet another example of English Canadian intransigence and arrogance.

If the premiers knew the Declaration was doomed before the ink was dry, then why go through the exercise? There were two obvious reasons that were more or less publicly admitted by the premiers in the aftermath of the Declaration. First, the Declaration was the premiers' contribution to Ottawa's "get tough" Plan B. After months of angry threats to Quebec sovereigntists by these same premiers, this ray of sweet reason came in the context of bellicose threats from Ottawa on partition, high voting thresholds and the illegality of separation, and stonewalling refusals to discuss anything to do with sovereignty. It also came quickly on the heels of Chrétien's June re-election. The message to the people of Quebec was clear: take it or leave it; this is all that's on offer; and, by the way, the road to sovereignty will be as painful and dangerous as we can make it. And as the Declaration was shredded in Quebec, as everyone knew it would be, the finger pointing began to the tune of "we tried again, but the Quebec nationalists are unreasonable and unyielding." This calculated, inevitable failure, as expected, hardened hearts in English Canada against Quebec even more.

Second, the Declaration was, however shoddy, a gift to the beleaguered federalist forces in Quebec as the Quebec election neared. No matter how short the document's life was — and it was very short indeed — it lived long enough initially to give the Quebec Liberal party "an offer from English Canada" to wave during a possible election. Federalists in Quebec were in a panic and, however inadequate the Calgary Declaration, their looming defeat at the hands of Bouchard appeared even more certain without some kind of offer to soften Ottawa's Plan B provocations. It was an indication of just how desperate Quebec federalists had become that they continued to give the Calgary Declaration heavily qualified support, despite attacks from Bouchard that Quebec's Liberal leader had become "the official candidate of English Canada for the position of Premier of Quebec…[whose]…election platform was written…in Calgary by the anglophone provinces."

In retrospect, the Calgary Declaration, though designed to fail in achieving a renewal of the federation, had one lasting effect in English Canada. English Canadians, at the end of the day, were even angrier at Quebec for once again rejecting what their premiers smugly decided ought to be enough to satisfy Québécois aspirations. Despite being passed quickly by all provincial legislatures but Quebec, the Calgary Declaration hit a stonewall in less than a year in the Quebec National Assembly when even the Quebec Liberals, now led by Jean Charest, refused to support the document. Bouchard declared that the National Assembly had concluded that the Declaration "denies the existence of the people of Quebec, blending it into the Canadian reality…in blatant contravention of the pact between two founding nations." Liberal leader Charest would only say that the Declaration was "a statement of goodwill from the other provinces," stopping short of the full endorsement that former leader Johnson had initially given a few months earlier.

12

The 1998 Watershed

There were significant developments in the national unity struggle in Quebec in 1998, beginning with the Ice Storm in January and ending with the 30 November Quebec election. In between those events much of great significance happened: Daniel Johnson was replaced as Quebec Liberal leader by federal Tory leader Jean Charest; the Supreme Court held hearings on the legality of secession; Bouchard joined the nine English-Canadian premiers in the Social Union talks; and the rifts in the PQ deepened as Bouchard faced down internal opponents.

The Ice Storm as national unity football
The Ice Storm of 1998, one of the costliest natural disasters in recorded history according to the Institute for Catastrophic Loss Reduction, was centred in Quebec, though parts of Ontario and New Brunswick were also afflicted. At the end of the disaster, an estimated twenty-four people had died, although the toll could have been much higher had not the Quebec government, with help from Ottawa, been so effective, particularly during the ten days that one million people and thousands of businesses and farms went without power in freezing temperatures. Insurance claims amounted to $1.44 billion. At first Ottawa and Quebec went to great lengths not to politicize the event by allowing it to be swept into the national unity standoff. After the immediate crisis, however, the Ice Storm became a political football. Quebec requested $1 billion in storm aid from Ottawa, including $600 million to repair damages incurred by Hydro-Québec. When Ottawa refused to fund Hydro-Québec losses Quebec complained that Ottawa had covered similar damage during ice storms in Manitoba and Newfoundland in 1984.

As the increasingly bitter negotiations went on, Ottawa held up disaster relief to Quebec businesses, pointing the finger of blame at the PQ government. Federal treasury board president Marcel Massé, one of the toughest Plan B advocates, asserted, "[It is] disappointing and pathetic to see Mr. Bouchard 'counting' how much he can 'take' from the generosity of our country." The Bouchard government accused Ottawa of Plan B destabilization tactics by refusing to compensate Hydro-Québec.

What began as a united effort to deal with a natural disaster degenerated into a debate about secession and national unity as a result of Ottawa's tactics. Ottawa's message to the Quebec people was clear: sovereigntists in power in Quebec are an impediment to the easy flow of federal largesse, and a separate Quebec would be on its own in such a case in the future. In English Canada, however, the view was that Ottawa had been overly generous in compensating both the Ice Storm of 1998 and the Saguenay floods of 1996. Throughout the drought on the Prairies from 2000 to 2002, and during the ongoing struggle in the world wheat wars with U.S. and EU subsidies, farmers lamented how their disaster relief was a pittance compared to that enjoyed by Quebec in 1996 and 1998. In 2003, during the SARS crisis in Toronto and with the mad cow crisis afflicting the beef industry in Alberta and Saskatchewan, the refrain was similar — Quebec always gets more and is always ungrateful. Thus the Ice Storm of 1998 was added to the mythic mix in the increasingly bitter national unity debate between Quebec and English Canada.

Johnson dumped; Charest crowned

After the 1995 referendum many prominent federalists in Quebec and Ottawa concluded that Daniel Johnson had to go. His failings were many: a dismal showing as leader of the No team in 1995; a failure to sign on to Plan B with enthusiasm; opposition to the Supreme Court reference; and an ineffectual performance against Bouchard. The conspiracy to unseat Johnson had become increasingly public. Back in November 1997, during a "secret" meeting (duly leaked to the press), business heavyweights and Liberal federalists suggested Pierre Pettigrew as an alternative if Jean Charest continued to resist the draft. The final daggers were plunged into Johnson by federal Liberal cabinet ministers Stéphane Dion and Marcel Massé who, in early 1998, declared they would take an active part in the next Quebec election as national unity defenders, a clear vote of non-confidence in Johnson from Ottawa. Ottawa's well-established Plan B involved pushing the soft nationalist element in the Quebec Liberal party out of positions of influence and leadership, and Johnson had resisted. It was clear Bouchard would crush Johnson in the coming election. On 2 March 1998 Johnson resigned.

The campaign to draft Charest was semi-publicly underway despite Charest's repeated public declarations of lack of interest. But there was no credible alternative in existing Quebec Liberal circles as no credible soft nationalist wanted the job under the Plan B circumstances. Jean Charest had impressive political credentials. As an avowed federalist, Charest held his Sherbrooke seat against formidable BQ challengers. He played a significant role on the No team in the 1995 debate. He took over the ruins of the federal Tory party and brought it back to life in the 1997 election, winning a handful of seats in Quebec. Charest was fluently bilingual, charming, articulate and handsome and thus, for many, the dream candidate to fight for Canada against Bouchard. Although a kind of "Charestmania" swept English Canada, where he was seen as a federalist saviour who would slay the separatist dragon, there was not a similar popular upsurge in Quebec. Charest carried a lot of political baggage and his wild popularity in English Canada was not seen positively in Quebec, where he was dubbed by Bouchard as English Canada's candidate. Charest's record in the Mulroney government was an instant issue, particularly his role in the Meech débâcle that led to Bouchard's rise and the Bloc's emergence. Therefore, as Quebec Liberal leader Charest would bear two potentially fatal burdens. First he would be smeared by the sovereigntists as English Canada's choice for Quebec premier. Second, Bouchard would repeatedly revisit Charest's key role in the Meech "betrayal." Therefore, with Charest as Liberal leader two old enemies, former mates in Mulroney's Tory caucus with scores to settle, would square off in the coming election. And given the charismatic mystique around Bouchard, many believed Charest stood no chance.

What tipped the scales in favour of Charest taking the plunge was a series of dramatic and startling polls showing Charest to be a serious contender. The most significant poll, conducted by Angus Reid and taken just before Johnson's resignation, suggested Charest could actually beat Bouchard. More significantly for Charest's decision, an April Ekos poll reported that Bouchard no longer held first place as the most trusted Quebec politician — now Charest outpolled Bouchard 40 per cent to 39. Other polls reported that with Charest as leader the No forces would win 58 to 42 per cent in a future referendum and that he would beat Bouchard in an election. Charest decided to go for it, announcing his decision in late March and winning the job unopposed on 30 April 1998.

Charest as Liberal leader created an unprecedented situation in Quebec politics. For the first time since before Jean Lesage, the Quebec Liberals were led by an ardent pro-federalist who frequently expressed a passionate commitment to Canada. Liberal leaders, beginning with Lesage and ending with Johnson, had typically expressed a "soft nationalist" abiding commitment to Quebec's "historic demands," to significant constitutional change to redress Quebec's grievances and to the constitutional doctrine of Canada as an equal partnership between two founding nations. Every pro-federalist Liberal leader since the Quiet Revolution had typically presented pragmatic economic arguments as the main reason for Quebec to stay in confederation: it was just a good deal for Quebec. And every premier of Quebec since the Quiet Revolution had been either a pragmatic pro-federalist or a committed sovereigntist. Charest was different. He did not pledge to press Quebec's "historic demands," he did not support the necessity for significant constitutional change and his defense of federalism mixed pragmatism and patriotism. Indeed, Charest argued that constitutional debates and referendums had to be abandoned in favour of quiet diplomacy with other provinces to reform the federation. As a result many believed that, after the honeymoon, his support in Quebec would collapse in inevitable bare-knuckled political debates.

The Supreme Court fiasco
During Charest's seduction as Liberal leader, the Supreme Court of Canada held its public hearings on Ottawa's 1996 secessionist reference questions, with oral arguments during the week of 16 February 1998. Briefs and documents submitted earlier were released to the public. Opinion in Quebec was overwhelmingly opposed to using the Supreme Court, a federal institution, to pass judgment on the right of the Québécois nation to its own state. A Léger & Léger poll found that 69.8 per cent of Quebeckers opposed the reference to the Supreme Court, insisting that it was the people of Quebec who must finally decide whether Quebec could declare unilateral independence. Opposition in Quebec united sovereigntist and federalist, including Jean Charest, Daniel Johnson and Claude Ryan. Quebec Liberal leader Johnson, and former Quebec Liberal leader Ryan, were forceful in their opposition to using the Supreme Court to block independence. Both men defended Quebec's unqualified right of self-determination and

insisted that a successful sovereignty referendum would have to be respected. Ottawa's position was that secession was illegal, referendum or not, and the only way Quebec could leave the federation was through a constitutional amendment, requiring the consent of seven of ten provinces representing 50 per cent of the Canadian population, as well as the assent of the House of Commons and the Senate. This was clearly a provocative position.

The fact was that Ottawa had no genuine interest in the legality of Quebec's separation. It was clearly a Plan B tactic. But it was a risky tactic, since it could open a Pandora's Box should the Supreme Court rule even marginally in the sovereigntists' favour. Nevertheless, back in 1996 when the reference was made, Ottawa was determined to take the risk, fearing Bouchard's success in a future referendum.

The context was important. First of all, the constitutional challenge to Quebec's drive to sovereignty was redundant. It was clear that any court would find unilateral secession unconstitutional. There was already a clear judicial opinion on the record. Mr. Justice Robert Lesage of the Quebec Superior Court, in the Bertrand case just before the 1995 referendum, had ruled that any attempt to secede was indeed unconstitutional, but that it would be a serious error for a court to try to block an exercise in democracy through vehicles such as referendums. And when constitutions cannot accommodate the democratic aspirations of a people, the well-established precedent is a unilateral declaration of independence followed by orderly negotiations in the context of international law. What Ottawa sought was legally self-evident and served no real legal purpose. Ottawa had already promised repeatedly not to force the people of Quebec to stay in Canada against their will. Therefore Ottawa's only conceivable motive was to intimidate the Québécois in order to keep them from continuing down the road to separation.

The legal challenge was politically dishonest. Ottawa had already qualified any constitutional initiative to outlaw a sovereignty referendum or to refuse to honour the result. Having already allowed three referendums under Quebec's referendum law, any effort by Ottawa to disallow that law retroactively would be difficult to justify. The active participation of many premiers and three prime ministers in previous referendums implied not only a respect for the process, but also a willingness to honour the outcome. In the Charlottetown referendum, all players — premiers, prime minister, legislatures and the House of Commons — accepted the expression of the will of the people as final. Further, back in 1970 when the federal government imposed the *War Measures Act*, Ottawa sent a clear message to the Quebec sovereignty movement that undemocratic, illegal methods would not be tolerated in a campaign for sovereignty. As a result, Québécois nationalists and sovereigntists put all their energy into the democratic drive for independence. The results, evidenced through victories in provincial elections for the PQ, two referendums and the election of Bloc MPs, were respected and recognized. To challenge that thirty-year history of democratic struggle as unlawful and unconstitutional was a monumental act of bad faith.

A key reason for Ottawa's decision to make the reference was the PQ government's argument that the Quebec National Assembly was sovereign in matters related to secession. Further, the PQ government insisted, as it always had, that the whole issue of secession was at heart a political and democratic matter, not a legal issue, and that any secession process by its nature must inevitably be addressed according to international law. The PQ government noted that there was a large body of international law, and multiple precedents involving secession, from which to draw guidance. The fundamental point, of course, was that existing constitutions are not typically designed to facilitate secession; quite the contrary, they are designed to protect the integrity of the existing constitutional order. These arguments had been a central part of the sovereigntist case since the founding of the PQ and had not only gained the status of a political axiom among the Québécois, but were widely supported by many specialists in English Canada. Indeed, such arguments seemed to have been implicitly accepted by all players since the sovereignty movement picked up the challenge to win through democratic means back in 1970. But Ottawa's Plan B strategists, like Dion and Chrétien, were convinced that these arguments had to be countered to block the momentum to sovereignty. When Ottawa intervened in the Bertrand case to refute these arguments, the PQ government withdrew from the case in protest, and when Ottawa referred the matter to the Supreme Court, the PQ government refused to participate since the National Assembly already enjoyed sovereignty in matters related to secession. To avoid the spectacle of a Supreme Court case on Quebec's right to secession attended by only Ottawa, the English-Canadian provinces and various other enemies of Quebec sovereignty, the Court appointed André Joli-Coeur to present the case for sovereignty.

Ottawa's reference questions were a biased exercise in card-stacking (See Appendix II). Clearly expecting a quick decision supporting Ottawa, the questions presented to the Supreme Court were: first, can Quebec unilaterally secede under the Canadian constitution? second, does Quebec have the right of unilateral secession; does the right of self-determination under international law include unilateral secession? and third, if there is a conflict between domestic and international law on these matters, which takes precedence? The unfairness in how the questions were worded and the order in which they were posed moved Alain Pellet, president of the United Nations' International Law Commission, to conclude his submission to the Supreme Court, made at the invitation of Joli-Coeur, with the following advice to the justices: "I am both deeply troubled and shocked by the partisan manner in which the questions were formulated and I allow myself to suggest that it be a court of justice's duty to react to that which seems to be a *too obvious attempt of political manipulation*" (emphasis added). Claude Ryan suggested in his brief that the Supreme Court refuse to answer the questions: "The Court would be wise to give back to the politicians the responsibility of finding answers to the democratic questions brought before the tribunal."

After the public hearings, Ottawa was less confident. The justices asked a series of sweeping questions that caught Ottawa's lawyers off guard and made it clear that the simple answers to the reference questions Ottawa wanted would not be forthcoming. Before the hearings, Dion confidently described Bouchard's pro-sovereignty arguments as "simplistic" and "weak," constituting "myths that [people]...ended up believing." After the hearings, Dion began uncharacteristically to talk about Plan A and all the good news it held for Quebec in the federation. Ottawa's fears were justified when the Supreme Court released its answers on 20 August 1998 (See Appendix II). Both federalists and sovereigntists instantly claimed victory. Prime Minister Chrétien asserted that the Court established "a barrier that you have to go over," and insisted that the decision could only be interpreted as demanding a majority far greater than 50 per cent plus one on a clear question on secession. Premier Bouchard, on the other hand, argued that the decision dealt a serious blow to federalist forces by stating that there was an obligation to negotiate in the event of a successful referendum on sovereignty.

While the Supreme Court decision was sufficiently carefully worded to allow both sides some solace, on balance there was a clear case that the sovereigntists won more than they lost. Clearly Ottawa lost on the overall gambit of getting the Supreme Court to

234 DEBTS TO PAY

give clear answers ruling out unilateral secession. Additionally, Ottawa lost in three crucial areas.

First, the Court ruled that Ottawa has an obligation to negotiate with Quebec sovereigntists in the event of a clear majority supporting a clear referendum question on sovereignty. A central feature of federalist strategy in both the 1980 and 1995 sovereignty referendums was the repetition of the mantra: No matter what the outcome, there will be no negotiations on sovereignty, none whatsoever, never. This had a tremendous impact on Quebec voters, contributing significantly to the No sweep in 1980 and even more so to the No squeaker in 1995. Many in Quebec worried about both the futility and uncertainty that would result from a Yes victory followed by an impenetrable federalist stonewall. The only options in that circumstance were self-evident: forget sovereignty and surrender, or go down the rocky path of a unilateral declaration of independence. Now the Supreme Court had ruled clearly: Ottawa and the other provinces are obliged to negotiate in good faith following a Yes victory.

Second, the Court ruled that a clear question on sovereignty must be presented in a referendum. The ruling solved a serious problem for the sovereigntists. Both the 1980 and 1995 questions were designed to reassure voters that the sovereigntists wanted to negotiate. In fact, the 1980 question only asked for a mandate to negotiate sovereignty-association and did not even ask for permission to move on to sovereignty. In 1995 the question was clearer, but still included a negotiation clause regarding a new partnership. In 1995, however, a failure to negotiate on the part of Ottawa would have triggered a move to independence after a twelve-month period. Now that the Supreme Court ruled that negotiations must occur, the sovereigntists could actually embrace a clear question. Indeed, Bouchard suggested that the wording of the question could be extracted from the very text of the Supreme Court decision which, in turn, would be rather disarming to the federalist cause.

Third, the Court ruled that this clear question must be approved by a clear majority. The sovereigntists, as well as many federalists in Quebec, including Liberal leader Charest, argued forcefully that a clear majority remains what it has always been in our system of democracy, 50 per cent plus one. Ottawa continued to argue otherwise, suggesting a larger majority was required. Here the sovereigntists have the constitutional edge. Fifty per cent plus one has always been the magic number in most democracies, unless otherwise explicitly stated. This level was accepted by all actors, sovereigntist and federalist, in the referendums of 1980 and 1995, thus there exists a clear precedent in recent constitutional history. Perhaps of more constitutional significance was the 1949 Newfoundland referendum in which 52 per cent was enough to trigger admission to the federation.

On balance, therefore, the sovereigntists arguably benefited most from the Supreme Court decision. The sovereigntist cause was legitimized as never before by the declaration of the highest court of the land that negotiations must follow a clear majority Yes vote on a clear question. Further, the Court directed that these negotiations "would address the potential act of secession as well as the possible terms should in fact secession proceed." Indeed, the Court went so far as to declare, "The other provinces and the federal government would have no basis to deny the right of the government of Quebec to pursue secession, should a clear majority of the people of Quebec choose that goal." In the long run the federalist cause may have been mortally wounded, thanks to the failed Plan B gamble that a tame Supreme Court would checkmate the sovereignty movement.

Bouchard gambles on the Social Union

After the failure of the Calgary Declaration, the nine premiers of the English-Canadian provinces rummaged around in the ashes in an effort to salvage something. They proposed that Canada and the provinces craft a Social Union Framework agreement, which would not be a constitutional change but could be realized through administrative and legislative means. Ottawa indicated a willingness to listen. The provinces were increasingly fiscally desperate. Ottawa's unilateral cuts in social, health and education spending during the fight against the deficit downloaded the problems onto provincial treasuries, and the provinces faced increasing popular anger and anxiety, particularly concerning the underfunding of medicare.

As Ottawa's deficits turned into surpluses and the federal government signalled an intention to embark on significant program development in health and education, the provinces argued that the priority should be restoring federal funding in areas like health, education and social welfare, and that transfers should be provided to the provinces to develop and implement the programs. Fearful of an intrusive federal government moving into areas of provincial jurisdiction, the provinces produced a Social Union proposal with the following elements: 1) the right to opt out of federal social pro-

236 DEBTS TO PAY

grams with full financial compensation as long as the province pursues a program with similar objectives; 2) an end to national standards in social programs enforced by Ottawa and the substitution of a provincial consensus on standards with no significant enforcement mechanism; 3) the restoration of federal funding to the provinces, especially in health, with guarantees against arbitrary future reductions; 4) strict limits on Ottawa's use of federal spending power for future social and health programs, like pharmacare, home care and daycare, requiring provincial consultation and consent; and 5) the transfer of the administration of social programs, including those heavily funded by Ottawa, to the provinces. Taken together, these proposals, like the Meech, Charlottetown and Calgary constitutional proposals, sought heavy curbs on the autonomy and power of the central government and devolution of considerable additional powers to the provinces. Though the Social Union proposal sought only a legislative and administrative agreement, easily changed by future governments, the successful forging of such an agreement with Ottawa could, in some minds, set the stage for the swift passage of the Calgary Declaration as a constitutional amendment.

The same old alliance of provincial rights premiers and the neo-conservative business lobby emerged to push the Social Union proposals. A weakened central government, stronger provincial governments and a massive devolution of control of social programs had been central aspects of the business lobby's efforts since the election of Mulroney in 1984. The business lobby continued to view a strong central government as a real threat to the expanding political hegemony it increasingly enjoyed. The lobby strongly supported Meech and Charlottetown, and had in fact drafted the Calgary Declaration. The devolution of social programs, and curbs on the federal spending power as a source of central discipline on the provinces, were both key to a number of long-term corporate objectives. The business lobby wanted to continue downsizing social programs and the public sector, both to remove government as a central actor in the social and economic life of Canadians and to speed up the harmonization necessary for successful free and global trade. The lobby also wanted to open up the social spending basket, especially the huge budgets in education and health, to the private sector, something right-wing premiers had already advocated. National standards and national enforcement made this difficult. Further, many of the provinces were already clearly more amenable to two-tiers in education and health: a second tier funded publicly and characterized by under-funding and low quality, and a first tier funded jointly by governments and consumers and open for private business.

In August 1998 Bouchard surprised many by joining the other nine premiers in a common front on the Social Union. In doing so, Bouchard ended Quebec's boycott of the Social Union initiative and yielded on a central demand that all Quebec's premiers had pursued as the bottom line. Bouchard dropped the position that Quebec must be able to withdraw unilaterally from federally funded programs and receive full financial compensation with no strings attached; i.e., the same amount of money that would have been spent by Ottawa on the federal program in Quebec would be paid to the Quebec government for use in any manner the government determined. Sovereigntist critics of Bouchard in Quebec were quick to warn of the dangers of being betrayed by the anglophone provinces, as had happened in the past, as well as to point out that by participating in such talks Quebec was de facto conceding that it was a province just like the others. Federalist critics of Bouchard warned that he was intent on manipulating the process in order to confront Ottawa with unreasonable demands and thus engineer another spectacular failure of federalism. Clearly the decision to join the talks was of enormous significance, as Bouchard conceded, "This is a concession that we have made. I know that it is very important because it's a move that Quebec has never made."

From Bouchard's perspective participation in the talks was part of an exceedingly complex manoeuvre. Federalists in Quebec were hopeful that the Social Union talks would produce something that could be characterized as a renewal of federalism, even if only a comprehensive administrative agreement on social programs. If such an agreement were reached by the nine provinces and Ottawa without Bouchard and Quebec's participation, it would be ammunition in coming elections and a future referendum. Charest was proving more popular than expected and continued to push the argument that a pragmatic, low-key approach at an administrative and legislative level would be more effective in making gains for Quebec than noisy constitutional clashes. Bouchard noted that Ottawa was poised to introduce some big-ticket intrusions into areas of provincial jurisdiction like health (pharmacare and home care, for example) and education (postsecondary scholarships and pre-kindergarten, for example), and it was essential for Quebec to join the other provinces in fighting such intrusions. Bouchard reasoned that since the people of Quebec had voted to stay in Canada in 1995, his obligation as premier included defending Quebec's interests while it remained trapped in the federation. From the perspective of advancing sovereignty, Bouchard reasoned that if the provinces held firm against Ottawa and stuck together, at some point Ottawa, unwilling to yield on its powers and control over funding, would pull the plug on the whole process, proving once again that the federation did not work. Finally, Bouchard saw the meetings around the Social Union as an opportunity to begin presenting to the premiers aspects of the PQ's latest partnership proposal in an atmosphere that was private and quiet, away from federal hyperbole and media hype.

Splits in the PQ

Many committed sovereigntists in the PQ doubted the depth of Bouchard's devotion to sovereignty, and decisions such as participating in the Social Union talks did nothing to reassure them. Top former Bloc staffer André Néron described Bouchard as a "sovereigntist in mutation," since he had switched between federalism and sovereignty four times in his political career. During the 1995 referendum campaign Parizeau had relinquished leadership of the Yes campaign only reluctantly, distrusting Bouchard's soft approach to sovereignty. Many sovereigntists believed Bouchard would be quick to accept a constitutional accommodation including the Meech minimum. As well, many in the PQ were angered by Bouchard's fiscal conservatism in the fight against the deficit, deeply cutting education, health and social spending. Bouchard's obsession with rapidly reducing the deficit to zero and beginning to generate surpluses prior to the election was criticized. Finally, Bouchard's proposal to use any surplus primarily for tax cuts, with a smaller portion going to social spending, was unpopular.

In April 1998, Parizeau publicly rebuked Bouchard and the PQ government for equivocating on a referendum commitment. He advised them to stop agonizing on a referendum, to stop appearing apologetic for supporting sovereignty, and to paint Charest for what he was, "a right-wing federalist." Parizeau, quite correctly in retrospect, advised Bouchard to quickly polarize the province to undercut Charest's strategy of placing himself in the middle ground between Chrétien and Bouchard, successfully tapping into the fundamental ambivalence of the Québécois' divided loyalties between Quebec and Canada. Parizeau also criticized Bouchard's deficit-fighting strategy, warning him that the cuts in education and health spending had been "too drastic and indiscriminate."

Parizeau renewed his attack in October 1998 against the "winning conditions" position on a future referendum. Bouchard had not heeded Parizeau's earlier warnings, and Charest's ascension to the Liberal leadership and his strength in the polls haunted the PQ. Charest attacked the PQ's endless referendum strategy, arguing that it created uncertainty and divisiveness. Polls reported that more than 60 per cent of Quebeckers did not want another referendum in the near future. Bouchard responded by bobbing and weaving, now saying there would definitely be a referendum, then saying that a referendum might not occur, then saying he would hold a referendum only under "winning conditions." This was seen for what it was — the typical equivocations of an insecure politician — and did nothing to reassure dedicated sovereigntists or to win public confidence. As André Néron said, "If the leader's position is ambiguous, how can he make sovereigntists out of people who are undecided?" Parizeau very publicly shared a similar view, arguing forcefully that Bouchard's "winning conditions" position on the referendum would not only hurt the sovereignty movement but also put the PQ's chance of re-election at risk. Parizeau's position, to make sovereignty the central issue, to unconditionally promise a referendum if re-elected and to devote all efforts to a general campaign to win the referendum, had always remained constant. Parizeau's October 1998 criticisms deeply wounded the government, since they occurred just days before the planned election call. Deputy premier Bernard Landry denounced Parizeau as an enemy of sovereignty since he had positioned himself in "an objective alliance with our adversaries and the adversaries of sovereignty."

By the end of October Bouchard tried to heal the rift. The day before the 1998 election call, Bouchard promised to hold a referendum if re-elected, but still focussed on "winning conditions" when he said, "My commitment is to hold a referendum that will be won." Landry continued to insist that a referendum would not be held during a new mandate if "winning conditions were not met." Bouchard also announced that Parizeau, the "enemy of sovereignty" of a few weeks before, would carry the PQ's campaign to the colleges and universities, clearly hoping that Parizeau could reassure those with doubts about the PQ government's dedication to sovereignty. Parizeau may have been a thorn in Bouchard's side, but his stature in the province remained formidable, particularly among committed sovereigntists.

Bouchard humbled: the 1998 Quebec election

The 30 November 1998 Quebec election was the second major test of Ottawa's Plan B. Bouchard's strategy after the near win of 1995 had been clear: he would seek a new mandate which, given his popularity, would be a crushing win over the federalist Liberals. Very soon thereafter there would be a "winning" referendum. In the meantime, the sovereigntists entertained the hope that Chrétien would fail to win a majority government, while the Bloc would sweep Quebec's federal seats. Alas for the sovereignty movement, things had not worked out. Chrétien had won in 1997. Ottawa's relentless attacks on Bouchard, and the effective destabilization of the political situation in Quebec, had gnawed away at Bouchard's popularity. Bouchard's own policy of deficit fighting through deep cuts in education and health had further undermined his popularity and led to public splits in the PQ. Charest had arrived on the scene, initially outpolling Bouchard.

Then in the run-up to the election, and doubtless firming up the PQ's decision to call an election, Bouchard was handed a number of political gifts. The militant anglophone rights group, Alliance Quebec, began a campaign in September 1998 to pressure major retailers in Montreal to post more English signs. This was perfectly legal under Quebec's language law after Bourassa's famous com-promise, which allowed languages other than French as long as the French version was at least twice the size of the other. Back in 1996 the PQ wanted to remove this right from the legislation, but Bouchard had persuaded them not to do so. Most large retailers, like Eaton's and the Bay, had not bothered to post English signs. Alliance Quebec demanded they do so and began a picketing cam-paign. Very quickly four major retailers relented under the pressure (Eaton's, the Bay, Wal-Mart and Sears). Bouchard met with these retailers and unsuccessfully urged them to continue with French-only signs in the interests of "linguistic peace." Charest refused to take a clear position on the matter. The crisis reminded francoph-one Quebeckers that the PQ government remained the major bulwark against English language incursions and that prominent anglophone retailers were overly eager to succumb to pressure from Quebec's small anglophone minority.

Prime Minister Chrétien gave Bouchard a boost when he told reporters in early October that constitutional change recognizing Quebec's "distinct" or "unique" character was no longer an option for the foreseeable future. But such change was not really neces-sary, he argued, since Ottawa had already fulfilled its promises out of the referendum. This created such a stir that a week later Chrétien clarified his position by telling reporters, "We're ready. If the provinces want to do it and Quebec wants to do it, it will be done. I can't do it if Quebec is opposed...Look, it will be very easy if Mr. Charest is there...When he will be premier, we will be able to put it in the constitution — if the provinces maintain their support for...Calgary..." This only made matters worse for Charest, since Chrétien's remarks supported the PQ's widely broadcast claim that Charest was English Canada's candidate for premier of Quebec.

And then, throughout the month of October, Charest and the Liberal party carried out a major propaganda campaign on the party's new, right-of-centre program: a less intrusive government; privatization; more tax cuts; a bigger role for the private sector; and economic growth through constitutional peace and co-operative federalism. Earlier, Charest had raised doubts about his support for Quebec's $5-per-day daycare program. Bouchard baited Charest, calling him Quebec's version of Ontario's Tory premier Mike Harris whose savage cuts were the talk of the land. In the spring Charest and the Liberals had outpolled Bouchard and the PQ with 52 per cent support. After the October media campaign, public support for Charest and his party had fallen seven points to 45 per cent.

The final gift to Bouchard was presented when, in the run-up to the campaign and during its early stage, Charest played the economic fear card. Charest had obviously failed to learn from the failure of economic scare tactics during both the Charlottetown and sovereignty referendum debates. Attacking the PQ for economic mismanagement and heartlessness, Charest lamented the high unemployment rate, poor economic growth and Bouchard's obsession with reducing the deficit through deep cuts, complaining that "dollars come before patients." A healthy economy could be achieved in two stages, Charest argued: first, eliminate the threat of sovereignty, and second, jettison economic nationalism and join the new global economy. The threat of another referendum on sovereignty had shackled Quebec's economic growth and dimmed its future economic prospects. The PQ drag on Quebec's economy was threefold: "too much government...too much intervention...we pay too much in taxes." Eliminating the separatist threat in Quebec would generate $17 billion in new private investment and create 131,000 new jobs over five years. These figures, Charest insisted, "illustrate...what Quebec can go out and get as long as it gets rid of the referendum threat."

Charest had thereby set up his own repeated economic ambush

and Bouchard was delighted to oblige. Pointing to a Liberal pro-
jection error in using expenses over four years and revenues over
five, Bouchard declaimed, "These are people who don't even know
how to count." He described Charest's scenario as "a monumental
joke," "ridiculous" and "surrealistic." The PQ accused the Liberals
of embarking on a dishonest and overstated economic fear campaign, something that had been used repeatedly in the past.

The Quebec economy was in fact doing very well, even
according to outside experts. An October ranking by *The Globe
and Mail Report on Business* (5 October 1998) declared that Quebec's economy was the healthiest of the ten provinces. While this
had a lot to do with reconstruction after the Ice Storm, the fact
was that on every measure, be it consumer spending, capital
spending, manufacturing shipments, wholesale and retail activity,
job creation or GDP forecasts, Quebec was performing excep-
tionally well. Quebec's 1998–99 budget reported a drastically
reduced deficit, projected to disappear in 2000 and creating thereafter an estimated $2 billion annual surplus. Despite Quebec's
cuts in spending, the province still enjoyed the strongest and most
generous safety net in the country, particularly its family support
programs. Further, in addition to fighting the deficit, Quebec had
promised tax cuts to business starting in 2000. Bouchard was thus
able to defend his credentials against Charest as both a social
spending interventionist and a fiscal conservative determined to
trim the deficit and debt.

As for Quebec's general and persisting structural economic
problems, the sovereigntists continued to lay the blame at the
door of Canada's federal system, which shackled the province
into a second-class economic status, unable to realize its full
potential. Freed of federal constraints and liberated from a dying
and inefficient national economy, a sovereign Quebec would be
vibrantly prosperous. Sovereigntists had taken this position ever
since the 1988 free trade debate. Quebec's poverty and unemployment figures were always higher than the more prosperous
anglophone provinces, whether a sovereigntist or a federalist
government was in power. Quebec's lower per capita income, 14
per cent behind Ontario's in 1997, reflected how the burdens of
federalism smothered Quebec's economic potential. Further,
Quebec still hadn't closed the linguistic income gap. (In 2001 the
Census reported those who spoke only French in Quebec earned
8 per cent less than those who spoke English only, while bilingual
speakers earned around 40 per cent more on the average.) These

facts represented the second-class economic role imposed on Quebec in the traditional national economy. Only full sovereignty would finally erase such lingering legacies of Quebec's colonial past. Therefore, sovereigntists had never taken responsibility for these structural problems but had always argued that only sovereignty would provide Quebec with the economic tools necessary to erase this inequity.

Charest had opened up a debate that he couldn't hope to win, particularly given the good performance of the Quebec economy in 1998 and the positive forecasts into 1999 and 2000. Though Charest continued to raise economic issues throughout the campaign, he did so in a more muted fashion.

Bouchard's economic platform was unapologetic: aggressive government intervention including a $2 billion economic development agency; aggressive use of the Caisse de dépôt et placement du Québec; and no deficit by 2000 followed by annual $2 billion surpluses for tax cuts and social programs. Bouchard's social program platform promised further major additional programs: a twenty-six-week improvement on Ottawa's parental leave program, including a guarantee of 70 per cent of incomes between $20,000 and $51,000; expansion of $5-per-day daycare spaces; all-day kindergarten for five year olds; and an immediate injection of $2.1 billion into the health system. The contrast with Charest's program could not have been greater. Further, Bouchard appealed to federalist voters and soft nationalists, arguing that the PQ would stand up for Quebec within Canada and provide good government.

Two groups disappeared from view in the campaign. Quebec's anglophone minority was ignored by both Bouchard and Charest. Bouchard had no hope of making significant inroads among anglophones, and campaigning aggressively in those seats would be provocative and potentially confrontational. Charest knew he had the anglophone vote in his pocket, and too much presence in such ridings would feed the "Charest as English-Canada's candidate" accusation among francophones. Further, Charest needed to focus on the francophone voters if he hoped to win. Francophones were a majority in 80 of the 125 ridings and the election would be won or lost in 30 to 35 swing seats outside Montreal. Charest knew he would rack up huge majorities in the anglophone and allophone seats in Montreal, but this would not translate into a large number of seats won. To win, given the concentration of the federalist vote in Montreal, Charest needed to outpoll Bouchard by about 5 per cent overall to win enough francophone seats to form a government.

The late Pierre Bourgault, founder of the RIN and militant sovereigntist, described the anglophone minority as "the great forgotten
people of this election campaign" who had been conveniently "dis-
guised as thin air."

The Action Démocratique du Québec also failed to be a major
player in the campaign. Dumont had distanced himself from his
former support for sovereignty-association and his participation on
the Yes team in 1995, calling for a moratorium on all referendums.
His platform was markedly right-of-centre, advocating the abolition of sixty-one government agencies and departments; a massive
reduction in the role of government, both provincial and federal;
huge tax cuts; more free enterprise; and a fair deal for Quebec's
youth. Reporters noted his platform was to the right of Charest's
and asked Dumont if he would consider a coalition with the Liberals. Dumont bristled, declaring all Charest had were old ideas.

Facing increasingly unfavourable poll results, Charest took a
huge gamble midway through his campaign and decided to focus
almost exclusively on the referendum issue. He had his bus repainted
with the slogan, "Fini Les Référendums," and began aggressively
denouncing the PQ's intention to hold a referendum, describing in
the darkest terms the resulting uncertainty. It was a classic, highly
emotional scare campaign that focussed in a very personal way on
Bouchard's separatist agenda, including his determination to hold a
referendum even if the public didn't want one.

On 30 November 1998 Bouchard failed to get his sweep;
indeed, though easily winning a majority government, he was
politically wounded. The Liberals won the popular vote, 43.7 per
cent to the PQ's 42.7 per cent. But Bouchard enjoyed a sweep in
seats won: 75 to the Liberals' 48 (the ADQ's Dumont held his
seat). Only 124 seats were counted on election night because PQ
candidate Yves Blais in Masson died during the campaign, neces-
sitating a by-election in December. It appeared that Charest's
eleventh-hour referendum scare campaign had a dramatic effect.
Nevertheless, Charest still failed to make the needed breakthrough among francophone voters, winning only one in four.

* * *

No matter how the results were probed and prodded, the fact
remained that Bouchard's drive to create a necessary "winning condition" for the next referendum had suffered a serious setback.
Ottawa's Plan B authors, though upset that Bouchard remained pre-

mier, found solace in his failure to obtain his expected electoral land-slide. Michel David of *Le Soleil* described Bouchard's win as "a very bitter victory," and Michel Auger of *Le Journal de Montréal* said Bouchard "triumphed without glory." A humbled Bouchard con-ceded the point: "Obviously...Quebeckers want us as a government...But they are not prepared to give us the current con-ditions for a referendum right now." Therefore, the PQ government would spend the first part of the new mandate delivering on the cam-paign platform and dealing with Ottawa. But, according to Bouchard, federalism would again fail and the prospect of a "win-ning" referendum later in the mandate would again open up. These were fighting words for Ottawa, and the constitutional confronta-tions continued.

13

The Fall of Lucien Bouchard and the Rise of Paul Martin

The first major battles of 1999 were joined over the Social Union Framework and Ottawa's 1999–2000 budget. As expected, the nine premiers of the anglophone provinces abandoned Quebec's bottom line, despite having earlier agreed when Bouchard signed on, giving up the right to opt out of new federal programs with financial compensation. In exchange for more immediate health-care cash ($23.4 billion), the provinces surrendered their central demands, proving, as they had in 1981–82, that Ottawa can usually buy all the English-Canadian premiers it needs to isolate Quebec. The provinces also caved on the demands that Ottawa not unilaterally cut federal transfers for health, post-secondary education and social assistance, and that it refrain from unilateral future intrusions into provincial jurisdictions. Quebec refused to agree and Parizeau declared that the other nine provinces "gave up their birthright for a plate of lentils." Bouchard accused Ottawa of "extortion" and "using federal surpluses to bring the provinces to their knees."

Quebec was punished in the new federal budget, according to Bouchard. As a result of not signing, the budget denied Quebec a fair share of the new funding. Noting that Quebec has 24 per cent of Canada's population, Bouchard complained that the province received only 8 per cent of the fresh federal health infusion. Overall, the budget again treated Quebec inequitably and continued the same old discriminatory pattern. Bouchard declared, "We estimate Ottawa deprives Quebec of 30,000 jobs." With this action, Ottawa has made a clear threat. Canada was becoming "a unitary government where we have…no right to affirm our distinctiveness."

Bouchard also declared that Ottawa's war against Quebec was continuing: "The battle undertaken against the Quebec model is a battle against Quebec identity…to convince us to dissolve our identity in the great Canadian bath." Such remarks clearly indicated that Bouchard had not given up on achieving "winning conditions" for a referendum during his new mandate. Accordingly, Ottawa's pit bull, Stéphane Dion, was again unleashed, describing Bouchard's linking of the Quebec economic model to Quebec identity as "odious…the Quebec model [of state intervention] has nothing to do with Quebec identity." Dion again attacked Bouchard's claim that 50 per cent plus one was enough to effect secession. Rather, Dion argued, in speeches, at press conferences and in articles in the press, a majority for secession had to be something approaching "a consensus." To effect secession on a "slim majority" would be undemocratic and "irresponsible." According to Dion, 50 per cent plus one was not enough, dismissing the Newfoundland precedent with the assertion that "it is customary in a democracy to require a higher majority for separating from a union than for entering it." Dion urged Bouchard to abandon another referendum, but insisted that if he chose to go ahead with one there had to be a clear majority on a clear question, as required by the Supreme Court. And Dion warned that Canada would not negotiate if neither the question nor the majority were clear. Indeed, he warned that "the government of Canada…might have to outline the reasonable requirements of clarity without which it would not undertake the negotiation of the secession of Quebec from Canada." With these provocative words, which had a chilling effect on the sovereignty movement, Dion snatched back the partial victory the sovereigntists won in the Supreme Court decision.

While the constitutional war of words continued, Bouchard saw another of his "winning conditions" jeopardized by an illegal strike by Quebec's 47,500 nurses in late June/early July of 1999. Labour peace was essential to building toward a successful referendum, and Quebec's powerful and militant unions, especially in the public sector, were strong sovereignty supporters. Yet these same unions were not shy about pressing their demands upon a sovereigntist government. This contradictory relationship frequently created political problems for the sovereignty movement. For example, just prior to the 1980 referendum, Lévesque had bought labour peace with generous settlements, which the PQ government tried to take back with a 20 per cent wage rollback in 1983, provoking some bitter strikes. In 1999 Bouchard faced unrest among Quebec's 400,000 public sector workers, particularly over his guideline of a maximum of a 5 per cent wage increase over three years. This guideline was essential, Bouchard

declared, if the deficit was to be eliminated and the necessary surplus generated for the tax cuts promised in 2000. Thus two of
Bouchard's "winning conditions," labour peace and deficit elim-
ination/tax cuts, were in contradiction. The nurses were the first
test of this guideline, demanding 6 per cent over two years and a
10 per cent catch-up. Entry-level nurses in Quebec were the lowest paid in Canada, while top-level nurses earned $5 an hour less
than those in Ontario. Determined to close that gap, Quebec's
nurses embarked on an illegal strike, enjoying strong popular
support. The Quebec government imposed harsh penalties. The
nurses persisted, however, defying Bouchard's ultimatum to go
back to work. The back-to-work law was passed, but 93 per cent
of the nurses voted to continue the illegal strike. Finally, with
Bouchard's political reputation damaged among trade unionists
and a large section of the public, the nurses broke the impasse by
offering a truce and returning to work. The government won in a
legal sense, but it suffered heavy political damage and began to
slip in the polls. Labour's disaffection with Bouchard increased
when, at a premiers' summit in Quebec City in early August
1999, Bouchard allied himself with premiers Harris of Ontario
and Klein of Alberta, arguing that the growing federal surplus
should be devoted, as a first priority, to federal tax cuts.

Throughout 1999 polls reported fading support for sovereignty.
Support for sovereignty among francophones in Quebec had
slipped from just over 60 per cent in 1995 to between 52 and 54 per
cent throughout 1999. Furthermore, Québécois opinion had firmed
up in opposition to holding a referendum during Bouchard's current
mandate, with 72 per cent opposed by July 1999. The prospect of
holding a winning referendum appeared beyond Bouchard's grasp.
Sovereigntist critics argued that if Bouchard placed sovereignty on
the front burner, used all the government's resources to push a pro-
sovereignty agenda and sharply polarized the province around the
issue, it was still possible to create political momentum toward a
Yes victory. But such an approach would take an element of reckless political courage and determined political will that Bouchard
did not possess. Bouchard was driven by the polls and unprepared
to take the risk involved in confronting public opinion in order to
turn it around. Given the volatility of public opinion during the preceding twenty years in Quebec, such a scenario was not completely
bizarre. Indeed, that was precisely the approach that Parizeau had
taken during his mandate and that was the advice Parizeau continued to give Bouchard. But Bouchard refused to take the plunge.

Though an unshakeable foundation of sovereignty support of 40 to 44 per cent disappointed Bouchard, it was enough to worry Ottawa. As long as Bouchard was in power, the risk of a successful referendum remained. Furthermore, the Supreme Court had ruled that Ottawa must negotiate if there were a Yes victory, stripping Ottawa and the English-Canadian premiers of their "no negotiations" trump card in the next referendum campaign. Chrétien and Dion determined that Plan B therefore remained dangerously incomplete and in December 1999 they pushed Bill C-20, "An act to give effect to the requirement for clarity as set out in the opinion of the Supreme Court of Canada in the Quebec secession reference," through cabinet despite the initially strong reservations of ministers like Paul Martin, Pierre Pettigrew and Lucienne Robillard. The so-called *Clarity Act* gave the House of Commons the power to rule on whether a "proposed secession" referendum question was clear (see Appendix II). Referendum questions that seek a mandate to negotiate, or that include any references to possible associations with Canada, would not pass the clarity test. As well, the law gave the House of Commons the power to rule on what constituted a "clear majority." Finally, the law identified the complex negotiations that would follow a clear majority on a clear question: "the division of assets and liabilities, any changes to the borders of the province, the rights, interests and territorial claims of the Aboriginal peoples of Canada, and the protection of minority rights."

Chrétien argued that Bouchard wanted another referendum and therefore, "It's time to act so that things are clear. People want clarity…They can ask the question; they can ask any question they want. It is for us to decide if we will negotiate…" And Dion made it clear that 50 per cent plus one was not, in the opinion of the present government, a clear majority, "If you try to negotiate at 50 per cent plus one, it's a mess." Such comments made it self-evident that this wasn't really a law, but rather a threat and an instrument of propaganda. The *Clarity Act*, according to the prime minister, made things clear. It did not. There was no definition of either a "clear question" or a "clear majority" in the law. Apparently, Dion and Chrétien wanted to place a high bar, say 60 per cent, in the law but their lawyers noted they might lose this on a challenge before the Supreme Court, which might well conclude that 50 per cent plus one constitutes a "clear majority." Consequently it was decided not to define "clear majority" in the law.

Since no clarity was provided, the law was really smoke and

mirrors. Under the law, the House of Commons would determine whether any referendum question was clear and whether any majority the pro-sovereignty forces might win constituted a clear majority. It was a foregone conclusion that any referendum question proposed by the Bouchard government would be deemed unclear, and any majority he might win in what would inevitably be a close vote would be deemed not to be a clear majority. The only real clarity achieved by the law was a clear warning to the Québécois: no matter what you do, the road to sovereignty will be closed by the House of Commons. But, if you happen to vote for sovereignty with a clear majority on a clear question, then the negotiations will be arduous, costly and humiliating. Clearly, as political propaganda the law was aimed at the soft nationalists who might embrace sovereignty if it were quickly and painlessly achieved, but who feared a long and uncertain political struggle.

Overlooked in the immediate firestorm the law provoked in Quebec was an unintended consequence. The law applied to all provinces. This might prove to be a final fatal step in Ottawa's determination to treat all provinces the same in order to deny Quebec's special status. Had the law just referred to Quebec, it would have instantly made that province unique in the federation. This was how absurd the situation had become — everyone knew that the law referred to Quebec's secession and that it was clearly targeted at the Quebec sovereignty movement because the entire Supreme Court case was devoted to the Quebec scenario. But to single out Quebec with a special law was not constitutionally acceptable. By refusing to grant the Québécois nation the right of self-determination through the evasive manoeuvre of recognizing the right of all provinces to secede, Ottawa opened a veritable Pandora's Box. Many Canadians recognize Quebec's right to secede only because it is the political home of the Québécois nation, and that nation, as do all nations, enjoys the right of self-determination. Canadians do not recognize the right of Alberta or British Columbia to secede because they are merely provinces and constitute part of the English-Canadian nation. With the *Clarity Act* Ottawa declared that each province has the right to secede and clearly laid out the legal process for provincial secession. By this law, therefore, Ottawa has arguably irreparably weakened the federation and undermined the power of the central state as the pre-eminent political instrumentality of the English-Canadian nation. Anyone who believed then, or believes now, that the *Clarity Act* strengthened the federation is dead wrong.

Ironically, this law may be first invoked not to deal with Quebec, but with Alberta or British Columbia.

Bouchard immediately denounced the *Clarity Act* as an effort to "restrict the exercise of democratic choices by Quebeckers." On 15 December 1999 Bouchard, in a province-wide television broadcast, savaged the *Clarity Act*. He invited the citizens of Quebec to join in a consultation on Quebec's legislative reply to Ottawa, characterized as a "self-determination bill" and "Quebec's charter of collective political rights." The last time a premier had held a dramatic province-wide television address was in 1995 when Parizeau initiated the referendum campaign. Clearly, Bouchard hoped to use Ottawa's provocation to build momentum towards a possible "winning" referendum. The consultations were not particularly effective, however, and though polls confirmed that 60 per cent of Quebeckers opposed the *Clarity Act*, as did all three parties in the National Assembly and a substantial majority of Quebec MPs in the House of Commons, this opposition did not translate into a surge in support for sovereignty or for another referendum. What many initially feared was a gift from Ottawa to Bouchard to help him build toward "winning conditions" did not work out that way. Sovereigntist critics of Bouchard suggested that responding with a long, drawn-out consultation revealed weakness and that perhaps a quick passage of Quebec's self-determination law followed by a snap call for a referendum might have awakened the public and polarized the province to the sovereignty movement's advantage. But again, this was a very risky strategy that Bouchard was unprepared to take.

Bouchard's law, "an act respecting the exercise of the fundamental rights and prerogatives of the Quebec people and the Quebec state," confronted the *Clarity Act* head-on. Like the *Clarity Act*, Quebec's *Fundamental Rights Act* was an instrument of political propaganda (see Appendix II). The law declared that the "Quebec people" have the right to "self determination...in fact and in law" and "the inalienable right to freely decide the political regime and legal status of Quebec." Further, the people of Quebec, through the National Assembly, "shall determine alone" the manner in which they make decisions about Quebec's status. Moreover, a victory in a referendum was defined as 50 per cent plus one. The law defined "the Quebec national state," as deriving its legitimacy from the National Assembly, as "sovereign in the areas assigned to its jurisdiction" and as having the duty to protect the rights and freedoms of the Quebec people. The law also defended Quebec's borders, asserting that the borders cannot be changed without the consent of the National Assembly, and it provided recognition to Quebec's aboriginal nations. Finally, and perhaps most importantly, the law stated "No other parliament or government may reduce the powers, authority, sovereignty or legitimacy of the National Assembly, or impose constraint on the democratic will of the Quebec people to determine its own future."

While the Bouchard government was in the midst of its consultation on the *Fundamental Rights Act* (which was not passed by the National Assembly until 7 December 2000), Chrétien called a federal election for 27 November 2000. From Chrétien's perspective it was a perfect opportunity for a variety of reasons that came together neatly. The Reform Party of Canada had metamorphosed into the Canadian Alliance in pursuit of an elusive Ontario breakthrough and, in an act of political self-mutilation, had replaced Preston Manning with former Alberta Treasurer Stockwell Day, widely seen as shallow and ineffectual. Paul Martin was also eagerly buying up the Liberal party, constituency by constituency, and his supporters (with considerable help from the media) had commenced a backstabbing campaign to oust Chrétien before he sought a third mandate. But these were secondary reasons.

The main reason for the timing of the election had to do with developments in Quebec. Bouchard was in the midst of trying to build momentum against the *Clarity Act*, but the effort was failing. Quebeckers were demoralized. Yes support slipped to 42.4 per cent; No rose to 57.6 per cent. Satisfaction with the PQ government was falling. Support for the federal Liberals in Quebec was on the rise, particularly among francophone voters. As a result, the Bloc was vulnerable and could lose its domination of Quebec's federal seats. The fall in morale, however, was not just afflicting the sovereignty movement. Charest was facing increasing disillusionment among voters and by May 2000, 57 per cent of Quebeckers stated the Liberals would fare better without Charest as leader, including 37 per cent of Liberal supporters. The Quebec Liberal party was in disarray: the soft nationalists were annoyed at Charest's pro-Canadian stance; key party members were upset that Charest had surrounded himself with his former Tory advisers and refused to consult meaningfully; and membership numbers were falling. Chrétien believed a successful federal campaign would rekindle the hopes of the provincial Liberals and shore up Charest.

Ignoring warnings of disaster, Chrétien proved his political shrewdness again, winning 171 of 301 seats with 42 per cent of the popular vote, an increase of sixteen seats and 3 per cent over 1997.

The freshly minted Canadian Alliance under Stockwell Day failed to make its elusive Ontario breakthrough, winning sixty-seven seats with 23 per cent of the vote; sixty-five of the seats were in Western Canada and only two were in Ontario. The Tories and the NDP clung to existence with eleven and fifteen seats respectively, both with 9 per cent of the popular vote. The Liberals won 13 of 88 seats in the West, compared to fifteen in 1997; 19 of 32 seats in Atlantic Canada, compared to 11 in 1997; and 100 of 103 seats in Ontario, compared to 101 in 1997. Again, Ontario voters voted strategically to checkmate the regional threat from the Alliance in the West and the separatist threat in Quebec. Atlantic Canada had forgiven Chrétien for some of his earlier sins of fiscal conservatism, reflecting the emergence of federal surpluses and Chrétien's rediscovery of his credentials as a social Liberal.

From the perspective of Ottawa's Plan B the results in Quebec were particularly gratifying for Chrétien and Dion. The Liberals carried thirty-seven of Quebec's seventy-five seats with 44.2 per cent of the popular vote, matching the Bloc's thirty-seven seats and besting the Bloc's popular vote of 39.8 per cent. Thus the Liberals could now claim to speak for Quebec in Ottawa with a legitimacy equal to that of the Bloc. Indeed, given that the Liberals outpolled the Bloc in votes, they could claim more political legitimacy. But there was a disturbing side to the results. The general collapse in political morale in Quebec, as a result of the years of constitutional wrangling leading to an irreconcilable impasse, was reflected in a steep fall in voter turnout — only 63.5 per cent of Quebec's voters turned out, down steeply from 73.3 per cent in 1997. Close to two million Quebec voters stayed home on election day.

Nevertheless, Chrétien was elated, insisting the results were a "warning" to separatists that "Quebeckers do not want another referendum." "The cause of separatism is weaker than it was before," Chrétien gloated. "For the federalists in Quebec, it's been a very, very big day." For sovereignty supporters it was indeed a major setback. Two days before the election, speaking to a large Montreal rally, Bouchard issued a personal challenge to Chrétien: "We must not accept someone who wants to handcuff, to hinder, our ability to decide our political future. On November 27 the Quebec people is going to vote for itself, its existence, and that means voting against Jean Chrétien." And as Parizeau had declared on more than one occasion during the campaign, a Bloc victory over the Liberals "will be one more step toward our country." As a result of Chrétien's masterful sense of the political mood of the country and his decision to gamble on an election, the sovereignty movement suffered its worst setback since 1995, the Alliance remained locked up in the West and Paul Martin's campaign to replace Chrétien sooner rather than later was temporarily derailed. Chrétien's gamble had paid huge dividends. We were not to learn of the size of Chrétien's win against sovereignty until forty-five days later.

* * *

On 11 January 2001 a tearful Lucien Bouchard announced his resignation in the National Assembly. His speech was blunt and his message simple: he had failed. "I recognize that my efforts to quickly revive the debate on the national question were in vain…[I] failed to revive the flame…[I] regret…not having been able to realize…the new Quebec nation." He lamented the indifference of Quebeckers and their failure to realize "the gravity of the situation":

> Quebeckers were astonishingly impassive in the face of federal offensives like the social union…[and] the adoption of Law C-20 [the *Clarity Act*], which aims at nothing less than limiting our capacity to choose our political future…[I]f there was anger, it certainly didn't show up in…the last federal election.

Bouchard warned the Québécois nation that it was "absolutely necessary to shake the indifference…toward the asphyxiation that is in store for us." Off the record, reaction in Ottawa was jubilation; on the record, remarks were more restrained. Prime Minister Chrétien noted, "our visions…were irreconcilable…[Bouchard] fought for his beliefs with passion and determination." Industry Minister Tobin described the resignation as a "blow to separatism" and "a vindication" of Chrétien's national unity strategy. Stéphane Dion cryptically noted that the resignation was "good for Canadian unity," but warned that separatism was definitely "not dead."

Bouchard was a complex man who was hurt deeply and personally by defeat. Just before the 1998 Quebec election Bouchard said, "Those defeats [the 1980 and 1995 referendums] have left their mark on me. Very much so. I don't ever want to go through another defeat like that. Never." An aide reported that Chrétien's triumph in Quebec in the 2000 federal election "was very hard on him." Bouchard was also deeply wounded by the way English-Canadians and the English-Canadian media demonized him, and complained about it frequently, insisting on one occasion, "I am not the great Satan." Some critics suggested that this desire to be respected by English Canada made Bouchard overly eager to work with the other premiers, losing sight of the hard negotiations necessary for sovereignty while not getting trapped in, and then betrayed by, a united front of provinces. On the other hand, Bouchard was also described by some close to him as authoritarian in the imposition of his own agenda on the government and the PQ and in his demands for devotion and hard work. Bouchard frequently fluctuated between anger and injured perplexity when dealing with opposition within the PQ over his allegedly lukewarm commitment to sovereignty and his allegedly excessive pandering to the shrill anti-sovereignty of the Jewish lobby in Quebec and other anglophone enemies of sovereignty. It was unclear what hurt him more: his inability to win sufficient numbers of the people of Quebec over to an enthusiastic support for sovereignty or his inability to win the undivided loyalty of his own party and the broader sovereignty movement. And there is no doubt that Bouchard was an ideologically committed fiscal conservative, as the nurses and other unions had learned, and that the social democratic mantle of the PQ did not sit easily on his shoulders.

The fact remained that Plan B had worked: the campaign of destabilizing the Bouchard government; the personal attacks on Bouchard's character and motives; the harsh message from Ottawa that the road to sovereignty would be either blocked by the House of Commons or made so difficult as to be truly daunting; and the punitive federal approach to a Quebec governed by Bouchard. The success was greater than expected. No one expected Bouchard to be driven from office. *The Globe and Mail*'s Jeffrey Simpson summed the event up succinctly: "Secessionists have lost their best political weapon; federalists their most dangerous political foe."

* * *

Ironically, in national politics Jean Chrétien's successes in dealing with the sovereignty movement and the other key problems inherited from the Mulroney disaster led to increasing attacks upon him and gradually escalating calls for his departure from office. These demands were orchestrated by Paul Martin's cabal in the Liberal party, the national business lobby and elements in the national media. As Chrétien's successes accumulated, particularly after the departure of Bouchard, the campaign to oust him from office gathered momentum. Initially there was not a great deal of public support for it, with approval ratings for both Chrétien and the Liberal government remaining very high, sometimes even astronomical. But the ouster campaign was well financed, well orchestrated and relentless and, accordingly, public support for Chrétien's departure began to increase. It appeared that now that Chrétien's job for the English-Canadian political and economic elites was successfully finished, those elites wanted him out. Paul Martin's personal ambition knew no bounds — he had never forgiven Chrétien for wresting the leadership from his grasp — and Chrétien's continuing successes put that ambition at risk. Rivalry between the two men dominated the national political news from Chrétien's second victory in 1997 onward, increasing in intensity after Chrétien's third victory in 2000.

According to most commentators, Chrétien behaved very badly in these skirmishes. It was clear their sympathies were with Martin, variously portrayed as a victim of an increasingly irrational prime minister, a political giant dealing with a pygmy and a dignified prime minister in waiting. The national business lobby supported Martin who was, and remains, one of their own. Not only is Martin the champion of corporate Canada, he is also a dapper and smooth member of the exclusive club of Canada's economic elite. Chrétien is an outsider, an *arriviste*, a rags-to-riches political scrapper. He is neither dapper nor smooth. Paul Martin is the business lobby's dream of the perfect prime minister. Jean Chrétien is, for them, an unpredictable nightmare: rough, crude, shrewd and, above all else, willing to use his power not always in accord with the wishes of the business lobby.

While many Canadians were tempted to see the battle as a struggle between two very big egos, as a clash of Shakespearean proportions between two very ambitious men, the facts arguably told a different story. Paul Martin instigated the confrontations. Martin's arrogance and ruthless ambition finally proved too much even for Chrétien. Martin and his supporters repeatedly crossed the line of restraint expected of heirs apparent.

From 1997 on, Chrétien's back had many daggers in it, all with Paul Martin's fingerprints. Martin and his supporters brazenly conspired to oust Chrétien in the run-up to the leadership review after his 1997 victory. The conspiracy was exposed, and Chrétien went on to win more than 90 per cent among his own party and, in 2000, another majority government. Meanwhile, Martin and his supporters, with a vast war chest (by October 2003, more than $10 million) continued to build a party within the party, taking over constituency organizations and provincial executives and hiring a huge paid staff from coast to coast. Further, Martin's people began leaking documents to discredit his leadership opponents and rivals and to undermine the prime minister's credibility. Martin was determined to leave nothing to chance, including the outside possibility that Chrétien might seek yet another electoral mandate, an event that could forever deny an aging Martin the office he coveted.

Martin, then, is a man who allows his personal ambition to take priority over the interests of the Liberal party and the Liberal government. If Martin were not so well loved by the business lobby and high-profile media pundits, he would have been pilloried for his Byzantine tactics. But Martin's sins were largely overlooked, and all blame was laid at the prime minister's door. Martin got away with violating virtually all the norms governing leadership rivals in the Liberal party. When John Turner differed with Trudeau and aspired to Trudeau's office, he quit the government and worked from the outside to replace him. When Chrétien could not reconcile Turner's leadership with his own personal ambition, he quit the House of Commons and organized in preparation for the day he could go for the leadership. Paul Martin had neither the integrity nor the political courage to do likewise. Instead, he remained at the prime minister's right hand as a powerful cabinet minister, and used this position of power, together with inexhaustible financial resources from corporate donors, to orchestrate the ouster of Chrétien and the discrediting of other leadership hopefuls. After Martin was hailed by the business lobby and celebrated by neo-conservatives up and down the land for his years of tax-cutting, program-cutting budgets, Chrétien sandbagged him by announcing he would increase social spending outside the budget cycle as federal surpluses became available. Subsequently Chrétien embarked on renewed social spending, especially after his re-election in 2000, and began lecturing all governments that it was time to become increasingly interventionist on a social agenda while putting the tax cuts demanded by the business lobby on the back burner, a position Martin could never fully accept, given his principled fiscal conservatism. For his part, by May 2002, Chrétien had reached his limits in tolerating public attacks and open disloyalty, almost all of which emanated from the Martin cabal. Chrétien angrily and harshly laid down the law for all cabinet members: cabinet leadership candidates had to cease fundraising, organizing and publicly criticizing the government and the prime minister. Further, all funds raised and their sources had to be disclosed. He also threw down the gauntlet to Martin — Chrétien would go through the leadership review in February 2003 and finish out his full term as prime minister before retiring. When pressed by the media about whether he was willing to accept these limits, Martin declared he was "review[ing] his options." On Sunday, 2 June, Chrétien fired Martin, though he refused to use such blunt words, insisting that Martin was simply "leaving the cabinet." To this day, Martin supporters claim he was unceremoniously fired, while Chrétien supporters insist he resigned. Perhaps we can agree that Chrétien merely transferred Martin to the back benches. But it was too late — the pressure to push Chrétien out was irresistible, and Martin had the leadership locked up.

Though his critics remain loath to admit it, Chrétien's achievements during his decade as prime minister were considerable. He won three back-to-back majority governments. He engineered the effective temporary containment of the separatist threat in Quebec and, while he almost lost the 1995 referendum, he recovered and his tough tactics pushed the soft nationalist Liberals in Quebec into the wilderness, drove Bouchard from office and set the stage for Charest's victory. Chrétien contained the Reform/Alliance threat in the West. He defeated the Mulroney deficit, contained the federal debt and ushered in an era of balanced budgets and huge surpluses. In later years Chrétien refurbished his image as a social Liberal with federal budgets containing considerable increases in social spending. In his twilight in office, he embarked on a significant reform of political party and election financing through proposed controls and limitations on corporate political funding. Chrétien refused, with strong public backing, to be browbeaten into joining the U.S. invasion of Iraq. For these achievements he gets little recognition from the coalition that effectively drove him from office.

In his last months in office Chrétien did everything he could to deny the leadership to Martin. He delayed his departure as long as he could, thus ensuring that Martin would take office as an old man. Chrétien beat the bushes for a candidate to stop Martin. His last forlorn hope was John Manley, to whom Chrétien gave everything he could, boosting Manley without apology. Manley was elevated to the two most powerful posts next to the prime minister:

minister of finance and deputy prime minister. Chrétien's preference for Manley, or virtually anybody, over Martin was widely known. But Chrétien failed. John Manley, with an eye on his political future after a Martin government, wimped out. Not satisfied with simply withdrawing from the race, Manley was obsequious to Martin, declaring, "Paul Martin will be the next leader of the Liberal Party and the next prime minister of Canada...And I believe he will make an excellent prime minister."

It is important to note the bigger reasons Chrétien was so opposed to Martin. Certainly part of it was very personal and grounded in Chrétien's anger at Martin's arrogance, disloyalty and repeated conspiracies to oust him. But there is more to it than that. Chrétien sincerely believed Martin would be a disaster as leader and prime minister after his initial electoral sweep. He saw Martin as too much in the corporate elite's pocket. Martin is a principled fiscal conservative, whereas Chrétien is a moderate social Liberal willing to adopt fiscal conservatism when necessary. Chrétien believes Martin is too aloof and patrician, unable to read the mood of the public and therefore incapable of riding that mood while shaping it. More importantly for Chrétien, Martin is too soft and weak on Québécois nationalism. Martin supported Meech, had reservations about the Supreme Court legal challenge and initially opposed the *Clarity Act*. Chrétien fears that under Martin, particularly if Martin fails to achieve something tangible to accommodate Quebec's aspirations, the Quebec sovereigntists will rise even stronger from the ashes of Bouchard's departure. Martin is also a weak and vacillating champion of federal power and Chrétien fears Martin will be over-inclined to cave in to the provincial rights premiers and travel too far down the road of devolution of federal powers to the provinces.

The premiers seemed to agree with Chrétien's assessment of Martin. They waited eagerly for Chrétien to go, ready to aggressively press their demands on Martin. And the business lobby also seemed to agree with Chrétien, expecting Martin to be more sympathetic to bank mergers and other corporate strategies that may not be in the national or public interest.

The fates of Bouchard and Chrétien were therefore linked. Bouchard's fall, a great triumph for Chrétien, became the signal for the final chapter in Chrétien's political demise as the gloves of his opponents in his own party, among the provincial premiers, in the national business lobby and in the national media came off, and the campaign to drive him from office became more vicious and brazen.

14

Charest Defeats the PQ:
Plan B Vindicated?

Those sovereigntists who hoped Bouchard's departure would lead to a vigorous debate about strategy and a wide-open leadership contest resulting in the election of a younger leader were disappointed. Deputy Premier Bernard Landry easily won the contest, replacing Bouchard as premier on 8 March 2001, the day before Landry turned sixty-four. Landry had been active in the PQ from the beginning, serving in the cabinets of Lévesque, Johnson, Parizeau and Bouchard. For the latter two he served as deputy premier as well as occupying key cabinet posts, including minister of finance and revenue under Bouchard. For Parizeau and Bouchard, Landry played the role of "hard cop," enforcing discipline on the cabinet and caucus and defending the premier with absolute loyalty. He fully supported Bouchard's "winning conditions" approach, and was seen by many in the movement as overly cautious on sovereignty and overly responsive to the federalist business lobby. While not a strategist of Parizeau and Bouchard's calibre, he was a careful poll watcher, as he himself admitted. He lacked a charismatic ability to connect with the people, so crucial in advancing sovereignty. In English Canada Landry was seen as a second-stringer.

Surprisingly, Landry was quick off the mark with a series of confrontations with federalism during his first few months as premier. Describing the Canadian flag as "a piece of red rag," he provoked outrage in English Canada. He complained of being "gagged" by Ottawa at the Summit of the Americas meeting in Quebec. He asserted that federalism had "no usefulness" for Quebec, and was "very harmful" to Quebec's economy. He supported Culture Minister Diane Lemieux's comment that "there is no real Ontario culture." He refused to co-operate with Roy Romanow's review of medicare, citing Romanow's role in stabbing Lévesque in the back in 1982. He complained of Ottawa's "fiscal strangulation" of Quebec. Boldly, Landry declared that Quebec constituted a nation and would act as a nation within Canada. Charest denounced Landry as "confrontational," "hard-line" and "a radical nationalist...obsessed with sovereignty." Paul Martin described Landry's comments as "barbaric," while Prime Minister Chrétien dismissed them as acts of desperation due to the crisis created by Bouchard's sudden departure and a serious fall in PQ membership. For a brief moment, Landry's approach worked: in April, Léger & Léger reported that support for the Yes side rose to 45.7 per cent, and support for the PQ had rebounded to 41.6 per cent, four points ahead of Charest and the Liberals.

The turning point marking the beginning of the fall of Landry and the PQ was the loss of the Mercier by-election on 10 April 2001. The PQ's problems in Mercier reflected the bigger contradictions the party faced. The sovereignty vote in the riding was split between a popular left-wing nationalist and an official PQ parachute candidate. (The official candidate was damaged during the campaign by revelations of a charge for wife assault the year before.)

The PQ had also been wounded by *l'affaire Michaud* the previous year. In seeking the nomination in the riding, Yves Michaud made a controversial comment about the Jewish vote in 1995, leading to accusations of anti-Semitism. Bouchard sponsored a motion in the National Assembly denouncing Michaud, seen by many in the movement as an over-reaction and excessive deference to the anti-sovereignty lobby. Therefore, in Mercier the PQ faced the local expression of some of the bigger problems of the party: the split between militant and moderate wings; the arrogant efforts of the PQ and premier's central apparatus to ensure the nomination of "acceptable" candidates; and the issue of how to handle the campaign of vilification the movement faced from the anti-sovereignty lobby.

After the Mercier defeat Bernard Landry engaged in a political St. Vitus' Dance on sovereignty up until his defeat by Charest in April 2003. In August 2001 Landry promised a sovereignty referendum in 2005, and talked grandly of a 1,000-day deadline. Then in March 2002 Landry changed his position, declaring there was no definite deadline since it depended on "winning conditions." A month later Landry affirmed the focus of the election as sovereignty. In September 2002 Landry withdrew the promise of a referendum if re-elected, but would await "winning conditions." In October 2002 he was emphatic: "Sovereignty will be promoted when a majority of Quebeckers show support for it." Then in March 2003 Landry, desperate to win disgruntled federalists and soft nationalists, created confusion and division when he unilaterally changed the PQ's election platform to seeking a new confederal union with Canada rather than sovereignty. During the campaign in April 2003 he declared that the election was not on sovereignty, but on good government.

As an earlier effort to set the sovereignty issue aside, in December 2002 Landry created the Council for Sovereignty to advance the cause of independence. To prevent the Council from doing anything aggressive, Landry tied its hands. He declared it "immoral" to spend significant public funds on advancing sovereignty, immediately disarming the Council against Ottawa's heavy spending to promote federalism. Days after the creation of the Council, Landry fired his senior advisor on sovereignty, Josée Legault, appointed in 1998 as part of Bouchard's renewal efforts. Legault was a principled sovereigntist dedicated to, in her own words, "the promotion and defence of sovereignty in a stronger, clearer manner." Only "reliable" moderate sovereigntists were appointed to the Council. Parizeau and Legault were not among the appointments, nor were some of the most prominent sovereigntists with recognized expertise in studying the costs and benefits of sovereignty. Landry hoped to pass off the hot issue of sovereignty to a parapolitical agency where it would rest quietly. Yet the Liberals, the ADQ, Ottawa and the media would not let Landry evade the issue, and maintained a constant barrage on his supposed secret referendum agenda and his unqualified adherence to independence. And the more Landry bobbed and weaved the more relentless his opponents were in sticking the "separatist" and "referendum" labels on his forehead. To the public Landry looked evasive. To his opponents Landry looked desperate.

The fallout from this evasive posturing on sovereignty hit Landry hard. Eight cabinet ministers announced their departure from politics between Landry's swearing in as premier and his defeat in April 2003. The optics of this were not lost on the public — ministers frequently abandon a sinking government. Seven of the eight resignations were tendered quietly. One resignation, however, hurt Landry badly. Paul Bégin, former minister of justice, resigned in October 2002 citing Landry's refusal to promote independence and a referendum. He complained that Landry took the same "disappointing approach as Bouchard" and that such an approach would "kill the idea we say we are promoting." Down that path, warned Bégin, lies "certain defeat." Bégin declared his raison d'être for entering politics was to achieve an independent Quebec, and stated that the PQ should make that its clear focus as a government. It was not surprising that rank-and-file activists, the key to any election victory, reported increasing demoralization and defeatism in the PQ.

Responding to Landry's equivocations in November 2002, Jacques Parizeau set up a new sovereignty coalition, La Rassemblement pour la souveraineté du Québec (RSQ). Parizeau insisted this was not a new political party, but rather an organization for committed sovereigntists to advocate more forcefully for sovereignty. Since sovereignty appeared to be more popular than the PQ, according to the polls, this move was an effort to break the PQ's ideological monopoly on independence and to allow sovereigntists an independent means to carry out pro-sovereignty research and advocacy. Parizeau was particularly interested in having the RSQ take on the task of documenting the benefits of sovereignty for Quebec.

Landry's shifting positions on sovereignty contributed to a series of more dramatic by-election losses following the Mercier defeat. Landry elevated the significance of the first package of four by-elections in October 2001 by staking the government's reputation and commitment to sovereignty on the outcome, predicting a sweep in four PQ fortresses won handily in 1998, including Bouchard's seat of Jonquière in the Saguenay region, the strongest pro-sovereignty area in Quebec. The PQ lost two of the four seats, including Jonquière and another twenty-five-year bastion of PQ power. In April 2002 the PQ lost three of four seats, one to the ADQ. The biggest by-election shake-up occurred in June 2002, when the ADQ won three of four seats, pulling francophone voters from both parties. This loss of francophone voters to the ADQ was particularly worrisome for the PQ, since significant split in the francophone vote undermined their confidence outside Montreal. But Charest and the Liberals were also concerned, because if the alienated francophone vote went to the ADQ in large numbers the Liberals were unlikely to win a majority.

Due to the electorate's volatility Landry was not alone in his unseemly scrambling. Jean Charest faced unhappiness with his performance, especially as the ADQ's popularity surged. In 1998 and in subsequent polling, Charest's failure to appeal to francophone voters was clear. As francophone voters unhappy with the PQ shifted to the ADQ, prominent federalist Liberals suggested Charest's replacement by Pierre Pettigrew. Charest denounced this interference and the cabal backed off. ADQ leader Mario Dumont was put in the spotlight, forced to justify his controversial policies. When Dumont made a major speech to business high rollers in Toronto in September 2002, where he affirmed his right-wing platform and his commitment to the privatization of aspects of health care, the gloves came off. Charest denounced Dumont as right of Klein of Alberta and Harris of Ontario, further noting Dumont's inconsistencies: "a sovereigntist in Baie Comeau and a federalist in Toronto." Wrapping himself in the Quebec flag, Charest ridiculed Dumont for speaking in Toronto to the business establishment, with lots of national media coverage, and squandering the opportunity by making "not a single demand for Quebec." The media, which had given Dumont a free ride, began a public dissection of his platform. Meanwhile, the PQ carried out an unrelenting attack on the ADQ's dangerously right-wing platform and its failure to stand up for Quebec. Dumont, convinced he was on the threshold of a possible victory, unapologetically defended his platform, declaring at the ADQ's October 2002 convention, "Every action I take each day in preparing for the next election is to win the election, nothing less."

From 2001 to 2003 Quebec was on a veritable political rollercoaster. In October 2001 the Liberals held a commanding lead. By August 2002 the ADQ was on top. In December 2002, the Liberals again took the lead. In March 2003 the PQ pulled ahead with a comfortable lead at 42 per cent, with the Liberals at 34 per cent and the ADQ at 24 per cent. This spike in PQ support led Landry to call the election for 14 April 2003.

The PQ moved up slightly at the campaign's start to 44 per cent, to the Liberals 36 and the ADQ's 17. It appeared Landry just might win a majority. Though his confederal union proposal had offended staunch sovereigntists, it appeared to appeal to soft nationalists and unhappy federalists. Landry promised to add to the PQ's social-democratic legacy: partial reimbursement for those who holidayed in Quebec; a promise to students to write off half of any student loan if the student had a baby within five years of graduation; a proposal for a four-day work week for parents; a promise to maintain $5-per-day daycare and to reduce the waiting list by increasing the number of spaces; and aggressive economic intervention. The PQ's strong opposition to America's war against Iraq also dovetailed neatly with

Quebec opinion, the most anti-war province in Canada. Charest stuck to his themes: the economy languished under the heavy hand of the state; taxes were too high and needed deep cuts; the PQ's sovereignty/referendum agenda, now hidden, was still there and a victorious PQ would hold another destructive referendum. Charest held firm to his pro-Canada stance, arguing Quebec must work for positive change in the existing federal system. Charest also pandered to his anglophone base by promising to reconsider the amalgamation of municipalities in the greater Montreal area, something the anglophones in more prosperous communities had fought bitterly. The ADQ soldiered on, adhering to its platform, now in tatters; seen as a non-contender; and having served as a gigantic voting parkade for the brief use of unhappy voters before the campaign. The main issue during the campaign was how many votes the ADQ would pull among francophones to the detriment of the PQ outside Montreal.

The leaders' debate held on 31 March, two weeks before voting day, was the turning point in the campaign. Charest hit Landry hard on two issues. One, the PQ's secret sovereignty/referendum agenda to be trundled out if they won again, was expected. The second was unexpected. In an act of dishonest demagoguery Charest attacked Landry for a remark Parizeau allegedly made to junior college students in Shawinigan, in which he blamed money and the ethnic vote for the 1995 referendum loss. Actually, according to the transcript, Parizeau, responding to a student's question, noted he had said that back in 1995, and explained why he had said it, but went on to suggest that such an explanation was simplistic, even more so given the integration of what he called "Law 101 children" into Quebec society. But Landry was caught off-guard, failing to deflect Charest or defend Parizeau. Landry made matters worse by presuming Parizeau's guilt and asking him to withdraw from the campaign. In the days following the debate Landry denied that Parizeau's speaking campaign at colleges and universities was part of the official PQ campaign. Indeed, Landry jumped on the "attack Parizeau" bandwagon by suggesting that while Parizeau's vision of Quebec excluded ethnic communities, his did not. This was indeed ironic, given that back in August 1998 Premier Bouchard had publicly rebuked Landry for his comment, defending the 50 per cent plus one rule for winning a referendum, saying that "Everyone knows very well that if we put the bar too high, it would be like giving a veto to our compatriots from the cultural communities over our national project. We can't do that." The Parizeau incident brought to a head the growing panic among PQ strategists. The focus by

Charest and the media on a victorious PQ's secret intention to push the sovereignty project, including a referendum, was hurting. The PQ's dogged adherence to the confederal plan, and the assertion that sovereignty and a referendum were not issues in the campaign, were unconvincing to the public.

After the debate, a CROP poll reported that the Liberals surged ahead to 38 per cent of decided voters, compared to 30 per cent for the PQ and 15 per cent for the ADQ. When undecided voters were factored in according to a formula that accounted for firmness of support, federal versus sovereigntist sympathies and a desire for change, the Liberals held a thirteen-point lead. More than half believed Charest won the debate and Charest outpolled Landry for best premier 34 to 32. The PQ lost heavily among francophone voters after the debate. Before the debate the PQ held a twenty-point lead over the Liberals among francophone voters. This was cut to five points after the debate. Perhaps more ominously, 57 per cent of Quebeckers wanted a change in government. On election day the CROP poll was confirmed as the Liberals won 76 seats with 45.9 per cent, the PQ won 45 with 33.2 per cent and the ADQ won 4 with 18.2 per cent. *The Globe and Mail* headline of 15 April 2003 captured the essence of what had happened: "Grit win shows sovereignty dormant." Federalists and the business community were delighted.

The results certainly suggested a Liberal sweep. But closer scrutiny suggested otherwise. The total Liberal vote was nearly 200,000 less than that won in 1998. The PQ, on the other hand, lost more than 500,000 votes and, although most of these were among the francophone electorate, a substantial portion went to the ADQ. But probably the bulk of the PQ's lost votes simply stayed home. Only 70 per cent of the electorate voted, the lowest turnout since 1927 and 8 per cent below the 1998 figure. And turnout rates in francophone ridings were lower than in anglophone and allophone ridings. Polls continued to report pro-sovereignty support ranging between 40 and 45 per cent. Therefore, it was the PQ under Landry, not sovereignty, that lost the election. The widespread demoralization among pro-sovereignty forces, and public defeatism after the 1995 loss and the subsequent federal assault on sovereignty, were among the most important broader contextual factors shaping the outcome. Finally, the Quebec electorate's extreme volatility made the election a bit of a crap shoot, with the PQ on the threshold of winning up until the leaders' debate. This was an election whose outcome was uncertain until election day. And given the volatile source of Charest's mandate — disgruntled francophones voting ADQ or staying home — his tenure as premier is far from secure. Certain things are clear, however. The Quebec election was a vote against Landry's PQ government as well as a vote against an early referendum. It was not, however, a vote against sovereignty for Quebec, at least not for that core 40 per cent of Québécois who continue to champion that national aspiration.

Four days after the election, premier-designate Charest released a document, *A Project for Quebec: Affirmation, Autonomy and Leadership*, advocating the establishment of a Council of the Federation, a permanent body appointed jointly by Ottawa and the provinces to negotiate issues of contention. Down this road, Charest declared, will lie a "new alliance" between Ottawa and the provinces leading to a "new partnership in a united country." It was time, he said, to break from the past and show Canadians that "this federation can work more effectively." Charest reiterated his pro-Canada position clearly: "Canada must be a strong country...the Canadian identity must be strong," but this will be achieved through "co-operation" not "unilateral action." Signaling that he was about to join the provincial rights premiers as an equal partner, Charest advocated giving "the provinces greater responsibility in the management of the common good of the Canadian state." Such pro-federalist words had not been uttered by a Quebec premier since Jean Lesage. Nor had any Quebec premier dared to go so far down the road of a de facto admission that Quebec was a province just like the others when it came to federal-provincial relations. At his swearing-in as premier, standing before both the Canadian and Quebec flags together in the National Assembly for the first time in a decade, Charest staked out his position clearly: "We will reclaim Quebec's position as a leader in the Canadian federation." This may be Charest's greatest political challenge in maintaining his credibility as an effective premier of Quebec. And as if to emphasize this new position of Quebec in the Canadian federal constellation, Charest refused to make an official appearance as premier on 19 May 2003 at the first celebration of National Patriots' Day, a holiday established by the PQ to honour the *Patriotes* of 1837–38.

Charest was quick off the mark in beginning to dismantle the PQ's social democratic legacy. In May 2003 he fired the CEOs of the two major state funds for steering the economy in Quebec's national interest — the Société générale de financement and Investissement Québec — characterizing this as a first step in downsizing the state. Charest proposed an end to $5-per-day daycare through a mixture of privatization and increased rates, provoking a major protest demonstration. In June 2003, during his first session of the National Assembly as premier, Charest announced there would be referendums on reversing the urban amalgamations. Charest's first budget reduced the role of the state by cutting business subsidies while promising major corporate tax cuts. Finance Minister Yves Séguin articulated the credo of the new Charest government: "Rather than asking what the state can do for us, we should ask ourselves what we can do without it." A month later this doctrine was applied vigorously to those able to work who were on social assistance. Charest's new "work for welfare" program was considerably harsher than the one introduced by the PQ government, proposing further cuts in welfare payments for "the able-bodied" of between $75 to $300 per month for those who either refused work or job training.

Lest there were doubts about Charest's commitment to a right-wing, pro-business agenda, they were laid to rest in autumn 2003. In September Charest announced the amendment of Section 45 of Quebec's Labour Code to permit contracting-out government work to non-union, private firms and organizations. In response to immediate protests from labour, Charest declared war on the labour movement with an open letter published in all major dailies in Quebec in late October, accusing labour of a "corporate" mentality determined to benefit from the status quo while opposing positive change in the interest of all Quebeckers. The comprehensive nature of the government's plans were fleshed out by Quebec Treasury Board President Monique Jérôme-Forget, who noted that private investments were needed to construct and manage roads, bridges, hospitals, prisons, the water treatment infrastructure and drinking water distribution systems. Charest's seriousness was underlined by an October 2003 trip to New York to tell investors that the days of sovereigntists in power and referendums were over and that "Quebec is open for business."

Charest's project was nothing less than the "re-engineering" of Quebec in order to bring it in line with the other provinces. This reconstruction required an end to "cumbersome and intrusive" government, a large role for the private sector and big eliminations in Quebec's generous social safety net. It also meant an end to the freeze on tuition fees that made Quebec's post-secondary education system the most affordable in North America, and more non-union contracting out creating more low-wage jobs. The task involved dismantling the social institutions and economic levers that

allowed the Quebec government to play both an active and paternalistic role, selectively and partially sheltering both the economy
and the population from the cold winds of unfettered market forces.
Public reaction to the Charest government became increasingly
negative, and its approval rating fell in October 2003 to 46 per cent
generally and 41 per cent among francophones. Even at its lowest
ebb just before defeat, the former PQ government had bottomed
out at 51 per cent. Senior Liberal statesman the late Claude Ryan
publicly warned Charest against going too far right in his imposition of "a narrow economic vision" on Quebec. And PQ leader
Landry happily reversed his decision to leave before the next election since "the [Charest] government will self-destruct by causing
agony in all directions, even in business circles."

Charest reaffirmed his government's commitment to joining the
provinces as an equal partner in battles with Ottawa over *le
deséquilibre fiscal* (the fiscal imbalance) that the provinces insist
exists in Canadian federalism. Indeed, Charest agreed that, as a concession to Ottawa, his government would give up Quebec's
traditionally independent levers of economic intervention and allow
Ottawa to invest directly in areas of provincial jurisdiction, like
municipalities, if Ottawa provided increased funding to the
provinces for health, education and welfare. Failing that, Ottawa
must back off on its taxation regime, giving the provinces more
room to generate revenue. Charest joined the chorus of premiers
expressing eagerness for Chrétien's quick departure and replacement by Martin, who was perceived as more likely to accede to
provincial demands. Suggesting that the same old federal-provincial war would resume, just before becoming prime minister Martin
flatly declared, "I don't believe there is a fiscal imbalance," while
ambiguously conceding that more money was needed to fund health
and post-secondary education. The difference when Martin squares
off to deal with provincial demands is clear. Martin faces a united
front of provinces, including Quebec as a full partner. And the sovereignty trump card that enabled previous prime ministers to isolate
PQ premiers from Lévesque to Landry, and thereby to shatter
provincial unity, has disappeared. There will be no prime ministerial calls to the premiers of the English-Canadian provinces to get
on side to defend national unity by not allowing themselves to be
manipulated by Quebec sovereigntists. As a result, federal-provincial relations in the future could become messier should Martin
prove unable to deliver on the premiers' elevated expectations.

The dismantling of "Quebec Inc.," the aggressive use of the

state to intervene to build Quebec's national economy and infrastructure, a nation-building strategy embraced by all Quebec governments since the Quiet Revolution, will provoke resistance. And dismantling the PQ's social safety net and family support system, the most generous in Canada, will prove politically costly for Charest. Undermining $5-per-day daycare and Quebec's policy of the lowest post-secondary fees in Canada, for example, will lead to large anti-government rallies and demonstrations. If Charest continues down this two-track road to make Quebec an active and equal partner with the other provinces in the federation and to dismantle the PQ's social-democratic edifice, politics in Quebec will experience a new and different kind of turbulence. Now the generally pro-sovereignty students and the pro-sovereignty trade unions are unencumbered in their anti-government campaigns by the self-restraint imposed previously when attacking a PQ government. Finally, Charest's plan to join the other provinces as an equal partner in dealings with Ottawa, a concession that Quebec is a province like the others, will deeply offend Québécois nationalist sensibilities, leading to a revival of nationalist sentiment and a resurgence of the sovereignty movement, fed by growing support from soft nationalist elements for whom the Quebec Liberal party had been the political home of choice since the Quiet Revolution.

This scenario very quickly became a reality in December 2003 when Charest rammed the first stage of his agenda through the National Assembly: $7-per-day daycare in the public system and more subsidies for private daycare centres; a ban on unionization of private nursing homes and home daycare centres; the amendment of the labour code to allow contracting out; the forced integration of health services provided by local agencies; the forced merger of hospital bargaining units; and a law permitting referendums on reversing urban amalgamations. On 11 December, Quebec's labour movement united to stage *une journée de perturbation* (a national day of disruption): major highways and ports were blocked; public transit was shut down for the morning rush hour; hundreds of workers walked off the job for four hours; and thousands of parents of 40,000 children shut down 500 daycare centres as they joined demonstrations. This was the culmination of almost daily protests beginning in October. Quebec's labour movement had never been so united and angry since the campaign against Bourassa in the early 1970s. President Réjean Parent of the Centrale des syndicates du Québec, representing teachers and workers in daycares and health facilities, declared, "This is a message of social solidarity...to the government and their friends in the business community...I had to hold my people back...[They] are just livid."

On 15 December Premier Charest invoked closure in the National Assembly, insisting, "Quebec is at a point in its history where it must do things differently." Gilles Taillon, CEO of Quebec's largest business organization, le Conseil du patronat, supported the move: "If the government backs down Charest will not be able to do anything for the next four years." More than 3,000 angry labour demonstrators came close to storming the National Assembly, restrained only by their leaders, as Henri Massé of the Quebec Federation of Labour declared in disgust, "Never in forty years have I seen such filth by a government...There's not a goddamn closure big enough in Quebec to gag the working class." PQ House Leader André Boisclair warned the government that by invoking closure, "Charest is sending the debate back into the streets." In the wake of these events Quebec's labour leaders announced the formation of a united front of all organized labour and began preparations for a general strike as contract negotiations opened for almost half a million government employees.

After eight short months in office, Charest had galvanized the creation of a coalition of organized labour and many social activist organizations, setting the stage for unceasing turmoil in Quebec. His ineptitude, heavy hand and lack of political skills were reminiscent of his role in the final unravelling of Meech and the emergence of the Bloc. Prime Minister Paul Martin, sworn in on 12 December 2003, already faced declining popularity in Quebec as a result of Charest's actions, as well as Martin's own announcements of a freeze on government spending and the possible cancellation of many of the projects and programs announced by Chrétien.

* * *

The departure of Bouchard and the defeat of the PQ led to a not unexpected response in English Canada, in addition to the departure of Chrétien. English Canadians fell asleep again, just as they had after the defeat of the PQ in 1985 and the re-election of Bourassa. They were helped into their slumber by the bragging confidence of Prime Minister Chrétien himself who after Charest's victory, declared that he was proud that Canada was now "more united than ever" and that on the "national unity file" he could declare, "mission accomplished." Now, he went on, with "a proud Quebecker and a proud Canadian" as Quebec premier, for the first time in a very long time there were governments in Ottawa and Quebec City with "a common commitment to Canada." Peter C. Newman, writing in the 12 May 2003 *Maclean's*, declared that Charest had "a chance to bring down the curtain on Quebec's independence movement" with its "delusions and excesses." He went on, "Quebec's voters realize that their...interests are better protected within...Canada" rather in the "neurotic isolation" of "independence." And he noted that Charest is a fighter, but he will fight "...for tax points, to be spent within a united Canada."

Such opinions will prove to be misguided. Sovereignty in Quebec — with support at 40 per cent — is far from dead. It is now more like a sleeping volcano that could erupt at any time, given the right combination of circumstances and provocations. What circumstances and provocations would be sufficient to lead to an eruption? That is always hard to predict, given the unexpected rise of sovereignty after the failure of Meech and Charlottetown. But certain factors are obvious. We have to recall that Quebec remains the only province that has failed to approve the 1982 constitution — a legally irrelevant fact but one laden with political significance. And, given the events of the last decade, it is clear that any serious reopening of the constitutional question could be the catalyst for a resurgence of sovereignty sentiment. If Charest attempts to get the National Assembly to approve the 1982 constitution, all hell could break loose. And Charest will face considerable pressure from English Canada to approve the constitution in order to "normalize" and to "legitimize" the constitutional situation. There may also be pressure on Charest to get National Assembly approval of the Calgary Declaration, a document approved by all provinces except Quebec. There may be pressure for Charest to repeal Bouchard's *Fundamental Rights Act*, another very risky gambit. If Ottawa follows the advice of some of its advisors and seizes upon the election of Charest to bypass the Quebec government in a massive intervention, directly funding infrastructure renewal in municipalities and more extensive post-secondary programs, a serious political crisis could ensue. Or should Charest appear to pander to the anglophone lobby excessively, particularly in weakening Quebec's language law, negative reaction in Quebec would be strong and swift. Should Ottawa continue, as it has in the past, to stonewall the provinces in their devolution campaign, now led by a loyal and federalist Quebec, Charest's failures will be noted brutally by Quebec sovereigntists. Or if Prime Minister Martin and Premier Charest —

who claimed, like all the other premiers, to have been waiting for Martin in order to get down to serious federal-provincial business — are unable to work out agreements that sell in Quebec as victories, then the longevity of this interlude of national unity may be much shorter than expected. In particular, Charest has awaited the arrival of Martin to persuade him to join the Council of the Federation, the latest phrase for the abattoir that awaits federal power. Should Martin resist efforts to dismantle federal power, the sovereigntists will declare another failure for federalism.

The next eruption of militant sovereignty sentiment in Quebec will take a much harder line than the "reasonable" sovereigntist proposals of Lévesque in 1980 and Parizeau/Bouchard in 1995. English Canada, represented by the other nine provinces and the domination of the Ottawa government, refused to negotiate, refused to grant acceptable concessions. In 1980 Lévesque held a referendum asking Quebeckers for permission to negotiate sovereignty-association with Canada. He lost heavily, but part of that loss had to do with a refusal on the part of Ottawa and the other provinces to engage in negotiations even if the Yes side won. In 1995, Parizeau held a referendum asking for the approval of the Quebec people for a declaration of independence that would take effect after one year of negotiations on a new partnership with Canada, if those negotiations failed. Again, English Canada stonewalled. Parizeau and Bouchard almost won. After 1995, rather than seeing the narrow victory for the No side as a wake-up call to engage in serious negotiations, Ottawa, to the applause of the provincial governments and most English Canadians, commenced a brutal campaign to discredit the sovereignty movement and to smear its leadership.

There is a pattern here. Each refusal by English Canada has led to an escalation in the tactics and demands that characterize each subsequent eruption of militant sovereignty sentiment in Quebec. Next time the sovereignty movement, having learned from English Canada's repeated refusals, will perhaps not even want to negotiate a partnership. Rather, perhaps a renewed PQ, freshly committed to aggressive and unapologetic sovereignty, will simply hold a referendum on secession and issue a unilateral declaration of independence if it passes. Or, as some among the PQ's youth wing are now advocating, next time the PQ could make sovereignty the central issue of an election campaign and, if a majority of seats are won, the National Assembly would simply declare independence. Such a scenario might include following such a declaration with a

referendum affirming the action of the National Assembly. However the next sovereignty scenario plays out, one thing is certain —
the next eruption will be more militant and less inclined to link sovereignty to either a partnership or negotiations.

The future of a revitalized sovereignty movement and PQ is not
as dark as many in English Canada predict. Demographically, the
sovereignty option is the option of the young; that is, as you go down
the age scale in Quebec, the proportion supporting sovereignty goes
up. Furthermore, the nature of the sovereignty movement is changing slowly but relentlessly. The old sovereignty movement, which
produced Bourgault, Lévesque, Parizeau, Bouchard and Landry,
was, in its origins, an expression of "ethnic nationalism." *La nation
Québécoise* — white, French-speaking, *pure laine* descendants of
the original conquered population — struggled for self-determination and independence. Ottawa and federalists in Quebec were able
to use this successfully to persuade the so-called "ethnic vote" to
stay on side against sovereignty (the anglophone minority in Quebec
needed little persuasion to oppose sovereignty). But in the last
decade ideologues and intellectuals in Quebec's sovereignty movement have successfully re-defined the foundation of the movement
to be rooted in "civic nationalism," much like English-Canadian
nationalism. This transformation has occurred with surprising ease
and success among younger Quebeckers. Among the older generation of sovereigntists, the intellectual and political arguments in
favour of civic nationalism have been won, but at an emotional level
older sovereigntists often still revert in their hearts to ethnic nationalism. During the election Premier Landry insisted, "Quebec forms
a nation. It is a civic nation that is inclusive and transcends all forms
of ethnicity." This is the official doctrine of the new nationalism of
the sovereignty movement and the PQ, but Landry and those of his
generation are not completely believed or trusted by many allophones in Quebec. A new generation of leaders in the sovereignty
movement and the PQ, likely to come to the fore during the PQ's
period out of power, will be more comfortable with the idea of civic
nationalism at both the intellectual and emotional levels, and could
prove very effective in making gains for sovereignty among Quebec's allophone communities. Add to this the fact that younger
francophones tend to be more committed to sovereignty than older
francophones, increasing the chances that the Yes side in the next
referendum will win 63 or 65 per cent of the francophone vote rather
than the 60 per cent won in 1995. Bouchard's elusive "winning conditions" could well be present next time.

Polls in Quebec in 2003 found that sovereignty support continues to be highest among the young. But the polls also report that 40 per cent of Quebeckers under thirty-five who are members of the so-called "ethnic communities" — they are either children of immigrants or immigrants themselves — would vote Yes in a referendum. Parizeau referred to these, and all those non-francophone young people who have been educated in French in Quebec, as "the Law 101 children." These new additions to the Québécois nation and culture are transforming and recreating that nation and culture daily, just as waves of immigrants transformed and recreated the English-Canadian nation and culture. The next eruption of militant sovereigntist sentiment, led by a new layer of leaders articulating a more compelling vision of *la nation et la culture Québécoise* — a vision more in touch with the daily reality — will make the next sovereignty referendum, if there is one, a much different political event than those of 1980 and 1995. And this time the sovereignty movement will be reminding English-Canada of new and additional debts to be paid: for the harsh and arrogant Plan B campaign of the 1990s; for the degradation and corruption of the millions spent by Plan A in a barrage of simplistic, pro-federalist propaganda; for the glee and exultation expressed upon the humbling of Quebec's nationalist leaders and the defeat of Québécois nationalism; and for the refusal to recognize, let alone talk about, the grievances and aspirations of the Québécois nation.

In 1980, Lévesque won 40 per cent. In 1995, Parizeau and Bouchard won 49.4 per cent. Next time, if the impasse continues, the sovereigntist movement could be poised for victory.

15

Separation or Special Status?

From the beginning of the Quiet Revolution, the Québécois have appealed to English Canadians to understand their national grievances and to provide the minimum accommodation necessary to allow Quebec to find a secure place in Confederation. And it was clear to all but the most willfully blind in English Canada that Quebec would eventually separate unless large structural concessions were made to the new progressive Québécois nationalism. The demands of the Québécois were simple — a recognition of the right to national self-determination and a willingness to negotiate a new, mutually acceptable set of relationships between the two nations.

Rather than rising to the challenge, English Canada papered together a federal system based on historical misperceptions, a rejection of the reality of Canada's two nations and a trivialization of Quebec's fears as merely questions of language. Furthermore, English Canada commenced to construct a series of political and constitutional myths. These myths concealed the reality of Quebec as the political and constitutional home of the Québécois nation, while providing a false but reassuring sense of Canadianism.

English Canadians will have to free themselves of these myths, which make a settlement impossible. One is the assertion that the Québécois are only one small piece in the Canadian mosaic, no more or less distinct than other groups in other provinces. This belief is absurd. We cannot make a constitutional choice about whether or not Quebec is a distinct society as if it were simply a matter of opinion. Quebec is a distinct society and always has been. What we are debating is whether our constitution will explicitly recognize that reality in a substantially meaningful way. And it must be said from the outset that constitutions that bloody-mindedly refuse to recognize reality are recipes for political strife. Trudeau's eloquent sophistry convinced us that somehow if we refused to recognize Quebec's distinctiveness constitutionally, that somehow if we denied the existence of the Québécois nation, they would not exist. Throughout the entire Trudeau and Chrétien eras, the reality of Quebec was denied. The constitutional recognition of Quebec as a distinct society is a minimum demand of the Québécois. In Quebec, it is seen as merely a recognition and affirmation of historical and sociological reality.

Multiculturalism is the second myth we will have to abandon. Before we can reach a successful resolution of our differences, English Canadians will have to stop embracing multiculturalism as an alternative to the reality of Canada's three nations: English Canadian, Québécois and First Nations. Section 27 of the 1982 *Constitution Act* says, "This Charter shall be interpreted in a manner consistent with the preservation and enhancement of the multicultural heritage of Canadians." This is an important principle with which no one should quarrel — the rich cultural and ethnic diversity of Canada should be maintained, encouraged and protected. But we must recall how the doctrine of official multiculturalism emerged, was used to bludgeon the Québécois (and later, the First Nation) and found final reflection in the constitution that Quebec rejected.

In October 1971, Trudeau promulgated the doctrine of official multiculturalism in a clear effort to avoid a central recognition of non-aboriginal Canada's binational, bicultural and bilingual reality. The doctrine stems from *The Cultural Contribution of the Other Ethnic Groups*, volume IV of the B and B Commission's report. This formal official statement by the prime minister in the House of Commons retroactively rewrote the mandate of the B and B Commission, flatly rejecting the thrust of the commission, which did not recommend multiculturalism as a state policy, but rather the integration of the diverse ethnocultural groups to one or the other of the two main founding nations. The multiculturalism doctrine, in contrast, proposes that *the* key feature of Canada is its composition by a variety of diverse ethnocultural groups, among which Canada's francophones are but one among many. While ethnocultural diversity is a key feature of Canada, it is a malicious fiction to insist it is the key feature of Canada when three out of four Canadians have British or French roots and when all Canadians have integrated with either the English or French language groups.

The most convenient aspect of multiculturalism, used quite cynically by Trudeau, is that while masking the reality of anglophone domination, it diminishes the significance of the French fact in Canada. English Canadians, and the many ethnic minorities that justifiably felt excluded, grasped the concept to offset demands both from francophone minorities across English Canada and from the Québécois nation.

The doctrine is not in accord with historical and contemporary fact, and its promulgation has only served to increase tensions. Canada is composed of two nations. The Québécois nation enjoys the province of Quebec as a political and constitutional home. The English-Canadian nation enjoys a considerably stronger political and constitutional home: nine provinces and three territories. It dominates the House of Commons, the Senate and all other federal institutions, and it has a well-protected and privileged minority status in Quebec. More recently, Canadians have also conceded we must add a third founding nation to Canada's constitutional design: the First or aboriginal nations. Because Canada's aboriginal people do not have a clearly defined and established constitutional and territorial home, because small populations are scattered across the country and because the aboriginal peoples themselves are composed of a diversity of nations and language groups, Canadians, including aboriginals, have yet to come to grips with how to deal with the First Nations principle fully, other than by recognizing aboriginal rights, conceding the inherent right of self-government and making a vague promise of fairness in land claims settlements. Canada's two-nation reality, however, is recognized in the *Official Languages Act* and in the language rights enumerated in the constitution. It was also recognized at the founding of Canada in the *British North America Act*. To live and work comfortably in Quebec, one must be able to do so in French. To live and work comfortably in the rest of Canada, one must be able to do so in English.

Finally, before English Canada can resolve its differences with Quebec, it will have to give up the myth of the equality of provinces. Confederation was not premised on the doctrine of the constitutional equality of provinces as a federal principle. Indeed, such a principle was explicitly rejected in favour of enumerating a specific and limited list of provincial powers while granting the federal government a list of specific powers, a series of key dominant powers and all "residual powers." All provinces were constitutionally equal in the exercise of the powers assigned to them within their borders, but that notion of equality did not extend to an equal say in the federation, to an equal share of power in the central government. On the contrary, the basic doctrine underlying the federal power was a slightly modified version of "representation by population." That is, each province would enjoy and exercise a share of power in the central government commensurate with the size of its population. This principle was modified to the extent that when readjustments were made in representation in the House of Commons after each census, the number of MPs for any province was not to be allowed to fall below the number of senators designated for that province. This provides the safeguard that, despite the principle of "rep by pop," each province will continue to enjoy reasonable levels of representation in the House of Commons.

Not all provinces were equal at the time of their entrance into Confederation. Each of the four original provinces — Ontario, Quebec, New Brunswick, Nova Scotia — entered Confederation under somewhat different arrangements in 1867, including a very special and "distinct" status for Quebec, and different deals were struck as each additional colony opted to join. The three Prairie provinces were in an entirely different constitutional category. Ottawa acquired the region as a colonial possession, and the Prairie provinces were simply the constitutional creations of the central government. Upon their creation, Ottawa denied them control of their lands and natural resources, a clear provincial power enumerated in the *BNA Act*, yet successfully withheld by Ottawa until 1930, "for the purposes of the Dominion." Nothing makes clearer the historical supremacy of Ottawa than this power to create provinces by federal statute and, furthermore, to create a different constitutional class of province, that is, those whose attainment of full constitutional provincial status could be delayed at the pleasure of Ottawa.

A further confirmation of federal supremacy lies in the fact that Ottawa retains key powers that can be exercised in the national interest and at the peril of provincial powers. These include the power to disallow or reserve any provincial statute, all residual powers, the general power "to make laws for the peace, order and good government of Canada" and the power to declare that any local work in a province is "to be for the general advantage of Canada or for the advantage of two or more of the provinces." The federal powers of disallowance and reservation have not been routinely exercised since the 1930s, during the heady days of Social Credit under William Aberhart of Alberta. But these powers have not atrophied from a lack of use. Indeed, they are designed not to have to be used. Their mere existence imposes a certain self-discipline on the provinces, particularly in the face of an assertive federal government. Any federal system that abandons such powers will slowly bleed to death as a result of a self-inflicted wound.

The relatively recent emergence of the doctrine of the constitutional equality of provinces was another device in the arsenal developed by Trudeau to deal with Quebec. By insisting that all provinces were constitutionally equal, Trudeau was able to insist that Quebec was a province just like the others. Quebec's demands should therefore simply be put on the list along with the demands of all other provinces. In this way, Trudeau was able to sidestep Quebec's demand for a bilateral negotiating process between Ottawa, representing English Canada, and the Quebec government, representing the Québécois nation. But it was a doctrine that Trudeau invoked with deft opportunism. To Quebec he would say he couldn't give what the Québécois wanted when the other provinces refused. Yet he was equally able to plead with Canadians to elect a strong central government "to speak for Canada." On one day he could determine to use Ottawa's power unilaterally to patriate and amend the constitution. Yet on another, when Lévesque appealed to him after the 1981 débâcle to help get Quebec's veto back, for example, he could insist that though he personally might favour such a concession to Quebec, the other provinces would have to agree, and that until that agreement was obtained, his hands were tied. In the post-1995 sovereignty referendum period, Chrétien proved to be a good student, invoking promises of constitutional change in Quebec in order to defeat the Yes, yet, right after the vote, pleading powerlessness in the face of the other provinces. Chrétien could threaten to assert maximum federal powers to stop the sovereigntists, yet insist he could do nothing on Quebec's constitutional concerns without the agreement of the premiers.

Ironically, Trudeau's opportunistic use of the doctrine gave it a degree of respectability, turning it into a Canadian constitutional convention and achieving a degree of realization in the amending formula adopted in 1982 (changes to the constitution require the consent of Ottawa and seven of 10 provinces, representing more than 50 per cent of the population). Provincial rights premiers and Mulroney were able to use the doctrine in nearly successful efforts to transform Confederation into a loose amalgamation of powerful provinces presided over by an increasingly impotent central government. Furthermore, the doctrine allows provincial rights premiers to insist that Quebec can obtain nothing not granted to all other provinces. This doctrine makes our current Quebec/English Canada impasse insoluble. To give all provinces exactly what Quebec needs to advance and protect its uniqueness will destroy the federation. Yet not to give Quebec at least some of what it needs also risks the breakup of Canada.

This brings us to the final logical expression of the doctrine of the equality of the provinces — the Triple-E Senate, composed of equal numbers of senators from each province, democratically elected and with some real and significant powers to exercise, first proposed by Manning and the Reform party and imperfectly expressed in the defeated Charlottetown Agreement. Quebec will never agree to such a proposal, nor will most English Canadians, preferring abolition. In arguing the Triple-E case, some have suggested that one of the original intentions of the Canadian Senate was to provide, in an imperfect way, a place to deal with regional grievances in the federation. Nothing could be further from the truth. The Fathers of Confederation explicitly rejected the model provided by the American Senate. They wanted neither a powerful nor a regional body. Although the *BNA Act* distributes equal number of senators to each of the four regions — Ontario, Quebec, Atlantic Canada and the West — the Senate was never conceived as a house of the regions. Rather, it was seen quite explicitly, in John A. Macdonald's words, as "the representative of property" and the place for second thoughts regarding the actions of the Commons. The Senate has no real effective power, other than that of delay and inconvenience, and the Commons can always finally prevail in any clash. In practice, the Senate became and remains simply a secure place at the public trough for former party bagmen and hacks, public figures past their partisan usefulness and assorted cronies of prime ministers, past and present. As such, it has long outlived its usefulness and deserves to be abolished, something about which there appears to be a near consensus in post-Charlottetown Canada.

If Canadians seriously want to address the problem of regional representation and deepening Canadian democracy by coming closer to realizing the principle of representation by population, without offending Quebec or most English Canadians, the remedy is available. First, abolish the Senate and establish a constitutional minimum number of House of Commons seats below which a province or a territory cannot fall should its population decline (say, for example, two seats for each territory, two seats for PEI, eight seats for the western and other Atlantic provinces at 500,000 or below, with "rep by pop" kicking in for populations above that number). Second, amend the constitution to require that the Commons seats granted to each province be assigned on a proportional basis to each political party according to levels of popular support. This would ensure that each province, or at least each region, would send MPs from all major political parties to Ottawa, forcing each party caucus to grapple with and reconcile regional and national interests at the same time. It would also ensure that splinter parties and regional protest parties, though small, would obtain a platform in the Commons sooner rather than later. Further, in the event that a regional protest party becomes strong, proportional representation would ensure a fair representation of all points of view among the voting population, avoiding a sweep of seats based on a plurality of votes in a "first past the post" system. The results of the 1997 and 2000 elections, roughly calculated to reflect proportional representation, would have been quite different under such a system, as the tables on pages 290 and 291 show.

The House of Commons would be a very different place if these had been the 1997 and 2000 results, and our recent political history would probably have been less divisive and crisis-ridden. The basic principles of fair and democratic representation would have been more perfectly realized. There would be the clash of debate including class, region, nation and party. Each party would have to deal with regional issues — language for Quebec, energy resource policy for the West, the fisheries in B. C. and Atlantic Canada — in the context of the party's ideological line. On occasion, cross-party regional alliances could occur. The chance of the kind of regional polarization by which Trudeau could write off the West, or the pre-Mulroney Tories could write off Quebec, or the Chrétien Liberals could write off Quebec, would be greatly lessened, indeed, would be highly unlikely.

A House of Commons based on proportional representation would be difficult to effect in Canada. The major parties would resist it, and it would be a disaster, critics allege. There would rarely be a majority government, the "Italian disease" would afflict us, and Canada would become ungovernable. Prime ministers would be constantly jockeying for majorities, governments would fall and we would have annual elections. One easy remedy is to have fixed elections — elections shall occur on the second Monday of June every fourth year, for example. In between, the parties would have to work harder at putting together ministries with the confidence of the House, which, after all, is the basic principle of parliamentary democracy and responsible government. Furthermore, Canada's experience with minority governments — Diefenbaker in 1957–58,

the Pearson years from 1963–68, Trudeau in 1972–74 (let's forget
Joe Clark in 1979, who pretended he had a majority) — have not
been particularly bad. Some argue such governments are the most
sensitive and productive. They have to work harder at governing
and refrain from arrogant assertions of undiluted power, not necessarily bad things. Indeed, one could argue that the governments of
Mulroney in 1988 and those of Chrétien in 1993, 1997 and 2000
may prove to have been the worst in our history — these governments won strong parliamentary majorities with minority popular
support and proceeded to brutally impose controversial, divisive
and damaging policies contrary to the popular will, and contrary to
much of what was promised before election.

English Canadians want and need a strong central government,
though one which is able and willing to share power in good faith
with the regions and the provinces on issues of vital provincial and
regional concern — forestry and the fishery in British Columbia,
energy resources and agriculture in the West, industrial policy in
Ontario, the fishery in Atlantic Canada. But after a failure of good-
faith efforts to reach a national strategy with regional support,
English Canadians want a central government with the power to do
what is best for Canada as a whole. Unlike Quebec, where a clear
majority of residents feel a primary allegiance to their province as a
result of Québécois nationalism, in the English-Canadian regions
residents feel a primary allegiance to Canada as a whole. The nine
English-Canadian provinces need and want a strong federal government to maintain a sense of Canadian nationhood through a
series of national strategies, particularly to offset regional dispari-
ties as well as to resist the American pull, a pull that has increased
dramatically in this era of free trade and "harmonization." They
want and need a prime minister and a House of Commons at the
centre that can not only speak for Canada but that can also act decisively for Canada. Canadians in English Canada want a government
at the centre that can continue existing national programs, like
medicare and support for post-secondary education, and develop
new ones in areas like daycare and culture. They want an effective
national government able to act on the popular will against the glob-
alization forces of the triumphant corporate millennium, not one
incapable of governing, fearful of asserting its democratic will
against the forces of economic dictatorship, characterized by so
many checks and balances that popular desires cannot be realized in
national policy.

Canadians in English Canada can never achieve such a strong

central government until the Quebec question is resolved satisfactorily. Québécois fears continue to block the realization of a more
potent national government. Intrusions of federal power, such as
federally funded programs in areas of provincial jurisdiction, have
always been viewed as threatening by the Québécois. English
Canada desperately needs a more aggressive national strategy on
culture, something the Québécois resist. English Canada cries out
for a well-developed, co-ordinated program in secondary and post-
secondary education, and manpower training and job strategies;
again there is profound resistance in Quebec. English Canada
urgently needs a new national economic policy: the regional pillars
of the old policy are collapsing — forestry in British Columbia,
agriculture in the West, industry in Ontario, the Atlantic fishery —
as global corporate power seeks to impose its anti-social market
logic on us. Yet Quebec, recalling a century of exploitation as a
source of cheap labour and cheap resources as well as its exploitation as a captive market, would undoubtedly resist such an initiative
if it was merely one of ten provinces at a table chaired by Ottawa.
Intrusions of the federal spending power in various areas of Québécois life have always provoked resistance, whereas English
Canadians realize, despite resistance from their provincial premiers,
that such assertions of federal power have been essential to bringing
us medicare, fairer access to university education, public pensions,
unemployment insurance and programs to fight regional disparity. It
is as a result of this federal power that all Canadians are assured a
reasonable minimum standard of living and of access to universal
publicly funded programs with national standards. Typically, English-Canadian provincial rights premiers, eager to expand provincial
at the expense of federal power, opportunistically ally themselves
with Quebec in order either to bring Ottawa to a standstill or to
extract additional revenues and administrative powers. As a result,
the national government has become increasingly ineffectual and
more and more the object of scorn among Canadians. It is, therefore,
in the interest of all Canadians in English Canada who yearn for an
effective and responsive national government to join together in a
final resolution of the Quebec question, if only as a necessary first
step in allowing English Canadians to address their national question with the same devotion and focus with which the Québécois
continue to address theirs.

English Canadians have two choices, now starkly clarified.
Either we grant Quebec some special constitutional status within
Confederation or we reconcile ourselves to further years of impasse

and conflict leading to Quebec's ultimate separation. Perhaps it is too late. We have squandered so many opportunities. Had English Canada responded with grace and intelligence to the B and B Commission, the Quiet Revolution, the October Crisis, the election of the PQ, the results of the 1980 sovereignty referendum, the post-Meech crisis, the defeat of Charlottetown in both Quebec and English Canada, the near win of the Yes in 1995 — we could have achieved a reconciliation and a meaningful compromise. But we did not respond, forcing the situation to the point where we wallow in a bitter impasse. And so here we are, dancing on the same precipice where the dance started forty years ago.

What sort of special status will satisfy Quebec? In the first place, most Québécois who support separation or sovereignty-association are reluctant separatists who yearn for even a minimal settlement with dignity. Bourassa clearly believed that his government's five conditions derived from Meech were the minimum: 1) recognition of Quebec as distinct society in the constitution; 2) more power over immigration; 3) limits on the use of the federal spending power; 4) a veto; and 5) a say in the appointment of Quebec's three judges on the Supreme Court. Obviously, clear and unfettered constitutional authority over language, education, culture and immigration are bottom lines for Quebec. Furthermore, a special mechanism to deal with intrusions of the federal spending power into Quebec (opting-out with financial compensation) would need to be developed. In addition, a Quebec veto over constitutional changes that have a significant impact on Quebec would need to be granted. The point is that the precise form of the special status will have to be negotiated. It might include some form of special status or asymmetrical federalism, or a confederal system, both of which would see the withdrawal of Quebec MPs from consideration of those matters before the House of Commons which have been devolved to the Quebec National Assembly. But the reality is clear: either we negotiate special status while Quebec is still part of Confederation, or we will negotiate at some future time with an independent Quebec the terms of the association we will inevitably want.

Certainly, the Charlottetown Agreement went some distance toward Quebec's minimum, but it proved finally insufficient. The recognition of Quebec as a distinct society was so heavily hedged and qualified that the Québécois decided it was not enough. The special status granted Quebec, such as it was, though enough to offend Trudeau, was not the sort Québécois nationalism had in mind. Québécois nationalism never asked for a perpetual guarantee of 25 per cent of House of Commons seats. Québécois nationalism never asked for a reformed Senate and a double majority on language and culture. Special status for Quebec was never seen as more power at the centre, power to threaten or frustrate the aspirations of English Canadians, but rather it was seen as uniquely granting the province of Quebec the special powers necessary to sustain the Québécois nation. Not only were the Charlottetown provisions insufficient for Quebec, but they provoked profound concern in English Canada. That concern was certainly a mixed ideological bag, including anti-Québécois sentiment at its rawest; fears of a loss of too many powers by Ottawa; a desire for a strong central government to articulate a vision of Canada acceptable in English Canada; a yearning for new national social programs in areas like daycare and for the defence of existing national social programs; concerns that the rights of women, especially aboriginal women, would be given short shrift under the deal; and so on.

The failure of Charlottetown followed quickly by the narrow victory for the No in the 1995 sovereignty referendum could have set the stage for another effort on the part of English Canada to resolve the Quebec crisis. But it did not, and our constitutional situation remains tattered and incomplete. In our inevitable efforts to reconstruct the constitution, perhaps we have learned not to do so in a crisis atmosphere. Next time let us proceed a careful step at a time: the Quebec/Canada impasse; the aboriginal question; the vision of English Canada in the context of the grievances of the English-Canadian peripheries; the Social Charter; expansion of gender-equity measures; and so on. That way our constitutional reconstruction can be deliberate, careful and solid, rather than haphazard jerrybuilding in a crisis atmosphere. Above all, constitutional reconstruction should not again be allowed to be made part of the personal, urgent re-election agendas of incumbent politicians, as was the case in Meech and Charlottetown. One approach worth considering is that of the constituent assembly, elected popularly and assigned the task of formulating constitutional solutions for presentation to the people in a referendum and then to the House of Commons and the provincial legislatures for ratification. Given the continuing urgency of the Quebec/Canada stalemate, the first task assigned such an assembly might be to formulate recommendations on reconciling the national question in the Canadian constitution, including special status for the Québécois and the aboriginal nations.

Critics have contended that special status for Quebec, no matter how limited initially, will turn out to be a half-way house to separation. This argument has considerable merit. Given any form of special status, the argument goes, Québécois nationalism will simply use these unique powers as levers to win more and more. In the end, only full sovereignty, followed by binational negotiations on association, will be enough. The argument became more compelling as Quebec's demands escalated in response to English Canada's repeated rebuffs, so compelling that it has taken on the character of a self-fulfilling prophecy. Perhaps we in English Canada have refused Quebec once too often, have denied the Québécois nation too repeatedly and with too much hostility and contempt. Perhaps the trajectory of the Québécois nation cannot now be deflected from ultimate sovereignty. If that is true, we in English Canada or our descendants will be forced to deal with it. But to continue to use it as an argument for yet more refusals will ensure that English Canada fulfils its own worst prophecy about Quebec.

Ottawa's Plan B has left a lot of rancour among Québécois nationalists and sovereigntists. The chasm has increased between the two solitudes. The possibility of reconciliation seems remote. But it is well to recall that together Québécois and English Canadians have forged one of the best places on the planet in which to live. If we can continue our unique experiment in seeking unity through diversity, if we can retain the two great cultures together in one federal or confederal structure, Canada could yet become a model for the entire world. But if we fail, it will not be a disaster. Life will go on, our economies will continue to function in much the same way, and Quebec and Canada will then compete for the UN title of the most desirable place in the world to live. We will muddle through, seeking some practical working arrangement. But the Canada we could have become, had we achieved an effective reconciliation between the two nations in a single federal or confederal state, will be lost, perhaps forever.

The Québécois nation has the political will to seek a reconciliation. It always has. Indeed, the last forty years have been characterized by increasingly urgent appeals from the Québécois for just such a reconciliation. But it cannot be on English Canada's terms, as it always was in the past. The reconciliation the Québécois seek insists that we in English Canada accept the fundamental legitimacy and correctness of their historical grievances. It also insists that English Canada abandon its notorious habit of declaring sympathy for the Québécois while imposing measures smugly judged by English Canada to be sufficient remedies. Just as English Canada reluctantly accepted the Québécois nation's right to self-determination only after the election of the PQ, English Canada must now yield to the Québécois nation the powers it needs to protect, strengthen and enhance that nation. To do otherwise, to try to turn back the clock and deny the existence of the Québécois nation, to threaten and bully that nation with the use of legal technicalities and superior federal power, will provoke an uglier confrontation at the next eruption of Quebec nationalism and sovereignty.

As we have seen, English Canada and Quebec have two quite different versions of the same history. Understandably this makes dialogue difficult. English Canadians, searching for positive, upbeat themes and justifications, prefer versions of history that ignore or diminish the oppression of the Québécois. Undeniably negative events — military conquest and suppression; the use of exile, prison and the noose; insults and degradations — are overlooked or attributed either to the actions of defective individuals who happened to hold power at the time or to the temper of the times. As victor, English Canada wrote the official history, selected the national symbols and controlled the myths, rituals and rites of official national self-celebration.

The Québécois, on the other hand, carefully husbanded their own history, holding it close to their hearts. Even when absent from, or reflected badly in, official versions, the history of the Québécois became deeply embedded in their collective consciousness. It was passed down from generation to generation in the private circle of family, neighbourhood and parish. The myths and symbols of that history became the litmus test for local political leaders. Efforts by English Canada to distort or prettify the history of oppression had an opposite effect. The Québécois resented what they saw as an arrogant attempt to rob them of their heritage and more determinedly clung to the truths they had learned at their parents' knees. English Canadians saw this tendency as evidence of backwardness, romanticism, an imprisonment by tradition, thus heaping insult on the original injury.

This circle can be broken only with the greatest of effort and only when English Canada admits the injustices done to the Québécois nation. For English Canada to admit publicly that the Québécois have been oppressed will involve the acceptance of critical public scrutiny and the humbling admission that all along much of what they said was true. It will also involve a fundamental change in self-perception. There will be shame and guilt and, inevitably, a need to make amends, an effort to pay historical debts.

Do English Canadians have the political will to go through this process? A crucial step in achieving that political will among English Canadians is for us to admit there are debts yet to be paid to the Québécois. Persuading English Canadians of this fact has been the purpose of this book. Do we acknowledge a debt to the descendants of those we conquered, reconquered and oppressed? Do we owe anything to the descendants of those we exploited as cheap labour? Can we be called to account again for the years of English privilege in Quebec? Have we settled accounts with the Québécois regarding the *War Measures Act*, or the dirty tricks of our secret police against the PQ, or the mole we placed in the Lévesque cabinet or the ganging up of 1981–82? Have we erased the impact of the insults and affronts when Meech fell? Did we really test our limits in the Charlottetown Agreement? Are we prepared to use domineering federal powers and the threat of force in an effort to checkmate a democratic decision by the Québécois to separate? Can we seek amends for the exultation and glee we expressed upon the crushing of the recent sovereignty initiative and the humiliation of Quebec's nationalist leaders? Can we in English Canada truly say that our collective conscience as a nation is now clear and that we have made a full historical accounting to the Québécois nation?

The Québécois nation does not believe we have yet paid our debts. Nor do many of us. We can pay them now, or we can pay them later. But pay them we must.

1997 Federal Election: Popular Vote, Seats Won and

	Total Seats	Conservative			Liberal		
		Vote %	1997 Result (seats)	PR (seats)	Vote %	1997 Result (seats)	PR (seats)
Quebec	75	22	5	17	37	26	27
Ontario	103	19	1	20	50	101	50
Manitoba	14	18	1	3	35	6	5
Saskatchewan	14	8	0	1	25	1	4
Alberta	26	14	0	4	24	2	6
British Columbia	34	6	0	2	29	6	10
New Brunswick	10	35	5	4	33	3	3
Nova Scotia	11	31	5	4	28	0	3
Prince Edward Is	4	38	0	3	45	4	2
Newfoundland	7	37	3	3	38	4	3
Yukon	1	14	0	0	22	0	0
North West Terr	2	17	0	0	43	2	1
	301	19%	20	60	38%	155	114

2000 Federal Election: Popular Vote, Seats Won and

	Total Seats	Conservative			Liberal		
		Vote %	2000 Result (seats)	PR (seats)	Vote %	2000 Result (seats)	PR (seats)
Quebec	75	6	1	5	44	36	33
Ontario	103	14	0	15	51	100	55
Manitoba	14	14	1	2	32	5	5
Saskatchewan	14	5	0	1	21	2	2
Alberta	26	14	1	4	21	1	5
British Columbia	34	7	0	2	28	5	10
New Brunswick	10	31	3	3	42	6	4
Nova Scotia	11	29	4	3	57	4	4
Prince Edward Is	4	38	0	2	47	4	2
Newfoundland	7	35	2	3	45	5	3
Yukon	1	8	0	0	33	1	1
North West Terr	1	10	0	0	46	1	1
Nunavut	1	8	0	0	68	1	1
	301	12%	12	40	41%	171	126

Estimates of Seats under Proportional Representation (PR)

NDP			Reform			Bloc Quebecois		
Vote %	1997 Result (seats)	PR (seats)	Vote %	1997 Result (seats)	PR (seats)	Vote %	1997 Result (seats)	PR (seats)
2	0	2	0.3	0	0	38	44	29
11	1	11	19	0	21	0	0	0
23	4	3	24	3	3	0	0	0
31	5	4	36	8	5	0	0	0
6	0	2	55	24	14	0	0	0
18	3	6	43	25	16	0	0	0
18	2	2	13	0	1	0	0	0
30	6	3	10	0	1	0	0	0
15	0	0	1	0	0	0	0	0
22	0	1	3	0	0	0	0	0
29	1	1	25	0	0	0	0	0
21	0	1	12	0	0	0	0	0
11%	13	36	19%	60	61	11%	44	29

Estimates of Seats under Proportional Representation (PR)

NDP			Alliance			Bloc		
Vote %	2000 Result (seats)	PR (seats)	Vote %	2000 Result (seats)	PR (seats)	Vote %	2000 Result (seats)	PR (seats)
2	0	2	6	0	5	40	38	30
8	1	8	24	2	25	0	0	0
21	4	3	31	4	4	0	0	0
26	2	4	48	10	7	0	0	0
6	0	2	59	23	15	0	0	0
11	2	4	49	27	18	0	0	0
12	1	1	16	0	2	0	0	0
24	3	3	10	0	1	0	0	0
9	0	0	5	0	0	0	0	0
13	1	1	4	0	0	0	0	0
32	0	0	28	0	0	0	0	0
27	0	0	18	0	0	0	0	0
19	0	0	-					
9%	13	28	25%	67	77	11%	38	30

When I first proposed the idea for this book to the publisher, I had in mind an essay that would make the basic "debts to pay" and "denial of nation" arguments, while providing a reinterpretation of the well-known events of Quebec's history. As I began to write, I found myself forced both to revisit a variety of old sources to refresh my memory and to visit some new ones to update myself on more recent events. I have included a list of those sources most heavily relied upon. However, the book is still first and foremost an essay.

Additionally, I made a great deal of use of my own newspaper clipping files from *The Globe and Mail*, the Regina *Leader Post*, *Maclean's* and selected editions of *Le Devoir*, particularly for the periods of the October Crisis of 1970 and the rise and fall of the Meech Lake Accord and the Charlottetown Agreement, and the 1995 sovereignty referendum. I also made frequent use of *The Gallup Report*, to which I have subscribed for many years before it ceased publication in Canada. I followed the constitutional debates between the demise of Meech and the Charlottetown effort in *The Network*, the newsletter of the Network on the Constitution, published out of the University of Ottawa and edited by Donald G. Lenihan. And I followed the extent and impacts of federal budget cuts through the *CCPA Monitor*, published by the Ottawa-based Canadian Centre for Policy Alternatives. The material on the Charlottetown Agreement, the 1992 and 1995 referendums, and events until 2004, is based on coverage provided in *The Globe and Mail*, Regina *Leader Post*, *Maclean's*, the Montreal *Gazette* and *Le Devoir*, as well as on the CBC-TV and CTV national networks.

My discussion of the October Crisis might provoke some controversy. The facts on which I base the characterization of the events of October 1970 are all now on the public record. For the skeptical among you, I refer you to the books on the crisis by Haggart and Golden, Pelletier, Rotstein, Smith, and Vallières. Some excellent investigative work, including interviews with paroled FLQers, was published in *The Globe and Mail* on the tenth and fifteenth anniversaries of the crisis (October 1980 and October 1985). I found John Twigg's unpublished paper to be very useful, and I kept a very detailed clipping file during the crisis. One cannot overlook the information contained in the report of the McDonald Commission on the RCMP Security Service and the press clippings about the Quebec Keable Commission.

For basic statistics, which I tried to use sparingly, I appealed often to Urquhart and Buckley's *Historical Statistics of Canada,* Langlois's *Recent Social Trends in Quebec, 1960–1990,* to census reports and reports by various electoral officers. Additionally, I found myself forced to revisit some of the major government reports regarding Quebec, most importantly the reports of the Royal Commission on Bilingualism and Biculturalism, the Task Force on Canadian Unity and Quebec's Gendron Commission.

Selected Bibliography

Armstrong, E. *The Crisis of Quebec, 1914–1918*. Toronto: McClelland and Stewart, 1974 (1937).

Arnaud, N., and Dofny, J. *Nationalism and the National Question*. Montreal: Black Rose, 1977.

Arnopoulos, S.M., and Clift, D. *The English Fact in Quebec*. Montreal: McGill-Queen's University Press, 1980.

Behiels, M.D. (ed.). *The Meech Lake Primer*. Ottawa: University of Ottawa Press, 1990.

————. *Prelude to Quebec's Quiet Revolution: Liberalism versus Neo-nationalism, 1945–1980*. Montreal/Kingston: McGill-Queen's University Press, 1985.

Bercuson, D.J., and Cooper, B. *Deconfederation: Canada without Quebec*. Toronto: Key Porter, 1991.

Berger, C. (ed.). *Conscription 1917*. Toronto: University of Toronto Press, n.d.

Bergeron, L. *The History of Quebec: A Patriote's Handbook*. Toronto: NC, 1971.

Bernard, A. *What Does Quebec Want?* Toronto: Lorimer, 1978.

Bernard, J.P. (ed.). *Les Rébellions de 1837–1838: Les Patriotes du Bas-Canada dans la mémoire collective et chez les historiens*. Montreal: Boréal, 1983.

Black, C. *Duplessis*. Toronto: McClelland and Stewart, 1976.

Blais, André et. al. *Anatomy of a Liberal Victory: Making Sense of the Vote in the 2000 Canadian Election*. Toronto: Broadview, 2002.

Bliss, J.M. (ed.). *Canadian History in Documents, 1763–1966*. Toronto: Ryerson, 1966.

Bloc Québécois. "Chantier de réflexion sur la citoyenneté et la démocratie," document de travail, *La souveraineté: pour le monde à venir*, Rivière-du-Loup, 1999.

―――. "Chantier de réflexion sur la défense et la promotion des intérêts du Quebec," document de travail, *La souveraineté: pour le monde à venir*, Rivière-du-Loup, 1999.

―――. "Chantier de réflexion sur le partenariat," document de travail, *La souveraineté: pour le monde à venir*, Rivière-du-Loup, 1999.

―――. "Chantier de réflexion sur la mondialisation," document de travail, *La souveraineté: pour le monde à venir*, Rivière-du-Loup, 1999.

Boris, S.T. *The Language of the Skies: The Bilingual Air Traffic Control Conflict in Canada*. Montreal: McGill-Queen's University Press, 1983.

Bouchard, L. *A visage découvert*. Montreal: Boréal, 1992.

―――. (dir.) *Un nouveau parti pour l'étape décisive*. Montreal: Fidès, 1993.

Brebner, J.B. *Canada: A Modern History*. Ann Arbor: University of Michigan Press, 1960.

Brown, R.C., and Cook, R. *Canada, 1896–1921: A Nation Transformed*. Toronto: McClelland and Stewart, 1974.

Browne, G.P. (ed.). *Documents on the Confederation of British North America*. Toronto: McClelland and Stewart, 1969.

Brunet, M. *La Présence Anglaise et Les Canadiens*. Montreal: Beauchemin, 1964.

Buchanan, A. *Secession: The Morality of Political Divorce from Fort Sumter to Lithuania and Quebec*. Boulder: Westview Press, 1991.

Burroughs, P. *The Colonial Reformers and Canada, 1830–1849*. Toronto: McClelland and Stewart, 1969.

Burt, A.L.R. *The Old Province of Quebec*. Toronto: McClelland and Stewart, 1968.

Campbell, K. *Time and Chance: The Political Memoirs of Canada's First Woman Prime Minister*. Toronto: Doubleday, 1996.

Canada. First Ministers' Meeting. *Consensus Report on the Constitution*. Ottawa, 1992. (Charlottetown Agreement.)

―――. Royal Commission on Bilingualism and Biculturalism. *Preliminary Report*, 1965; *The Official Languages*, Vol. I, 1967; *Education*, Vol. II, 1968; *The Work World*, Vol. III, 1969; *The Cultural Contribution of the Other Ethnic Groups*, Vol. IV, 1970. Ottawa: various years.

————. The Task Force on Canadian Unity. *A Future Together*. Ottawa, 1979.

Carens, J.H. (ed.) *Is Quebec Nationalism Just?* Montreal/ Kingston: McGill-Queen's University Press, 1995.

Chaput, M. *Pourquoi je suis séparatiste*. Montreal: Editions du Jour, 1961.

Chodos, R., and Hamovitch, E. *Quebec and the American Dream*. Toronto: Between the Lines, 1991.

Cleroux, R. "L'affaire Morin." *Canadian Forum*, June 1992.

Clouthier, E., Guay, J.H., and Latouche, D. *Le virage: l'évolution de l'opinion publique au Québec depuis 1960, ou comment le Québec est devenu souverainiste*. Montreal: Editions Québec/ Amérique, 1992.

Constitutional Forum Constitutionnel. "Perspectives on the PQ Plan for Sovereignty, 'Quebec in a New World,'" Special issue. Edmonton: Centre for Constitutional Studies, University of Alberta, Fall 1994.

Conway, J.F. *The West: The History of a Region in Confederation*. Toronto: Lorimer, 1994.

————. "The Mulroney Counter-Revolution, 1984–1993," unpublished paper, Canadian Sociology and Anthropology Association, Learneds. Calgary: University of Calgary, 1994.

————. "Reflections on Canada in the Year 1994," in de Finney, J., et. al., (eds.), *Canadian Studies at Home and Abroad*. Montreal: Association for Canadian Studies, 1995.

Cook, R. *Canada and the French-Canadian Question*. Toronto: Macmillan, 1966.

————. (ed.). *Confederation*. Toronto: University of Toronto Press, 1967.

Coon Come, M. "The Status and Rights of the James Bay Crees in the Context of Quebec Secession from Canada," *Constitutional Forum Constitutionnel*, Fall 1994.

Cornellier, M. *The Bloc*. Toronto: Lorimer, 1995.

Coyne, D. *Roll of the Dice*. Toronto: Lorimer, 1992.

Craig, G.M. (ed.). *Lord Durham's Report*. Toronto: McClelland and Stewart, 1963.

Creighton, D.G. *British North America at Confederation*. Ottawa: Queen's Printer, 1963.

————. *Dominion of the North: A History of Canada*. Toronto: Macmillan, 1957.

————. *Empire of the St. Lawrence*. Toronto: Macmillan, 1972.

Dafoe, J.W. *Laurier*. Toronto: McClelland and Stewart, 1963.

Dawson, R. MacGregor. *The Government of Canada*. (revised by Norman Ward). Toronto: University of Toronto Press, 1964 (1947).

den Otten, A.A. *Civilizing the West: The Galts and the Development of Western Canada*. Edmonton: University of Alberta Press, 1982.

Delacourt, Susan. *Juggernaut: Paul Martin's Campaign for Chretién's Crown*. Toronto: McClelland and Stewart, 2003

Desbarats, P. *René: A Canadian in Search of a Country*. Toronto: McClelland and Stewart, 1976.

Dion, L. *Quebec: The Unfinished Revolution*. Montreal: McGill University Press, 1976.

Dion, S. "The Dynamic of Secession: Scenarios after a Pro-separatist Vote in a Quebec Referendum," *Canadian Journal of Political Science*, September 1995.

————. "Why is Secession Difficult in Well-Established Democracies? Lessons from Quebec," *British Journal of Political Science*, 1995.

Dobbin, M. *Preston Manning and the Reform Party*. Toronto: Lorimer, 1991.

Drache, D. (ed.). *Quebec: Only the Beginning*. Toronto: New Press, 1972.

————., and Perin, R. (eds.). *Negotiating with a Sovereign Quebec*. Toronto: Lorimer, 1992.

Duhamel, P. "Anglo-Quebec: A Distinct Society." *Report on Business Magazine*, April 1991.

Dunham, A. *Political Unrest in Upper Canada, 1815–1836*. Toronto: McClelland and Stewart, 1963.

Eccles, W.J. *The Ordeal of New France*. Montreal: CBC, 1966.

Flanagan, T. *Waiting for the Wave: The Reform Party and Preston Manning*. Toronto: Stoddart, 1995.

Fournier, P. A *Meech Lake Post-Mortem: Is Quebec Sovereignty Inevitable?* Montreal/Kingston: McGill-Queen's University Press, 1991.

————. *The Quebec Establishment*. Montreal: Black Rose, 1976.

Frances, Diane. *Fighting for Canada*. Toronto: Key Porter, 1996.

Fraser, G. *PQ: René Lévesque and the Parti Québécois in Power*. Toronto: Macmillan, 1984.

Freeman, A., and Grady, P. *Dividing the House: Planning for a Canada without Quebec*. Toronto: HarperCollins, 1995.

Frizzel, A., Pammett, J.H., and Westell, A. *The Canadian General Election of 1993*. Ottawa: Carleton, 1994.

Gagnon, Alain (ed.) *L'union sociale canadienne sans le Québec.* Montréal: St-Martin, 2000.

———. (ed.). *Quebec: State and Society.* Toronto: Metheun, 1984.

———., and Rocher, F. (eds.). *Répliques aux détracteurs de la souveraineté du Québec.* Montreal: VLB éditeur, 1992.

Gibson, G. *Plan B: The Future of the Rest of Canada.* Vancouver: Fraser Institute, 1994.

Gourgeon, G. *The History of Quebec Nationalism.* Translated by R. Chodos. Toronto: Lorimer, 1996.

Gourlay, R. *Statistical Account of Upper Canada.* Toronto: McClelland and Stewart, 1974 (1822).

Granatstein, J.L., and Hitsman, J.M. *Broken Promises: A History of Conscription in Canada.* Toronto: Oxford University Press, 1977.

———., and McNaught, K. (eds.). *"English Canada" Speaks Out.* Toronto: Doubleday, 1991.

Haggart, R., and Golden, A.E. *Rumours of War.* Toronto: Lorimer, 1979.

Harrison, R. *Of Passionate Intensity: Right-Wing Populism and the Reform Party of Canada.* Toronto: University of Toronto, 1995.

Hartt, S.H., et. al. *Tangled Web: Legal Aspects of Deconfederation.* Toronto: C.D. Howe Institute, 1992.

Héroux, M. *The Office of the Commissioner of Official Languages. A Twenty-Year Chronicle from 1970 to Mid-1989.* Ottawa, 1989.

Hughes, E. *French Canada in Transition.* Chicago: University of Chicago Press, 1963.

Keilty, G. (ed.). *1837: Revolution in the Canadas.* Toronto: NC, 1974.

Kwavnik, D. (ed.). *The Tremblay Report.* Toronto: McClelland and Stewart, 1973.

Laidler, D.E., and Robson, W.B. (eds.). *Two Nations, One Money?* Toronto: C.D. Howe Institute, 1991.

Langlois, S., et. al. *Recent Social Trends in Quebec, 1960–1990.* Montreal: McGill-Queen's University Press, 1992.

Language and Society, Special Report, 25th Anniversary of the Royal Commission on Bilingualism and Biculturalism, Summer 1989.

Laurendeau, A. *Witness for Quebec.* Toronto: Macmillan, 1973.

LeDuc, L., and Pamett, J.H. "Referendum Voting: Attitudes and

Behaviour in the 1992 Constitutional Referendum," *Canadian Journal of Political Science*, March 1995.

Lemco, J. *Turmoil in the Peaceful Kingdom: The Quebec Sovereignty Movement and Its Implications for Canada and the United States*. Toronto: University of Toronto, 1994.

Lester, Normand. *The Black Book of English Canada*. Toronto: McClelland and Stewart, 2002 (with an introduction by the translator, Ray Cologne).

Lévesque, R. *An Option for Quebec*. Toronto: McClelland and Stewart, 1965.

———. *Memoirs*. Toronto: McClelland and Stewart, 1986.

———. *My Quebec*. Toronto: Methuen, 1979.

Levitt, J. *Henri Bourassa and the Golden Calf: The Social Programme of the Nationalists of Quebec, 1900–1914*. Ottawa: University of Ottawa Press, 1969.

Liberal Party. *Creating Opportunity: The Liberal Plan for Canada*. (The Red Book) Ottawa: Liberal Party of Canada, 1993.

Linteau, P.-A., Durocher, R., and Robert, J.-C. *Quebec: A History, 1867–1929*. Toronto: Lorimer, 1983.

———., et. al. *Quebec Since 1930*. Translated by R. Chodos. Toronto: Lorimer, 1995.

Lower, A.R.M. *Colony to Nation*. Toronto: Longmans, Green, 1946.

MacDonald, L. Ian. *From Bourassa to Bourassa*. Second edition. Montreal/Kingston: McGill-Queen's, 2002.

Macli, C. "Duelling in the Dark." *Report on Business Magazine*, April, 1991.

Mallory, J.R. *The Structure of Canadian Government*. Toronto: Gage, 1984.

Mann, Susan. *The Dream of Nation: A Social and Intellectual History of Quebec*. Second edition. Montreal/Kingston: McGill-Queen's, 2002.

Maroney, Heather Jon. "'Who has the baby?' Nationalism, pronationalism and the construction of a 'demographic crisis' in Quebec 1960–1988," *Studies in Political Economy*, 39, Autumn 1992, pp. 7–36.

Martin, P. "Association after Sovereignty? Canadian Views on Economic Association with a Sovereign Quebec," *Canadian Public Policy*, 1995.

———. "Générations politiques, rationalité économique et appui á la souveraineté au Québec," *Canadian Journal of Political*

Science, June 1994.

Masters, D.C. *The Reciprocity Treaty of 1854*. Toronto: McClelland and Stewart, 1963.

McRoberts, K. (ed.). *Beyond Quebec: Taking Stock of Canada*. Montreal/Kingston: McGill-Queen's University Press, 1995.

————., and Monahan, P.J. (eds.). *The Charlottetown Accord, the Referendum and the Future of Canada*. Toronto: University of Toronto Press, 1993.

————., and Postgate, D. *Quebec: Social Change and Political Crisis*. Toronto: McClelland and Stewart, 1980.

McWhinney, E. *Quebec and the Constitution, 1960–1978*. Toronto: University of Toronto Press, 1979.

Milne, D. *The Canadian Constitution*. Toronto: Lorimer, 1991.

Milner, H. *Politics in the New Quebec*. Toronto: McClelland and Stewart, 1978.

Milner, S.H., and Milner, H. *The Decolonization of Quebec: An Analysis of Left-Wing Nationalism*. Toronto: McClelland and Stewart, 1973.

Monahan, P.J. *Cooler Heads Shall Prevail: Assessing the Costs and Consequences of Quebec Separation*. Toronto: C.D. Howe Institute, 1994.

Monière, Denis. *Pour compendre le nationalisme du Québec et ailleurs*. Montréal: Université de Montréal, 2001.

Morin, Claude. *Le Pouvoir québécois...en négociation*. Montreal: Boréal, 1972.

————. *Les prophètes désarmés? Que faire si un réferendum gagnant sur la souveraineté n'était possible?* Montreal: Boréal, 2001.

————. *Quebec vs. Ottawa: The Struggle for Self-Government, 1960–72*. Toronto: University of Toronto Press, 1976.

————. *Les choses comme elles étaient*. Montreal: Boréal, 1994.

Morissette, Yves-Marie. *Le renvoir sur la sécession du Québec: bilan provisoire et perspectives*. Montréal: Varia, 2001.

Morisson, A. (ed.) *The Canadian Strategic Forecast 1992: Divided We Fall: The National Security Implications of Canadian Constitutional Issues*. Toronto: Canadian Institute for Strategic Studies, 1991.

Morton, W.L. *The Kingdom of Canada*. Toronto: McClelland and Stewart, 1969.

Nash, K. (ed.) *Visions of Canada*. Toronto: McClelland and Stewart, 1991.

Noel, Alain. *Without Quebec: Collaborative Federalism with a*

Footnote? Montreal: Institute for Research on Public Policy, March 2000.

Ouellet, F. *Economic and Social History of Quebec, 1760–1850.* Toronto: Carleton University Press, 1980.

———. *Lower Canada, 1791–1840: Social Change and Nationalism.* Toronto: McClelland and Stewart, 1980.

Owram, D. *Promise of Eden: The Canadian Expansionist Movement and the Idea of the West, 1856–1900.* Toronto: University of Toronto Press, 1980.

Papineau, Louis-Joseph. *Histoire de la Résistance du Canada au gouvernement anglais.* Matrical: Comeau and Nadeau, 2001.

Parti Québécois. *Quebec in a New World.* Translated by R. Chodos. Toronto: Lorimer, 1995.

Parizeau, Jacques. *Pour un Québec souverain.* Montreal: VLB éditeur, 1997.

Pellet, Allain, President, United Nations International Law Commission. "Reference Concerning Specific Questions Pertaining to the Secession of Québec from Canada: Legal Opinion on Certain Questions of International Law Raised by the Present Reference," Supreme Court of Canada, 2 December 1997.

Pelletier, G. *The October Crisis.* Toronto: McClelland and Stewart, 1971.

Philpot, R. *Oka: dernier alibi du Canada anglais.* Montreal: VLB éditeur, 1991.

Québec. *Québec's Political and Constitutional Status: an overview.* Québec: Gouvernement du Québec, 1999.

———. *Rapport de la commission d'enquête sur la situation de la langue française et sur les droits linguistiques au Québec.* Gouvernement du Québec, 1972 (Gendron Commission).

———.*Quebec-Canada: A New Deal.* Gouvernement du Québec, 1979.

———. *The Political and Constitutional Future of Quebec.* Gouvernement du Québec, 1992 (Bélanger-Campeau Commission).

———. "Les implications de la mise en oeuvre de la souveraineté: les aspects économiques et les finances publiques." *Exposés et études.* Assemblée Nationale du Québec, 1992 (Vol. 4).

Quebec Liberal Party. *A Quebec Free to Choose.* Quebec City, 1991 (Allaire Report).

Quinn, H. *The Union Nationale: Quebec Nationalism from Duplessis to Lévesque.* Toronto: University of Toronto Press, 1979.

Reid, M. *The Shouting Signpainters*. Toronto: McClelland and Stewart, 1968.

Reid, Stuart. *Wolfe: The Career of General James Wolfe from Culloden to Quebec*. Cambridge, Mass.: Da Capo: 2000.

Resnick, P. *Letters to a Québécois Friend*. Reply by D. Latouche. Montreal/Kingston: McGill-Queen's University Press, 1990.

———. *Toward a Canada-Quebec Union*. Kingston/Montreal: McGill-Queen's University Press, 1991.

———. *Thinking English Canada*. Toronto: Stoddart, 1994.

Richler, M. *Oh Canada! Oh Quebec! Requiem for a Divided Country*. Toronto: Penguin, 1992.

Rioux, M. *Quebec in Question*. Toronto: Lorimer, 1978.

———., and Martin, Y. (eds.). *French Canadian Society*. Toronto: McClelland and Stewart, 1964.

Ritchie, G., et. al. *Broken Links: Trade Relations After a Quebec Secession*. Toronto: C.D. Howe Institute, 1991.

Robin, M. *Shades of Right: Nativist and Fascist Politics in Canada, 1920–1940*. Toronto: University of Toronto Press, 1992.

Rocher, G. "Preface," in Conway, J.F. *Des comptes á rendre*. Montreal: VLB éditeur, 1995.

Rothwell, Robert. *Canada and Quebec: One Country, Two Histories*. Vancouver: UBC, 1998.

Rotstein, A. (ed.). *Power Corrupted: The October Crisis and the Repression of Quebec*. Toronto: New Press, 1971.

Royal Bank. *Unity or Disunity: An Economic Analysis of the Benefits and Costs*. Montreal: Royal Bank of Canada, 1992.

Ryan, Claude. "The Reference Pending Before the Supreme Court of Canada Concerning Certain Questions Relating to the Secession of Quebec: Memoir sent to the Amicus Curiae Concerning the First Question of the Reference," 31 January 1998, in possession of author.

Ryerson, S. *1837: The Birth of Canadian Democracy*. Toronto: Francis White, 1937.

———. *The Founding of Canada*. Toronto: Progress, 1960.

———. *French Canada*. Toronto: Progress, 1953.

———. *Unequal Union*. Toronto: Progress, 1968.

Sarra-Bournet, M. *Le Canada anglais et la souveraineté du Québec: deux cents leaders d'opinion prononcent*. Montreal: VLB éditeur, 1995.

Sawatsky, J. *Mulroney: The Politics of Ambition*. Toronto: Macfarlane, Walter and Ross, 1991.

Saywell, J. *The Rise of the Parti Québécois*. Toronto: University of Toronto Press, 1977.

Scott, F.R., and Oliver, M. (eds.). *Quebec States Her Case*. Toronto: Macmillan, 1964.

Schull, J. *Rebellion: The Rising in French Canada, 1837*. Toronto: Macmillan, 1971.

Seidle, F.L. (ed.). *Seeking a New Canadian Partnership: Asymmetrical and Confederal Options*. Montreal: Institute for Research on Public Policy, 1994.

Seymour, Michel. *Le pari de la démesure: L'intransigence canadienne face au Québec*. Montréal: l'Hexagone, 2001.

———. "Quebec and Canada at the Crossroads: a nation within a nation." *Nation and Nationalism*, 6 (2), 2000.

Sharpe, S., and Braid, D. *Storming Babylon: Preston Manning and the Rise of the Reform Party*. Toronto: Key Porter, 1991.

Siegfried, A. *The Race Question in Canada*. Toronto: McClelland and Stewart, 1966.

Silver, A.I. *The French-Canadian Idea of Confederation, 1864–1900*. Toronto: University of Toronto Press, 1982.

Smith, D. *Bleeding Hearts...Bleeding Country: Canada and the Quebec Crisis*. Edmonton: Hurtig, 1971.

Smith, D.E. *The Regional Decline of a National Party: Liberals on the Prairies*. Toronto: University of Toronto Press, 1981.

Stanley, G.F.G. *The Birth of Western Canada: A History of the Riel Rebellions*. Toronto: University of Toronto Press, 1960.

Stewart, W. *Shrug: Trudeau in Power*. Toronto: New Press, 1972.

Trofimenkoff, S.M. *The Dream of Nation*. Toronto: Gage, 1983.

Trudeau, P.E. *Federalism and the French-Canadians*. Toronto: Macmillan, 1968.

Turp, Daniel. *La nation baillonnée*. Montreal: VLB: 2000.

———. "Québec's Right to Secessionist Self-Determination: The Colliding Paths of Canada's Clarity Act and Québec's Fundamental Rights Act," paper presented at the Americas' Regional Conference on Secession and International Law, Santa Clara University Law School, 2 February 2001 <www.danielturp.org>.

Twigg, J. "Press Reaction to the October 1970 Crisis in Quebec." Unpublished paper, 1971.

Urquhart, M.C., and Buckley, K.A.H. (eds.). *Historical Statistics of Canada*. Ottawa: Statistics Canada, 1983.

Vallières, P. *White Niggers of America*. Toronto: McClelland and Stewart, 1971.

————. *Choose!* Toronto: NewPress, 1972.

————. *The Assassination of Pierre Laporte: Behind the October '70 Scenario*. Toronto: Lorimer, 1977.

Varcoe, F.P. *The Constitution of Canada*. Toronto: Carswell, 1965.

Venne, Michel. *Vivé Québec! New Thinking and New Approaches to the Quebec Nation*. Lorimer, 2001 (translated by Robert Chodos and Louisa Blair).

Wade, M. *The French-Canadian Outlook*. Toronto: McClelland and Stewart, 1964.

————. *The French-Canadians: 1760–1967*. Toronto: Macmillan, 1968 (Vols. I and II).

Waite, P.B. *The Life and Times of Confederation, 1864–67*. Toronto: University of Toronto Press, 1962.

————. (ed.). *The Confederation Debates in the Province of Canada, 1865*. Toronto: McClelland and Stewart, 1963.

Wallot, Jean-Pierre. (ed.). *Le débat qui n'a pas eu lieu: La Commission Pepin-Robarts, quelque vingt ans après*. Ottawa: Universite de Ottawa, 2001.

Ward, N. *The Canadian House of Commons*. Toronto: University of Toronto Press, 1950.

Weaver, R.K. (eds.). *The Collapse of Canada?* Washington, D.C.: Brookings Institute, 1992.

Young, R.A. *The Breakup of Czechoslovakia*. Kingston: Queen's University Press, 1994.

————. "How Do Peaceful Secessions Happen?" *Canadian Journal of Political Science*, December 1994.

————. *The Secession of Quebec and the Future of Canada*. Kingston/Montreal: McGill-Queen's University Press, 1995.

APPENDIX I:
THE CHARLOTTETOWN AGREEMENT

The Charlottetown Agreement went much further than Meech in the devolution of powers from Ottawa to the provinces. The new powers the Agreement proposed to extend to the provinces were considerable:

- Exclusive jurisdiction over labour market development and human resources training, including the right to eject the federal government from all activities in the area. Ottawa, however, would still maintain the unemployment insurance program. Surely this was a bizarre idea: Ottawa would pay for unemployment insurance, but Canada could conceivably have ten different human resources development policies unrelated to the national unemployment insurance program.
- Exclusive jurisdiction over culture, but Ottawa would continue to maintain national cultural institutions. How this would work in practice challenged the imagination. Would Ottawa be allowed to pay for and to run the CBC, but with provinces determining provincial programming?
- Exclusive jurisdiction over forestry, mining, tourism, housing, recreation and municipal and urban affairs. These areas were already considered to be provincial jurisdictions, but Ottawa has not hesitated to act in these areas using the federal spending power. What remained unclear was how much of the federal spending power came with this exclusive jurisdiction.
- The constitutional power to compel Ottawa to negotiate regional development programs. This was an effort to give some force to the already existing constitutional commit-

ment to equalization payments and comparable levels of services and taxes across the country. The new proposal also added a commitment to "comparable economic infrastructures of a national nature," whatever that meant.

- A share in power over immigration, something Quebec already enjoyed by intergovernmental agreement as a result of post-Meech bilateral negotiations between Quebec and Ottawa.
- A share in power over the regulation of the telecommunications industry.
- The right to opt out of new national shared-cost programs with financial compensation.
- A constitutional right to protect future intergovernmental agreements from unilateral change by Ottawa.
- The right to submit a list of names from which Ottawa must select appointees for the Supreme Court.
- A veto over constitutional changes affecting the Senate, the House of Commons, the Supreme Court (except the nomination and appointment process) and the constitutional amending formula.
- A right to opt out, with financial compensation, of any constitutional change that transfers provincial powers to Ottawa.

In addition to these new provincial powers, Charlottetown also proposed to hamstring federal power. Ottawa's power of disallowance and/or reservation of provincial legislation was to be repealed. Ottawa's power to declare a provincial "work" in the interests of two or more provinces, or the nation as a whole, thereby taking over jurisdiction, was now to be exercised only with the consent of the province in which the "work" was located. These are presently unqualified, clear and unchallengeable central powers to be exercised at the pleasure and discretion of Ottawa. With these gone, Ottawa would only retain the "peace, order and good government" power, a vague and unsatisfactory central power, subject to arguments about meaning and justification and ultimately arguable in front of the Supreme Court, which, over time, would tilt more and more toward provincial rights.

These were enormous new powers for the provinces and a dramatic shackling of federal power. One can understand why nine premiers, under the decentralizing guidance of Joe Clark and

Brian Mulroney, would agree to allow such burdens to be imposed upon them. Interestingly, they also, taken together, more or less amounted to a significant portion of the wish-list Quebec had developed over the past thirty years. The only thing missing, of course, was that the Charlottetown Agreement did not grant each province constitutional recognition as a "distinct society." Only Quebec received that recognition. Now, if this had remained the package on offer — new powers for the provinces, the profound weakening of the federal power, distinct society status for Quebec — then Quebec might have signed on eagerly. If the only way it can get special constitutional status is by giving special status to every other province, then Quebec won't argue. With the support of the prime minister, the nine English-Canadian premiers were playing the same game that the premiers had played during Meech and have more or less played since the Quiet Revolution. If Ottawa wants to solve the Quebec constitutional crisis, the only way it can be done is if each and every concession to Quebec is given to all provinces. In exchange, the nine English-Canadian premiers agreed to yield, reluctantly, on distinct society for Quebec.

The Charlottetown Agreement included commitments to both "the vitality and development of official language minority communities throughout Canada" and the "equality of provinces" in the Canada clause to stand uneasily beside Quebec's distinct society clause. Both proposals struck at the very root of Quebec's continuing grievances. The first was seen as a potential trump card to be used in future Supreme Court tests of Quebec's language laws. It did not take much imagination to anticipate a flurry of challenges by Quebec's English-Canadian minority to many aspects of Quebec's language laws on the grounds that the laws did not respect the vitality and development of the English-speaking minority in Quebec. Public opinion in Quebec would hesitate to accept any measure that appeared to threaten the right of the Québécois to secure and to enhance the French language in Quebec.

The equality-of-provinces clause was also deeply offensive to many Québécois, though perhaps not as immediately threatening as the minority-language clause. Quebec has always resented being treated as a province just like the others and has always maintained an official position that it is distinctive. Clearly, the equality-of-provinces clause could be seen as a direct counterweight to Quebec's distinct society clause. But Quebec had long

ago learned to live with the uneasy co-existence of the two contradictory concepts in practice. The proposal to insert the
equality-of-provinces provision explicitly in the constitution,
however, created agitated concern in Quebec. But given the post-
Meech mood, if it had remained merely words, Quebec might
well have swallowed the pill in exchange for all the other gains.
But Charlottetown proceeded to give that clause substantial effect
in a new reformed Senate.

The Senate that was initially proposed in the July Premiers'
Accord was unacceptable to Quebec. It was truly Triple-E —
equal, elected and effective. It was so large — eight senators for
each province, two for each territory, as well as eventual aboriginal representation — that it would have had a significant impact
and could conceivably frustrate the will of the House of Commons. As popularly elected politicians, senators would enjoy a
power base relatively independent of either the provincial legislatures or the House of Commons, allowing them to become
credible brokers and mediators of regional interests in Ottawa.
Furthermore, the premiers proposed to give this Senate a great
deal of power, thus a simple majority could veto natural resource
taxation measures; a majority of 60 to 70 per cent could force a
joint sitting of the two houses to decide any question by a majority vote of the combined chambers; and a majority of 70 per cent
or more could defeat measures approved by the House of Commons. Although money bills in general were to be immune from
the Senate, the 60 to 70 per cent rule would apply to "fundamental policy changes to the tax system." Finally, the Senate would
also enjoy the power to ratify or to reject Ottawa's appointments,
"of heads of the national cultural institutions, the heads of the federal regulatory boards and agencies" and the governor of the
Bank of Canada.

The premiers' Triple-E Senate was flatly rejected by Quebec.
It was so large and so powerful that Quebec could never agree to
an equal number of senators with the other smaller provinces. Not
only was this undemocratic in principle, but, more practically, it
would dilute Quebec's voice on behalf of the Québécois in the
central government. Furthermore, the prospect of another sepa-
rately elected, powerful group of potential federalist politicians
representing the Québécois was unthinkable. For years, the Quebec government, speaking on behalf of the Québécois through the
National Assembly, had had to contend with federalist MPs also
speaking for the Québécois and often carrying contradictory mes-

sages. To add a third independent and powerful voice to the mix would further reduce the impact of the National Assembly in Ottawa. Quebec preferred abolition of the Senate or, failing that, the status quo.

In order to overcome Quebec's refusal to accept the loss of so much power at the centre, the premiers' Triple-E Senate proposal was eviscerated and rendered virtually meaningless. In the Charlottetown Agreement, the Senate proposal gave each province six senators and each territory one, for a total of sixty-two senators. The new Senate's powers were strictly limited: a Senate majority vote could force a joint sitting where a majority of both Houses would decide an issue; could kill a bill approved by the House of Commons regarding natural resource taxation; could initiate bills to go to the Commons, other than bills on money matters; could veto government appointments of heads of national institutions; and could block Commons bills on the French language and/or French culture.

In exchange for accepting equal numbers of senators, the provinces with large populations received additional seats in the House of Commons. Quebec and Ontario each got eighteen additional seats; British Columbia got four in addition to an early redistribution in 1996 to deal with the province's rapidly growing population; and Alberta got two. Thus, the proposed House of Commons was increased by forty-two seats.

In addition, Quebec received a form of special status. Quebec was permanently guaranteed 25 per cent of seats in the House of Commons, essentially freezing and protecting its current share of seats. Furthermore, Quebec was allowed to select its six senators through the National Assembly, ensuring that its Senate seats would be occupied by individuals with the confidence of the National Assembly. Finally, French linguistic and/or cultural matters were subject to a double Senate majority, requiring the approval of a majority of the sixty-two senators, including a majority of francophone senators. This limited special status, in addition to the distinct society clause, significantly offset the equality-of-provinces clause and gave Bourassa room to argue in favour of the deal.

In order to obtain Quebec's agreement, aboriginal negotiators also made some serious concessions in the final Charlottetown Agreement. In exchange for Quebec's acceptance of the inherent right of self-government for aboriginals, aboriginal negotiators and the first ministers agreed that this right would not involve new land rights, and that all native laws would be subordinate to federal and provincial laws in "matters of peace, order and good government." As well, Charlottetown included a guarantee of aboriginal representation in the Senate, but the matter of numbers, method of selection and special powers of aboriginal senators were set aside for a future political accord.

On the issue of the creation of new provinces, Quebec failed to obtain a clear veto. Under the Charlottetown Agreement, Ottawa could create new provinces after negotiations with the territories. But each province retained an imperfect partial veto, since the important details of becoming a functioning province, like the details of representation in Senate and establishing constitutional rights, required unanimous provincial consent. This, in fact, amounted to a temporary de facto veto. As well, Quebec and every other province received a veto over future constitutional changes to the Senate, the House of Commons and the Supreme Court (except for the selection process, which would follow the 7/50 rule; that is, seven provinces with more than 50 per cent of the population).

In the final analysis, the Charlottetown Agreement was a power grab by the premiers. To mollify Quebec, as well as the premiers of the more populous English-Canadian provinces, the Triple-E Senate was gone and replaced by a Single-E Senate: equal. Given the increase in the numbers of Commons seats going to Quebec and Ontario and the dramatic reduction in powers, the proposed Senate ceased to be effective, except on natural resource taxation (the National Energy Program clause). And with Quebec allowed to appoint senators through the National Assembly, the Senate ceased to be elected. Furthermore, though it had yet to be finalized, most premiers other than Bourassa assumed that senators in the nine English-Canadian provinces would be elected on a province-wide basis. This meant that those wishing to have a serious chance at winning a seat would have to get their names included on a central party list. Since the election was to be province-wide, the mechanism for the selection of a party's list of candidates would of necessity be highly centralized and the party leader, particularly if he or she were also premier, would play the key role in determining the names to be included. The senators would thereby owe their first allegiance to the movers and shakers of the provincial party apparatus, not of the federal party apparatus. And if senators wished to be included on the party list the next time around, they would accept the discipline of the provincial party and, most importantly, provincial party leaders. Provincial party leaders, particularly those who were premiers, would thus have exercised enormous power and influence at the centre, power and influence potentially sufficient to frustrate the will of the House of Commons, especially when no party enjoyed a clear majority. Hence, the new Senate was essentially a House of the Premiers.

When the Canada Round was finally over, having brought forth the Charlottetown Agreement, the politicians, civil servants and negotiators involved and the journalists covering the process expressed relief that it was finally over, having complained endlessly and loudly about constitutional fatigue. Many shared this view, especially editorial writers. Many others, however, expressed differing levels of disbelief and shock about the Agreement, since it failed to address many crucial concerns and appeared to have overlooked so many of the views presented both before and after the death of the Meech Lake Accord.

One major strength of the Charlottetown Agreement was the satisfactory inclusion of the inherent right of aboriginal self-government. Another strength was the Social Charter that Ontario's NDP premier Rae succeeded in obtaining with the support of the other two NDP premiers, Romanow of Saskatchewan and Harcourt of British Columbia. Though declaring a commitment to existing joint federal-provincial programs in health, social assistance and education; to workers' rights to collective bargaining; and to environmental protection, the Social Charter clause remained toothless since it was not enforceable through the courts, only through a "monitoring mechanism" to be established at a future first ministers' meeting. The inclusion of a Social Charter was a largely meaningless legal victory, though perhaps a positive moral and political one. Finally, a third strength of the Agreement was the inclusion of a mechanism preventing Ottawa from making unilateral reductions in the federal funding share of any future joint programs, or in renewals of agreements in medicare, social assistance or post-secondary education.

Charlottetown's greatest failure was that it did not address one of the major fears in English Canada that had contributed to the death of Meech: that provincial powers had been unduly enhanced and that the powers of the central government had been unduly diminished. These fears were completely ignored. Indeed, the Charlottetown Agreement went further down the road of decentralization than Meech had gone. After Charlottetown, the federal government would be left weak and impotent, unable to speak, let alone act, for Canada by providing effective national leadership. At the centre of this fear had been the conviction that the opting out/financial compensation feature of Meech would ensure that no new universal national programs with enforceable national standards could ever again be established. That feature of Meech remained intact in the Charlottetown Agreement. Provincial governments would be allowed to opt out of any future nationally run shared-cost social programs, yet still receive federal funds in compensation. The only requirement was that to be eligible for federal tax dollars, the province would have to establish a program "compatible with national objectives." But these "national objectives" would not be established and enforced by Ottawa. Rather, they would be set by the first ministers. Ottawa would thereby lose its ability to use the federal spending power to discipline the provinces to adhere to a national program's principles and objectives. Yet, enforcing adherence is something Ottawa has had to do repeatedly, first to establish and then to maintain the integrity of the national medicare program. Under the Charlottetown Agreement, national shared-cost programs like medicare in new areas of urgent public need, such as daycare, for example, could never be established, even if the public demanded them.

Those loudly applauding the Charlottetown Agreement, if only because of constitutional fatigue and a desire to get on with other issues, were also in for a disappointment once they examined the text carefully. Fully twenty-nine separate, complex elements of the Agreement required further negotiations in order to achieve final working arrangements that could be included in future political accords. In other words, the Charlottetown Agreement was a recipe for a continuing and virtually endless negotiating process. The areas requiring these negotiations included not only aboriginal self-government, but also every new power transferred to the provinces. This was a "settlement" hardly worth the name. Rather, much of Charlottetown amounted to an agreement to continue negotiating! Canadians who thought that concluding the Agreement had ended the constitutional nightmare were in for a rude awakening.

And what did the West get? Were western grievances effectively addressed, grievances that had been central in precipitating both the isolation of Quebec in 1981–82 and the unravelling of Meech? Charlottetown's Single-E Senate allegedly gave the West one clear victory — a simple majority of the new Senate could defeat House of Commons bills relating to natural resource taxation. The substantive meaning of this power remained undefined. In the words of the Agreement, "The precise definition of this category of legislation remains to be determined." If the Agreement were passed, the only real winners in the West would be the natural resource companies, especially the oil and gas interests. Given the Senate's small size and the probability of at-large, province-wide Senate elections, these natural resource companies would do their best to buy all the senators they could. It was a remarkable testimony to the enormous power and influence of the oil and natural gas industry to realize that the only western grievance effectively addressed by the new Senate was that rooted in the industry's deep-seated, continuing anger over Trudeau's National Energy Program. Seldom, if ever, has a single industry's lobbying effort been so effective, not only in creating a Senate but in giving it the single power the lobby wanted.

The apparent gain for the West and Atlantic Canada of an equal Senate was more than offset by the thirty-six new seats added to Central Canada's representation in the House of Commons. Though the Senate could force joint sittings of the combined chambers, the Senate's sixty-two members, already divided among themselves, would be more than effectively drowned out by the 337 members of the new House of Commons. It seemed hardly worth the estimated annual price tag of $140 million the Charlottetown Senate would cost the taxpayer. Exactly how this new Senate was a victory for the West remained murky.

While the western premiers hailed the transfer of many new powers to the provinces and the opting out/financial compensation clause as real victories for the West, many westerners (and Atlantic Canadians) were profoundly uneasy. What good was exclusive provincial jurisdiction in areas like forestry, tourism, housing, culture and so on, if federal money didn't come with it or if additional fiscal powers were not transferred? What good was the provinces' opting out/financial compensation right, if it provided the justification for Ottawa's refusal to bother developing any future national programs in areas of public need? Westerners were well aware that had not access to federal funding been dependent on implementation of an acceptable version of medicare, British Columbia, Alberta and perhaps Manitoba might never have implemented medicare as we know it. Indeed, a careful examination of Western-Canadian history informed westerners and Atlantic Canadians that the major concessions won over the years of serious and lasting benefit to the people of these regions resulted from decisions made by the House of Commons and enforced by a strong central government in Ottawa. The unemployment insurance program; shared-cost programming in health, social assistance and post-secondary education; and many smaller-scale programs would never have happened had we had as weak a federal government as that proposed in the Charlottetown Agreement. When examined in the clear light of history, and in terms of the real gains of the past, the new provincial powers and the opting out/financial compensation clause seemed victories that had more the character of defeats, at least from the perspective of rank-and-file westerners.

Finally, the central question about the Charlottetown Agreement was whether it would be enough to satisfy Quebec. Regardless of what the Allaire Report and the Bélanger-Campeau Commission had demanded as Quebec's minimum, demands seen almost universally in English Canada as outrageous, Bourassa had insisted from the outset that the five elements in the Meech Lake Accord were his bottom line. The Meech minimum had to be conceded to Quebec.

First, Quebec required constitutional recognition as a "distinct society." English-Canadian crankiness about the distinct society clause had been the most significant single factor in the death of Meech. In the post-Meech phase, however, particularly during the elaborate constitutional discussions, English Canadians had become somewhat more receptive to this concession to Quebec. Indeed, many English Canadians had even begun again to toy with the idea of "special status" for Quebec, though preferring the more neutral phrase, "asymmetrical federalism." Still, the hostility to Meech's distinct society clause had emerged abruptly and with surprising ferocity. Therefore, the English-Canadian first ministers approached the issue gingerly. On the other hand, for Bourassa, "distinct society" was non-negotiable.

Bourassa got the words "distinct society" not once but twice in the Charlottetown Agreement. Section 2.(1)(c) of the Canada clause said, "Quebec constitutes within Canada a distinct society, which includes a French-speaking majority, a unique culture and a civil law tradition," while section 2.(2) said, "The role of the legislature and Government of Quebec to preserve and promote the distinct society of Quebec is affirmed." But these affirmations were twice trumped in the Canada clause, making the distinct society provision of the agreement significantly weaker than that included in Meech. Section 2.(1)(d) committed "Canadians and their governments...to the vitality and development of official language communities throughout Canada." And Section 2.(1)(h) enunciated "the principle of the equality of the provinces," for the first time proposing the constitutionalization of that fundamentally controversial doctrine. In a clash regarding Quebec's language laws, which would prevail, "distinct society" mentioned twice or the double trump? Furthermore, as Clyde Wells put it, a "fence" was put around Quebec's distinct society by specifying its meaning to include only "a French-speaking majority, a unique culture and a civil law tradition," the concessions made to Quebec in the 1774 *Quebec Act*. Meech's distinct society clause had not been so precisely defined, allowing the possibility of expanding upon its meaning and extending its application into new areas. Just days after the Charlottetown Agreement, eight constitutional experts from five Quebec universities published an open letter in *La Presse* and *Le Devoir* emphatically stating "the distinct society clause found in the Charlottetown agreement is of virtually no value for Quebec [ensuring] that the integrity of the Charter of the French Language will be more precarious than ever... We consider that its adoption may even represent a setback with respect to the current situation...The Charlottetown agreement, in defining the distinct society and putting it on an equal footing with the commitment of governments to the vitality and development of the English-speaking minority in Quebec, may put into question what has already been recognized."

Second, Quebec required a veto. In Quebec this was widely seen as a return of Quebec's historic veto given up by Lévesque in order to cement his participation in the Gang of Eight in 1981. Although the Supreme Court had later ruled that no such veto had ever existed, the political convention had indeed prevailed and Quebec had exercised this veto often in the past — most dramatically in 1971 to torpedo the Victoria Charter. Bourassa wanted a Quebec veto over all aspects of the constitution that directly affected Quebec, including the creation of new provinces. Quebec and every other province had obtained such a veto in the Meech Accord.

The Charlottetown Agreement gave all provinces veto power over constitutional changes to the Senate, the House of Commons and all aspects of the Supreme Court, except the nomination and appointment procedure. On the creation of new provinces, Quebec, and every other province, obtained only an imperfect, partial and temporary veto. This veto was much less than Meech had offered. Again, the issue of creating new provinces struck at the heart of one of Quebec's historical anxieties, an anxiety that had increased with the emergence of the doctrine of the equality of provinces. Now one province of ten, Quebec looked forward to an uncertain future when it would become one of eleven, then twelve, then thirteen, as provincial status was granted to Canada's northern territories. The prospect of becoming increasingly marginalized as the one French-speaking province among so many "equal" English-speaking provinces recalled Lord Durham's prescription of gradually pushing the French fact to the margins of society and politics. The Charlottetown Agreement struck an unsatisfactory compromise. Ottawa would have the pre-1982 power to create new provinces following consultation with the first ministers. But each existing province would have a de facto veto over the inclusion of the new province in the constitutional amending formula and over any increase in representation in the Senate. Granted, in the realities of political life, such a de facto veto could not be used to deny full provincial status forever, but it could provide an important bargaining chip in seeking new concessions. In addition, Bourassa received a backdoor veto he had not requested in the Senate he didn't want, that is, Commons bills affecting the French language and culture required a double majority in the Senate before final approval.

On the third and fourth elements of Meech, there was little controversy. Meech had promised all provinces a significant share in power over immigration if they requested it. This had been such a sore point with Quebec that, after the collapse of Meech, Quebec had received this through direct bilateral negotiations with Ottawa. Charlottetown extended the right to all provinces that wished to pursue it. In Meech, Quebec had also gained the constitutional recognition of three of nine members on the Supreme Court, as well as a say in the nomination and selection procedure. Charlottetown easily granted these demands to Quebec as well as granting all provinces the guarantee that Ottawa would only select members of the Supreme Court from lists submitted by the provinces.

Similarly, there was little controversy on the fifth element of Meech crucial for Quebec: opting out and financial compensation. The Charlottetown Agreement reiterated Meech. Quebec, together with all provinces, could opt out of future national shared-cost programs in areas of provincial jurisdiction and receive financial compensation, as long as the province in question developed a program "compatible with national objectives." Furthermore, a province could opt out in the event of a future constitutional transfer of a provincial jurisdiction to Ottawa with "reasonable compensation." The "national objectives" aspect of the opting-out right caused some continuing anxiety in Quebec, and was seen as a major concession by many Québécois since it allowed Ottawa to maintain a significant role in exercising the federal spending power in the province.

Did the Charlottetown Agreement meet the minimum demands of Meech? At the time, Bourassa and the Agreement's supporters insisted that it did. But on sober reflection, one had to conclude it was nowhere near the Meech minimum. One must recall that at the time Meech was negotiated, the Québécois considered the demands that it addressed as skeletal. After the death of Meech, Québécois demands escalated. With Charlottetown, Quebec was asked not only to accept a watered-down Meech, but at the same time to swallow a Senate it did not want, the entrenchment of aboriginal self-government which created profound unease, a flat refusal even to contemplate a new division of powers based on Quebec's aspirations and a total rejection of any consideration of "special status" beyond the minimum granted in the 1774 *Quebec Act*. It hardly appeared a serious effort to save or renew Canadian federalism. Granted, the English-Canadian premiers had tried to sugar the pill with Quebec's 25 per cent guarantee regarding seats in the House of Commons, the double majority in the Senate on French language and culture and the right of the National Assembly to select Quebec's six senators. Many in English Canada complained about this "special status" — and it was a kind of special status, albeit not the kind Quebec wanted. Once again, English Canada had decided virtually unilaterally what the Québécois should have and then imposed it upon them. Certainly, Québécois nationalism could, and would, use these concessions in the future, as it had with previous concessions, but only as tools to continue to struggle toward one of the two options Québécois nationalism had insisted since the Quiet Revolution constituted the real choices for Quebec and English Canada — real special status involving a new division of powers satisfactory to the Québécois nation or some form of sovereignty. In short, like all earlier accommodations devised and imposed by English Canada, the Charlottetown Agreement really settled nothing, but rather, merely attempted once again to postpone the day of final reckoning.

The tragedy for Canada of the Charlottetown Agreement was that the English-Canadian premiers and the prime minister had squandered yet another opportunity to recommend changes that could have taken a large step toward a resolution of the Quebec crisis without jeopardizing the integrity of the whole country. The nine English-Canadian premiers proved unwilling to do so, preferring to use the moment to make a grab for more provincial power under the cover of salvaging Canada. Bourassa was politically vulnerable and desperate for a deal, desperate for any piece of paper he could wave triumphantly as he stepped off the plane at Quebec City. To the surprise of most, including his own top negotiators, Bourassa quickly and easily grasped the straw thrown to him by his colleagues and ushered in another destructive and divisive episode in the history of relations between the Québécois and English Canada.

The Reference Questions and the Court's Answers

Question 1: Under the Constitution of Canada, can the National Assembly, legislature or government of Quebec effect the secession of Quebec from Canada unilaterally?

Question 2: Does international law give the National Assembly, legislature or government of Quebec the right to effect the secession of Quebec from Canada unilaterally? In this regard, is there a right to self-determination under international law that would give the National Assembly, legislature or government of Quebec the right to effect the secession of Quebec from Canada unilaterally?

Question 3: In the event of a conflict between domestic and international law on the right of the National Assembly, legislature or government of Quebec to effect the secession of Quebec from Canada unilaterally, which would take precedence in Canada?

(1) Supreme Court's Reference Jurisdiction

Section 101 of the Constitution Act, 1867 gives Parliament the authority to grant this Court the reference jurisdiction provided for in s. 53 of the Supreme Court Act. The words "general court of appeal" in s. 101 denote the status of the Court within the national court structure and should not be taken as a restrictive definition of the Court's functions. While, in most instances, this

Court acts as the exclusive ultimate appellate court in the country, an appellate court can receive, on an exceptional basis, original jurisdiction not incompatible with its appellate jurisdiction. Even if there were any conflict between this Court's reference jurisdiction and the original jurisdiction of the provincial superior courts, any such conflict must be resolved in favour of Parliament's exercise of its plenary power to establish a "general court of appeal." A "general court of appeal" may also properly undertake other legal functions, such as the rendering of advisory opinions. There is no constitutional bar to this Court's receipt of jurisdiction to undertake an advisory role.

The reference questions are within the scope of s. 53 of the Supreme Court Act. Question 1 is directed, at least in part, to the interpretation of the Constitution Acts, which are referred to in s. 53 (1)(a). Both Questions 1 and 2 fall within s. 53 (1)(d), since they relate to the powers of the legislature or government of a Canadian province. Finally, all three questions are "important questions of law or fact concerning any matter" and thus come within s. 53(2). In answering Question 2, the Court is not exceeding its jurisdiction by purporting to act as an international tribunal. The Court is providing an advisory opinion to the Governor in Council in its capacity as a national court on legal questions touching and concerning the future of the Canadian federation. Further, Question 2 is not beyond the competence of this Court, as a domestic court, because it requires the Court to look at international law rather than domestic law. More importantly, Question 2 does not ask an abstract question of "pure" international law but seeks to determine the legal rights and obligations of the legislature or government of Quebec, institutions that exist as part of the Canadian legal order. International law must be addressed since it has been invoked as a consideration in the context of this Reference.

The reference questions are justiciable and should be answered. They do not ask the Court to usurp any democratic decision that the people of Quebec may be called upon to make. The questions, as interpreted by the Court, are strictly limited to aspects of the legal framework in which that democratic decision is to be taken. Since the reference questions may clearly be interpreted as directed to legal issues, the Court is in a position to answer them. The Court cannot exercise its discretion to refuse to answer the questions on a pragmatic basis. The questions raise issues of fundamental public importance and they are not too imprecise or ambiguous so as not to permit a proper legal answer. Nor has the Court been provided with insufficient information regarding the present context in which the questions arise. Finally, the Court may deal on a reference with issues that might otherwise be considered not yet "ripe" for decision.

(2) Question 1

The Constitution is more than a written text. It embraces the entire global system of rules and principles which govern the exercise of constitutional authority. A superficial reading of selected provisions of the written constitutional enactment, without more, may be misleading. It is necessary to make a more profound investigation of the underlying principles animating the whole of the Constitution, including the principles of federalism, democracy, constitutionalism and the rule of law, and respect for minorities. Those principles must inform our overall appreciation of the constitutional rights and obligations that would come into play in the event that a clear majority of Quebecers votes on a clear question in favour of secession.

The Court in this Reference is required to consider whether Quebec has a right to unilateral secession. Arguments in support of the existence of such a right were primarily based on the principle of democracy. Democracy, however, means more than simple majority rule. Constitutional jurisprudence shows that democracy exists in the larger context of other constitutional values. Since Confederation, the people of the provinces and territories have created close ties of interdependence (economic, social, political and cultural) based on shared values that include federalism, democracy, constitutionalism and the rule of law, and respect for minorities. A democratic decision of Quebecers in favour of secession would put those relationships at risk. The Constitution vouchsafes order and stability, and accordingly secession of a province "under the Constitution" could not be achieved unilaterally, that is, without principled negotiation with other participants in Confederation within the existing constitutional framework.

Our democratic institutions necessarily accommodate a continuous process of discussion and evolution, which is reflected in the constitutional right of each participant in the federation to initiate constitutional change. This right implies a reciprocal duty on the other participants to engage in discussions to address any legitimate initiative to change the constitutional order. A clear majority vote in Quebec on a clear question in favour of secession would confer democratic legitimacy on the secession initiative which all of the other participants in Confederation would have to recognize.

Quebec could not, despite a clear referendum result, purport to invoke a right of self-determination to dictate the terms of a proposed secession to the other parties to the federation. The democratic vote, by however strong a majority, would have no legal effect on its own and could not push aside the principles of federalism and the rule of law, the rights of individuals and minorities, or the operation of democracy in the other provinces or in Canada as a whole. Democratic rights under the Constitution cannot be divorced from constitutional obligations. Nor, however, can the reverse proposition be accepted: the continued existence and operation of the Canadian constitutional order could not be indifferent to a clear expression of a clear majority of Quebecers that they no longer wish to remain in Canada. The other provinces and the federal government would have no basis to deny the right of the government of Quebec to pursue secession should a clear majority of the people of Quebec choose that goal, so long as in doing so, Quebec respects the rights of others. The negotiations that followed such a vote would address the potential act of secession as well as its possible terms should in fact secession proceed. There would be no conclusions predetermined by law on any issue. Negotiations would need to address the interests of the other provinces, the federal government and Quebec and indeed the rights of all Canadians both within and outside Quebec, and specifically the rights of minorities.

The negotiation process would require the reconciliation of various rights and obligations by negotiation between two legitimate majorities, namely, the majority of the population of Quebec, and that of Canada as a whole. A political majority at either level that does not act in accordance with the underlying constitutional principles puts at risk the legitimacy of its exercise of its rights, and the ultimate acceptance of the result by the international community.

The task of the Court has been to clarify the legal framework within which political decisions are to be taken "under the Constitution" and not to usurp the prerogatives of the political forces that operate within that framework. The obligations identified by the Court are binding obligations under the Constitution. However, it will be for the political actors to determine what constitutes "a clear majority on a clear question" in the circumstances under which a future referendum vote may be taken. Equally, in the event of demonstrated majority support for Quebec secession, the content and process of the negotiations will be for the political actors to settle. The reconciliation of the various legitimate constitutional interests is necessarily committed to the political rather than the judicial realm precisely because that reconciliation can only be achieved through the give and take of political negotiations. To the extent issues addressed in the course of negotiation are political, the courts, appreciating their proper role in the constitutional scheme, would have no supervisory role.

(3) Question 2

The Court was also required to consider whether a right to unilateral secession exists under international law. Some supporting an affirmative answer did so on the basis of the recognized right to self-determination that belongs to all "peoples." Although much of the Quebec population certainly shares many of the characteristics of a people, it is not necessary to decide the "people" issue because, whatever may be the correct determination of this issue in the context of Quebec, a right to secession only arises under the principle of self-determination of people at international law where "a people" is governed as part of a colonial empire; where "a people" is subject to alien subjugation, domination or exploitation; and possibly where "a people" is denied any meaningful exercise of its right to self-determination within the state of which it forms a part. In other circumstances, peoples are expected to achieve self-determination within the framework of their existing state. A state whose government represents the whole of the people or peoples resident within its territory, on a basis of equality and without discrimination, and respects the principles of self-determination in its internal arrangements, is entitled to maintain its territorial integrity under international law and to have that territorial integrity recognized by other states. Quebec does not meet the threshold of a colonial people or an oppressed people, nor can it be suggested that Quebecers have been denied meaningful access to government to pursue their political, economic, cultural and social development. In the circumstances, the "National Assembly, the legislature or the government of Quebec" do not enjoy a right at international law to effect the secession of Quebec from Canada unilaterally.

Although there is no right, under the Constitution or at international law, to unilateral secession, the possibility of an unconstitutional declaration of secession leading to a de facto secession is not ruled out. The ultimate success of such a secession would be dependent on recognition by the international community, which is likely to consider the legality and legitimacy of secession having regard to, amongst other facts, the conduct of Quebec and Canada, in determining whether to grant or withhold recognition. Even if granted, such recognition would not, however, provide any retroactive justification for the act of secession, either under the Constitution of Canada or at international law.

(4.) Question 3

In view of the answers to Questions 1 and 2, there is no conflict between domestic and international law to be addressed in the context of this Reference.

BILL C-20

The Clarity Act

Approved by the House of Commons, 29 June 2000

An Act to give effect to the requirement for clarity as set out in the opinion of the Supreme Court of Canada in the Quebec Secession Reference

WHEREAS the Supreme Court of Canada has confirmed that there is no right, under international law or under the Constitution of Canada, for the National Assembly, legislature or government of Quebec to effect the secession of Quebec from Canada unilaterally;

WHEREAS any proposal relating to the break-up of a democratic state is a matter of the utmost gravity and is of fundamental importance to all of its citizens;

WHEREAS the government of any province of Canada is entitled to consult its population by referendum on any issue and is entitled to formulate the wording of its referendum question;

WHEREAS the Supreme Court of Canada has determined that the result of a referendum on the secession of a province from Canada must be free of ambiguity both in terms of the question asked and in terms of the support it achieves if that result is to be taken as an expression of the democratic will that would give rise to an obligation to enter into negotiations that might lead to secession;

WHEREAS the Supreme Court of Canada has stated that democracy means more than simple majority rule, that a clear majority in favour of secession would be required to create an obligation to negotiate secession, and that a qualitative evaluation is required to determine whether a clear majority in favour of secession exists in the circumstances;

WHEREAS the Supreme Court of Canada has confirmed that, in Canada, the secession of a province, to be lawful, would require an amendment to the Constitution of Canada, that such an amendment would perforce require negotiations in relation to secession involving at least the governments of all of the provinces and the Government of Canada, and that those negotiations would be governed by the principles of federalism, democracy, constitutionalism and the rule of law, and the protection of minorities;

WHEREAS, in light of the finding by the Supreme Court of Canada that it would be for elected representatives to determine what constitutes a clear question and what constitutes a clear majority in a referendum held in a province on secession, the House of Commons, as the only political institution elected to represent all Canadians, has an important role in identifying what constitutes a clear question and a clear majority sufficient for the Government of Canada to enter into negotiations in relation to the secession of a province from Canada;

And WHEREAS it is incumbent on the Government of Canada not to enter into negotiations that might lead to the secession of a province from Canada, and that could consequently entail the termination of citizenship and other rights that Canadian citizens resident in the province enjoy as full participants in Canada, unless the population of that province has clearly expressed its democratic will that the province secede from Canada;

Now, Therefore, Her Majesty, by and with the advice and consent of the Senate and House of Commons of Canada, enacts as follows:

1. (1) The House of Commons shall, within thirty days after the government of a province tables in its legislative assembly or otherwise officially releases the question that it intends to submit to its voters in a referendum relating to the proposed secession of the province from Canada, consider the question and, by resolution, set out its determination on whether the question is clear.

(2) Where the thirty days referred to in subsection (1) occur, in whole or in part, during a general election of members to serve in the House of Commons, the thirty days shall be extended by an additional forty days.

(3) In considering the clarity of a referendum question, the House of Commons shall consider whether the question would result in a clear expression of the will of the population of a province on whether the province should cease to be part of Canada and become an independent state.

(4) For the purpose of subsection (3), a clear expression of the will of the population of a province that the province cease to be part of Canada could not result from

(a) a referendum question that merely focuses on a mandate to negotiate without soliciting a direct expression of the will of the population of that province on whether the province should cease to be part of Canada; or

(b) a referendum question that envisages other possibilities in addition to the secession of the province from Canada, such as economic or political arrangements with Canada, that obscure a direct expression of the will of the population of that province on whether the province should cease to be part of Canada.

(5) In considering the clarity of a referendum question, the House of Commons shall take into account the views of all political parties represented in the legislative assembly of

the province whose government is proposing the referendum on secession, any formal statements or resolutions by the government or legislative assembly of any province or territory of Canada, any formal statements or resolutions by the Senate, any formal statements or resolutions by the representatives of the Aboriginal peoples of Canada, especially those in the province whose government is proposing the referendum on secession, and any other views it considers to be relevant.

(6) The Government of Canada shall not enter into negotiations on the terms on which a province might cease to be part of Canada if the House of Commons determines, pursuant to this section, that a referendum question is not clear and, for that reason, would not result in a clear expression of the will of the population of that province on whether the province should cease to be part of Canada.

2. (1) Where the government of a province, following a referendum relating to the secession of the province from Canada, seeks to enter into negotiations on the terms on which that province might cease to be part of Canada, the House of Commons shall, except where it has determined pursuant to section 1 that a referendum question is not clear, consider and, by resolution, set out its determination on whether, in the circumstances, there has been a clear expression of a will by a clear majority of the population of that province that the province cease to be part of Canada.

(2) In considering whether there has been a clear expression of a will by a clear majority of the population of a province that the province cease to be part of Canada, the House of Commons shall take into account

(a) the size of the majority of valid votes cast in favour of the secessionist option;
(b) the percentage of eligible voters voting in the referendum; and
(c) any other matters or circumstances it considers to be relevant.

(3) In considering whether there has been a clear expres-

328 DEBTS TO PAY

sion of a will by a clear majority of the population of a
province that the province cease to be part of Canada, the
House of Commons shall take into account the views of all
political parties represented in the legislative assembly of
the province whose government proposed the referendum
on secession, any formal statements or resolutions by the
government or legislative assembly of any province or territory of Canada, any formal statements or resolutions by
the Senate, any formal statements or resolutions by the representatives of the Aboriginal peoples of Canada,
especially those in the province whose government proposed the referendum on secession, and any other views it
considers to be relevant.

(4) The Government of Canada shall not enter into negotiations on the terms on which a province might cease to be
part of Canada unless the House of Commons determines,
pursuant to this section, that there has been a clear expression of a will by a clear majority of the population of that
province that the province cease to be part of Canada.

3. (1) It is recognized that there is no right under the Constitution of Canada to effect the secession of a province from
Canada unilaterally and that, therefore, an amendment to
the Constitution of Canada would be required for any
province to secede from Canada, which in turn would
require negotiations involving at least the governments of
all of the provinces and the Government of Canada.

(2) No Minister of the Crown shall propose a constitutional
amendment to effect the secession of a province from
Canada unless the Government of Canada has addressed, in
its negotiations, the terms of secession that are relevant in
the circumstances, including the division of assets and liabilities, any changes to the borders of the province, the
rights, interests and territorial claims of the Aboriginal peoples of Canada, and the protection of minority rights.

Québec's *Fundamental Rights Act*
Approved by the National Assembly, 7 December 2000

An Act respecting the exercise of the Fundamental Rights and Prerogatives of the Québec People and the Québec State

WHEREAS the Québec people, in the majority French-speaking, possesses specific characteristics and a deep-rooted historical continuity in a territory over which it exercises its rights through a modern national state, having a government, a national assembly and impartial and independent courts of justice;

WHEREAS the constitutional foundation of the Québec State has been enriched over the years by the passage of fundamental laws and the creation of democratic institutions specific to Québec;

WHEREAS Québec entered the Canadian federation in 1867;

WHEREAS Québec is firmly committed to respecting human rights and freedoms;

WHEREAS the Abenaki, Algonquin, Attikamek, Cree, Huron, Innu, Malecite, Micmac, Mohawk, Naskapi and Inuit Nations exist within Québec, and whereas the principles associated with that recognition were set out in the resolution adopted by the National Assembly on 20 March 1985, in particular their right to autonomy within Québec;

WHEREAS there exists a Québec English-speaking community that enjoys long-established rights;

WHEREAS Québec recognizes the contribution made by Québeckers of all origins to its development;

WHEREAS the National Assembly is composed of Members elected by universal suffrage by the Québec people and derives its legitimacy from the Québec people in that it is the only legislative body exclusively representing the Québec people;

WHEREAS it is incumbent upon the National Assembly, as the guardian of the historical and inalienable rights and powers of the Québec people, to defend the Québec people against any attempt to despoil it of those rights or powers or to undermine them;

WHEREAS the National Assembly has never adhered to the Constitution Act, 1982, which was enacted despite its opposition;

WHEREAS Québec is facing a policy of the federal government designed to call into question legitimacy, integrity and valid operation of its national democratic institutions and proclamation of the Act to give effect to the requirement for clarity as set out in the opinion of the Supreme Court of Canada in the Québec Secession Reference (Statutes of Canada, chapter 26);

WHEREAS it is necessary to reaffirm the fundamental principle that the Quebec people is free to take charge of its own destiny, determine its political status and pursue its economic, social and cultural development;

WHEREAS this principle has applied on several occasions in the past, notably in the referendums held in 1980, 1992 and 1995;

WHEREAS the Supreme Court of Canada rendered an advisory opinion on 20 August 1998, and considering the recognition by the Government of Québec of its political importance;

WHEREAS it is necessary to reaffirm the collective attainments of the Québec people, the responsibilities of the Québec State and the rights and prerogatives of the National Assembly with respect to all matters affecting the future of the Québec people;

THE PARLIAMENT OF QUÉBEC ENACTS AS FOLLOWS:

CHAPTER I

THE QUÉBEC PEOPLE

1. The right of the Québec people to self-determination is founded in fact and in law. The Québec people is the holder of rights that are universally recognized under the principle of equal rights and self-determination of peoples.

2. The Québec people has the inalienable right to freely decide the political regime and legal status of Québec.

3. The Québec people, acting through its own political institutions, shall determine alone the mode of exercise of its right to choose the political regime and legal status of Québec.

    No condition or mode of exercise of that right, in particular the consultation of the Québec people by way of a referendum, shall have effect unless determined in accordance with the first paragraph.

4. When the Québec people is consulted by way of a referendum under the Referendum Act, the winning option is the option that obtains a majority of the valid votes cast, namely fifty percent of the valid votes cast plus one.

CHAPTER II

THE QUÉBEC NATIONAL STATE

5. The Québec State derives its legitimacy from the will of the people inhabiting its territory.

    The will of the people is expressed through the election of Members to the National Assembly by universal suffrage, by secret ballot under the one person, one vote system pursuant to the Election Act, and through referendums held pursuant to the Referendum Act.

    Qualification as an elector is governed by the provisions of the Election Act.

6. The Québec State is sovereign in the areas assigned to its jurisdiction within the scope of constitutional laws and conventions.

7. The Québec State is free to consent to be bound by any treaty, convention or international agreement in matters under its constitutional jurisdiction.

    No treaty, convention or agreement in the areas under its

jurisdiction may be binding on the Québec State unless the consent of the Québec State to be bound has been formally expressed by the National Assembly or the Government, subject to the applicable legislative provisions.

The Québec State may, in the areas under its jurisdiction, establish and maintain relations with foreign States and international organizations and ensure its representation outside Québec.

8. The French language is the official language of Québec.

The duties and obligations relating to or arising from the status of French language are established by the Charter of the French language.

The Québec State must promote the quality and influence of the French language. It shall pursue those objectives in a spirit of fairness and open-mindedness, respectful of the long-established rights of Québec's English-speaking community.

CHAPTER III

THE TERRITORY OF QUÉBEC

9. The territory of Québec and its boundaries cannot be altered except with the consent of the National Assembly.

The Government must ensure that the territorial integrity of Québec is maintained and respected.

10. The Québec State exercises, throughout the territory of Québec and on behalf of the Québec people, all the powers relating to its jurisdiction and to the Québec public domain.

The State may develop and administer the territory of Québec and, more specifically, delegate authority to administer the territory to local or regional mandated entities, as provided by law. The State shall encourage local and regional communities to take responsibility for their development.

CHAPTER IV

THE ABORIGINAL NATIONS OF QUÉBEC

11. In exercising its constitutional jurisdiction, the Québec State recognized the existing aboriginal and treaty rights of the aboriginal nations of Québec.

12. The Government undertakes to promote the establishment and maintenance of harmonious relations with the aboriginal nations, and to foster their development and an improvement in their economic, social and cultural conditions.

CHAPTER V

FINAL PROVISIONS

13. No other parliament or government may reduce the powers, authority, sovereignty or legitimacy of the National Assembly, or impose constraint on the democratic will of the Québec people to determine its own future.

14. The provisions of this Act come into force on dates to be fixed by the government

Index

Aberhart, William, 101
aboriginal peoples: and Charlottetown
    Agreement, 309–10; as founding
    nation, 278; and Meech Lake Accord,
    131, 200; and Quebec sovereignty,
    188, 191–92, 208; self-government,
    141, 151, 311
Acadians, expulsion of, 22
l'Action démocratique du Québec
    (ADQ), 12, 168, 196, 197, 203, 217,
    244, 264
Act of Union, 38–39
l'Actualité, 163
l'affaire Michaud, 261
l'affaire Wilhelmy, 162–63
air controllers dispute, 93–94
Alberta: and bilingualism, 133–34; cen-
    sorship, 85; Charlottetown referen-
    dum, 164; and constitutional amend-
    ments, 142; and energy resources,
    104–8; patriation of constitution, 112,
    114–15; ratification of Meech Lake
    Accord, 134
Alcan, 155
Allaire, Jean, 161, 168, 196
Allaire Report, 139
Alliance for the Preservation of English
    in Canada, 191
Alliance Quebec, 240
amending formula, 280
American War of Independence, 27–28
*An Act to promote the French language
    in Quebec* (Bill 63), 73
Andre, Harvie, 144
Anglophone Assault Group, 217
Article 80, of *BNA Act,* 43, 89
assimilation, policy of, 38

l'Association des manufacturiers du
    Québéc, 155
Atlantic Canada: control of offshore
    energy resources, 107; 1979 federal
    election, 106; 1980 federal election,
    108; 1997 federal election, 222; and
    oil crisis, 105
Auger, Michel, 245
Axworthy, Lloyd, 187

Bank of Montreal, 194
Batoche, 47
Bay, the, 240
B & B Commission. *See* Royal
    Commission on Bilingualism and
    Biculturalism (B and B Commission)
beau risque, 119–21
Bédard, Pierre, 27
Bégin, Paul, 262
Bélanger-Campeau Commission, 139
Bertrand, Jean-Guy, 215
bilingualism, 65, 130
Bill 22. *See Official Languages Act* (Bill
    22)
Bill 63. *See An Act to promote the
    French language in Quebec* (Bill 63)
Bill 101. *See La Charte de la langue
    française*
Bill C-20. *See Clarity Act*
Bill C-110, 213
Blakeney, Allan, 104, 112, 114, 115, 136
Bleus, 43–42
Bloc Populaire, 178
Bloc Québécois, 138; and Charlottetown
    Agreement, 11–20; electoral support,
    217; 1993 federal election, 174,
    179–81; 1997 federal election, 222;

political influence of, 15; and sovereign Quebec, 15

Boisclair, André, 271

Borden, Robert, 51

Bouchard, Lucien, 12, 132, 138, 165; and *l'affaire Michaud*, 261; economic platform, 243; and federal funding, 246; "flesh-eating disease," 200; in Opposition, 187; popularity, 211; as PQ premier, 211, 217–18; and 1994 Quebec provincial election, 191, 193–94, 195; and 1998 Quebec provincial election, 240–45; Quebec territorial question, 190, 218; resignation, 254–55; and rift in PQ, 238–39; and Social Union initiative, 237–38; soft question, 203; and sovereignty referendum, 202–3, 206, 208; target of personal attacks 223–24; and "winning conditions," 239, 247–48

Bougainville, Louis Antoine, Comte de, 21

Bourassa, Robert, 16, 76, 91, 121; and Bill 22, 92–93; and Charlottetown Agreement, 139, 141–42, 160–61, 163; Charlottetown referendum, 149; and Meech Lake Accord, 124–25, 138; and October Crisis, 80, 81; and Plan B, 219; Quebec nationalism of, 60; retirement, 168; and Victoria Charter, 92

Bourgault, Pierre, 69, 75, 244

British colonial merchants, 23, 28, 32

British Columbia: Charlottetown referendum, 164; and constitutional amendments, 142; and English unilingualism, 137; and October Crisis, 84–85; patriation of constitution, 115; ratification of Meech Lake, 131

British Columbia Employers' Council, 155

British immigration, 34, 38

British laws, 24

British North America Act (BNA Act), 43, 89

business lobby: and Charlottetown Agreement, 155; and curbs on social spending, 236; flight of capital, 76–77, 101; Plan B and, 221; and Quiet Revolution, 76–77; and 1995 sovereignty referendum, 205–6; support for Martin, 256, 257

Caisse de dépôt et placement du Québec, 66, 206

Calgary Declaration, 224–26

Callwood, June, 150

Campbell, Kim, 170–71, 174–75, 176, 180

Campeau, Jean, 206

Canada: electoral system, 182; national flag, 66; and Quebec impasse, 11–20

Canada clause, 141, 151

Canada Information Office (CIO), 214

"Canada Round," 140

Canada Yes Committee, 147, 150

Canadian Alliance, 15, 252, 253; merger with Progressive Conservative Party, 13

Canadian Federation of Independent Business, 155

Canadian Imperial Bank of Commerce, 149

Canadian Labour Congress (CLC), 150, 155

Canadian Pension Plan, 66

Canadian Radio-television and Telecommunications Commission (CRTC), 145–46

Canadian Union of Postal Workers, 155

Caouette, Réal, 85

capitalism, and reform movement, 34

Carleton, Guy, 23, 26

Carstairs, Sharon, 130, 154

Catholic church: conservatism of, 59; leadership of, 25, 26, 43; and Patriotes, 36; rights of, 39

Catholic Farmers' Union, 80

CBC radio, 85

Centrale des syndicats du Québec, 270

Centre d'Archives et de Documentation (CAD), 95–96

Chambre de Commerce du Québec, 155

CHAN Toronto, 85

Charest, Jean, 132, 171–72, 183, 214, 221–22, 225; and federal funding, 269; 2003 leaders' debate, 265; Quebec Liberal leader, 229–30, 252; and 1998 Quebec provincial election, 240–44; and 2003 Quebec provincial election, 263–64, 265–66; and quiescent sovereignty sentiment, 272–75; right-wing agenda, 267–71

Charlottetown Agreement, 305–18; and aboriginal peoples, 309–10, 311; aftermath of, 11–13; approval mechanism, 142–53; delayed release of text, 146–47, 157–58; devolution of powers to provinces, 140–42, 305–6; equality-of-provinces clause, 307–8; and French-English impasse, 18; opting-out provision, 312; public opinion, 145, 148, 163; selection of judges, 316; Senate reform, 309, 310–11; Social Charter, 311; veto power, 310, 315–16

Charlottetown referendum, 11; *l'affaire Wilhelmy*, 162–63; business lobby and, 155; NDP and, 154; No campaign, 150–53, 161–62; No vote, 164–65; organized labour and, 155; outcome, 165; Quebec campaign, 159–63; unpopularity of Mulroney, 153; wording of question, 143; Yes campaign, 146–50, 157–59, 159–61

La Charte de la langue française, 100–1, 135

Charter of Rights and Freedoms, 111

Chénier, Jean-Olivier, 37

Choquette, Jérome, 79

Chrétien, Jean, 115, 169, 189, 240, 254; avoidance of separatist issue, 187; and Charlottetown Agreement, 154; and 2000 federal election, 252–53; 1993 federal election campaign,

176–77, 180; and neo-conservative agenda, 186–87; offensive Tory election ad, 175; rivalry with Martin, 255–59; and soft nationalists, 219–20; and 1995 sovereignty referendum, 199, 204, 207

Cité Libre, 59

Civil law, 39

Clarity Act, 249–51, 324–32

Clark, Joe, 106–8, 141, 144, 148, 204

Cleroux, Richard, 117, 118

Colbourne, John, 37

Confederation, 17, 19, 41–43

Conquest of 1759, 17; Anglo-French rivalry and, 22–23; and loyalty of Québécois, 23–24, 26; and Old Quebec, 21–30; and Québécois social structure, 24–25, 26, 27–28; and ruralization, 25

conscription crises: World War I, 50–54; World War II, 54, 144

le Conseil du patronat, 271

conservatism: of Catholic Church, 36, 43, 59; of Charest, 267-71; of Duplessis, 57, 59, 62

Conservative Party of Canada, 13. *See also* Progressive Conservative Party

constituent assembly, 286

Constitution Act, 1982, 277

Constitutional Act of 1791, 29

constitutional renewal: and French-English impasse, 11–17; 1980 No campaign promises, 110–11; unilateral patriation of constitution, 111–15. *See also* Meech Lake Accord

Coon Come, Matthew, 200

Copps, Sheila, 200

Corn Laws, 41

Council for Sovereignty, 262

Coyne, Deborah, 154

Créditistes, 76, 77, 85

Cross, James, 77, 79

David, Michel, 245

Day, Stockwell, 252

debt, and deficit, 175, 176, 180, 217, 221
DeLorimier, Chevalier, 37
Demers, Robert, 80
Devine, Grant, 136
Le Devoir, 59
Diefenbaker, John, and Quebec, 64–65
Dion, Stéphane, 214, 223, 228, 247, 249
disallowance, powers of, 279–80
distinct society: B and B Commission,
    71; Charlottetown Agreement, 141;
    House resolution on, 212, 214; Lower
    Canada, 30; Meech Lake Accord,
    124, 127, 131, 315; nature of Quebec,
    276–77
Doer, Gary, 132
Douglas, Tommy, 82, 101
Drapeau, Jean, 85, 86
Dumont, Mario, 12, 161, 168, 196, 199,
    203, 206, 218, 244, 264
Duplessis, Maurice, 57, 59, 62
Durham, Lord, 32, 37, 38

Eastern Townships, 43
Easter riot, 53
Eaton's, 240
education: of English minority in
    Quebec, 72–73, 93, 100; in Manitoba,
    45, 46, 48, 50; in Ontario, 50
elected assembly, 23, 24, 26, 28–29
energy crisis, 103–8
English Canada: and Bill 22, 93; and
    Bloc Québécois, 179, 183–84, 184;
    national identity, 56; nationalism, 56;
    and negotiation with sovereign
    Quebec, 204–5; 1980 No campaign,
    111; No vote to Charlottetown
    Agreement, 165; and October Crisis,
    84–85, 88; opposition to Quebec,
    13–20; posturing of, 200, 204–5,
    216–17; and PQ 1976 election victo-
    ry, 91–92; and 1994 Quebec provin-
    cial election, 188–89, 190, 197–98;
    and Quebec signage issue, 135–37;
    and Quiet Revolution, 64–67; and
    reconciliation, 287–89; and St.

Léonard crisis, 72–73; scare tactics,
    191–93; and 1995 sovereignty refer-
    endum, 200, 204–5, 207; and strong
    central government, 283–84
English language, use of, 24
equality-of-provinces: clause, 307–8;
    doctrine, 141; myth, 278–81
étapiste strategy, 97–99
"ethnic politics," 208–211, 275. *See also*
    immigrants, education of

Family Compact, 32
fear campaign: Charlottetown referen-
    dum, 148–50; of Plan B, 215–16;
    1994 Quebec provincial election, 189,
    191–93, 194; 1980 referendum,
    109–110, 111; 1995 sovereignty ref-
    erendum, 204–5, 207–8
federal civil service, reforms, 66
federal election: of 1958, 64; of 1963,
    65; of 1965, 67; of 1968, 71; of 1972,
    89; of 1979, 106–7; of 1980, 108; of
    1984, 120; of 1993, 11–12, 174–84;
    of 1997, 221–22; of 2000, 252–53
federalism: new nationalism vs. new lib-
    eralism approach to, 60; Trudeau and,
    60
federal-provincial relations: constitution-
    al patriation, 111–15; energy
    resources, 103–9; Mulroney and, 124;
    Social Union Framework agreement,
    235–38, 246. *See also* Meech Lake
    Accord
Ferguson, Max, 85
Filmon, Gary, 130, 136, 157, 189, 204
Finn, Ed, 155
"first past the post" system, 182
Flood, Al, 149
Fontaine, Leo, 117, 118
Francis, Diane, 216
free trade, 167, 176, 180, 192; British
    North America, 41–42; and English-
    Canadian backlash, 14, 134–35; with
    U.S., 42
French-English impasse: constitutional

renewal and, 11–17; English-Canadian intelligentsia and, 14–15; in historical perspective, 17–18; regionalism and, 13–14; and separate Quebec, 15

French language: air controllers dispute, 93–94; Bill 22, 92–93; Bill 63, 73; Bill 101, 100–1; and economic status, 74–75, 94, 193; Gendron Commission, 92; in Manitoba, 45, 48; new nationalism and, 59; in North-West Territory, 48; in Quebec, 24, 26, 62, 73, 92–94, 128, 135–36; signage issue, 135–37, 240

Front de Libération du Québec (FLQ): bombing campaign, 63–64, 69; 1970 manifesto, 78–79. *See also* October Crisis

Fundamental Rights Act, 251–52, 329–33

fur trade, 23

Gagnon, Jean-Louis, 117–18

Galt, Alexander, 42

Gang of Eight, dissenting premiers, 114–16

Garcia, Claude, 204–5

Gaulle, General Charles de, 69

Gendron Commission, 73, 92

Les Gens d l'Air, 93

Gérin-Lajoie, Paul, 61

Getty, Don, 157

Godfrey, John, 223

Godin, Gérald, 91, 127, 129

Gregg, Allan, 175

GST, 176

Harcourt, Mike, 157, 172, 173, 188, 189, 224, 311

Harris, Mike, 204, 241

Hatfield, Richard, 130

Horsman, James, 157

Hudson Bay Company, 44, 45

Hydro-Québec, 61

IBM Canada, 155

Ice Storm, 1998, 227–28

immigrants, education of, 72–73, 93, 100

immigration, British, 34, 38

Intercolonial Reciprocity Agreement, 42

Irwin, Ron, 188

Jacob, Jean-Marc, 216

Jérôme-Forget, Monique, 268

job creation, 175, 176

Johnson, Daniel, Jr.: and Plan B, 218–19; and secessionist reference questions, 230; and 1995 sovereignty referendum, 199, 200, 204, 205; television debate, 168–69; Quebec territorial question, 190; unseated, 228

Johnson, Daniel, Sr., 195

Johnson, Pierre-Marc, 121–22, 129–30

Johnson, Rita, 170

Joli-Coeur, André, 232

Jonquière by-election, 263

Keable Commission, 86

Keehr, Orris, 85

Kierans, Eric, 155

King, Mackenzie, 54, 144

Klein, Ralph, 189, 204

labour legislation: Lesage government, 63; Lévesque government, 96

labour militancy, 63, 64; Quebec nurses strike, 247–48

labour movement: and Charest government, 268, 270–71; and Charlottetown Agreement, 155; and Meech Lake Accord, 131; and October Crisis, 80; and PQ, 119; support for independent Quebec, 69

Lafontaine, Louis, 40

Lagacé, Loraine, 116

Landry, Bernard, 239, 260–66; 2000 leaders' debate, 265

Langdon, Steven, 173, 182

Laporte, Pierre, 80, 83–84

Laurier, Wilfrid, 51

Legault, Josée, 262
Le Hir, Richard, 206
Lemieux, Diane, 260
Lemieux, Robert, 80
Lesage, Jean, 60–63, 67–68, 195
Lévesque, René, 15, 16, 75; and *beau risque*, 119–21, 178; betrayed by Morin, 116–19; break with provincial Liberals, 68–69; and constitutional patriation, 112, 113–15; death, 128–29; electoral defeats, 77, 89; erratic behaviour, 119; *étapiste* referendum strategy, 95, 97–98; French language issue, 100–1; and Gang of Eight, 114–15; in Lesage cabinet, 61; moderate approach of PQ government, 95–101; new nationalism of, 60; and October Crisis, 88; retirement, 121; social democratic programs, 96–97; and sovereignty, 97–98, 121–22
Liberal Party of Canada: aftermath of Charlottetown referendum, 169; and Charlottetown Agreement, 154; 1993 election, 176–77; English minority and, 77; under Pearson, 65–67. *See also* Trudeau, Pierre
Liberal Party of Quebec, 15; aftermath of Charlottetown referendum, 168–69; and Charlottetown Agreement, 161; 1994 election, 186, 194–97; 2003 election, 263–66; 1970 election victory, 76; hard federalist wing, 168; Lesage government, 60–63, 67–68. *See also* Bourassa, Robert; Charest, Jean
Lougheed, Peter, 104, 112, 114–15
Lount, Samuel, 33
Lower Canada: and American Revolution, 26–27; British minority, 29; creation of, 29–30; "distinct" nature of, 30; elections, 33; political representation, 29; Rebellion of 1837–38, 33–38. *See also* Quebec
Loyalists. *See* United Empire Loyalists

Loyola College, 64

Macdonald, John A., 46, 47–48, 281
Mackenzie, Michael, 194
Mackenzie, William Lyon, 32, 33
Maclean Hunter, 153
mad cow crisis, 228
"*Maître chez nous*", 62–63
Manitoba: abolition of French language rights, 48; and constitutional amendments, 142; creation of, 44–46; education, 45, 46, 48, 50; language rights, 54; and Meech Lake Accord, 132, 133, 136
Manley, John, 258–59
Manning, Preston: No campaign, 151; opposition to Quebec, 13–14; and 1994 Quebec provincial election, 190
Marchand, Jean, 66
Martin, Paul, 205, 207, 249, 252; fiscal conservatism, 259; neo-conservative agenda, 187; political ambitions, 255–59
Massé, Henri, 271
Massé, Marcel, 228
Matthews, Peter, 33
McCrae, Justice Minister, Manitoba, 157
McDonald Royal Commission, 86
McDougall, William, 45
McGill University, 64
McKenna, Frank, 130, 190, 200
McLaughlin, Audrey, 150, 154, 173–74, 177, 181
McMurtry, Roy, 115
media, self-censorship, 86
Meech Lake Accord: deadline for ratification, 126; death of, 132–33; decentralization of power, 125–26; "distinct society" clause, 124, 127, 131, 315; free trade and, 134–35; and French-English impasse, 18; opposition to, 130–31; public opinion, 126; Quebec's five conditions, 124–25, 285; Quebec signage issue and, 136–38; and regional polarization, 13

mercantalism, end of, 41
merchants. *See* British colonial merchants; Québécois merchant elite, displacement of
Mercier by-election, 261
Métis, 45
Michaud, Yves, 261
Military Voters Act, 51, 52
minority governments, 282–82
modernization, of Quebec: and interventionist state, 60–61. *See also* Quiet Revolution
Montreal, and Quiet Revolution, 58–59
Montreal Stock Exchange, 64
Morin, Claude, 113, 116–18; *étapiste* strategy, 97–99
Le Movement souveraineté-association (MSA), 69
Mulroney, Brian, 222; casualty of Charlottetown referendum, 166–68; and Charlottetown Agreement, 139–41, 148, 159; Charlottetown referendum, 148, 149; and federal-provincial relations, 124, 125; and Meech Lake Accord, 131–32, 133; neo-conservative agenda, 167; and PQ, 120, 121; unpopularity of, 153, 167
multiculturalism, 92, 277–78
Munez, Osvaldo, 210
Murray, General James, 22, 24
Murray Hill, 63

National Action Committee on the Status of Women (NAC), 151
National Bank of Canada, 155
National Energy Program, 109
nationalism. *See* English Canada, nationalism; Québécois nationalism
Native Women's Association of Canada (NWAC), 151
Navigation Acts, 41
neo-conservatism, 167
Néron, André, 238, 239
New Brunswick: Charlottetown referendum, 164; and Meech Lake Accord, 131, 132; official bilingualism, 74; patriation of constitution, 112
New Democratic Party (NDP), 67; aftermath of Charlottetown referendum, 172–74; and Charlottetown Agreement, 154; 1993 economic policies, 174; 1993 federal election, 181–82; 1993 federal election campaign, 177; and Meech Lake Accord, 131; and *War Measures Act,* 82
Newfoundland: Charlottetown referendum, 164; and constitutional amendments, 142; and Meech Lake Accord, 131, 133; patriation of constitution, 115
new liberalism, 59–60
Newman, Peter C., 272
new nationalism, 59–60
"Ninety-two Resolutions" (Papineau), 35
North American Free Trade Agreement (NAFTA), 176
Northern Telecom, 155
North-West Rebellion, 47
Northwest Territories, and Charlottetown referendum, 164
North West Territories Act, 133
North-West Territory, and French language rights, 48
Notre Dame de Grâce by-election, 129
notwithstanding clause, 136
Nova Scotia: Charlottetown referendum, 164; patriation of constitution, 115; ratification of Meech Lake Accord, 131

oath of loyalty, 179, 184n–185n
October Crisis, 77–89; censorship, 85; FLQ demands, 78; hardline approach of Trudeau, 80–81; impact of, 88–89; kidnapping and murder of Pierre Laporte, 80, 83–84; kidnapping of James Cross, 77, 79; public reaction, 79, 84–85; RCMP security services and, 86–88; and suspension of civil

rights, 82, 84–85; and *War Measures Act,* 81–83
Official Languages Act (Bill 22), 92–93
Official Languages Act (Ottawa), 71–72, 278
oil. *See* energy crisis
Oka crisis, and English-Canadian backlash, 14
Ontario: Charlottetown referendum, 164; and 1979 federal election, 106; and 2000 federal election, 253; French education, 50; and oil crisis, 105; patriation of constitution, 112; ratification of Meech Lake Accord, 131
Organization of Petroleum Exporting Countries (OPEC), 103
Ottawa: and aftermath of 1995 referendum, 95–96
Ottawa Valley, 43

Paillé, Daniel, 194, 206
Papineau, Louis-Joseph, 33
Parent, Raymond, 117, 118
Parent, Réjean, 270
Parizeau, Jacques, 12, 121, 129–30, 139, 161, 165, 262; analysis of sovereignty referendum, 208–9; and Bouchard, 202–3, 206, 238–39; and Dumont, 203; and economic impact of sovereignty, 193–94; hardline approach to sovereignty, 201, 202; 1994 Quebec provincial election, 189–90; La Rassemblement pour la souveraineté du Québec, 263; resignation, 211; and 1995 sovereignty referendum, 199–203, 205, 206
Parti Nationaliste, 119, 120, 179
Parti Québécois (PQ): criticisms of Bouchard, 238–39; deficit and debt reduction, 221; 1976 election victory, 91; fall of Johnson, 129–30; and 1979 federal election, 197; and 1984 federal election, 119–121; founding of, 69; impact of October Crisis on, 88–89; Landry government, 260–67; and

minorities in Quebec, 208–9, 210–11, 217; 1970 provincial election, 76–77; 1973 provincial election, 89; 1985 provincial election, 122; 1994 provincial election, 12, 189–90, 194–95, 197; 1998 provincial election, 240–44; 2003 provincial election, 264–66; and sovereign Quebec, 15; target of smear campaign, 224. *See also* Bouchard, Lucien; Lévesque, René; Parizeau, Jacques
partitionist movement, 216
Patriotes, 34–38
Pawley, Howard, 130
Pearson, Lester, and Quebec, 65–67
Peckford, Brian, 107
Pelletier, Gérard, 66
Pettigrew, Pierre, 214, 228, 249
Plan A, federal strategy, 215
Plan B, 215–26; appeal to English Canada, 220–21; business patronage, 221; Calgary Declaration, 224–26; constitutional question of sovereignty, 215; destabilization strategy, 220; polarization strategy, 220; and secessionist reference questions, 231–32; smear campaigns, 223–24; and soft nationalists, 201–2, 229
Prince Edward Island, Charlottetown referendum, 164
Progressive Conservative Party: aftermath of Charlottetown referendum, 166–68; Clark government, 106–8; Diefenbaker government, 64–65; 1993 federal election, 174–75, 181, 182; 1997 federal election, 222; leadership contest to replace Mulroney, 169–72; merger with Canadian Alliance, 13
proportional representation, 282
Prudential, 101

Quebec: boundaries, 24, 26–27; under British rule, 21–30; and Charlottetown Agreement, 314–18; Charlottetown referendum, 164; as

colony of English Canada, 63; conservative leadership bloc, 26, 27; and
constitutional amendments, 142; and
constitutional patriation, 112, 113–15;
emigration, 49; English minority, 29,
43, 63–64, 72–73, 77; 1979 federal
election, 107; 1980 federal election,
108; 1997 federal election, 222; 1993
federal election campaign, 178–81,
183; industrialization and urbanization, 57–58; and Meech Lake Accord,
13; middle-class leadership, 27–28;
population, 25, 58; provincial flag,
62; reaction to Plan B, 217–18; sign
law, 135–36; sovereignty, 16; territorial question, 189–90, 191, 215; trade
with U.S., 192; and western frontier,
43–45. *See also* Lower Canada
Quebec Act, 26–27, 29–30
Quebec Federation of Labour, 155
Québécois merchant elite, displacement
of, 24–26
Québécois nationalism: "civic" nationalism, 274–75; conservatism, 42–43,
57; federalist/nationalist, 55; insular,
55; land and, 25, 34; "*maître chez
nous*", 61–62; new liberalism, 59–60;
new nationalism, 59–60, 60; *pure
laine* "ethnic" nationalism, 274;
Quebec nationalism (Bourassa), 60;
radicalism, 42; and Rebellion of
1837–38, 34–38; sovereign Quebec
state, 15, 33; survival of nation, 25
Québecor Inc., 206
Quebec provincial election: of 1966,
67–68; of 1970, 75–77; of 1973, 89;
of 1976, 91; of 1985, 122; of 1994,
12, 186–98; of 1998, 240–44; of
2003, 264–67
"Quebec round," 125–26
Quiet Revolution, 57–70, 90; and culture, 62; and flight of capital, 76–77;
intellectual ferment, 59–60; labour
militancy, 63; and modernization,
57–62; nature of, 58–64; political

violence, 63–64

Rae, Bob, 172, 173, 184, 311
Rakoff, Vivian, 223
Ralfe, Tim, 80, 81
Ralliement National (RN), 67, 69
La Rassemblement pour la souveraineté
du Québec (RSQ), 263
La Rassemblement pour l'Indépendance
Nationale (RIN), 67–68, 69, 178
RCMP security service, 86–88, 116–18
Rebellions of 1837–38, 17; land ques-
tion, 32, 34–35; in Lower Canada,
33–38; outcomes, 38–40; political
impasse, 32, 35; and political reform,
39–40; in Upper Canada, 32–33
Rebick, Judy, 151–51
Reciprocity Treaty, 42
Red River Rebellion, 44–46
referendum: of 1980, 18, 109–110; of
1995, 12, 17; divisive nature of, 144;
federal law, 145; 1992 Quebec deadline, 139; Quebec law, 146; 1995 sovereignty referendum, 12, 17, 199–211;
"winning conditions" position, 239
Reform movement (Upper Canada),
32–33, 39
Reform party: and anti-Quebec anger,
213–14; 1993 federal election,
177–79, 181, 182; 1997 federal election, 222; opposition to Quebec,
13–14. *See also* Canadian Alliance
regionalism: constitutional renewal and,
13–14. *See also* Western Canada
representation by population, 281–82
residual powers, 279
resources: energy, 101–9; and patriation
of constitution, 114–15
responsible government, 38, 39, 41
Richler, Modecai, 14
Riel, Louis, 17, 44–48
Robillard, Lucienne, 249
Romanow, Roy, 114, 115, 172, 173,
188–89, 200, 204, 224, 260–61, 311
Rouges, 42

Royal Bank, 149, 194, 205
Royal Commission on Bilingualism and
    Biculturalism (B and B Commission),
    16; on bilingualism, 71–72; on eco-
    nomic disparity, 74–7; on education,
    71, 72–74; on ethnocultural groups,
    7; 1965 interim report, 66
Royal Proclamation of 1763, 24
Royal Trust, 76–77
Russell, Lord John, 36
Ryan, Claude, 204, 230

Saint-Jean-Baptiste Day demonstration,
    71
St. Benoit, 37
St. Denis, 37, 38
St. Eustache, 37
St. Léonard crisis, 72–73
SARS crisis, 228
Saskatchewan: and bilingualism,
    133–34; Charlottetown referendum,
    164; and constitutional amendments,
    142; and energy resources, 104–8;
    patriation of constitution, 112, 114;
    ratification of Meech Lake Accord,
    134
Sauvé, Paul, 61
Scott, Thomas, 46
Sears, 240
Seaton, Lord. See Colbourne, John
secessionist reference questions: clear
    majority decision, 234; clear referen-
    dum question, 234; on conflicting
    laws, 324; obligation to negotiate
    with sovereigntists, 234; Quebec
    opposition to, 230–32; rulings,
    234–35, 319–33; secession under
    international law, 323–24; supreme
    Court's reference jurisdiction,
    319–21; unilateral right to secede,
    321–23
secularization, 59. See also Quiet
    Revolution
Séguin, Yves, 268
self-determination, Quebec: FLQ and,

63–64; founding of Parti Québécois,
    69; 1966 provincial election of 1966,
    67–68; and public opinion, 75–76
Senate, 281
separatism: public opinion, 95. See also
    self-determination, Quebec
Sihota, Moe, 16, 158
Simpson, Jeffrey, 255
Single-E Senate, 310, 312–13
Social Charter, 311
Social Union Framework agreement,
    235–38
La Société Saint-Jean-Baptiste, 69
soft nationalists, 201–2, 252
sovereignty: constitutionality of, 215;
    sovereignty association, 69; sover-
    eignty-association, 97–99. See also
    self-determination, Quebec
sovereignty referendum: and Bouchard's
    leadership, 206; Canada Place rally,
    207; Cree and Innu and, 208; draft
    bill, 200; economic question, 199;
    "ethnic" politics, 208–10; outcome,
    205; posturing of English Canada,
    200, 204–5; public consultation
    process, 201; public opinion, 201,
    206, 207; referendum question,
    202–3; soft nationalists, 201–2;
    timetable for, 199–200
special status, of Quebec, 92, 111,
    285–286, 307
Spicer Commission, 140, 153
sponsorship program, for federal propa-
    ganda, 214
spying, political, 96; on Carstairs and
    Doer, 132; on PQ, 116–18. See also
    RCMP security service
Standard Life Assurance, 205
Stanfield, Robert, 71
strategic voting, spontaneous, 182–83
Sun Life Insurance, 101
Sydenham, Lord, 39

Taillon, Gilles, 271
Task Force on Canadian Unity, 16

Taylor, Allan, 149
"Ten Resolutions" (Russell), 36
Terrana, Anna, 216
Timber and Sugar Duties, 41
Tobin, Brian, 254
trade unions. *See* labour movement
Treaty of Utrecht, 22
Tremblay, André, 162
Triple E-Senate, 13, 141, 281, 308
Trudeau, Pierre: attack on Meech Lake
    Accord, 130; and Charlottetown
    Accord, 152–53, 162; constitutional
    patriation, 111–16; and equality-of-
    provinces myth, 280; 1980 federal
    election, 108; and 1993 federal elec-
    tion, 184; and federalism, 60, 67, 70;
    Liberal leadership, 70–71; and
    October Crisis, 80–81, 89; political
    background, 69–70; promises of con-
    stitutional renewal, 110–11; and
    Quebec special status, 92; recruitment
    to federal politics, 66; unilateral patri-
    ation of constitution, 111–15; and the
    West, 103–9
Turner, John, 120

unemployment, 175
Union government, 51–54
Union Nationale, 54; and Bill 63, 73, 76;
    under Duplessis, 57, 60–61, 62; and
    1966 provincial election, 67; and
    1970 provincial election, 76, 77;
    under Sauvé, 61
Union Populaire, 178
United Empire Loyalists, 28–29
University of Quebec at Montreal, 205–6
Upper Canada: creation of, 29; Reform
    movement, 32–33

Vallières, Pierre, 63
Vancouver Liberation Front, 84
Vander Zalm, Bill, 170
veto, 111, 112, 114, 212, 315–16
Victoria Charter, 91–92

Wal-Mart, 240
War Measures Act (WMA), 18, 81–83
War-time Elections Act, 51, 52
welfare state, 67
Wells, Clyde, 131, 132, 150, 157
western Canada: abolition of minority
    rights, 48; annexation of Prairie West,
    44–45; and Charlottetown
    Agreement, 312–14; control of
    resources, 112, 114–15; energy
    resources, 103–9; and Joe Clark, 106,
    107–8; and patriation of constitution,
    114–15; political estrangement,
    101–6; regionalism, 13–14; resource
    development, 101–2; settlement,
    44–49
Westmount, 64
White, Bob, 150
Wilhelmy, Diane, 162
Wilson, Gordon, 154
"winning conditions" position, 239, 261,
    262
Wolfe, General James, 22–23
women's organizatons, and Meech Lake
    Accord, 131

Yorkton western premiers meeting, 213
Yukon, and Charlottetown referendum,
    164

AGMV Marquis

MEMBER OF SCABRINI MEDIA

Quebec, Canada
2004